Organizations as Systems

THE OPEN UNIVERSITY SYSTEMS GROUP

Professor R. J. Beishon
Ms. M. Blunden
Mr. K. Chidsey — Visiting Lecturer
Mr. R. C. Forrester-Paton
Mr. J. J. Hamwee
Dr. J. N. T. Martin
Mr. W. M. Mayon-White

Dr. R. M. Morris — Senior Lecturer
Mr. J. J. Naughton
Mr. G. Peters
Mr. R. G. Spear
Ms. J. Tait
Mr. A. R. Thomas
Mr. A. Thomas — Visiting Lecturer

Research and Support Staff

Mr. B. Bloomfield
Ms. S. Brown
Ms. M. Campbell
Mr. P. Chaplin
Ms. P. Cheney
Ms. C. M. Cooper
Mr. C. Cornforth
Ms. R. Daggett
Mr. J. Frederickson
Mr. S. Lawson

Mr. G. Mantle
Ms. D. Manning-Clift
Ms. J. McGowan
Mr. C. Pym
Ms. V. Risby
Ms. S. Snelling
Ms. S. Stone
Ms. E. Tynan
Mr. H. Ward
Ms. C. Willemstyn

Organizations as Systems

edited by Martin Lockett and Roger Spear

The Open University Press
Milton Keynes

The Open University Press
12 Cofferidge Close, Stony Stratford
Milton Keynes MK11 1BY, England

Made and printed in Great Britain by Eyre & Spottiswoode Ltd, Thanet Press, Union Crescent, Margate, Kent

---

British Library Cataloguing in Publication Data

Organizations as systems.
   1. Organization — Addresses, essays, lectures
   2. System analysis — Addresses, essays, lectures
   I. Lockett, Martin II. Spear, Roger
   301.18'32   HM131

ISBN 0-335-00263-3

Acknowledgements

The editors would like to thank all those who have contributed to the development of this book of readings. They are grateful for the discussions with the members of the Open University T243 course team on *Systems Organization: the Management of Complexity;* in particular Karl Chidsey, Rob Paton, Professor John Beishon, Margaret Blunden, John Hamwee and Chris Pym, whose own preferences and ideas they have tried to integrate into the overall framework of this reader. In addition, other members of the Open University Systems Group and the Department of Social and Economic Studies at Imperial College have provided helpful comments on their ideas; Sue Snelling made their handwriting into a legible typescript; and Godfrey Smart made it fit for publication.

Martin Lockett, *Lecturer in the Department of Social and Economic Studies, Imperial College*
Roger Spear, *Lecturer in the Systems Group, Open University*

Grateful acknowledgement is made to the following for permission to reproduce material in this reader:

Reading 1   Checkland, P. B. 'The origins and nature of hard systems thinking', *Journal of Applied Systems Analysis,* Vol. 5 No. 2, pp. 99–110, 1978. Reprinted by permission of P. B. Checkland, University of Lancaster.

Reading 2   Ackoff, R. L. 'The systems revolution', *Long Range Planning,* Vol. 7 No. 6, pp. 2–5, December 1974, *and* Ackoff, R. L. 'Resurrecting the future of operational research', *Journal of the Operational Research Society,* Vol. 30 No. 3, pp. 189–93. Both reprinted by permission of Pergamon Press.

Reading 3   Buckley, W. *Sociology and modern systems theory* (© 1967), Chapter 3, pp. 41–80, Prentice-Hall. Reprinted by permission of Prentice-Hall, Inc., Englewood Cliffs, New Jersey.

Reading 4   Watzlawick, P. (Ph.D), Weakland, J. H. (Ch.E) and Fisch, R. (M.D.) *Change: principles of problem formation and problem resolution* (© 1974), Chapters 1 and 2, pp. 1–28, W. W. Norton & Co Ltd. Reprinted with the permission of W. W. Norton & Company Inc.

Reading 5   Trist, E. L. 'A social-technical critique of scientific management' in Edge, D. O. and Wolfe, J. N. (1973) *Meaning and control: essays in social aspects of science and technology,* pp. 95–116, Tavistock Publications Ltd.

Reading 6   Silverman, D. *The theory of organizations* (1970), pp. 109–24, Heinemann Educational Books Ltd, and Basic Books Inc.

Reading 7   Bowey, A. M. 'Approaches to organization theory' in *Social Science Information,* Vol. 11 No. 6, 1972, pp. 109–28.

Reading 8   Hall, R. H. *Organizations: structure and process* (© 1977) 2nd edn., Chapter 3, 'Goals and effectiveness', pp. 67–85, Prentice-Hall Inc. Reprinted by permission of Prentice-Hall, Inc., Englewood Cliffs, New Jersey.

6

Reading 9   Child, J. *Organisation* (1977), Chapter 1, 'The contribution of organisation structure', pp. 8–23, Harper & Row Ltd.

Reading 10   Galbraith, J. R. 'Organizational design: an information processing view' in *Interfaces,* Vol. 4 No. 3, May 1974, pp. 28–36. Reprinted by permission of *Interfaces*, published by the Institute of Management Sciences and the Operations Research Society of America.

Reading 11   den Hertog, J. F. 'The role of information and control systems in the process of organizational renewal: roadblock or roadbridge?' in *Accounting, Organizations and Society,* Vol. 3 No. 1 1978, pp. 29–45. Reprinted by permission of Pergamon Press.

Reading 12   Argyris, C. and Schön, D. *Organizational learning* (© 1978), Chapter 1, 'What is an organization that it may learn?', pp. 8–29, Addison-Wesley. Reprinted by permission of Addison-Wesley Publishing Co., Reading, Mass.

Reading 13   Elliott, Ruth *Conceptual approaches to power and authority,* Chapter 1, Ph.D. thesis for University of London. Reprinted by permission of the author.

Reading 14   Benson, J. K. 'Organizations: a dialectical view' in *The Administrative Science Quarterly,* Vol. 22 No. 1, March 1977, pp. 1–21. Reprinted by permission of *The Administrative Science Quarterly.*

Reading 15   Bonis, J. 'Organization and environment' in *International Studies of Management and Organization,* Fall 1972, pp. 314–43. © Éditions du Seuil. First published in *Sociologie du Travail,* Paris. Reprinted by permission of M. E. Sharpe Inc., N.Y., and Éditions du Seuil, Paris.

Reading 16   Stern, L. W. 'Potential conflict management mechanisms in distribution channels: an interorganizational analysis' in *Contractual marketing systems,* ed. Thompson, D. N. (Lexington Mass.: Lexington Books, D. C. Heath and Company, copyright 1971, D. C. Heath and Company). Reprinted by permission of the publisher.

Reading 17   Crozier, M. 'Comparing structures and comparing games' in Hofstede, G. and Kassem, M. S. *European contributions to organization theory,* pp. 193–207, 1975, Assen. Reprinted by permission of the publishers, Van Gorcum, The Netherlands.

Reading 18   Vickers, G. *Freedom in a rocking boat: changing values in an unstable society* (Allen Lane, The Penguin Press, 1970) pp. 43–55. © Geoffery Vickers, 1970. Reprinted by permission of Penguin Books Ltd.

Reading 19   Schön, D. *Beyond the stable state,* Chapter 4, 'Diffusion of innovation', Pelican Books. Copyright © Donald A. Schön, 1971. Reprinted by permission of Elaine Greene Ltd., and Random House, Inc.

Reading 20   Baumgartner, T., Buckley, W. and Burns, T. 'Meta-power and relational control in social life' in *Social Science Information,* Vol. 14 No. 6, 1975, pp. 49–78. Reprinted by permission of SAGE Publications (originally published by Mouton Publishing Co.).

Front cover: The 'Molok' from 'Metropolis', reproduced by permission of Transit-Film GmbH, Munich.

The Open University Systems Courses

The Systems Group have produced four systems courses, each of half credit rating which entails 16 weeks' study totalling about 160–200 hours study time. The courses have radio and television programmes as integral parts of the teaching material and two have home kits for experiments and practical activities which can be done in the students' homes. All students on systems courses attend a one week summer school.

Systems Behaviour (T241)

The idea of this course is to introduce students from many different backgrounds, scientists, technologists, social scientists, to the study and understanding of systems and systems behaviour. The course is at second level which approximates to a second year undergraduate course at a British University. The course contains eight modules of about two weeks work each covering a different case study in a correspondence text together with radio and TV programmes and computer exercises and home experiments where appropriate. Each case study is linked to the teaching of a specific technique or method in the systems area. The eight studies are:

Deep sea container berth

Air traffic control

Telephone system

Work group systems

Local government

The human respiratory system

Sheep farming-grass ecosystem

Economic case studies

The techniques developed include: data collection and statistical analysis, simulation and modelling both in digital and analogue forms and systems dynamics.

Systems Organization: the Management of Complexity (T243)

Organizations as Systems is associated with this course.

The course explains how the discipline of systems can be used to tackle endemic problems in the organization of work and services, and how its distinctive approach can suggest solutions to these problems.

It starts from a wide perspective of the organization of human activities from football crowds to financial and health systems. This perspective forms the context for more detailed consideration of the organization of work, and colours the whole of the course, distinguishing it from both management science and the sociology of organizations.

The first specific focus of the course is on people, operations and groups. Some of the material, develops different models of human interactions and shows how people work in groups, how they can best be divided from each other by the allocation and design of work and how their efforts can be co-ordinated to meet overall ends.

The next area of detailed treatment considers what can be loosely thought of as the organization—clubs, companies, co-operatives or schools. From that assumption of unity it considers organizational structure and overall control of the various groupings within it, but in developing the idea of organizations as systems it emphasizes processes such as information flow, conflict and bargaining, planned and unplanned change, and the relationships between interdependent parts of different organizations.

The last point is developed further in the section on multiorganizations, where organizations are viewed as members of wider systems such as housing finance, markets and industrial conglomerates in which the roots of endemic organizational problems may be sought, and on whose operations many of our social expectations are based.

The final section of the course considers the picture of organizations which emerges from these views in terms of some themes which recur in any analytical consideration of the organization of people—conflicts over goals, the demands of stability and change and the issues of power and control.

Systems Modelling (T341)

This is a third level course which as the title implies,

8

deals with the modelling of systems. The aim is to break down the mystique that surrounds the use of quantitative models and computer methods in the making of major decisions.

The course concentrates on the problems of formulating models of complex systems and of interpreting the results they give. It draws on a range of case studies to illustrate the use of linear models and simulation modelling. Two units deal with modelling community decisions and large scale economic modelling (including world modelling).

Systems Performance: Human Factors and Systems Failures (TD342)

This is also a third level course and it deals comprehensively with analyses of the performance of systems concentrating particularly on the human element in systems and the problems of failures. It develops techniques for the analysis of failures such as failure modes and effects analysis and it critically deals with a wide range of systems failures. These cover catastrophic failures such as the Aberfan tip disaster, the Summerland fire and the Hixon level crossing train smash; and organizational studies in the field of science policy, mental health provisions and a major case study of the Bay Area Rapid Transport system in California. There are 16 TV and radio programmes which deal with these and other case studies including earthquakes and air crashes in depth. The course also studies concepts of reliability and safety in relation to the design of safe and effective systems. A unique home kit is included with the course which illustrates the range of problems which can arise in systems and shows how many of them can be avoided.

Contents

Introduction

This book of readings aims to provide an introduction to the application of systems ideas in the general field of organizations. From its early development in subjects like biology, control theory, structural functionalism, the systems approach has become a pervasive influence in a wide range of disciplines. At the same time as its scope has widened, the original idea of a 'general systems theory' which could be of universal validity has quite correctly receded. Thus there are a plurality of systems approaches, rather than just one set of ideas, which might be more correctly seen as a systems movement. Given this diversity, it would not be useful to define what is, or is not, a 'genuine' systems approach. In this reader we do not attempt to do this—rather we are concerned with some of the underlying factors which make these readings useful for those interested in applying systems ideas to organizations. Amongst the factors that can be identified are:

1 holism—a perceived need to see parts of a society in relation to other parts; hence for example one cannot consider the subgroups of an organization in isolation from the organization as a whole and the wider society.

2 open systems—in the process of analysis we will draw boundaries around the units we are studying for we cannot study everything at once; however such boundaries are not impenetrable and do not make organizations 'closed systems'—instead one of their main features is the extent and importance of the environment of the system.

3 inter-disciplinary approach—traditional disciplinary boundaries are seen as questionable, and it is necessary to combine the perspectives of, at times, widely disparate disciplines.

4 applied emphasis—demonstrating a concern not only for theoretical analysis but also for the resolution of practical problems, or, more correctly, attempts to resolve complex sets of problems which have arisen in modern industrial societies. Thus systems ideas can be used in such areas as urban transport, the promotion and guidance of technological innovation, the regulation of complex ecosystems and the problems associated with new technological developments like microprocessors, which will have wide-ranging effects on areas as far apart as the skills of industrial workers and the shape of leisure activities.

These general factors behind systems approaches are reflected in this reader, although we have concentrated on some of the theoretical underpinnings of systems approaches to organization. However, despite the force of this idea, the historical development of certain systems ideas within the structure of our economic and political system have not been without criticism.

Firstly, systems approaches to organizations have given rise to an 'organic analogy', which derives from some apparent similarities between complex biological organisms and organizations, and which has been over-extended. We would warn against the dangers of such an approach, despite its initial attractiveness and simplicity.

In particular, some central concepts of social science have not until recently received adequate consideration by many systems theorists of organizations. Most notable has been the neglect of meaningful human action as a valid theoretical category in favour of structural and/or functional analyses, although this neglect has been recognized amongst more recent writers. Combined with this has been insufficient emphasis on the role, sources and exercise of power, both within organizations and within society as a whole.

Secondly, the applied systems approaches have in practice often led to a rather uncritical identification with the currently dominant centres of power in society. Furthermore, we would argue that although many systems ideas are by no means 'conservative', the development of applied systems approaches has tended to have a managerial bias. Thus, for example, management information systems are given much attention in contrast to workers' information systems in organizations. In this reader we have presented a variety of perspectives, although the above criticisms are reflected in many of the readings.

Historically there has been an excessive concentration on the organization as the level of analysis. The fact that the organizational level is the one at which effectiveness is usually measured, and, in the case of business organizations, profits realized, has no doubt been influential. However, there has always been a concern with smaller groups within organizations, which is the subject of the second section of the reader, 'People and groups'. Such subgroups cannot be understood except in the context of organizations; thus our third section is on 'Organizations'. Concern with the limitations of this focus has been expressed both from (1) the rather false assumptions about the lack of effect of organizations, particularly large business corporations and state institutions, on their environment; and (2) the concern of state policy-makers with the complex set of organizations and the inter-relationships between them, which will affect the formulation and implementation of policy. So our fourth section is on 'Multiorganizations'. This can in turn be seen within the context of societies as a whole, and even perhaps necessarily within a world context—for as many writers concerned with the under-development of the Third World have stressed, the technology, attitudes and social structure of, say, an African village are intimately connected with the development of modern capitalist society in the West. However these higher 'societal' and 'world' levels are outside the scope of our particular concerns in this book.

The organization of this book is therefore along the lines of *levels of analysis*, which we would argue to be a useful approach both analytically and from a teaching point of view. However this fairly traditional categorization has its drawbacks, as the limitations of each theoretical level are revealed in the next level. For example, the limited diffusion of the Scandinavian job design experiments can be explained by an analysis of the threats to the power relationships of middle management; similarly organizational behaviour can only be partly understood by analysis of reality *within* the organization since interorganizational networks, market forces, and so on, also shape its behaviour. This realization has broadened the focus of organization theory. At the *group* level the readings cover the historical development of job design from scientific management, through sociotechnical systems, to action theory. But rather than presenting ideas historically, the readings provide theoretical explanations for different aspects of current practice. Similarly the section on Organization covers the many disparate strands of organization theory. Although this apparently chaotic state of theory does not assist the task

of understanding organizational behaviour as a whole, it is possible to utilize different theories to answer different questions or to assist the illumination of different problems. This is consistent with the aims of this reader, which are to provide the basis for the development of practical action or 'praxis', by first understanding the different perspectives on the problems studied, their limitations and the potential for change.

The *multiorganization* theories are, as we have argued, vital for a full understanding of organizational behaviour, but the relatively recent appreciation of this fact means that, rather than being faced with a full range of disparate theories (as in the section on Organization) we have in this section not only different perspectives, but also significant theoretical gaps in the field, particularly in respect of the development of ideas about the effect of economic forces on the organization and on networks of organizations. The multiorganization section, condensed and highly selective as it is, attempts to cover the field *both* from the point of view of the organization attempting to control its environment *and* from the point of view of an agency attempting to intervene in a field of several interacting organizations in order to modify the overall system behaviour. Again, this section in many ways reflects existing power relationships, for the impetus for such studies and action has usually come 'from above', from state agencies or large business corporations. Such perspectives are by no means confined to the West, for in the USSR there are systems theorists who argue for the 'scientific management of society'.

To sum up, we have not selected the readings to establish a unified systems view of how organizations do and should work. Rather we are presenting a set of more or less related theoretical contributions to assist you in building up a perspective on organizations which will more or less explicitly include the valid insights and concepts developed within systems frameworks. Your perspective will necessarily depend on your values and interests, and we hope that these readings will expand your awareness of *both* the problems associated with organizations in society today *and* the range of possible prescriptions for change which can be put forward.

As a result, this reader should be relevant to all students of organizations—whether from social science, systems, business, scientific or engineering backgrounds, or just as someone who is affected fundamentally by organization in his daily life. We hope to assist all of these readers in broadening their perspectives on organizations, as well as appreciating the possible alternatives for the future.

Section I   Systems

Introduction

In this section there are two papers on systems as a prescriptive approach to change and one paper on systems as a theoretical framework. These two perspectives are obviously related, as it is only through adequate theoretical understanding of situations that prescriptions for change can be effectively made. This distinction between theory and change is to some degree artificial but it is nevertheless useful as a way of distinguishing between management science (or non-managerial approaches and strategies for change) on the one hand, and organization theory on the other. It does not, however, imply that such theoretical approaches are 'value-free', for theory has been very much dependent upon its social context.

Even within these categories there is considerable variation among the views of practitioners as to what constitutes a systems approach or a systems theory of organizations. The concepts and ideas have been absorbed into different paradigms and whilst the original major characteristic of the systems paradigm—holism—is still important, many people would now add the following necessary characteristics of a valid approach: an emphasis on process, a relativistic perspective and a self-reflexive approach to social reality. Combined with this has come a persistent emphasis on change—the applied emphasis of systems thinking. This is our starting point. With systems approaches to prescriptive change there are many schools of thought and we have selected two important papers in the area. Checkland (Reading 1) deals with 'hard' systems approaches and Ackoff (Reading 2) with 'soft' systems thinking. Checkland studies the history of approaches, showing the reliance on 'means–end' rationality in less complex 'engineering' problems can be a powerful methodology. But he challenges this rationality in soft systems, which involve people and organizations. Ackoff recognizes some of the difficulties of isolating and defining problems which can then be 'solved'. In practice he argues that the word 'mess' vividly and more accurately describes the sets of interconnected problems which characterize actual situations. Thus simple problem-solving methodologies are inappropriate. Instead he argues for a continuous, interactive process of planning to deal with the difficulties.

The other paper in this section deals with the theoretical side of systems. Buckley (Reading 3) develops, in a difficult but worthwhile paper, some basic systems ideas into a sophisticated theory of organizations, perhaps illustrating the extent to which systems can act as an overarching framework for a range of theories. Consequently Buckley's paper would be equally well placed at the end of this book.

Further Reading

There are so many articles and books to suggest, especially in the prescriptive change area (although much of it with a managerial bias). Checkland has published several articles in the *Journal of Applied Systems Analysis* (previously called the *Journal of Systems Engineering*), itself a useful reference, the most notable being 'Towards a systems-based methodology for real-world problem solving'. Kramer and de Smit in *Systems thinking* provide a brief overview of the area. The design and management of large socio-technical projects is discussed in A. D. Hall, *Systems engineering*. Stafford Beer, in *Brain of the firm* introduces some interesting ideas, despite his tendency to over-extend the use of an organic analogy. A historical perspective on recent systems ideas and their current development is given in a series of papers in *Systems thinking* ed. F. E. Emery, although several of the papers are rather difficult. Papers in *Systems behaviour,* Beishon and Peters (eds.) illustrate the application of the systems approach in a broad range of fields (such as physiological, ecological and political areas). C. W. Churchman deals with more philosophical issues in two very readable books, *Challenge to reason* and *The systems approach;* a later book, *Design of inquiring systems* is more difficult but discusses important methodological issues. W. Buckley in *Sociology and modern systems theory* and later papers, has significantly developed systems ideas as a theoretical framework for studying social issues.

Beer, S. (1972) *The brain of the firm,* McGraw-Hill.

Beishon, J. and Peters, G. (1972) *Systems behaviour,* Open University Press.

Buckley, W. (1967) *Sociology and modern systems theory,* Prentice Hall.

Checkland, P. B. (Winter 1972) 'Towards a system-based methodology for real-world problem solving', *Journal of Systems Engineering,* **3,** No. 2.

Churchman, C. W. (1968) *Challenge to reason,* McGraw-Hill.

Churchman, C. W. (1969) *The systems approach,* Dell.

Churchman, C. W. (1972) *Design of inquiring systems,* Basic Books.

Emery, F. E. (ed.) (1970) *Systems thinking,* Penguin.

Hall, A. D. (1962) *A methodology for systems engineering,* Van Nostrand.

Kramer, N. and de Smit, J. (1977) *Systems thinking: concepts and notions,* Martinus Nijhoff Social Sciences Division, Leiden.

Ryan, A. (1970) Wholes, parts, purposes and functions, Chapter 8 in *The Philosophy of the Social Sciences,* Macmillan.

1   The origins and nature of 'hard' systems thinking

P. B. Checkland

Introduction

Within the systems movement as a whole there are two distinct traditions which stem respectively from the thinking of biologists and engineers. The existence of the two traditions is usefully marked by the two collections of readings. *Systems Thinking* edited by Emery[1], and *Systems Analysis* edited by Optner[2]. In his introduction to the former, Emery remarks

> . . . we have kept to the strand of thought that runs from *theorising* about biological systems in general to social systems. We have practically ignored the strand that arises from the design of complex engineering systems . . . (my italics).

while for Optner

> . . . Systems analysis should be viewed as the most recent and perhaps most comprehensive vehicle for complex *problem solving* . . . (my italics).

This emphasis in the engineering tradition on *practice* is hardly surprising, coming from that source, but as the movement's aspirations spread from the solution of technical problems to the tackling of societal problems it is not obvious that the engineering tradition contains all the intellectual resources called for by the task. An eventual requirement may be that the two strands come together.

It is certainly the case at present that attempts to apply systems analysis to social problems have not been greeted with universal acclamation. Hoos[3, 4], Boguslaw[5] and Churchman[6] have all discussed the difficulties involved and the modest results achieved so far. In order to understand the weaknesses as well as the strengths of systems analysis as a 'vehicle for complex problem solving', and to lay the foundations for improved methods, it is necessary to understand the way in which the nature of engineers' thinking both shapes and limits systems analysis. This paper, extracted from a work in progress, examines the origins and nature of this strand of the systems movement. It examines the difference between science and engineering or technology, reviews the emergence of 'systems engineering' and 'systems analysis' and finds a single pattern or model underlying all 'hard' systems thinking.

Science, engineering and technology

The intention behind the activity of science is to establish well-tested knowledge about the world and our place in it. Its method, the carrying out of reductionist, repeatable experiments which aim to test hypotheses to destruction, has been very successful, and much knowledge of a special kind—public knowledge—has been established by the use of it. In our civilization the *application* of scientific knowledge through technology has so dominated the man-made world that we may forget the crucial differences between science and technology, and between the aims and methods of professional scientists and engineers or technologists.

All human communities have faced problems arising from man's basic need for food, shelter and, from an early stage of cultural development, transport; and all societies have developed technologies to solve the problem of meeting these needs. In our civilization the incorporation of science into technological problem solving has produced a uniquely powerful cultural force, so much so that some writers (for example Bunge)[7] would describe mud hut building, or ancient Chinese paper making as 'crafts', restricting the label 'technology' to the combination of a craft with science. But however the word is used, there is no doubt that its Greek origin *techne* has to do with objects produced artificially by man, and it is in this that the crucial distinction between science and technology (or engineering) lies.

Any purposeful human activity implies commitment to a particular ranking of values. Science implies the belief that the highest value attaches to the advancement of knowledge. Engineering and technology, on the other hand, prize most highly the efficient accomplishment of some defined purpose. Where the scientists ask: 'have we learnt anything?' the engineer and the technologist ask 'does it work?'

This difference of aim and motivation is on the whole reflected in statements about science and technology in the rather sparse literature concerned with the philosophy of technology. Thus, according to Wisdom[8]: 'The difference is not *in rerum natura* but in aim: the one to understand structure, the other to create a structure for a certain purpose'. Skolimowski[9], discussing the structure of thinking in technology, summarizes the distinction in the sentence: 'In short, science concerns itself with what *is*, technology with what *is to be*', while Jarvie[10] in commenting on Skolimowski's paper argues that the epistemological distinction is that 'Scientific statements are posed to solve scientific problems; technological statements allow that certain devices are not impossible'.

These theoretical discussions, which I would summarize in the crucial difference between the value systems of science and technology, match well my own experiences as a Research and Development manager in science-based industry. In the 1960s, for example, the largest team in my group, ten science or technology graduates under the leadership of a very able scientist-turned-technologist, were trying to define a synthetic shoe upper material and a process to make it economically. The technological base was our knowledge of polymers and our expertise in making synthetic fibres, and the composite leather-like product developed was what has been called a 'third generation' product in that industry[11]. In the experiments carried out we were not at all interested in refuting hypotheses, in gaining knowledge for its own sake, only in gaining *useful* knowledge in the shape of *rules* for obtaining a product which performed satisfactorily in shoe uppers. Such technological rules are very different from the laws which science seeks, being circumscribed by a range of considerations specific to a particular situation and purpose: we were trying to develop a new material within a certain time, at a certain cost, to meet a specific opportunity believed to exist in a particular market. Such considerations are determining factors in technology and engineering but are not fundamentally relevant to science. An individual scientist may be in a hurry to make the discovery which will gain him a Nobel prize, but the timing is intrinsically unimportant except to those who believe that new scientific knowledge is welcome for its own sake, and welcome early rather than late. In our technological projects we and a number of competitors were trying to meet a market need which, we believed, would exist in the mid-70s as a result of a world shortage of natural hides. As it happens the market forecasts were wrong, but that does not affect the fact that the timing was not just a factor in our objectives but a determining factor.

One other experience in that project also illustrated the difference between a scientific and a technological approach. Many groups with polymer and fibre-making skills were interested in the possibility of a 'synthetic leather'. In one research department which got left behind in the race, a research physicist was asked to report on the possibility of a project to make such a material. He assumed this to be a scientific question, one concerning knowledge, and his negative report was based on the following argument: 'the three-dimensional matrix of natural leather is so complex that it cannot at present be accurately described; therefore we cannot hope to simulate it'. Had he assumed the question to be a technological one he would have asked, not 'can we copy leather' but 'can we imagine a material which will perform satisfactorily in the *end uses* in which natural leather is now used?' Where science is interested in new knowledge, and whether it is true or false, technology and engineering are interested in action directed to a defined end, and whether it is *successful* or *unsuccessful*.

The fact that this thinking underlying technology and engineering is directed towards action makes it a very direct and explicit guide to exploring the possibilities of 'engineering' human activity systems. This strength eventually turns out to be also a weakness, as we shall see, but as a first basis for systems practice it is useful.

Systems engineering

It is not surprising that engineering as a professional activity attracts action-oriented people who value practical achievement above all else. A result of this is that engineers (and technologists) are impatient with theorizing; after a good design has been successfully realized in practice they are little inclined to analyse the way they went about achieving it. As a result the literature of engineering methodology is not extensive, in spite of the fact that public speculation on the role of engineers usually embodies rather grand visions: thus Sporn[12]

> The engineer is the key figure in the material progress of the world. It is his engineering that makes a reality of the potential value of science by translating scientific knowledge into tools, resources, energy and labour to bring them into the service of man . . . the engineer requires the imagination to visualise the needs of society and to appreciate what is possible as well as the technological and hard social understanding to bring his vision to reality.

Engineers have not in fact developed the broad systems approach which is implied by clarion calls of this kind, but nevertheless, there is one part of engineering in which methodological prescriptions are common. This is that area of the subject concerned with the engineering not of components but of systems (both physical and organizational) which involve the mutual interactions of many components: the engineering of the telephone network, for example, rather than the telephone instrument or the switching equipment in an exchange.

It is obvious that engineers throughout history have faced tasks of this kind, from the pyramid builders to the NASA engineers who worked on the moon-landing mission, although it is only in relatively recent times that the methodological principles for carrying out such projects have been defined. It is characteristic of the engineering world that principles should be learnt from experience and grasped intuitively long before they are codified and expounded. Eli Whitney in the 1790s in America contracted to produce 10,000 muskets by using jigs, thus enabling unskilled workers to make larger numbers of interchangeable parts; he must have had an intuitive grasp of what is now known as 'industrial engineering'. And in the 1830s in Lancashire, James Nasmyth produced standardized machine tools in a factory which was a pioneer of assembly lines. By 1913 the knowledge was available to enable Henry Ford to set up a moving assembly line on which a chassis was produced in 1 hour 33 minutes compared with the previous 12 hours 28 minutes; in 1914 he produced more than a quarter of a million cars[13]. Similarly, the history of the development of electrical engineering, including the provision of power, lighting and telecommunication systems abounds in examples of 'systems engineering' even though the phrase gets no mention in a standard history of the subject.[14]

The principles of work organization began to be codified around the turn of the century, with the work of Frederick Taylor, and the Gilbreth's, Frank and Lillian. Exposition of methodology for the total engineering of complex man-machine systems involving sophisticated machines as well as logistic support systems came rather later. It dates only from the 1950s, although since then a number of versions of this kind of 'hard' systems thinking have been described. The following dozen references illustrate the steady stream of discussion of 'systems engineering' over the last 20 years: Goode and Machol 1957, Eckman 1961, Williams 1961, Gosling 1962, Hall 1962, Chestnut 1965 and 1967, Miles 1971, de Neufville and Stafford 1971, Chase 1974, Daenzer 1976, Wymore 1976.

Both Goode and Machol[15], and Gosling[16], identify the increased complexity of human requirements, and hence of the engineer's task, as the prime reason for the development of 'systems engineering' as a new set of considerations which engineers must take into account. Gosling makes a good *systemic* point when he writes:

> The system engineer must also be capable of predicting the emergent properties of the system, those properties that is, which are possessed by the system but not its parts.

But in general the emphasis in both books is on a *systematic* approach to engineering design by means of model building and model optimization. For Goode and Machol the computer is 'the basic tool of interior system design', and their overall approach comprises: deciding what system has to be designed and suggesting some possible designs; mathematical and experimental evaluation of potential designs according to some defined 'measure of effectiveness'; principal design, a phase which 'may last from 1 year to 10 years'; prototype construction; and testing, training and evaluation, the purpose of the latter being 'to decide whether the design accomplishes its objectives'. In the case of large-scale systems designed and constructed over a number of years, evaluation in the field is not really possible, and in any case the problem itself may have altered. Thus 'evaluation at the end of the system-design process overlaps evaluation at the beginning of the system-design process'.

This picture of systems engineering as the total task of conceiving, designing, evaluating and implementing a system to meet some defined need—the carrying out, in other words, of an engineering *project*—is the one which persists throughout accounts of this activity; and, from the 1950s on, many engineers and project managers in large organizations were consciously formulating the procedures needed to make such projects successful, including the necessary sequencing of activities as well as approaches to the problem of co-ordinating the efforts of numerous specialists. Williams[17] gives an account of the approach adopted within the Monsanto company; but the leaders were probably Bell Telephone Laboratories[18] and the classic account of systems engineering methodology, that of Hall[19, 20] is the result of Bell Telephone experience.

Hall sees systems engineering as part of 'organised creative technology' in which new research knowledge is translated into applications meeting human needs through a sequence of plans, projects and 'whole programs of projects'. He goes on:

> Thus systems engineering operates in the space between research and business, and assumes the attitudes of both. For those projects which it finds most worthwhile for development, it formulates the operational, performance and economic objectives, and the broad technical plan to be followed.

Hall envisages, and illustrates, a sequence of steps in the systems engineering process, these being 'generalised from case histories' rather than developed theoretically. This an important indication of the spirit behind this approach.

The problem-solving sequence in Hall is as follows:

Problem definition (essentially definition of a need)

↓

Choice of objectives (a definition of physical needs and of the value system within which they must be met)

↓

Systems synthesis (creation of possible alternative systems)

↓

Systems analysis (analysis of the hypothetical systems in the light of objectives)

↓

Systems selection (selection of the most promising alternative)

↓

System development (up to the prototype stage)

↓

Current engineering (system realization beyond prototype stage and including monitoring, modifying and feeding back information to design).

As an initial example Hall quotes from Engstrom an account of the development in America of colour television. The need for such a system was examined, together with its technical and economic feasibility. These considerations introduced an important constraint into the statement of objectives: because of the existing investment in black-and-white receivers the systems engineers concluded that the new system must be compatible with the existing service. Systems synthesis to meet the objectives required some technical inventions to be made; system selection related to apparatus design, practical operation under normal broadcast service conditions and Federal approval of signal specifications. Then came the problems of establishing the service, which involved developing new studios, connecting broadcasting networks, installing transmitters and creating programme production groups. Finally the technical performance and public reaction to the new system had to be measured: all this Engstrom sees as a ' "text book" example of the systems concept

in action', with a systems project team 'working toward the single defined objective'. Hall's own major case history describes the 14 years of work on establishing and improving a continent-wide microwave radio relay system. Again there is careful emphasis on defining a range of precise objectives so that expected performance can be stated and the criteria named by which performance will be measured.

The pattern of Hall's exposition is recognizable in most later accounts of systems engineering. Chestnut [21] in an account broadly similar to Hall's emphasizes that the systems engineering process is itself a system which has to 'engineered':

> . . . the overall problem of systems engineering (is) composed of two parts, one being the systems engineering associated with the way that the operating system itself works and the other with the systematic process of performing the engineering and associated work in producing the operating system.

The 'operating system' itself, in Chestnut's account, is still a physical entity of the kind which has traditionally been the concern of the engineering profession, though the overall system will also include activity systems. More recent accounts have emphasized that logically the thinking applies equally to the kind which professional *planners* are now expected to design—for example health care or public water systems. Thus de Neufville and Stafford[22] address their account to managers as well as engineers, and, like Hall include a summary of welfare economics as one tool relevant to a systems study. Their emphasis is on the need for multiple criteria in evaluating public projects, and on the theory of welfare economics as a source of the various elements which will make up a function which measures 'social welfare'. They accept that the decision on how objectives should be traded off against each other in social projects is taken by means of the political process, and that the role of the systems study is to feed that process, improving the quality and range of information available to decision makers:

> It is important that engineers, planners, and economists recognise not only their incapacity to determine a social welfare function, but also the legitimacy of the political process to decide social priorities.

It is their inclusion of social projects, presumably, which causes their account to be restricted to the analysis phase of the whole systems engineering sequence. Within that phase they advocate five steps which match those in the accounts already discussed: definition of objectives; formulation of measures of effectiveness; generation of alternatives; evaluation of alternatives; selection of the proposed system.

A recent European account[23] emphasizes that the starting point for the systems engineering process is often only a feeling of unease, an awareness that things could be better than they are, a point made earlier by Jenkins[24]. The assumption is that improvements will follow the modification or restructuring of a system, and the recommended iterative problem-solving cycle begins with the 'Zielformulierung' phase, the formulation of objectives which are neutral with regard to possible solutions, complete, precise and intelligible, and realistic. This is followed by the search for possible solutions and the choice between alternatives, on the usual pattern.

Finally, in a recently published account of 'systems engineering methodology for interdisciplinary teams' we have an account which, in the claims made for it, goes beyond earlier versions. Wymore[25] claims as within the scope of the team's efforts, just those considerations which de Neufville and Stafford accept as 'political' and hence, in their view, outside the boundaries of the systems study as such. The interdisciplinary team is said to be concerned with 'the analysis and design of large-scale, complex, man/machine systems'. The claim made is that this category may include not only such obvious examples as communication, transportation and manufacturing systems but also education systems, 'health systems' and law enforcement systems!

The methodology Whymore expounds is said to be 'powerful enough to state *any* system design or analysis problem' and to be based on an earlier mathematical theory of systems[26] which is itself 'based rigorously on set theory'. The underlying structure of the methodology in fact fits the pattern which runs through earlier versions: define the proposed performance the system is required to achieve, generate alternative possibilities, and select one on the basis of defined criteria. The specific form of it involves a definition of what is required in terms of a set of input trajectories (varying over time) and a set of output trajectories. A potential *system* is an arrangement which matches an input trajectory to an output trajectory:

> ... (a) way to look at an input/output specification is as a formal description of the total range of possible performances by the system to be designed, from the possibility of abysmal failure to the possibility of perfect performance ...
> ... it is the function of the interdisciplinary system design team eventually to choose one possible (input/output) matching for the purposes of design and development of a system ...

Having generated a set of input/output matchings which meet the ultimate requirements—that is, having carefully specified what is *desirable*—the team now proceed to define the set of potential systems (i.e. input/output matchings) which are *feasible* with available technology. Any system which is a member of both the desirable set and the feasible set is a candidate for implementation, and selection is done on the basis of criteria such as: the input/output merit ordering, the technology merit ordering, profit, performance, quality/reliability, cost/benefit etc.

Wymore's account sets out in detail the logic involved in synthesising sub-systems into systems, and so designing the latter that objectives are met and constraints accommodated. It is the most elaborate exploration of the logic inherent in the kind of engineering process of which Hall gives the classic account. Whether or not we should accept the claim that 'soft' human activity systems, such as education or health care systems, can be engineered by this process unfortunately cannot be decided by a reading of the book. This restricts itself to spelling out the logic of the systems engineering process and claiming that it is universally applicable. This claim is really a version of the view which may be vulgarly expressed as the idea that there is a 'technological fix' for every problem. Early in the book Wymore points out that there are many models available which purport to describe and predict various aspects of human behaviour; he advocates using them, since 'we must be able to predict (the human being's) behaviour as a component in a system' and claims that:

> Extant insights from the behavioural sciences *are* sufficient to enable the development of the system-theoretic models of human behaviour in a restricted environment.

His advice is to bring in at the appropriate time the expert with the appropriate model, as when in discussion a notional example of an education system whose objective is to produce a person specializing in engineering he writes:

> Do you worry too much at this stage about how to measure social contributions or family contributions, for example, or the student's competence in self-education? We will enlist experts to serve on the interdisciplinary team who can help to design state-of-the-art symbols for levels or states of these various attributes and who can help to design instruments for assessing these levels or states ...

Only specific case histories could dispel the utopian ring of this. Such cases may be forthcoming in the future, but at this stage the relevant point is that here is the latest in the long line of accounts of how to go about the engineering of systems which has been appearing over the last two decades and which ought in principle to provide guidelines for attempts to solve real-world problems by seeking to 'engineer', in the broad sense of the word, that special class of system: the human activity system[27]. Another source of such guidelines is the tradition of 'systems analysis', which parallels and overlaps that of 'systems engineering'.

Systems analysis

Simultaneously with the development of systems engineering in the 1950s there emerged the strand of methodological thinking known as 'systems analysis', a development associated especially with the RAND Corporation, a non-profit making corporation in the advice-giving business. Though it is not easy to find explicit accounts of the methodological thinking which gradually evolved in the course of actual studies made by RAND professionals, the outlines of the methodology are quite clear, and what is being practised and developed at the International Institute of Applied Systems Analysis (IIASA) in the 1970s is undoubtedly RAND-style analysis[28].

The development which made possible the emergence of institutions like RAND Corporation was the involvement of scientifically-trained civilians in the planning of military operations during World War II. The success of operational research teams established in military thinking the value of scientific analyses of the kind OR could provide[29]. In the now-classic wartime OR studies the concern was usually tactical. Early applications included studies of anti-submarine tactics and the co-ordination of the use of radar with anti-aircraft guns and interceptor aircraft. In the immediate post-war years scientifically-based advisory work shifted to broader issues and there emerged what a historian of RAND Corporation describes as 'a broader and more refined sister discipline—"systems analysis"'. Actually, there is a strong case for describing systems analysis as *less* refined than OR! But we can agree that it was 'less quantitative in method and more oriented toward the analysis of broad strategic and policy questions'[30].

In 1944 and 1945, discussions among officials of the War Department and the office of Scientific Research and Development in Washington led to the idea of 'a contract with a private organization to assist in military planning, and particularly in co-ordinating planning with research and development decisions. Thus the concept of Project RAND began to emerge in nascent form in mid-summer 1945' (Smith)[30]. RAND is an acronym for 'research and

development', and *Project* RAND was a contract with the Douglas Aircraft Company for a study of 'inter-continental warfare, other than surface, with the object of advising the Army Air Forces on devices and techniques'. Work on the contract began in 1946, the initial four employees being located in the main Douglas building in Santa Monica. The first report carried the title 'Preliminary Design of an Experimental World-Circling Spaceship', and it is essentially a contribution to a systems engineering study. By 1947 Douglas felt that Project RAND was a commercial liability, in that the Air Force, in placing other contracts, tried hard to avoid the appearance of giving preferential treatment to Douglas; Douglas lost some contracts they expected to get. The result was that in 1948 the RAND Corporation separated from Douglas and was established as an independent non-profit advisory corporation funded initially by the Ford Foundation and some San Francisco banks.

The emphasis on systems engineering in early RAND studies was quickly replaced by an emphasis on cost and strategic considerations. In later years RAND's President described its role to a congressional committee in the following terms:

> RAND is engaged primarily in long-range research and analyses . . . as an aid to strategic and technical planning and operations. We have no laboratories . . . we do not manufacture hardware . . . we do not act as systems engineers as that term is usually used in industry[30].

During the 1950s the pattern of RAND style 'systems analysis' became clearer. The work done consisted of broad economic appraisal of all the costs and consequences of various alternative means of meeting a defined end. It was a refinement of the kind of cost-benefit analysis which had been developing in Government since the 1930s and of the 'requirements approach' especially associated with the Department of Defence, an approach characterized by definition, by officials, of a 'requirement' whose provision will solve a problem. The requirement might be a task, a piece of equipment or a complete system. Feasibility and performance characteristics of alternatives are then checked, and the analysis is passed to Government decision-makers for a decision on whether the necessary budget can be obtained. In one of the first book-length accounts of systems analysis, McKean of RAND Corporation takes the 'requirement approach' as given, and argues that systems analysis extends it by putting more emphasis on cost estimation during the course of the analysis[31]. Systems analysis asks, he says: 'what are the pay-offs *and the costs* of alternative programs?' He argues that there is a need for formal quantitative cost-benefit analysis in all aspects of Government, not merely in Defence, because Government spending lacks any 'natural' mechanism for promoting efficiency' such as a free-market price mechanism might provide. His discussion centres on the problems of choosing performance criteria, selecting alternatives to be compared, dealing with intangibles and uncertainties, and taking into account the fact that time is an important aspect of both gains and costs. The emphasis throughout is on the search for economic efficiency in Government-funded activities, and the same theme was developed in more detail for defence spending by Hitch and McKean[32]. They regard systems analysis as '*a way of looking* at military problems' which they insist can be treated as problems of economics in the sense that 'economics is concerned with allocating resources—choosing doctrines and techniques—so as to get the most out of available resources'. The search for economic efficiency can be helped by 'increased reliance on systematic quantitative analysis to determine the most efficient alternative allocations and methods'. By 1967, a book on Defence Management (edited by Enke)[33] could claim that the adoption of the RAND approach was 'a revolution' which was now in the past. That book could now address itself, in an article by McKean, to 'remaining difficulties'. The revolution referred to was the introduction of RAND-style systems analysis/cost-benefit analysis/program budgeting into the Pentagon by Secretary McNamara in the 1960s. McNamara selected Charles Hitch as his Comptroller, and by 1965 there was an 'Assistant Secretary of Defence for Systems Analysis'.

The formal methodology of systems analysis was described briefly by many RAND authors during the 1950s[2]. In a 1955 RAND report[34] Hitch gives an account which has many similarities with systems engineering (and OR) methodology which was emerging at the same time. The essential elements are described as:

1 An objective or objectives we desire to accomplish.
2 Alternative techniques or instrumentalities (or 'systems') by which the objective may be accomplished.
3 The 'costs' or resources required by each system.
4 A mathematical model or models; i.e. the mathematical or logical framework or set of equations showing the inter-dependence of the objectives, the techniques and instrumen-

talities, the environment and the resources.
5 A criterion, relating objectives and costs or resources for choosing the preferred or optimal alternative.

These are the elements in the approach. The making use of them, says Hitch is 'shot through with intuition and judgement'; systems analysis is 'a framework which permits the judgement of experts in numerous sub-fields to be combined'. It is clear that the word 'system' in systems analysis has two connotations. It is used in the same sense as in the phrase 'systems engineering', and this derives from the fact that, from the 1940s, defence requirements were usually expressed in terms of a total complex of equipment, personnel and procedures, rather than simply as a requirement for a specific piece of equipment. And the word is also used to indicate that the analyst tries to be comprehensive, to take into account many of the factors—financial, technical, political, strategic—which will affect decision on an important problem. The flavour of a RAND systems analysis is best described by Quade and Boucher[35].

> One strives to look at the entire problem, as a whole, in context, and to compare alternative choices in the light of their possible outcomes. Three sorts of enquiry are required, any of which can modify the others as the work proceeds. There is a need, first of all, for a systematic investigation of the decision-makers' objectives and of the relevant criteria for deciding among the alternatives that promise to achieve these objectives. Next, the alternatives need to be identified, examined for feasibility, and then compared in terms of their effectiveness and cost, taking time and risk into account. Finally an attempt must be made to design better alternatives and select other goals if those previously examined are found wanting.

Given the establishment of systems analysis as a way of tackling complex problems of resource allocation in defence, it is inevitable that it should be advocated as a methodology for business managers, who face problems of a similar kind. We have already noted that de Neufville and Stafford[22] address their account of what they call 'engineering systems analysis' to managers as well as engineers, and there are a number of accounts of systems analysis as an approach to business and industrial management[36, 37, 38] as well as systems-oriented accounts of management and organizational studies[39, 40, 41, 42]. In the business and management application area there is some confusion of 'systems analysis' in the broad, RAND, sense with the more limited kind of computer systems analysis which must precede the installation of computers, as when Schoderbek *et al.,* in a systems-based account of the management process, nevertheless define systems analysis as:

> the organised step-by-step study of the detailed procedures for the collection, manipulation and evaluation of data about an organisation for the purpose not only of determining what must be done, but also of ascertaining the best way to improve the functioning of the system[42].

However, when the broader sense of the term is used, we find the RAND methodology being urged upon managers. Lee, for example, advocates analysis and comparison of alternative solutions to the identified problem followed by the allocation of resources to 'a usable system, plan or method based upon the "best" solution'[38]. Advocacy of this kind tends to be more common than detailed accounts of specific case histories which we might hope would discuss the strengths and weaknesses of systems analysis in this area of application. Nevertheless the general concepts of RAND-style systems analysis are now part of the knowledge of any competent manager.

The nature of systems engineering and systems analysis

Systems engineering comprises the set of activities which together lead to the creation of a complex man-made entity and/or the procedures and information flows associated with its operation. Systems analysis is the systematic appraisal of the costs and other implications of meeting a defined requirement in various ways. Both are 'research strategies' rather than methods or techniques[43], and both require 'art' from the practitioner while making use of scientific methods wherever possible. It is obvious that the two overlap: S.E. is the totality of an engineering project in the broadest sense of that term; S.A. is a type of appraisal relevant both to the decision-making which ought to precede the setting up of any engineering project and to the early stages of such a project once it is started. Hall[19] acknowledges this in his statement that 'the RAND Corporation . . . developed a useful philosophy . . . similar to what we shall call later the first phase of systems engineering'. Both activities use the word 'system' to indicate their nature. Systems engineering is a systematic in the control engineers' sense of that word, while both S.E. and S.A. are *systematic* in the sense that they proceed by rational and well-ordered steps. Their similarities stem from this commitment to a systematic approach, and behind this, at the core of both S.E. and S.A., is the single idea which links them, the idea that an important class of real-world problems can be formulated in the following way: there is a desired state, S_1, and a present state, S_0, and alternative ways of getting from S_0 to S_1. 'Problem solving', according to this view, consists of defining S_1 and S_0 and selecting the best means of reducing the difference between them. Thus, in S.E., $(S_1 - S_0)$ defines 'the need', or the objective to be attained, and S.A. provides an ordered way of selecting the best among the alternative systems which could fulfil that need. *The belief that real-world problems can be formulated in this way is the distinguishing characteristic of all 'hard' systems thinking,* whether it emerges as S.E. or S.A. Faith in this belief has been strong, which explains why the literature of systems methodology has been insisting since the 1950s that at the start of a systems study it is necessary to define the need, the aim to be achieved, the system which when engineered will meet the need, the mission to be accomplished etc. The table collects some representative statements made in the period 1955–1976 about the initial phase of a systems study, whether it is called S.E., S.A. or the 'systems approach'. The words differ somewhat but the thought is always the same, that at the start of the study it is essential to know, and to state, what end we want to achieve, where we want to go. Given that definition, the systems thinking then enables us to select a means of achieving the desired end which is efficient, if possible *economically* efficient.

It is not surprising that this outlook underlies 'hard' systems thinking, it is inevitable, given the historical origins of systems engineering and systems analysis in the world of engineering and engineering economics. Hard systems thinking makes use of the kind of thinking which is natural to design engineers, whose role is to provide an efficient means of meeting a defined need. The design engineer exercises his professionalism in a situation in which *what* is required has been defined, and he must examine *how* it can be provided. His skill and flair are directed to providing ingenious possible answers to the question: how? The best design engineer is the man who generates the cheapest, most efficient and ingenious alternatives, the man, for example who first designs a bridge with arch and keystone where previous beam-based structures have required closely-spaced support pillars, thereby achieving a cheaper, more elegant and more efficient means of meeting a defined need. Much skill is called for in engineering design, and much resolution in converting design into realised artifact, but the relevant point here is that the design engineer's problem is a *structured* one: there is a gap to be bridged between the desired future state and the present state; *how* to bridge it is the problem. For the engineer as a professional, the need- and objective-defining are taken

Author	Date	Name given to the systems activity	Initial phases
Hitch [34]	1955	Systems analysis	The first element is 'an objective which we desire to accomplish'.
Hall [19]	1962	Systems engineering	'Problem definition is isolating, possibly quantifying, and relating that set of factors which will define the system and its environment . . . a problem is an outward expression of an unsatisfied need . . .'.
Quade [45]	1963	Military systems analysis	'Systems analysis is undertaken primarily to suggest or recommend a course of action. This action has an aim or objective. Policies or strategies, forces or equipment are examined and compared on the basis of how well and cheaply they can accomplish this aim . . .'.
Machol [46]	1965	Systems engineering	'In the first go around the general outlines of the system and one-significant-figure estimates of its performance can be drawn up'.
Chestnut [21]	1967	Systems engineering	'Establish the value or need for the system'.
Jenkins [24]	1969	Systems approach	'1.1 Recognition and formulation of the problem 1.2 Organisation of the systems project 1.3 Definition of the system . . .'.
Lee [38]	1970	Systems analysis	'Recognition that a problem or a challenge exists . . . . Research to find possible solutions . . . analysis and comparison of these alternatives to determine the 'best' one . . .'.
de Neufville and Stafford [22]	1971	Engineering systems analysis	'1. Definition of objectives . . . . The ultimate purpose . . . is to develop an application for the relative effectiveness with which selected alternatives meet some set of goals'.
Miles [47]	1973	Systems approach	'1. Goal definition or problem statement'.
Chase [48]	1974	Systems engineering	'Describe mission or use requirements'.
Daenzer [23]	1976	Systems engineering	The concrete and problem-oriented work begins with the formulation of objectives. 'What is involved . . . is systematic thinking concerning the formulation of objectives'.
Wymore [25]	1976	Systems engineering	'What is the system supposed to do, basically?'

The initial phases in a dozen accounts of 'hard' systems methodology published 1955–1976 [44]

as given at the start of his problem-solving, and we find this carried over into 'hard' systems methodology together with the structured model of problem-solving which objective-defining implies[49].

The ultimate identity of 'hard' systems thinking with engineering and economics is seen in the intermittent debate which goes on about whether 'systems engineering' is not simply 'good engineering'. Thus, where Gibson[50], for example, sees systems engineering as 'a branch of the art (of engineering) with problems, methods and objectives peculiar to itself', it is not surprising that *chemical* engineers fail to see any distinctive attribute which is not already present in their discipline. They are used to modelling complex designed physical systems, and to estimating the contribution of individual components to an overall economic measure of performance. Sargent sees the coining of the term 'systems engineering' as signalling

a determined take-over bid from the communications and control engineers, who say this as a natural extension of their own field, with perhaps a nervous look over their shoulders at the proponents of 'cybernetics'[51].

He concludes, fairly enough, that:

the basic systems approach is seen to be nothing more than the traditional engineering approach. Indeed chemical engineering owes its emergence as a separate discipline to the application of precisely this philosophy to analysis of complex chemical processes. The recognition that these processes were built up from a basic set of 'unit operations' would nowadays be hailed as brilliant 'systems' concept.

Conclusion

The strand of systems thinking which derives from engineering is embodied both in 'systems engineering' and in 'systems analysis'. Examination of the origin and nature of these approaches shows both to be based upon the assumption that the problem task they tackle is to select an efficient means of achieving a known and defined end. This in fact suggests a definition of what constitutes 'hard' systems thinking: it is any systems thinking which adopts this means-end schema.

Now, although this goal-seeking model of problem solving is useful in well-defined, or 'hard' problems, it is not surprising that the formulations of systems engineering and systems analysis are less successful in unstructured or 'soft' problems. Here, one aspect of the problem situation is precisely the impossibility of defining desirable ends or objectives [44, 49]. The 'soft' systems thinking which is applicable in such situations has to abandon the means-end model upon which 'hard' systems thinking is based[52].

References

[1] Emery, F. E. (Ed.), *Systems Thinking*, Penguin Books, 1969.
[2] Optner, S. L. (Ed.), *Systems Analysis*, Penguin Books, 1973.
[3] Hoos, I. R., *Systems Analysis in Public Policy: A Critique*, University of California Press, 1972.
[4] Hoos, I. R., 'Engineers as Analysts of Social Systems: An Enquiry', *J. Sys. Eng.*, **4** (2), 1976.
[5] Boguslaw, R., *The New Utopians: A Study of System Design and Social Change*, Prentice Hall, 1968.
[6] Churchman, C. W., *The Systems Approach*, Dell, 1968.
[7] Bunge, M., 'Technology as Applied Science', in Rapp, F. (Ed.), *Contributions to a Philosophy of Technology*, Reidel, 1974.
[8] Wisdom, J. O., 'Rules for Making Discoveries', in Rapp, F. (Ed.), see 7 above.
[9] Skolimowski, H., 'The Structure of Thinking in Technology', in Rapp, F. (Ed.), see 7 above.
[10] Jarvie, I. C., 'The Social Character of Technological Problems', in Rapp, F. (Ed.), see 7 above.
[11] Thompson, A. B., 'A Third Generation of Synthetic Fibre Materials', *Paper to British Association Meeting*, Leeds, 1967.
[12] Sporn, P., *Foundations of Engineering*, Pergamon, 1964.
[13] Armytage, W. H. E., *A Social History of Engineering*, Faber and Faber, 1961.
[14] Dunsheath, P., *A History of Electrical Engineering*, Faber and Faber, 1961.
[15] Goode, H. H. and Machol, R. E., *Systems Engineering*, McGraw-Hill, 1957.
[16] Gosling, W., *The Design of Engineering Systems*, Heywood, 1962.
[17] Williams, T. J., *Systems Engineering for the Process Industries*, McGraw-Hill, 1961.
[18] Hunt, M. M., 'Bell Labs' 230 Long Range Planners', *Fortune*, May, 1954.
[19] Hall, A. D., *A Methodology for Systems Engineering*, Van Nostrand, 1962.
[20] Hall, A. D., 'Three Dimensional Morphology for Systems Engineering', in Rapp, D. (Ed.), see 7 above.
[21] Chestnut H., *Systems Engineering Methods*, Wiley, 1967.
[22] De Neufville, R. and Stafford, J. H., *Systems Analysis for Engineers and Managers*, McGraw-Hill, 1971.
[23] Daenzer, W. F. (Ed.), *Systems Engineering*, Hamstein, 1976.
[24] Jenkins, G. M., 'The Systems Approach', *J. Sys. Eng.* **1** (1), 1969.
[25] Wymore, A. W., *Systems Engineering Methodology for Interdisciplinary Teams*, Wiley, 1976.
[26] Wymore, A. W., *A Mathematical Theory of Systems Engineering*, Wiley, 1967.
[27] Checkland, P. B., 'A Systems Map of the Universe', *J. Sys. Eng.* **2** (2), 1971.
[28] Quade, E., Brown, K., Levien, R., Majone, G., Rakhmankulov, V., ' "Systems Analysis": An Outline for the State of the Art Survey Publications', IIASA Report RR-76-16, also J. Appl. Sys. Anal 5(2), 1978.
[29] More, P. M., 'The History and Development of Operations Research', in Kelleher, G. J. (Ed.), *The Challenge of Systems Analysis*, Wiley, 1970.
[30] Smith, B. L. R., *The RAND Corporation: Case Study of a Non-profit Advisory Corporation*, Harvard University Press, 1966.
[31] McKean, R. N., *Efficiency in Government Through Systems Analysis*, Wileyn 1958.
[32] Hitch, C. J. and McKean, R. N., *The Economics of Defence in the Nuclear Age*, Harvard University Press, 1960.
[33] Enke, S. (Ed.), *Defence Management*, Prentice-Hall, 1967.
[34] Hitch, C. J., 'An appreciation of Systems Analysis' in Optner, S. L. (Ed.): see 2 above.
[35] Quade, E. and Boucher, W. I. (Eds.), *Systems Analysis and Policy Planning: Applications in Defence*, Elsevier, 1968.
[36] Optner, S. L., *Systems Analysis for Business and Industrial Problem-Solving*, Prentice-Hall, 1965.
[37] Optner, S. L., *Systems Analysis for Business Management* (3rd edition), Prentice-Hall, 1975.
[38] Lee, A. M., *Systems Analysis Frameworks*, McMillan, 1970.
[39] Johnson, R. A., Kast, F. E. and Rosenweig, J. E., *The Theory and Management of Systems*, McGraw-Hill, 1963.
[40] Litterer, J. A., *Organisations Vol. 1: Structure and Behaviour; Vol. 2: Systems, Control and Adaption*, Wiley, 1963.
[41] Beckett, J. A., *Management Dynamics: The New Synthesis*, McGraw-Hill, 1971.
[42] Schoderbek, P. P., Kefalas, A. G. and Schoderbek, C. G., *Management Systems: Conceptual Considerations*, Business Publications (Irwin-Dorsey International), 1975.
[43] Fisher, G. H., *Cost Considerations in Systems Analysis*, Elsevier, 1971.

[44] Checkland, P. B., 'The Problem of Problem Formulation in the Application of a Systems Approach', *International Conference on Applied General Systems Research*, Binghamton, New York, July, 1977 (Proceedings to be published).

[45] Quade, E., 'Military Systems Analysis', in Optner, S. L. (Ed.), see 2 above.

[46] Machol, R. E., *Systems Engineering Handbook*, McGraw-Hill, 1965.

[47] Miles, R. F. (Ed.), *Systems Concepts*, Wiley, 1973.

[48] Chase, W. P., *Management of Systems Engineering*, Wiley, 1974.

[49] Checkland, P. B., 'Towards a Systems-based Methodology for Real-world Problem Solving', *J. Sys. Eng.* **3** (2), 1972.

[50] Gibson, R. E., 'The Recognition of Systems Engineering', in Flagle, C. D., Huggins, W. H., and Roy, R. H. (Eds.), *Operations Research and Systems Engineering*, John Hopkins Press, 1960.

[51] Sargent, R. W. H., 'Forecasts and trends in Systems Engineering', *The Chemical Engineer*, June, 1972.

[52] Checkland, P. B. 'Science and the Systems Paradigm', *Int.J.Gen.Sys.* **3** (2), 1976.

2 The systems revolution
R. L. Ackoff

THE SYSTEMS REVOLUTION

I believe we are leaving one cultural and technological age and are entering another, and that we are in an early stage of changes in our conception of the world and in our way of thinking about it. These changes, I believe, are as fundamental and as pervasive as were those associated with the renaissance and its product, the industrial revolution. This socio-technical revolution may well come to be known as the *resurrection*.

The systems age

Although eras do not have precise beginnings or ends, the 1940s can be said to have contained the beginning of the end of the machine age and the beginning of the systems age. This new age is the product of a new intellectual framework in which the doctrines of reductionism and mechanism and the analytical mode of thought are being supplemented (not replaced) by the doctrines of *expansionism* and *teleology*, and a new *synthetic* or *systems* mode of thought.

Expansionism is a doctrine that maintains that all objects and events, and experiences of them, are parts of larger wholes. It does not deny that they have parts but it focuses on the wholes of which they are part. It is another way of viewing things, a way that is different from, but compatible with, reductionism. It turns attention from ultimate elements to wholes with interrelated parts, to *systems*. Preoccupation with systems emerged during the 1940s. Only a few of the highlights of this process are noted here.

In 1941, the American philosopher Suzanne Langer argued that over the preceding two decades philosophy had shifted its attention from elementary particles, events, and their properties to a different kind of element, the *symbol*. A symbol is an element whose physical properties have no essential importance. Charles W. Morris (1946), another American philosopher, built on Langer's work a framework for the scientific study of symbols and the wholes of which they were part, *languages*. The focus shifted to the latter. In 1949 Claude Shannon, a mathematician at Bell Laboratories, developed a mathematical theory that turned attention to a still more inclusive phenomenon, *communication*. Another mathematician, Norbert Wiener (1948), in his book *Cybernetics*, put communication into a still larger context, that of *control*. By the early 1950s it became apparent that interest in control and communication was only an aspect of an interest in an even larger phenomenon, *systems*, to which biologist Ludwig von Bertalanffy (1968) drew attention with his work. *Systems* has since been increasingly recognized as the new organizing concept in science. The concept is not new but its organizing role is.

A system is a set of two or more elements of *any* kind; for example, concepts (as in the number system), ideas (as in a philosophical system), objects (as in a telephone system or organism), or people (as in a society). Therefore, it is *not* an ultimate indivisible element but a whole that can be divided into parts. The elements of the set and the set of elements have the following three properties:

1   The properties or behavior of each element in the set has an effect on the properties or behavior of the set as a whole. For example, every organ in an animal's body affects the performance of the body.

2   The properties and behavior of each part and the way they affect the whole depends on the properties and behavior of at least one other element in the set. Therefore, no part has an independent effect on the whole and each is affected by at least one other part. For example, the effect that the heart has on the body depends on the behavior of the lungs, and its own behavior does as well.

3   Every possible subgroup of elements in the set has the first two properties; that is, each has an effect, and none has an independent effect, on the whole. Therefore, the elements cannot be organized into independent subgroups. A system cannot be divided into independent subsystems. For example, all the subsystems in an animal's body—such as the nervous, respiratory, digestive, and motor

subsystems—interact and each affects the performance of the whole.

Because of these properties a set of elements that form a system always has some characteristics, or can display some behavior, that none of its elements or subsystems can. A human body, for example, can write, but none of its parts can. Furthermore, membership in the set either increases or decreases the capabilities of each element. For example, a heart that is not part of a living body (or some substitute for it) cannot live. A government official can do some things he could not do if he were not a part of the government. On the other hand, a child in class cannot do some things he could do if he were not in class.

A system, viewed structurally, is a divisible whole; but viewed functionally it is an *indivisible whole* in the sense that some of its essential properties are lost in taking it apart.

The parts of a system may themselves be systems and every system may be part of a larger system.

Preoccupation with systems brings with it the *synthetic* mode of thinking. In the analytic mode, it will be recalled, an explanation of a whole is derived from explanations of its parts. In synthetic thinking something to be explained is viewed as part of a larger system and is explained in terms of its role in that larger whole. For example, universities are explained by their role in the educational system rather than by the behavior of their parts, colleges and departments. *The systems age is more interested in putting things together than in taking them apart.*

Analytic thinking is, so to speak, closed thinking; synthetic thinking is open thinking. Neither negates the value of the other but by synthetic thinking we can gain understanding that we cannot obtain through analysis, particularly of that large class of phenomena that cannot be accommodated within a mechanistic conception of nature.

The synthetic mode of thought, when applied to systems problems, is called the *systems approach*. This way of thinking is based on the observation that each part of a system performs as well as possible relative to the criteria applied to it. This follows from the fact that the sum of the functioning of the parts considered independently of each other is seldom equal to the functioning of the whole. This can be illustrated as follows:

Suppose we collect one each of every model of available automobile. Suppose further that we then ask some expert automotive engineers to determine which of these cars has the best carburetor. When they have done so we note the result. Then we ask them to do the same for transmissions, fuel pumps, distributors, and so on through each part required to make an automobile. When this is completed we ask them to remove the parts noted from their respective automobiles and assemble them into a new automobile each of the parts of which would be the best available. The engineers would not be able to do so because the parts *would not fit together*. Even if they could be assembled it is doubtful that they would *work well together*. System performance depends critically on how the parts fit and work together, not merely on how well each performs independently; it depends on interactions rather than on actions.

Furthermore, a system's performance depends on how it relates to its environment—the larger system of which it is a part—and to other systems in that environment. For example, an automobile's performance depends on the weather, the road on which it is driven, and how it and other cars are handled. Therefore, in systems thinking we try to evaluate the performance of a system by evaluating its functioning in the larger system that contains it. It will be recalled that in the machine age cause–effect was the central relationship in terms of which all explanations were sought. At the turn of this century the American philosopher of science, E. A. Singer, Jr., noted that cause–effect was used in two different senses. First, it was used in the sense already discussed: a cause is a necessary and sufficient condition for its effect. Secondly, it was also used when one thing was taken as necessary but *not* sufficient for the other. For example, an acorn is necessary but not sufficient for an oak. Various soil and weather conditions are also necessary. Despite 'womens' lib', a mother is not sufficient, however necessary she is, for a child. Singer chose to refer to this less restrictive use of cause–effect as *producer–product*. It can also be thought of as probabilistic or nondeterministic cause–effect.

Because a producer is not sufficient for its product, other producers, coproducers, are also necessary. Taken collectively the coproducers constitute the producer's environment. Hence use of this relationship yields an environment-full, not an environment-free, way of thinking.

Furthermore, Singer (1959) showed that an image of Nature based on the producer–product relationship was compatible with (complementary to) one based on deterministic cause–effect, but that it permitted functional, goal-seeking, and purposeful behavior (and, hence, free will) to be studied objectively and scientifically. Teleological concepts no longer needed to be declared illegal or exiled to metaphysics.

Later, biologist G. Sommerhoff (1951) independently came to the same conclusions Singer had. In the meantime, in a series of papers that laid the groundwork for cybernetics, Arturo Rosenblueth, Norbert Wiener, and J. H. Bigelow (1943 and 1950) showed the great value of conceptualizing certain types of machine and man-machine system as functioning, goal-seeking, and purposeful entities. In effect they showed that whereas in the past it had been fruitful to study man as though he were a machine, it was becoming at least equally fruitful to study some machines and man-machine systems, so to speak, as though they were men; that is, as goal-seeking or purposeful. Thus, in the 1950s, teleology, the study of goal-seeking and purposeful behavior, was brought into science. It provided an alternative to mechanism.

In mechanistic thinking behavior is explained by identifying what caused it, never its effect. In teleological thinking behavior can be explained either by what produced it or by what it is intended to produce. For example, a boy's going to the store can be explained either by the fact that his mother sent him or by the fact that he intends to buy ice cream for supper. Study of the functions, goals, and purposes of individuals and groups is yielding a greater ability to evaluate and improve their performance than mechanism did.

The post industrial revolution

The doctrines of expansionism and teleology and the synthetic mode of thought are both the producers and the products of the post industrial revolution. But this revolution is also based on three technological developments, the first two of which occurred during the (first) industrial revolution. One of these emerged with the telegraph in the first half of the 19th century, followed by the invention of the telephone by Alexander Graham Bell in 1876, and of the wireless by Marconi in 1895. Radio and television followed in this century. Such devices mechanized *communication*, the *transmission of symbols*. Since symbols are not made of matter, their movement through space does not constitute physical work (except in a trivial and irrelevant sense). The significance of this fact was not appreciated at the time of the invention of communication machines.

The second technology emerged with the development of instruments that can *observe* the properties of objects and events. They generate symbols that we call *data*; hence, they are data-generating machines. The thermometer, odometer, speedometer, and volt meter are familiar examples. Such instruments can observe what man unaided cannot observe but in doing so they do not perform physical work because they do not apply energy to matter in any essential way.

The third and key technology emerged in the 1940s with the development of the electronic digital computer, a machine that could *manipulate symbols logically*. They can convert data into information and information into instruction. Hence they are *data-processing* and *decision-making* machines.

These three technologies made it possible to observe, communicate, and use symbols. By combining them in various ways it became possible to mechanize *mental work,* to *automate*. This is what the post industrial revolution is all about. It is not a mere extension of the industrial revolution; it is fundamentally different in kind.

Development and use of automation requires an understanding of the mental processes that are involved in observing, recording and processing what is observed, communicating the results, and using them to make decisions and control our affairs. Since 1940 a number of interdisciplines have been developing to generate and apply knowledge and understanding of mental processes. I shall examine them and their impact on science in the last part of this paper.

Neither the hardware nor the software of the post industrial revolution provide panaceas. They can be used either to create or to solve problems. The ultimate outcome of this revolution will depend on the effectiveness with which we use its technology and the ends for which we do so. The revolution can fail because we fail to apply its products to the appropriate threats and opportunities.

The organizing problems of the systems age

Because the systems age is teleologically oriented it is preoccupied with systems that are goal-seeking or purposeful; that is, systems that can display *choice* of either means or ends, or both. Its interests in purely mechanical systems derive from their use as instruments by purposeful systems. Furthermore, the systems age is most concerned with those purposeful systems whose parts are purposeful, with *groups*. The most important class of groups is the one containing systems among whose parts there is a functional division of labor: *organizations*. Groups and organizations are themselves parts of larger purposeful systems.

There are three ways in which such systems can be studied. We can try to increase the effectiveness with which they serve (1) their own purposes, (2) the purposes of their parts, and (3) the purposes of the larger systems of which they are part. These are, respectively, the *self-control*, the *humanization*, and the *environmentalization* problems. They are obviously interrelated. I call them 'organizing problems' because most, if not all, of the problems that confront systems can be interpreted as manifestations of one or some combination of these problems.

The self-control problem

To direct a goal-seeking or purposeful system towards its goals or objectives from within that system is to exercise self-control. A subsystem whose function it is to control the larger system of which it is part is a *management* system. *Decision making* is essential for self-control because to decide is to choose and choice of ends and means is the essence of goal-seeking and purposeful behavior. When (1) a decision maker is dissatisfied with the state that he or the system he controls is in, (2) choice of means or ends is possible, and (3) he is in doubt as to which means or end to choose, he is in a *problematic situation*. Problem solving is the activity directed at removing the doubt, making a choice, and eliminating the dissatisfaction. Hence, problem solving appears to be a major aspect of self-control.

The first position that I will take is that problems exist only as *abstract subjective constructs*, not as concrete objective states. Furthermore, I will argue that even if they were objective states *they would not have solutions*, if by 'solutions' we mean actions that extinguish a problem or put it to rest. I will maintain that in dealing with problems and solutions we have been dealing with shadows rather than substance. I will *not* argue, however, that we have been wasting our time. The sleight of mind in which we have been engaged has been, and can continue to be, useful. But its usefulness is limited and there is a bigger, more difficult, and more important job to be done.

Now to elucidate. Problems have traditionally been assumed to be *given* or *presented* to an actor much as they are to students at the end of chapters in text books. Where they come from and why they are worth solving is implicitly assumed to be irrelevant to consideration of how they should be solved or what their solutions are. Books dealing with the methodology of research and problem solving seldom give more than a polite nod to problem generation, identification, and formulation. They move impatiently to problem solving. They do this despite advice to the contrary given by two eminent American philosophers, William James and John Dewey. They sought to make us aware of the fact that problems are *taken up by,* not *given to,* decision makers. William James argued that problems are extracted from unstructured states of confusion. John Dewey

referred to such states as *indeterminate* or *problematic*. I prefer to call then 'messes'.

What decision makers deal with, I maintain, are messes, not problems. This is hardly illuminating, however, unless I make more explicit and precise the meaning of 'mess'. A mess is a system of external conditions that produces dissatisfaction. It can be conceptualized as a *system of problems* in the same sense in which a physical body can be conceptualized as a system of atoms.

If the reality with which decision makers deal consists of messes from which systems of problems can be abstracted, then there are a number of important implications to the decision sciences. Let me explore some of them with you briefly.

First, then, a problem is an ultimate element abstracted from a mess. In this respect it is treated by decision scientists as other scientists have treated such elements as atoms and cells. It is important to recognize that ultimate elements are necessarily abstractions which *cannot* be observed. It is not possible for us to conceive of something which can be observed but cannot be divided into parts. We cannot see geometric points; they are abstractions. What we see and call points are small areas. Therefore, what we see and call problems are small messes, mini-messes.

Problems, even as abstract mental constructs, do not exist in isolation, although isolate them conceptually. They are elements of systems. Therefore, each affects the fate of the messes of which they are part; none has an independent effect on the fate of any of these messes; and every subgrouping of them also has these properties. This systematic property of problems has several important consequences for decision theory.

The 'solution' to a mess—whatever it may be—is not the simple sum of the solutions to the problems which are or can be extracted from it. No mess can be solved by solving each of its component problems independently of the others because no mess can be decomposed into independent problems. The optimal solution to a mess is not the sum of the optimal solutions to its component problems treated independently of each other.

Now I am not denying the existence of simple situations which can be improved by extracting one problem from them and solving it. After all, we can make an in-operative automobile work by replacing one defective part. But I deny that *all* problematic situations can be handled in this way or that any of the organizational, institutional, or societal messes which face us today can be so treated with any effectiveness.

Decision makers, particularly those with responsibility for others, must cope with messes. Improved methods of solving problems do not assure improved methods of coping with messes. On the other hand, decomposing messes into independent problems, even ones that are solvable optimally, does assure failure to cope with at least some messes as effectively as possible.

The attempt to deal with a system of problems as a system—synthetically, as a whole—is an essential property of *planning* in contrast to problem solving. Although a great deal of effort has gone into the development of methods of problem solving, we have only begun to develop a corresponding methodology of planning. Effective self-control depends critically on using the best planning methodology available and on improving what we have . . .

THE PARADIGM

I suggested earlier that the predict-and-prepare paradigm employed by OR be replaced by one directed at designing a desirable future and inventing ways of bringing it about, and that OR replace its problem-solving orientation by one that focuses on planning for and design of systems. I would like to amplify this alternative paradigm a bit. It has been developed at length in other places.

Operating principles

The planning paradigm I have proposed usually goes under the name *interactive*. (Some call it *proactive*.) It is based on three operating principles.

First, the *participative principle*. Most planners and consumers of plans believe that the principal benefit of planning comes from the consumption of the plans it produces. The interactive paradigm is based on a contrary belief: that *the principal benefit of planning comes from engaging in it*. In planning, process is the most important product. This belief has two important implications for the way planning is carried out.

It implies that no one can plan effectively for someone else: that it is better to plan for oneself, no matter how badly, than to be planned for by others, no matter how well. Interactive plans are not prepared by planning units either from within or without the organization planned for, and then submitted to its management for approval. Rather, management engages directly in the planning process. Doing so is one of its major responsibilities. This commitment to participation also calls for the involvement of all others who can be affected by the plans made, or their representatives. Such comprehensive participation and the co-ordination it requires can be and has been obtained even in very large systems by means of what I have called a 'circular organization' of the planning process. This design is described in my book, *A Concept of Corporate Planning*.

The participative principle also implies that planners should not emulate medical doctors by diagnosing the ailments of others and prescribing for them. Rather they should be like teachers who, although they cannot learn for their students, can facilitate their students' learning for themselves. Professional planners should be facilitators of the planning of others for themselves.

A major consequence of participation by stakeholders in the planning process is a reduction of the problems associated with implementing plans. People are considerably more inclined to implement plans in which they have had a productive hand than those that are handed down to, or imposed on, them.

Secondly, *the principle of continuity*. Most planning is done cyclically. It is carried out during a specified period after which implementation of its output is initiated. With implementation begun, planning stops until shortly before the end of the period covered by the plan. Such planning is discontinuous; *it should be continuous*.

No plan ever works exactly as expected because things happen that are not, and could not have been, anticipated. Therefore, plans should be continuously revised in light of (i) their performance, (ii) unexpected problems and opportunities that arise, and (iii) the latest information, knowledge and understanding available, much of which is derived from the implementation process.

Nor is any plan so complete as to dictate every decision that every manager must make during the period in which it is implemented. Those decisions not so dictated should be reviewed for their effects on the plan and the plan should be reviewed for its effects on them.

Furthermore, since the principal benefit of planning derives from engaging in it, why should it be discontinued?

Third, the *holistic principle*. The first part of this principle asserts that *all units at the same level of an organization should be planned for simultaneously and interdependently*. The reason for this is that a problem or opportunity that appears in any one unit may not be able to be treated as effectively in that unit as somewhere else. This should be as apparent as the fact that the best way to treat a headache may not be to treat the head. In fact, the best treatment may not involve treating the body at all, but changing its environment.

The second part of this principle asserts that *no level of a multilevel system can be planned for effectively without involving every level of that system.* Problems that occur at one level are often the consequence of what has been or has not been done at another level. Therefore, the best treatment of a problem or opportunity may consist of actions taken at a level above or below the one at which the problem or opportunity appears.

Combining these two parts of the holistic principle we obtain: *every part of a system and every level of it should be planned for simultaneously and interdependently.* This stands in opposition to two prevailing practices: top-down and bottom-up planning.

The content of interactive planning

Now consider the content of interactive planning. Planning should include (i) formulating the mess, (ii) setting organizational goals, objectives and ideals and selecting the means for pursuing them, (iii) providing the resources required by the pursuit, (iv) organizing and managing the pursuit and (v) implementing and controlling it. The order in which I have presented these aspects of planning is not necessarily the order in which they should be initiated and certainly not completed. In continuous planning none of them is ever completed. More important is the fact that these aspects of planning are interdependent, each of which affects and is affected by the others.

Formulating the mess involves identifying the problems and prospects facing the organization and revealing the relationships between them; that is, conceptualizing them as a system. Such conceptualization requires synthesis, not analysis. The mess is often best formulated as scenarios of likely futures of the organization which are based on the (not necessarily valid) assumption that no significant changes will be made in current organizational policies and practices.

Means-ends planning should be concerned with producing a design of a desired future and inventing ways of approximating it as closely as possible. I will return to this aspect of planning in a moment.

Resource planning is concerned with determining what resources will be required, when, how they are to be acquired or generated and how they should be allocated once available. Five types of resource should be taken into account: people, plant and facilities, materials and energy, money and information.

Organizational and management planning is concerned with designing the organization and the system for managing it so as to make possible effective execution and modification of plans, and effective organizational learning and adaptation.

Design of implementation and control is concerned with determining who is to do what, where and when; and how what they do and its effects should be monitored—that is, how performance should be compared with expectations, and how significant differences between them should be diagnosed and corrected.

Idealized design for the planned system

The key to interactive planning is the way that ends and means are selected in it. This selection is based on the preparation of an *idealized redesign* of the system planned for—a design of the system with which the designers would replace the existing system *now* if they were free to do so. Such a redesign is subject to only two constraints. First, the replacement should be *technologically feasible*; otherwise it could turn out to be science fiction. Secondly, the new system should be *operationally viable*—that is, capable of survival if it were brought into existence, but no attention should be given to whether or not it can be brought into existence.

The idealization process involves several design principles that significantly differentiate its product from a utopia. First, the design is subject to continuing change by its designers, particularly as a result of what is learned from efforts to implement it. Second, for those design questions which have no clear answer the designers should incorporate into the system-design an ability to determine experimentally how they should be answered. Thus they design into the system an ability to learn from its own experience and a capability of redesigning itself continuously. Third, because the system designed will have to face conditions not anticipated in its design, it should have designed into it an ability to monitor its environment and its own performance, so it can detect changes from expectations and improve its performance under these unexpected conditions. These abilities are necessary for adaptation to changing internal and external conditions.

Because of these three characteristics of the idealized-design process, its product is *not* a utopia, an ideal system, but the best *ideal-seeking* system its designers can currently conceptualize.

The remainder of the planning process is directed at approximating this ideal-seeking system as closely as possible. Thus, the role of an idealized design in interactive planning corresponds to that of a predicted future in conventional planning. The advantages of basing the planning process on such a design are many.

First, it *facilitates participation* in the planning process. Conventional planning usually requires an élite who have special planning and forecasting skills and detailed knowledge of the operations of the system planned for. But there are no experts when it comes to answering the question: what ought a system to be like? Here every stakeholder's opinion is as relevant as any other's.

Because engaging in such design is fun, participation is not hard to get. But it provides more fun. It provides its participants with an opportunity for learning how the parts of the system interact and how these interactions affect the performance of the whole. Such learning enables those engaged in the process to make decisions and take actions that have better effects on the performance of the whole. It is the acquisition and use of this ability that is the principal benefit of planning.

Second, *idealized design facilitates the incorporation of the aesthetic values of the system's stakeholders into its planning*. It provides a relatively unconstrained opportunity to those participating in it to insert their stylistic preferences and ideals, thereby removing the need for others to do so for them. Consideration of the quality of life within the organization and in its environment cannot be avoided, as it so often is in conventional planning.

Third, *participation in idealized design tends to generate a consensus among the participants*. Such consensus generally arises because the design process focuses more on ultimate values than on short-run objectives and means for pursuing them. There is usually more agreement about such values than there is about short-run objectives and means. When agreement is reached on ideals, differences over objectives and means are more easily resolved. Furthermore, when such differences cannot be resolved, the process requires that experiments be designed into the system that are capable of resolving them. Agreement on the design of such experiments is usually easier to obtain than on the issue they are directed at resolving. The amount of agreement generated in the design process usually comes as a pleasant surprise to the participants and reinforces their inclination to co-operate with each other.

Fourth, *idealized design mobilizes its participants into a crusade in pursuit of its product*. José Ortega y Gasset put this point much better than I can:

> . . . man has been able to grow enthusiastic over his vision of . . . unconvincing enterprises. He has put himself to work for the sake of an idea, seeking by magnificent exertions to arrive at the incredible. And in the end, he has arrived there. Beyond all doubt it is one of the vital sources of man's power, to be thus able to kindle enthusiasm from the mere glimmer of something improbable, difficult, remote.

Fifth, *idealized design releases large amounts of suppressed creativity and focuses it on organizational development*. Creativity is imprisoned in most people behind walls built of self-imposed constraints. Many of the self-imposed constraints that operate in conventional planning derive from considerations of *feasibility*. Because feasibility is not a requirement imposed on idealized design, this process tends to liberate the imagination and stimulate the desire and ability to invent and innovate. The fun derived from unconstrained creativity converts the work involved in such design into play.

Sixth and last, *the idealized-design process expands its participants' concept of feasibility*. In conventional planning the plan as a whole is arrived at only after considering each of its parts separately. Each part—policies, programmes, projects and practices—is separately put to the test of feasibility because a plan is taken to be like a chain, no more feasible than its least feasible part. This assumption is wrong and costly.

A plan is not like a chain. It is a *system* of policies, programmes, projects and practices. This means that it has properties that none of its parts does, and that its parts acquire properties by being a part of it that they do not have when considered separately. Therefore, it is possible to have a feasible plan no part of which is feasible when considered separately. It is also possible to have an infeasible plan each part of which appears to be feasible when considered separately.

After a group at my Center had participated in the design of an idealized National Scientific Communication and Technology Transfer System, I was asked to present it to a large meeting of the system's stakeholders. After the presentation one of them, a young man, commented from the floor as follows: 'This is the best thing that has happened in the field since I have been in it. It's exciting as hell. But why in the world do you call it *ideal*? We could have such a system right now if we really wanted it.'

That young man had got the point: *idealized design reveals that the largest obstruction between man and the future he most desires is man himself*. This obstruction can be removed by a set of mobilizing ideas. Idealized design can provide such ideas.

Now let me try to summarize in operational terms the planning paradigm sketched so briefly here. (i) When a problematic situation is presented do not cut it down to the size of a problem. Enlarge it by focusing on and formulating the largest relevant mess over which the management served has some control or influence. (ii) Subject the system whose mess you have formulated to participative idealized design so as to produce a concept of it that can either dissolve the initiating problematic situation or bring it under continuous and improving control. (iii) Finally, prepare an interactive plan for approximating that design as closely as possible.

Such a procedure substitutes planning and design for problem solving. Doing so facilitates the involvement of management, and it leads to enlargement of the organizational domain to which the researchers have access. Within a short time it enables them to work simultaneously at all levels of

an organization and thus deal with it both as a whole and as a part of a larger system.

References

R. L. Ackoff, *Redesigning the future,* Wiley, New York, 1974.

R. L. Ackoff, *A concept of corporate planning,* Wiley, New York, 1970.

José Ortega y Gasset, *Mission of the University,* Norton, New York, 1966.

R. L. Ackoff and J. R. Emshoff, 'Advertising research at Anheuser–Busch, Inc. (1963–68),' *Sloan Management Review,* Winter 1975, pp. 1–15; 'Advertising research at Anheuser–Busch, Inc. (1968–74),' *Sloan Management Review,* Spring, 1976, pp. 1–16.

3 Systems
W. Buckley

We shall not, in this reading, indulge to any great extent in the sport of defining the general concept of 'system' in formal terms. Our main emphasis will be on the differences among the major types of systems specified in terms of their structural arrangements and dynamics, and on the methodological problems of analysis they raise.

The kind of system we are interested in may be described generally as a complex of elements or components directly or indirectly related in a causal network, such that each component is related to at least some others in a more of less stable way within any particular period of time.[1] The components may be relatively simple and stable, or complex and changing; they may vary in only one or two properties or take on many different states. The interrelations between them may be mutual or unidirectional, linear, non-linear or intermittent, and varying in degrees of causal efficacy or priority. The particular kinds of more of less stable interrelationships of components that become established at any time constitute the particular structure of the system at that time, thus achieving a kind of 'whole' with some degree of continuity and boundary. Also, we are mainly interested in systems within which some process is continually going on, including an interchange with an environment across the boundary. It is generally agreed that when we deal with the more open system with a highly flexible structure, the distinction between the boundaries and the environment becomes a more and more arbitrary matter, dependent on the purpose of the observer.

In fact, it is becoming clear that we cannot make a neat division of those things that are and those that are not systems; rather, we shall have to recognize varying degrees of 'systemness.' And if we also recognize that the 'substances' or 'entities' that the various scientific disciplines study—nuclear 'particles,' atoms, molecules, solar systems, cells, organs, organisms, ecological communities, societies—are all sub-sumable under a definition of system, then we seem forced to accept the notion of varying degrees of 'entitivity.' If we continue to think in terms of 'real substances' this does not seem to make much

sense, for how can there be degrees of 'substance'? But if substances or entities represent systems whose characteristics or properties are due to a particular *organization* of lower-level components, and if we admit of varying degrees of organization, the mystery disappears. For we can understand that it is the *organization* that ceases to exist or is formed when, for example, a nuclear particle is 'annihilated' and another 'created,' or water is broken down into hydrogen and oxygen or table salt built up from sodium and chlorine atoms, or a living cell dies and becomes nothing but its constituent molecules while a new living cell is synthesized from such constituents, or a social group dissolves into its constituent individuals as another is created out of previously unrelated persons.

Thus, if social groups are not 'real entities' then neither are individual organisms, organs, cells, molecules or atoms, since they are all 'nothing but' the constituents of which they are made. But this 'nothing but' hides the central key to modern thinking—the fact of *organization* of components into systemic relationships. When we say that 'the whole is more than the sum of its parts,' the meaning becomes unambiguous and loses its mystery: the 'more than' points to the fact of *organization,* which imparts to the aggregate characteristics that are not only *different* from, but often *not found in* the components alone; and the 'sum of the parts' must be taken to mean, not their numerical addition, but their unorganized aggregation.

Generally speaking, we might say that the modern concepts of system and organization are now taking over the duty of the overworked and perhaps retiring concept of the 'organic.' This concept, along with that of mechanical equilibrium, has performed the essential job of bringing the social scientist to full recognition of the fact that the parts of society are not independent, that society is to some degree an interrelated whole. But further advance required that we come to appreciate the important ways in which society differs from the organic or the mechanical.

An important shift of focus occurred with the

growing recognition of the fact that, while phenomena of widely differing kinds are wholes constituted by more or less permanent relations of parts, a crucial distinguishing feature is *the particular nature of those relations*. After Spencer, it became clearer and clearer that whereas the relations of parts of an organism are physiological, involving complex physico-chemical *energy* interchanges, the relations of parts of society are primarily psychic, involving complex communicative processes of *information* exchange, and that this difference makes all the difference.

Comparative systems

We turn now to a more detailed consideration of the nature of the organization characterizing and differentiating types of systems. Our purposes are

1   To probe somewhat deeper into the intricacies of analysis of the nature of organization—beyond the mere interdependence of parts which characterizes any system;

2   To promote a deeper appreciation of the differences between the organization and dynamics of mechanical, organic, and sociocultural systems;

3   To introduce some key conceptions of modern systems analysis.

Since the types of systems we discuss here represent only three points along a series of possible system levels, our generalizations will only approximate any particular empirical system. And especially in the case of the mechanical system, our model is sometimes the man-made machine enthroned in the 18th and 19th centuries, the prototype often being the clock, rather than natural physical systems. The machine in this context will refer to the pre-cybernetic type, without deviation-regulating feedback loops. But to represent a system in equilibrium, our model may be a collection of gases or other substances at different temperatures, pressures, or concentrations, interacting in isolation from other influences long enough to reach an equilibrium state.

System parts: simple to complex

The *nature of the parts* or components of a mechanical system are, typically, relatively simple in their own structure, stable, and not appreciably or permanently affected by being part of the system. By contrast, as we proceed up through the organic and sociocultural levels the components that are interrelated become more complex in their own organization, more and more unstable (more easily subject to change by small forces), and more fundamentally

alterable by the workings of the system of which they are a part. These features, of course, are all prerequisite to the very development of higher levels of organization.

Systemic relations: energy links to information links

The *nature of the relations* among components varies importantly along many dimensions for different types of system. In mechanical systems of the machine type the interrelations are typically narrowly restricted, with very few degrees of freedom in the behavior of the components. The structure of the system is rigid, and we have an example of what Rapoport calls 'organized simplicity.'[2] In the typical equilibrium system of particle mechanics we find conditions at the opposite extreme, 'chaotic complexity.'[2] There are so many degrees of freedom in the relations of components that states of the system can only be specified statistically, and there is little or no stable structure.

Organic and sociocultural systems are examples of 'organized complexity.'[2] As we proceed up the various levels, the relations of parts become more flexible and the 'structure' more fluid with process as the set of alternative behaviors open to the components increases. Whereas the relations among components of mechanical systems are a function primarily of spatial and temporal considerations and the transmission of energy from one component to another, the interrelations characterizing higher levels come to depend more and more on the transmission of *information*—a principle fundamental to modern complex system analysis. Though 'information' is dependent on some physical base or energy flow, the energy component is entirely subordinate to the particular form or structure of variations that the physical base or flow may manifest. In the process of transmitting information, the base or carrier energy may change in many ways—as in the production and reproduction of phonograph records—but the structure of variations in the various media remains invariant over the carrier transformations. This structured variation—the marks of writing, the sounds of speech, the molecular arrangement of the genetic code substance DNA, etc.—is still only raw material or energy unless it 'corresponds' to, or matches in some important way, the structure of variations of other components to which it may thereby become dynamically related. A person speaking a language foreign to a companion is emitting only noise or vibrating energy as far as the latter is concerned, because there is no mapping of the structured variety of the vocal energy with the repertoire of meaningful sounds structured in the mind of the companion. If the latter did understand the language, however, and the information spoken was, 'Look out, a car is coming at you!'—the very small amount of vocal energy would trigger off a large amount of energy in the companion who is acting as the receiving system.[3]

Thus, 'information' is not a substance or concrete entity but rather a *relationship* between sets or ensembles of structured variety—to put it very generally. The implications of this shift from energy flow to information flow as a basis for the interrelations of components in higher level systems, are of central importance in distinguishing the nature and behavioral capabilities of the latter, as against lower-level systems. Thus, a minute amount of structured energy or matter from one component of a higher system is able to 'trigger' selectively a large amount of activity or behavior in other components in the system, at the same time overcoming limitations of temporal and spatial proximity as well as availability of energy. The components of systems thus become more autonomous in certain respects while still maintaining intimate and more intricate interrelation with one another. The structure of the system becomes more and more 'fluid' as it merges with process—the communication process which is its predominant feature. At the higher ecological, social, and sociocultural system levels, the component individuals need come into physical contact in the manner of mechanical systems only or principally in sexual union and physical combat.

Interactions among components mediated by the selective 'triggering' of information flows are possible, of course, only because (1) the system components are themselves organized and relatively unstable, or 'sensitive', or in 'tension,' such that they react easily to a small influence of the correct type (or code) and can release much larger amounts of bound energy than that embodied in the triggering signal; and (2) each of the alternative behaviors open to the system components have somehow become associated with one of the structural arrangements embodying the information code.

Donald M. MacKay is one of the small number of systems theorists who have tackled the question of *semantic* information from the perspective of modern information theory, and his work enlightens our present discussion. He begins by suggesting that so little progress is being made on the semantic side of information theory because of a failure to study the communicative process within a wide enough context to embrace, not only the channel and the nature of the signals flowing through it, but the terminal sender and receiver as goal-directed, self-adaptive systems.

Within this conceptual framework, MacKay then goes on to define information, meaning, and communication, in a generalized way that we believe to be especially congenial to, and an important theoretical underpinning for, the social interactionist perspective in sociology.

Information can now be defined as that which does logical work on the organism's orientation (whether correctly or not, and whether by adding to, replacing or confirming the functional linkages of the orienting system). Thus we leave open the question whether the information is true or false, fresh, corrective or confirmatory, and so on . . . The *meaning* of an indicative item of information to the organism may now be defined as its selective function on the range of the organism's possible states of orientation, or for short, its *organizing function* for the organism. It will be noted that this too is a relation . . .

A solitary organism keeps its orienting system up to date in response to physical *signs* of the state of the environment, received by its sense organs. This adaptive updating of the state of orientation we call *perception*. We can regard *communication* as an extension of this process whereby some of the organizing work in one organism is attempted by *another organism*. Normally this means that the receiving organism is induced to adapt itself in response to physical signs that are perceived as *symbols*—as calling for orienting (or other) activity over and above that which constitutes their perception as physical events.

The logical starting point for a semantic theory of communication would therefore seem to be the analysis of the organizing functions that are 'extensible' in this way from one organism to another.[4]

From closed to open systems

The transition from mechanical systems to adaptive, information-processing systems is closely related to the transition from the relatively *closed* to the *open* type of system. That a system is *open* means, not simply that it engages in interchanges with the environment, but that this interchange is *an essential factor* underlying the system's viability, its reproductive ability or continuity, and its ability to change. As L. J. Henderson was at great pains to point out in his book, *The Fitness of the Environment,* the environment is just as basic as the organic system in the intimate system-environment transactions that account for the particular adaptation and evolution of complex systems.[5] In fact, of course, the system and its environment make up sub-parts of a wider system which often must be treated on its own level. Indeed, this is a key principle underlying the field or transactional approach.

The typical response of natural, closed systems to an intrusion of environmental events is a loss of organization, or a change in the direction of dissolution of the system (although, depending on the nature and strength of the intrusion, the system may sometimes move to new level of equilibrium). On the other hand, the typical response of open systems to environmental intrusions is elaboration or change of their structure to a higher or more complex level. This is due to factors discussed above: the environmental interchange is not, or does not long remain, random or unstructured, but rather becomes selective due to the mapping, or coding, or information-processing capabilities (that is, its adaptiveness) inherent in this type of system. This is true whether the system is the lowliest biological organism or a complex sociocultural system. And as we proceed up the system levels we find the systems becoming more and more open in the sense that they become involved in a wider interchange with a greater variety of aspects of the environment, that is, are capable of mapping or responding selectively to a greater range and detail of the endless variety of the environment. At the sociocultural level the details of the natural environment become subordinate to the social, gestural, symbolic environment which is now mapped and responded to selectively in greater detail as the basis of group life.

System tension

As we noted earlier, the source of action and interaction of the parts of mechanical systems is expressed in the physical concept of energy, whereas in complex, adaptive systems raw energy plays a less and less important role as it gives way to a more complex form of organized and directed motive force that we refer to as the inherent 'irritability of protoplasm,' tension or stress in animals, and psychic energy or motive power in men. 'Tension,' in the broad sense, of which 'stress' and 'strain' are manifestations under conditions of felt blockage, is ever present in one form or another throughout the sociocultural system—sometimes as diffuse, socially unstructured strivings, frustrations, enthusiasms, aggressions, neurotic or normative deviation; sometimes as clustered and minimally structured crowd or quasi-group processes, normatively constructive as well as destructive; and sometimes as socioculturally structured creativity and production, conflict and competition, or upheaval and destruction. As Thelen and colleagues put it:

1   Man is always trying to live beyond his means. Life is a sequence of reactions to stress; Man is continually meeting situations with which he cannot quite cope.

2   In stress situations, energy is mobilized and a state of tension is produced.

3   The state of tension tends to be disturbing, and Man seeks to reduce the tension.

4   He has direct impulses to take action . . . [6]

Thus it can be argued that, far from seeing any principle of 'inertia' operating in complex adaptive systems, with 'tension' occurring only occasionally or residually as a 'disturbing' factor, we must see some level of tension as characteristic of and vital to such systems though it may manifest itself as now destructive, now constructive.

Feedback and purposive systems

Given the open, negentropic, information-processing nature of complex adaptive systems, we still need a more exact delineation of the mechanisms whereby these systems come to behave in a characteristic manner so different from physical systems—a manner usually expressed by the concept of 'purposive.' It is generally agreed among systems theorists that a basic principle underlying these purposive, or goal-seeking mechanisms is embodied in the concept of *feedback*. [7] The notion of feedback is seen as finally removing the ancient mysticism associated with teleology by redefining it in operationally respectable terms. As Anatol Rapoport has argued, the trend is definitely toward explanation in terms of 'efficient' causes operating here and now, and not of 'final' causes (or future events, system 'requirements,' or ultimate functions). Today we can treat 'purpose' causally in the former sense of forces acting here and now; if we can build a model of purposefulness, we can explain it.[8]

The concept of feedback has now been vulgarized, and is very often equated simply with any reciprocal interaction between variables. As a principle underlying the goal-seeking behavior of complex systems, however, it involves much more than that. As used here, it applies particularly to an open system:

1   Whose characteristic features depend on certain internal parameters or criterion variables remaining within certain limits;

2   Whose organization has developed a selective sensitivity, or mapped relationship, to environmental things or events of relevance to these criterion variables;

3   Whose sensory apparatus is able to distinguish any deviations of the systems' internal states and/or overt behavior from goal-states defined in terms of the criterion variables;

4   Such that feedback of this 'mismatch' information into the system's behavior-directing centers reduces (in the case of negative feedback) or increases (in the case of positive feedback) the deviation of the system from its goal-states or criterion limits.

Even the simple thermostat meets these basic requirements: it is a system of components open to one aspect of the environment, and contains: (1) A criterion variable representing the particular temperature setting selected, (2) An element sensitive to the temperature of the surrounding air such that (3) The system responds to deviations of the air temperature on either side of the setting by (4) Turning on or off the heating component such that the deviation is reduced (hence, an example of negative feedback). We shall refer to simpler closed causal loops, lacking in internal variables, as 'pseudo-feedback' loops.

Feedback-controlled systems are referred to as goal-*directed,* and not merely goal-*oriented,* since it is the deviations from the goal-state itself that direct the behavior of the system, rather than some predetermined internal mechanism that aims blindly. The significance of feedback control for complex systems can be partially expressed by a comparison of 'pre-cybernetic' machines with modern servomechanisms. In the former, the designer had to attempt to anticipate all the contingencies the machine was apt to meet in performing its task, and to build counter-acting features into the design; the modern machine, however, uses these very contingencies themselves as information which, fed into the machine, directs it against them. The great gain in capabilities is easily understood in these terms.

Of particular interest to us here in dealing with the evolution of complex adaptive systems is the development of more and more complex criterion-testing subsystems. Our concern is not so much with homeostatic mechanisms, which may or may not be made more comprehensible by translation into feedback terms, but rather with mechanisms that direct system behavior. These latter mechanisms run the gamut from tropistic, instinctual, and reflexive feedback testing mechanisms, to learned, conscious, symbol-actuated subsystems, to the mechanisms of social planning. It may be questionable whether all mechanisms on each of these levels involve true feedback, but it seems clear that higher levels of control, from cortical learning on, can only be adequately understood in terms of complex, often higher order feedback transactions.[9]

Other areas of psychology benefiting from the concept of feedback include those of stress, conflict, and disorganization, as represented by the work, for example, of Geoffrey Vickers and of Notterman and Trumbull.[10] Sociology, however, has yet to feel the impact of modern systems research. The little that has been written of sociological relevance by non-sociologists has not, for the most part, been presented in terms directly applicable to the field. The little that has been done with a cybernetic orientation by the sociologically minded will be discussed later. However, Karl W. Deutsch has provided a very useful discussion of the advances in social system analysis provided by the concept of feedback as contrasted with the notions of equilibrium or homeostasis. His views also add substantially to our earlier critique of these latter concepts as used in sociology, and will be presented briefly here. For Deutsch, feedback

... is a more sophisticated notion than the simple mechanical notion of equilibrium, and it promises to become a more powerful tool in the social sciences than the traditional equilibrium analysis.[11]

In Deutsch's view, to say that a social system is in equilibrium implies that: (1) it will return to a particular state when disturbed; (2) the disturbance is coming from outside the system; (3) the greater the disturbance the greater the force with which the system will return to its original state; (4) the speed of the system's reaction to disturbance is somehow less relevant—a sort of friction, or blemish having no place in the 'ideal' equilibrium; (5) no catastrophe can happen within the system, but once the equilibrium is disturbed, almost nothing can be said of the future of the society. Such equilibrium theories, Deutsch points out, are based on the very restricted field of 'steady state dynamics,' and are not well suited to deal with transient events, to predict the consequences of sudden changes. 'Altogether, in the world of equilibrium theory, there is no growth, no evolution, no sudden changes, no efficient prediction of the consequences of "friction" over time.'[11]

Feedback theory, on the other hand, does not push 'friction' into the background, but can deal specifically with the 'lag' and 'gain' between impinging events. Large 'lag' can be conceptualized as a swing away from common goals so far before feedback correction occurs that only violent reaction, for example, revolution, can bring the social system back to a more viable, goal-oriented state. A full appreciation of the role and nature of feedback permits a relatively objective attack on the problem of assessment and correction of the 'lag' in the system.

Deutsch further promotes our conception of feedback by suggesting the kinds of information required to 'steer' a society, the kinds or levels of feedback underlying system effectiveness, and the successive levels of purpose thereby made possible. For effective 'self-direction' a sociocultural system must continue to receive a *full flow* of three kinds of information: (1) information of the world outside; (2)

information from the past, with a wide range of recall and recombination; and (3) information about itself and its own parts. Three kinds of feedback, which make use of these types of information, include: (1) *goal-seeking*—feedback of new external data into the system net whose operational channels remain unchanged; (2) *learning*—feedback of new external data for the *changing of these operating channels themselves,* that is, a change in the structure of the system; and (3) *consciousness,* or 'self-awareness'—feedback of new *internal* data via secondary messages, messages about changes in the state of parts of the system itself. These secondary messages serve as symbols or internal labels for changes of state within the net. Finally, four successively higher orders of purposes can be recognized: (1) seeking of immediate satisfaction; (2) self-preservation, which may require overruling the first; (3) preservation of the group; and (4) preservation of a process of goal-seeking beyond any one group. These orders of purpose, of course, require successively higher-order feedback nets.[11]

These suggestion, of course, need extensive development but may serve here to make the point that, whereas the concept of 'equilibrium' is restricted to description of steady states, the cybernetic view is based on full dynamics, including change of state as an inherent and necessary aspect of complex system operation. In particular, it can be seen that cybernetics offers to restore the problem of purpose to a fuller share of attention, and even to help us make a much needed distinction between the attainment of actual external goals, and the reduction of goal-drive merely by internal readjustment that provides an ersatz satisfaction (or short-circuit), such as scapegoating, drug addiction, or other so-called 'mechanisms of control.' In Deutsch's view, more complex, goal-changing feedback conceptions take this distinction into account.

Morphostasis and Morphogenesis

The various features of complex adaptive systems sketched so far—openness, information-linkage of the parts and the environment, feedback loops, goal-direction, and so forth—provide the basic conceptional elements that underlie the general features characteristic of systems referred to as 'self-regulating,' 'self-directing,' and 'self-organizing.' These concepts all point to the fact that the behavior of complex, open systems is not a simple and direct function of impinging external forces, as is the case with colliding billiard balls or gravitational systems. Rather, as open systems become more complex

there develop within them more and more complex mediating processes that intervene between external forces and behavior. At higher levels these mediating processes become more and more independent or autonomous, and more determinative of behavior. They come to perform the operations of: (1) temporarily adjusting the system to external contingencies: (2) directing the system toward more congenial environments; and (3) permanently reorganizing aspects of the system itself to deal perhaps more effectively with the environment. The 'self' in 'self-regulation,' 'self-direction,' and 'self-organizing' points, of course, to these mediating processes, though we tend to use the term 'self' in its full sense only on the human level. However, the perspective we are taking argues that an understanding of the mediating processes on lower system levels should help us understand their nature and workings on the higher level: sharp discontinuities are not to be found.

Some of the connotations of these concepts of 'self-regulation' and the like are misleading, whether applied to modern machines, men, or groups, since the tendency is to overemphasize the independence of the internal system at the expense of situational or environmental variables. For this reason it might be profitable to utilize more neutral terms for the two basic processes of interest to us here, namely, *morphostasis* and *morphogenesis*. The former refers to those processes in complex system-environment exchanges that tend to preserve or maintain a system's given form, organization, or state. Morphogenesis will refer to those processes which tend to elaborate or change a system's given form, structure, or state. Homeostatic processes in organisms, and ritual in sociocultural systems are examples of 'morphostasis'; biological evolution, learning, and societal development are examples of 'morphogenesis'.

We have already discussed morphostatic processes in dealing with equilibrium, homeostasis, and negative feedback. These conserving, deviation-counterbalancing processes have come to be emphasized in the literature at the expense of structure-elaborating, deviation-promoting processes that are central to an understanding of higher level systems such as the sociocultural. Just as the concept of negative feedback has provided insight into the mechanisms underlying homeostatic processes, the concept of positive feedback provides insight into the mechanisms underlying structure-building, or morphogenesis. Magoroh Maruyama has recently argued very effectively the case for greater concern with the latter.

By focusing on the deviation-counteracting aspect of the mutual causal relationships . . . the cyberneticians paid less attention to the systems in which the mutual causal effects are deviation-amplifying. Such systems are ubiquitous: accumulation of capital in industry, evolution of living organisms, the rise of cultures of various types, interpersonal processes which produce mental illness, international conflicts, and the processes that are loosely termed as 'vicious circles' and 'compound interests': in short, all processes of mutual causal relationships that amplify an insignificant or accidental initial kick, build up deviation and diverge from the initial condition.[12]

Maruyama gives as one example the development of a city in an agricultural plain. A farmer starts a farm at some chance spot on the homogeneous plain. Other farmers are attracted and follow suit. Someone opens a tool shop, someone else a food stand, and gradually a village grows. The village facilitates the marketing of crops and attracts more farms. The increased activity and population necessitates the development of industry, and the village becomes a city.[13]

One of the many evolutionary examples is the adaptation of varieties of a species to colder and colder climates. In the beginning some mutants are enabled to live at a somewhat colder temperature than normal for the species. They move to a colder climate, where further mutations occur. Some of these are unfit for the colder climate and die off, but other mutants can stand even colder surroundings than their parents and move to a still colder climate. This deviation-amplifying process continues until some limit is reached.

Many illuminating examples in the sociocultural realm could also be given. Besides the above processes of growth or adaptive structural change, there are the often nonadaptive processes such as those embodied in Myrdal's 'vicious circle' theory of racial discrimination, whereby initial prejudice generates those personal and social characteristics of Negroes that are then seen to justify further discrimination which, in turn, aggravates further the Negroes' condition.[14] Another example is the process by which the malfunctioning of bureaucratic organizations may occur. March and Simon have traced out, in *Organizations,* a model of Robert Merton's theory of bureaucracy which, in simplified form, starts with the demand for control made on the organization by upper management. This demand takes the form of an emphasis on the reliability of behavior of lower-level administrators, operationalized in terms of accountability and predictability of behavior. This, in turn, leads to a rigid adherence to rules and mutual defense of members' positions. But this creates difficulties in administrator–client relations,

which lead to a felt need for defensibility of individual action. The net effect of client pressure on lower and higher officials is to tighten further the top official emphasis on reliability, thus closing the positive feedback loop leading back to a more rigid adherence to rules and a more vigorous defense of status. In sum, deviation from the goal of satisfying clients tends to reinforce the very factors creating the deviation.[15]

As Maruyama points out, there are a number of methodological implications to be drawn from the consideration of these morphogenetic processes. The classical principle of causality held that similar conditions produce similar effects, and consequently dissimilar results are due to dissimilar conditions. [16] Bertalanffy, in analyzing the self-regulating, or morphostatic, features of open biological systems, loosened this classical conception by introducing the concept of 'equifinality'.[17] This holds that, in ontogenesis for example, a final normal adult state may be reached by any number of devious developmental routes. Morphogenetic processes, however, go even further and suggest an opposite principle that might be called 'multifinality':[18] similar initial conditions may lead to dissimilar end-states. Thus, two cultures developing in very similar ecological environments may end up with very different sociocultural systems. In the example of city growth, Maruyama suggests that if a historian should try to find the 'cause' of the city's growth in that particular spot he will be unable to do so either in terms of the initial homogeneity of the plain or the decision of the first farmer.

The secret of the growth of the city is in the process of deviation-amplifying mutual positive feedback networks rather than in the initial condition or in the initial kick. This process, rather than the initial condition, has generated the complexly structured city. It is in this sense that the deviation-amplifying mutual causal process is called 'morphogenesis.'[19]

Such considerations provide a more precise and basic methodological rationale for the transactional approach to the study of complex adaptive systems. For example, the classical approach to the study of delinquent or criminal behavior was to look either at personality or at the environing situation. We now, however, can appreciate more fully the possibility that some deviation-amplifying transaction operating between the personality system and the situation has *generated* the deviant outcome. The initial conditions in either the personality or the situation may or may not be relevant or causally dominant.

A partial generalization of the morphogenic process is suggested in Maruyama's discussion of the biologist's puzzlement over the fact that the amount of information stored in the genes is much too small to specify the detailed structure of the adult individual. The puzzle can be resolved if we find that it is not necessary for the genes to carry all the detailed information, but rather that it suffices for them to carry *a set of rules to generate the information*. This can be conceptualized, for example, in terms of rules specifying the general direction and amount of cellular growth in terms of the immediate spatial and cellular environment of the growing tissues; the details are then generated by the *interactions* of the cells, tissues and other limiting boundaries and gradients. Thus, though the total process is deterministic, it is not possible or necessary to specify in the initial condition whether, for example, a particular part of an embryo is to become eye-tissue or skin-tissue. In Maruyama's words:

> The amount of information to describe the resulting pattern is much more than the amount of information to describe the generating rules and the positions of the initial tissues. The pattern is generated by the rules and by the *interaction* between the tissues. In this sense, the information to describe the adult individual was not contained in the initial tissues at the beginning but was generated by their interactions.[20]

This principle applies equally to the sociocultural system. There is not enough information, knowledge, or decision-making power when simply summed over all the relevant individuals or groups to account for the full-blown complex organization, the metropolitan agglomeration, the body of scientific theory, or the developed religious dogma. The sociocultural pattern is generated by the rules (norms, laws, and values—themselves generated in a similar manner) *and by the interactions* among normatively and purposively oriented individuals and subgroups in an ecological setting. Full understanding and explanation can appeal, alone, neither to early history nor common human characteristics (initial conditions), nor to final structure and functions. Attention must finally be paid to the interactions generated by the rules, seen as only limiting frameworks of action; to the new information, meanings, and revised rules generated by the interactions; and to the more or less temporary social products that represent the current state or structure of the ongoing process. Only one-sided, highly selective observation and conceptualization could lead us to see a principle of 'social inertia' or a predominance of morphostatic processes operating in the sociocultural realm.

An abstract model of morphogenesis
The conceptualizations of morphogenic processes

suggested by Campbell, Maruyama, and others,[21] have paved the way for the emergence of a highly generalized paradigm of morphogenesis or evolution applicable, in principle, to all complex system levels.

In these terms, then, the paradigm underlying the evolution of more and more complex adaptive systems begins with the fact of a potentially changing environment characterized by constrained variety and an adaptive system or organization whose persistence and elaboration to higher levels depends upon a successful mapping of some of the environmental variety and constraints into its own organization on at least a semipermanent basis. This means that our adaptive system—whether biological, psychological, or sociocultural—must manifest (1) some degree of 'plasticity' and 'sensitivity' or *tension* vis-à-vis its environment such that it carries on a constant interchange with environmental events, acting on and reacting to them; (2) some source of mechanism providing for *variety,* to act as a potential pool of adaptive variability to meet the problem of mapping new or more detailed variety and constraints in a changeable environment; (3) a set of *selective* criteria or mechanisms against which the 'variety pool' may be sifted into those variations in the organization or system that more closely map the environment and those that do not; and (4) an arrangement for *preserving and/or propagating* these 'successful' mappings.[22]

It should be noted, as suggested above, that this is a *relational* perspective, corresponding closely with the current conception of 'information,' viewed as the process of selection, from an ensemble of variety, of a subset which, to have 'meaning,' must match another subset taken from a similar ensemble. Communication is the process by which this constrained variety is transmitted in one form or another between such ensembles, involving coding and decoding such that the original variety and its constraints remain relatively invariant at the receiving end.

One point that requires much more discussion may be briefly mentioned here. With the transition from the higher primate social organization to the full-blown human, symbolically mediated, sociocultural system, the mapping of the subtle behaviors, gestures, and intentions of the individuals making up the effective social organization become increasingly central, and eventually equals or even overshadows, the mapping of the physical environment. The new, demanding requirements of co-ordination, anticipation, expectation, and the like within an increasingly complex *social* environment of interacting and interdependent others—where genetic mappings were absent or inadequate—prompted the fairly rapid elaboration of relatively new features in the social system. These included, of course: (1) the ever-greater conventionalizing of gestures into true symbols; (2) the development of a 'self,' self-awareness, or self-consciousness out of the symbolically mediated, continuous mirroring and mapping of each person's own behaviors and gestures in those of ever-present others (a process well described by John Dewey, G. H. Mead, Cooley, and others); and (3) the resulting ability to deal in the present with the predicted future as well as the past and hence to manifest conscious goal seeking, evaluating, self-other relating, norm-referring behavior.

The problem of causality in social theory

We are not primarily concerned here with the various types of (mathematical) functions relating two variables, but it is pertinent to call attention to them. Whereas our traditional methodological tools generally focus on or assume a simple linear relation, newer research is making clear the importance of other types of functions for an understanding of the dynamics of the development, maintenance, or change of social systems. One type of relation more and more frequently encountered is the special kind of nonlinear relation referred to as a *step function*, whereby a variable has no appreciable effect on others until its value has increased or decreased by some minimal increment. Consequently, research may fail to disclose any significant relationship even though a large potential interaction is in fact building up. A related kind of interrelation of variables involves the presence of *buffer mechanisms*, which delay the effects of a variable until some later point in a process. These two functions pose similar problems for the researcher. An especially important problem today involves the *primacy* of certain systemic variables over others, what might be called the problem of 'methodological pluralism'. We have overreacted against single-factor theories by assuming an equally radical 'equality of effectiveness' of a plurality of factors. Thus, as Andrew Hacker has remarked, 'Parsons' scheme has too many ideas which interact on a parity of causal significance.'[23] But modern systems theorists have long recognized that just because a number of variables are interrelated in a systemic manner does not necessarily mean /that each is of equal weight in producing characteristic states of the system: any systemic variable may run the gamut from insignificance to overwhelming primacy. Sociological discussions in this area will remain sophomoric until the principles of modern systems research are more widely ingested.

Important as these considerations are—in fact, just because they are so important—we must leave it to the expert methodologist to provide us with a much needed treatise on the research implications of modern (especially non-equilibrial) social systems analysis. We shall discuss below, rather, the more general ways in which social scientists have treated relations between variables or system parts, and the theoretical orientations built on them.

Traditional causal relations

The most common method of analyzing a given phenomenon X has been to relate it to *prior* phenomena, or 'causes,' a, b, c ..., in a one-way causal linkage. If the prior events are proximal to the event being explained, we speak of 'efficient causes'; if more distant, we speak of 'historical causes.'

Teleology or final cause

Here we attempt to analyze an event X in terms of its relation to *future* events (or purposes, functions, or consequences).

Reciprocal or mutual relations

Especially with the advent of the mechanical equilibrium model, the recognition of the importance of mutually interrelated events, variables, or system elements challenged the more simplified appeals to causality. For a period, an overreaction seems in fact to have occurred, associated with the claim that mutual interactionism completely replaces the older causality. However, moderation now seems to have set in, based on the recognition that (as is usually the case with new scientific theories) new perspectives usually refine and broaden older ones rather than replace them outright, such that the old come to be seen as special cases restricted in applicability. It can perhaps be argued that Robert M. MacIver's book, *Social Causation*, represents an attempt in social science to temper the claims of mutual interactionism to have done away with 'causality' entirely. In any case, recognition of reciprocal relations among parts of a larger complex was an important early step in the direction of a thoroughgoing systems analysis. Or, to turn it around, early treatments of society or the group in terms of physical or mechanical system models led to the widespread recognition that the parts of society are not typically independent, but are mutually interrelated and constitute a whole, at least to some degree. This historical point needs emphasis, as suggested earlier, in view of the current attempt, often ingenuous, of many functionalists to claim credit for this insight or, indeed, to *define* functional analysis in terms of its emphasis on mutual relations of parts rather than, more correctly, its emphasis on final causes or consequences for the larger whole.[24]

Circular causal chains (pseudo-feedback)

The concept of mutual relations of parts could not long remain a simple and undifferentiated one, since there are many subtypes to be recognized and analyzed. We have pointed to the growing centrality of the concept of organization for modern science; underlying this concept is the understanding and analysis of the complex ways the parts of a whole are interrelated to produce the structure and dynamics of what we now call systems. Of particular importance are those kinds of mutual relations that make up what have been called circular causal chains: the effect of an event or variable returns indirectly to influence the original event itself by way of one or more intermediate events or variables. This kind of interrelationship of parts came to be recognized as a kind of building block of higher-level, adaptive, self-regulating systems, and a prototype of the kind of organization manifesting 'purpose' or goal-seeking.

However, it becomes important to recognize that the simple circular causal chain is not to be identified with the true goal-directed feedback loop underlying the more advanced self-directing systems. Some examples of the circular causal chain are the re-equilibrating process in disturbed mechanical equilibrium systems, the chain reaction in nuclear fission, the ecological interrelations between population size and food supply, the 'vicious circle' of racial discrimination, etc. These are not true 'feedback' cycles in the cybernetic sense, inasmuch as there are no internal mechanisms which measure or compare the feedback input against a goal and pass the mismatch information on to a *control center* which activates appropriate system counter behavior. There is no 'control' here, only a blind reaction of the original variable to the forces it has helped to create and which are now reacting back on it.

We can argue that processes based on circular causal chains (for example, those underlying the evolution of lower living forms), are only superficially similar to purposeful behavior. The correlations found between the behaving object and its environment are due to blind processes involving circular causal chains, untested by criteria other than sheer survival and reproducibility. It is only at the higher levels of evolution or of cybernetic machinery that we find internal test parameters operating in accordance with signals or symbols standing for certain goal-states, which alone make possible goal-directed, 'purposeful' behavior. It is the matching of external events or objects against these internal test criteria that appears basic here, and fundamental to any satisfactory answer to Taylor's well-taken argument. He insists that at least one significant and irreducible difference between human purposive behavior and servomechanism behavior is the presumed fact that the latter can never positively seek objects which are non-existent, such as Holy Grails.[25] But once we recognize that purpose *must* involve some internal representation of a goal-state, and that it may lie in the future or even be non-existent, Taylor's objection loses force and we must allow that servomechanisms, as well as men, can seek to match the environment against an internal representation for which there is no external counterpart. The question of how that representation got into the system, whether it was designed into the servomechanism or learned as a belief or motive by the man, is a different question, one that should not prejudice the problem of the purposiveness of the behavior *per se*. And, to reiterate our main point, purposeful behavior involves true feedback loops, not just simple, circular causal chains. Higher level systems had to wait for the development of symbolically mediated internal representations and testing subsystems before true purposive behavior became possible.

True self-regulating *feedback loops*, then, constitute a higher level of interrelations of parts and underlie the complex organization and dynamics of higher level adaptive systems. Here we have gone beyond the kinds of interrelationships pertinent to mere aggregates of elements or to closed equilibrial systems, and are now dealing with open systems involving some degree of learning, purpose or goal-seeking, elaboration of organization, or evolution in general.

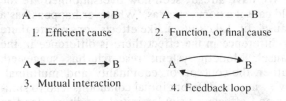

Figure 3.1   Relations between variables

[Returning to causality in social systems,] it is highly instructive to contrast the current, simple distinction between 'manifest' (conscious and intended) and 'latent' (unconscious and unintended) consequences of human behavior along with the view that social structures persist because they satisfy social system 'needs', on the one hand, with MacIver's conception of social structure and the role of purpose and 'dynamic assessment,' on the other. For most social patterns are a complex emergent product of both purposive and unintended consequences. When we *are* able to distinguish the two empirically, important questions remain. For example, for *which* individuals and groups are the consequences intended, and for which unintended or unrecognized? We have already suggested that MacIver's chapters on the 'dynamic assessment' constitute an important prolegomenon to the reviving concern with decision-making processes in social analysis. And, in fact, it is on this level—of the purposes and decisions of complexes of interrelated and interacting individuals and groups—that current research and theory is developing the important modern theories of tension, 'role-strain', exchange or bargaining, and the like (although it is not thereby necessary to reduce analysis to a framework of radical methodological individualism as some have argued).[26]

Modern systems analysis

We must certainly agree with MacIver's recent restatement of his belief that 'the advancement of the social sciences (and, not least, that of sociology) depends to a great degree on a more thorough grappling with the exceedingly complex problem of the causation of social phenomena.'[27] We argue that the most significant grappling occurring today is within the modern systems research movement, which is augmenting our traditional conceptions of causation to such a degree that it might be best, as many suggest, to avoid causal terminology altogether (though it would be misleading, if at all meaningful, to claim that the 'causal principle' has been 'overthrown').

We have already seen how oversimplified are the old causal axioms, such as, 'Whatever happens has a cause', or 'Like causes, like effects', or 'Where there is difference in the effect there is difference in the cause'. Modern systems research has suggested, rather, the concepts of 'equifinality' and 'multifinality', whereby different initial conditions lead to similar end effects, or similar initial conditions lead to different end effects. It has also demonstrated the inadequacy of traditional causal analysis to deal with such important phenomena as emergence, purpose or goal-seeking, self-regulation, adaptation, and the like.

In contrasting systems research with mutual interactionism, we have seen how the former transcends the static equilibrium reference of the latter in

recognizing the very different problem of the complex open, adaptive system which depends not simply on mutual relations of parts, but on very particular kinds of mutual interrelations. In addition, the important problems of primacy of some parts over others and the varying degrees of connectedness of some parts of the system to others are made subject to analysis. Thus, Karl Deutsch suggests that one test of importance for determining whether some component of a system is more critical than another is the answer to the question, 'Which part of the system gives you the maximum over-all change in system performance for the least change or smallest change in the subassembly structure?'[28]

Finally, in contrasting systems analysis with functionalism, we note that the concepts of teleology and purpose have been made respectable or precise by rendering them into 'efficient causes', or more particularly, into specifiable mechanisms involving feedbacks. Furthermore, the groundwork has been laid for elucidating the conditions making for self-regulation, development, or disintegration—instead of assuming automatic regulation or 'mechanisms of control' for any system we are dealing with. And the decision-making of learning, thinking, groups of individuals is given an important place as a psychosocial process that brings into conjunction previously unrelated events or conditions, by way of social action and transaction, to produce the current sociocultural structure. Thus, decision-making is seen as the exemplar, in the sociocultural system, of the general selective process occurring in every adaptive system, whereby variety is selectively organized and utilized for self-regulation and self-direction.

A brief but suggestive illustration of some of these points may be made in connection with the Midtown Manhattan Study of mental health, in which Leo Srole *et al*. started with a convergent view of causality that viewed sociogenic factors as leading to mental illness or health.[29] But the authors then recognized the importance of: (1) the possible reciprocal influences of the dependent variable back onto the independent variables, by way, for example, of the 'choices' of individuals of their particular social environments, and (2) the possible 'circular' or 'spiraling' interactions of these related factors through time. Thus, there were now seen to be at least three categories of factors or variables to be taken into account: (1) the dependent variable—mental health or illness, (2) the 'independent' factors—age, sex, ethnic origin, and so forth, (3) 'reciprocal variables'—marital status, socioeconomic status, religion, rural-urban migration. In commenting on these last four variables, the authors suggest that 'Variations on all four may be self-determined, and as such may well be consequences rather than independent antecedents of mental health'.[30] We note, then, that whereas any one of the approaches we have discussed might be used in such a study, only the modern systems approach promises to get at the full complexity of the interacting phenomena—to see not only the *causes* acting on the phenomena under study, the possible *consequences* of the phenomena, and the possible *mutual interactions* of some of these factors, but also to see the *total emergent processes* as a function of possible positive and/or negative *feedbacks* mediated by the *selective decisions,* or 'choices,' of the individuals and groups directly or indirectly involved. No less complex an approach can be expected to get at the complexity of the phenomena studied.

Notes and references

[1] A good statement of the concept of 'system' may be found in Arthur D. Hall and R. E. Fagen, 'Definition of Systems,' *General Systems*, 1 (1956), 18–28.

[2] Anatol Rapoport and William J. Horvath, 'Thoughts on Organization Theory,' *General Systems,* 4 (1959), 89.

[3] A more pertinent example for the social researcher is the central methodological problem of mapping the researcher's scientifically oriented cognitive structure into the research subject's common-sense mapping (interpretive understanding) of the structured variety of the external situation of action. This example is suggested by the extensive discussion of the problem in Aaron V. Cicourel, *Method and Measurement in Sociology* (New York: Free Press of Glencoe Inc., 1964).

[4] Donald M. MacKay 'The Informational Analysis of Questions and Commands' in *Information Theory: Fourth London Symposium*, ed. Colin Cherry, pp. 470–1.

[5] Lawrence J. Henderson. *The Fitness of the Environment* (New York: The Macmillan Company, 1915).

[6] Herbert A. Thelen, *Emotionality and Work in Groups,* in *The State of the Social Sciences*, ed. Leonard D. White (Chicago: University of Chicago Press, 1956), pp. 184–86. Such a conception also underlies the pragmatism or social behaviorism of William James. John Dewey, and G. H. Mead.

[7] Arturo Rosenblueth, Norbert Wiener, and Julian Bigelow, 'Behavior, Purpose, and Teleology,' *Philosophy of Science*, 10 (1943), 18–24; Arturo Rosenblueth and Norbert Wiener, 'Purposeful and Non-Purposeful Behavior,' *Philosophy of Science,* 17 (1950), 318–26; W. Ross Ashby, *An Introduction to Cybernetics* (London: Chapman & Hall Ltd., 1956); C. W. Churchman and R. L. Ackoff, 'Purposive Behavior and Cybernetics,' *Social Forces*, 29 (1950), 32–39. For a critical review, see Richard Taylor, 'Comments on a Mechanistic Conception of Purposefulness,' and 'Purposeful and Non-Purposeful Behavior: A Rejoinder,' *Philosophy of Science*, 17 (1950), 310–17, 327–32.

[8] Anatol Rapoport, in *Toward a Unified Theory of Human Behavior*, ed. Roy Grinker (New York: Basic Books, Inc., Publishers, 1956), Chap. 17.

[9] See, for example, Derek H. Fender. 'Control Mechanisms of the Eye,' *Scientific American*, 211 (July, 1964).

[10] Geoffrey Vickers, *The Concept of Stress in Relation to the Disorganization of Human Behavior*, in *Stress and Psychiatric Disorder*, ed. J. M. Tanner (Oxford: Blackwell Scientific Publications, Ltd., 1959), pp. 3–10; Joseph M. Notterman and Richard Trumbull, 'Note on Self-Regulating Systems and Stress,' *Behavioral Science*, 4 (1950), 324–27.

[11] Karl W. Deutsch, 'Mechanism, Teleology and Mind', *Philosophy and Phenomenological Research*, 12 (1951), pp. 185–222.

[12] Magoroh Maruyama, 'The Second Cybernetics: Deviation-Amplifying Mutual Causal Processes,' *American Scientist*, 51 (1963), 164–79. Quote is on p. 164.

[13] *Ibid.*, 165–66.

[14] Gunnar Myrdal, *An American Dilemma* (New York: Harper & Row, Publishers, 1944), pp. 75–78.

[15] James G. March and Herbert A. Simon, *Organizations* (New York: John Wiley & Sons, Inc., 1958), pp. 37–41.

[16] Myrdal, *An American Dilemma* (see [14] above).

[17] Ludwig von Bertalanffy, *Problems of Life* (New York: Harper & Row, Publishers, Torchbook ed., 1960), pp. 142 ff.

[18] This concept is perhaps implied in the biological notation of 'equipotential.'

[19] M. Maruyama, *The Second Cybernetics*, 166.

[20] *Ibid.*, 174.

[21] See J. W. S. Pringle, 'On the Parallel Between Learning and Evolution.' *Behavior,* 3 (1951), 174–215.

[22] Campbell. *Methodological Suggestions.*

[23] Andrew Hacker, *Sociology and Ideology*, in *The Social Theories of Talcott Parsons*, ed. Max Black (Englewood Cliffs, N.J.: Prentice-Hall, Inc., 1961), p. 297.

[24] An earlier argument attempting to equate functionalism simply with good sociological analysis, or even with scientific analysis in general, was quite unsuccessful, largely because it failed to appreciate this point. See Kingsley Davis, 'The Myth of Functional Analysis as a Special Method in Sociology and Anthropology,' *American Sociological Review,* 24 (1959), 757–72.

[25] Taylor, 'Purposeful and Non-Purposeful Behavior', pp. 329–30 (see [7] above).

[26] For two recent, perceptive discussions of the problem of function and cause see Ronald P. Dore, 'Function and Cause,' *American Sociological Review,* 26 (1961), 843–53; and Yonina Talmon, 'Mate Selection in Collective Settlements,' *American Sociological Review*, 29 (1964), 491–508.

[27] MacIver, *Social Causation*. p. vii.

[28] In Grinker, *Toward a Unified Theory*. p. 279.

[29] Leo Srole *et al., Mental Health in the Metropolis* (New York: McGraw-Hill Book Company, 1962).

[30] *Ibid.*, p. 18.

Section II People and groups

Introduction

Following our initial look at some of the main ideas behind systems approaches in general terms, this section concentrates on what are normally seen as the 'building blocks' of organizations—people and small groups. In no way does this section attempt to give a comprehensive picture of the subject matter, for it is easy to write whole books on the questions surrounding people in small groups. Rather, this section is an attempt to relate these to some of the issues we will deal with at the organizational and multiorganizational levels.

In Reading 4 by Paul Watzlawick and his colleagues we deal with a key issue; change. Watzlawick *et al.* put forward in the reading a general framework for looking at change, based on analogies with two mathematical theories, group theory and the theory of logical types, and their work on personal relationships. Such an approach is perhaps rather forced at times, but it is important to realize that they are only using these theories as analogies rather than arguing that such abstract ideas can adequately account for people's actions and perceptions. Their key point is that there are two main types of change. First there is change which is essentially a change in the state of a system whose basic structure remains intact. This is called *first-order change*. Then there is change which involves a transformation of the system itself, a change in its structure or mode of behaviour. This more radical change in terms of the system is *second-order change*.

Having drawn this distinction, they illustrate the concepts using a variety of situations, from films to the Chinese Cultural Revolution. In particular they use examples of personal relationships and ideas of relationships which have a similar structure even if the actions of those involved are changed in apparently major ways, so that almost any action is unable to resolve the contradictions of the system. Such a perspective enables us to see how important the conceptualization of a 'system' is, especially when we are trying to resolve problems within it.

Does a proposed solution merely alter the state of the system whilst not changing it at the higher second-order level which would be necessary to resolve its underlying contradictions? Further, it may be—as Watzlawick *et al.* argue about the Red Guards in China—that radical changes in one aspect of a society are carried out by mechanisms which do not use means radically different from those used in the past. A final question raised by the reading is, to what extent is a rigid division between first- and second-order change valid—to what degree are they closely related and how much do they depend on the objectives and perceptions of the observer?

However, in looking at the area of people and groups it would be wrong to concentrate entirely on the question of change and persistence.

One important aspect is the way in which work groups are created. It is widely argued that within work organizations, the technology used has a significant effect on the way in which work groups are formed and on their members' behaviour and attitudes. The application of systems ideas to the problems of work groups has been a focus of the 'socio-technical systems' approach outlined by Eric Trist (Reading 5) and critically analysed by David Silverman (Reading 6). Trist is a practitioner of change in work groups, usually through management consultancy. Like an increasing number of theorists, Trist argues that the traditional 'scientific management' way of designing jobs and organizing work leads potentially to more problems than it solves, with its emphasis on the subdivision of labour and the removal of skill and control from the workforce. The impetus behind the types of change suggested by Trist and others using similar analyses has come from the increasing problems for managers of an extreme division of labour, derived from a view that one can see people purely as 'factors of production'. Instead, argues Trist, one must see that production involves both a *technical* system of machines, work flow and so on, and a *social* system involving those doing the work and their relationships with each other and with management. He argues in effect that a concentration on one or the other will lead to problems, including that of lower profitability. The answer is primarily in terms of individual jobs and the small groups within which people should work. Thus the approach is primarily at the level of the work-group, and various methods at this level are suggested by Trist.

Silverman (Reading 6) is more critical of such approaches, which he outlines concisely in the first part of his reading. On theoretical grounds he argues that their use of 'organic analogies' for groups and organizations is theoretically deficient, and that their approach confuses other issues, such as the difference between analysis of what 'is' and prescription of what 'ought' to happen. Whilst such criticisms are well-directed, Silverman concedes that in general 'there is no reason why an adequate analytical theory . . . could not be constructed'. However Silverman himself is a prominent critic of systems approaches, preferring to adopt an 'action approach'—a type of theory discussed in Reading 7 by Angela Bowey, and one which has contributed to some of the more recent work, using systems ideas, such as that of Argyris and Schön (Reading 12).

Other criticisms of the practice of the socio-technical systems approach have been made, for example, by Kelly, who argues that the results claimed by Trist and others can be more accurately seen as the results of increased overall work pace through the sharing of responsibility and of payment incentives. Thus Trist's example of the productivity increases following a 'socio-technical experiment' could perhaps be the result of the motivation of 'take home pay-packets in excess of the most skilled workers in the plant'. Another point of view is that such experiments largely represent attempts by management to regain control of the work group's activities by giving it responsibility for 'means' whilst not allowing it any real choice of the 'ends' to be pursued.

Further reading

Watzlawick *et al.*'s model of change is extended and illustrated in the rest of their book on *Change* which concentrates on how to formulate and resolve problems in the light of their theoretical perspective. Another interesting approach is that of Gregory Bateson in *Steps to an ecology of mind*. One of the main areas where such 'social–psychological' approaches have been applied is that of small groups, which although not covered directly in this set of readings is a basis for much of the discussion in this area. Bion's *Experience in groups* and Bradford, Gibb and Benne's *T-group theory and the laboratory method* are standard introductions to the theory of small groups. Isobel Menzies uses these ideas in a powerful case study of work in hospitals in her *The functioning of social systems as a defence against anxiety* which indirectly relates to some of the work of the socio-technical theorists, who also worked at the Tavistock Institute of Human Relations.

A rather more analytical presentation of the basic socio-technical systems approach is provided by Emery and Trist's 1960 article *Socio-technical systems* widely reprinted, for example in Emery's collection *Systems thinking*. A summary of Norwegian experience is given by Thorsrud in Hofstede and Kassem. Critical perspectives are provided by Kelly. More general approaches to the design of jobs are given in L. Davis, ed., *Design of jobs* and a historical approach is given in Susman. Braverman's *Labor and monopoly capital* takes a more global perspective on changes in work in the twentieth century, arguing that the workforce is progressively being deprived of control and skill.

Bateson, G. (1975) *Steps to an ecology of mind*, Ballantine.
Bion, W. R. (1961) *Experiences in groups*, Basic Books.
Bradford, L. P., Gibb, J. R. and Benne, K. D. (eds.) *T-group theory and laboratory method*, J. Wiley.
Braverman, H. (1974) *Labor and monopoly capital*, Monthly Review Press.
Davis, L. E. and Taylor, J. C. (eds.) (1972) *Design of jobs*, Penguin.
Emery, F. E. (1970) *Systems thinking*, Penguin.
Goffman, E. (1959) 'Teams', Chapter 2 in *The Presentation of Self in Everyday Life*, Allen Lane.
Hofstede, G. and Kassem, M. S. (eds.) (1975) *European contributions to organization theory*, Assen.
Kelly, J. E. (December 1978) 'A reappraisal of socio-technical systems theory', *Human Relations*, Vol. 31, no. 12.
Menzies, I. (1961) *The functioning of social systems as a defence against anxiety*, Tavistock Pamphlet number 3.
Susman, G. I. (1976) *Autonomy at work*, Praeger.
Watzlawick, P., Weakland, J. H. and Fisch, R. (1974) *Change: principles of problem formation and problem resolution*, W. W. Norton and Co. Ltd., New York.

4 Change

P. Watzlawick, J. H. Weakland and R. Fisch

The theoretical perspective

Plus ça change, plus c'est la même chose.

The French proverb according to which the more something changes the more it remains the same is more than a witticism. It is a wonderfully concise expression of the puzzling and paradoxical relationship between persistence and change. It appeals more immediately to experience than the most sophisticated theories that have been put forth by philosophers, mathematicians, and logicians, and implicitly makes a basic point often neglected: that persistence and change need to be considered together, in spite of their apparently opposite nature. This is not an abstruse idea, but a specific instance of the general principle that all perception and thought is relative, operating by comparison and contrast.

In practice, however, this comparative stance has been difficult to achieve. In the Western world the philosophers of science seem to agree that change is such a pervasive and immediate element of our experience that it could become the subject of thought only after the early Greek philosophers had been able to conceptualize the antithetical concept of invariance or persistence. Until then there was nothing that change could be conceptually contrasted with (this is a matter of conceptualizing experience, not of finding 'reality'), and the situation must have been like one proposed by Whorf: that in a universe in which everything is blue, the concept of blueness cannot be developed for lack of contrasting colours.

While many theories of persistence and change have been formulated throughout the centuries of Western culture, these have mainly been theories of persistence, *or* theories of change, not theories of persistence *and* change. That is, the tendency has been either to view persistence and invariance as a 'natural' or 'spontaneous' state, to be taken for granted and needing no explanation, and change as the problem to be explained, or to take the inverse position. But the very fact that either position can be adopted so readily suggests that they are complementary—that what is problematic is not absolute and somehow inherent in the nature of things, but depends on the particular case and point of view involved. Such a conception is consistent with our experience of human affairs and difficulties. For example, whenever we observe a person, a family, or a wider social system enmeshed in a problem in a persistent and repetitive way, despite desire and effort to alter the situation, *two* questions arise equally: 'How does this undesirable situation persist?' and 'What is required to change it?'

In the course of our work, we have made some progress not only toward answering these questions in particular cases, but in moving toward a more general view. Rather than retracing this long road, however, we feel that two abstract and general theories, drawn from the field of mathematical logic, may be utilized to help present and clarify some of the conclusions at which we have arrived. These are (1) the theory of groups and (2) the theory of logical types.

In doing so, we are fully aware that our use of these theories is far from satisfying mathematical rigor. It should be taken as an attempt at exemplification through analogy.

[The] basic postulates [of group theory], concerned with relationships between elements and wholes, are quite simple—perhaps deceptively so. According to the theory, a *group* has the following properties:

(a) It is composed of *members* which are all alike in one common characteristic, while their actual nature is otherwise irrelevant for the purposes of the theory. They can thus be numbers, objects, concepts, events, or whatever else one wants to draw together in such a group, as long as they have that common denominator and as long as the outcome of any combination of two or more members is itself a member of the group . . .

The grouping of 'things' (in the widest sense) is the most basic and necessary element of our perception and conception of reality. While it is obvious that no two things will ever be exactly alike, the ordering of the world into (complexly intersecting and overlapping) groups composed of members which all share an important element in common gives structure to what would otherwise be a phantasmagoric chaos. But as we have seen, this ordering also establishes *invariance* in the above-mentioned sense, namely that a combination of any group members is again itself a member of the group—'a thing *in* the system, not out of it,' as Keyser puts it. Thus this first group property may allow for myriads of changes *within* the group (in fact, there are so-called infinite groups) but also makes it impossible for any member or combination of members to place themselves *outside* the system.

(b) Another property of a group is that one may combine its members in varying sequence, yet the outcome of the combination remains the same . . . One might, therefore, say that there is changeability in process, but invariance in outcome.

(c) A group contains an *identity* member such that its combination with any other member means that it maintains that other member's identity . . . In relation to our concerns the point is that a member may act without making a difference.

(d) Finally, in any system satisfying the group concept, we find that every member has its reciprocal or opposite, such that the combination of any member with its opposite gives the identity member . . .

It is our contention that the theory of groups, even in the primitive terms used here to describe its basic concepts (illustrating ways in which particular changes may make no difference in the group), provides a valid framework for thinking about the peculiar interdependence between persistence and change which we can observe in many practical instances where *plus ça change, plus c'est la même chose*.

What group theory apparently cannot give us is a model for those types of change which transcend a given system or frame of reference. It is at this point that we have to turn to the theory of logical types.

This theory, too, begins with the concept of collections of 'things' which are united by a specific characteristic common to all of them. As in group theory, the components of the totality are called *members*, while the totality itself is called *class* rather than group. One essential axiom of the theory of logical types is that 'whatever involves *all* of a collection must not be one of the collection,' as Whitehead and Russell state it in their monumental work *Principia Mathematica*. It should be immediately obvious that mankind is the class of all individuals, but that it is not itself an individual. Any attempt to deal with the one in terms of the other is doomed to lead to nonsense and confusion. For example, the economic

behavior of the population of a large city cannot be understood in terms of the behavior of one inhabitant multipled by, say, four million. This, incidentally, was precisely the mistake committed in the early days of economic theory and is now scornfully referred to as the Robinson Crusoe economic model. A population of four million is not just quantitatively but qualitatively different from an individual, because it involves systems of interaction among the individuals. Similarly, while the individual members of a species are usually endowed with very specific survival mechanisms, it is well known that the *entire* species may race headlong towards extinction—and the human species is probably no exception . . .

Outcomes of the kind mentioned are the result of ignoring the paramount distinction between member and class and the fact that a class cannot be a member of itself. In all our pursuits, but especially in research, we are constantly faced with the hierarchies of logical levels, so the dangers of level confusions and their puzzling consequences are ubiquitous. The phenomena of change are no exception, but this is much more difficult to see in the behavioral sciences than, for instance, in physics. As Bateson points out, the simplest and most familiar form of change is motion, namely a change of position. But motion can itself be subject to change, i.e., to acceleration or deceleration, and this is a change of change (or metachange) of position. Still one level higher there is change of acceleration (or of deceleration) which amounts to change of change of change (or metametachange) of position. Even we laymen can appreciate that these forms of motion are very different phenomena involving very different explanatory principles and very different mathematical methods for their computation. It can also be seen that change always involves the next higher level: to proceed, for instance, from position to motion, a step *out of* the theoretical framework of position is necessary. *Within* that framework the concept of motion cannot be generated, let alone dealt with, and any attempt at ignoring this basic axiom of the theory of logical types leads to paradoxical confusion . . .

Another one of Bateson's favorite examples is that usually only a schizophrenic is likely to eat the menu card instead of the meal (and complain of its bad taste, we would add).

Yet another useful analogy is supplied by an automobile with a conventional shift gear. The performance of the engine can be changed in two very different ways: either through the gas pedal (by increasing or decreasing the supply of fuel to the cylinders), or by shifting gears. Let us strain the analogy just a little and say that in each gear the car has a certain range of 'behaviors' (i.e., of power output and consequently of speed, acceleration, climbing capacity, etc.). *Within* that range (i.e., that class of behaviors), appropriate use of the gas pedal will produce the desired change in performance. But if the required performance falls *outside* this range, the driver must shift gears to obtain the desired change. Gear-shifting is thus a phenomenon of a higher logical type than giving gas, and it would be patently nonsensical to talk about the mechanics of complex gears in the language of the thermodynamics of fuel supply.

But the formulation that is perhaps most relevant to our subject matter is the one given by Ashby for the cybernetic properties of a machine with input: 'It will be seen that the word "change" if applied to such a machine can refer to two very different things. There is the change from state to state, . . . , which is the machine's behavior, and there is the change from transformation to transformation, . . . , which is *a change of its way of behaving,* and which occurs at the whim of the experimenter or some outside factor. The distinction is fundamental and must on no account be slighted'. There are, then, two important conclusions to be drawn from the postulates of the theory of logical types: (1) logical levels must be kept strictly apart to prevent paradox and confusion; and (2) going from one level to the next higher (i.e., from member to class) entails a shift, a jump, a discontinuity or transformation—in a word, a change—of the greatest theoretical and practical importance, for it provides a way *out of* a system.

To summarize what has been said so far: group theory gives us a framework for thinking about the kind of change that can occur within a system that itself stays invariant; the theory of logical types is not concerned with what goes on inside a class, i.e., between its members, but gives us a frame for considering the relationship between member and class and the peculiar metamorphosis which is in the nature of shifts from one logical level to the next higher. If we accept this basic distinction between the two theories, it follows that there are two different types of change: one that occurs within a given system which itself remains unchanged, and one whose occurrence changes the system itself. To exemplify this distinction in more behavioral terms: a person having a nightmare can do many things *in* his dream—run, hide, fight, scream, jump off a cliff, etc.—but no change from any one of these behaviors to another would ever terminate the nightmare. *We shall henceforth refer to this kind of change as first-order change.* The one way *out of* a dream involves a

change from dreaming to waking. Waking, obviously, is no longer a part of the dream, but a change to an altogether different state. *This kind of change will from now on be referred to as second-order change.* (The equivalence of this distinction with Ashby's cybernetic definition of the two kinds of change, quoted earlier, is evident.) Second-order change is thus *change of change.* . . . At this point of our inquiry we must retrace our steps and take another look at our very simplistic presentation of group theory. In the light of what we have now learned from the theory of logical types, we realize that the four properties of any group that are responsible for creating the particular interdependence of persistence and change within the group are not themselves members of the group. They are clearly about, and therefore *meta* to, the group . . .

We can now appreciate that groups are invariant only on the first-order change level (i.e., on the level of change from one member to another, where, indeed, the more things change, the more they remain the same), but are open to change on the second-order change level (i.e., to changes in the body or rules governing their structure or internal order). Group theory and the theory of logical types thus reveal themselves not only as compatible with each other, but also as complementary. Furthermore (and bearing in mind that when we talk about change in connection with problem formation and problem resolution we always mean second-order change), we find that the two theories equip us with a conceptual framework useful in examining concrete, practical examples of change. And finally, remembering that second-order change is always in the nature of discontinuity or a logical jump, we may expect the practical manifestations of second-order change to appear as illogical and paradoxical as the decision of the commandant of the castle of Hochosterwitz to throw away his last food in order to survive.

The practical perspective

I would not dream of belonging to a club that is willing to have me for a member.

GROUCHO MARX

While it is relatively easy to establish a clear distinction between first-order change and second-order change in strictly theoretical terms, this same distinction can be extremely difficult to make in real-life situations. Thus, inattention to this difference and confusion between the two levels of change can occur very easily, and actions may be taken in difficult situations which not only do not produce the desired change, but compound the problem to which the 'solution' is applied. However, before dealing with solutions, practical examples for the theoretical considerations contained above are needed.

(a) It is not difficult to find examples for the first group property (that any combination, transformation, or operation of group members gives again a group member, and thus maintains the group structure). In John Fowles' novel *The Collector*, a young man has abducted the beautiful art student Miranda, with whom he is in love, and is holding her prisoner in a remote and escape-proof house in the country. Although she is completely in his power, the situation that he has created makes him as much her prisoner as she is his. Because he hopes desperately that she will eventually begin to love him, he can neither coerce nor release her. Release is out of the question for practical reasons also: he would be arrested for a serious crime, unless, of course, she were to claim that she followed him voluntarily. She is willing to promise this, but he knows that this would at best be a ruse to obtain her freedom and that she would never return to him. Under these unusual circumstances, both she and he are desperately attempting to effect a change (he by trying to make her love him, she by trying to escape), but any move by either of them is of the first-order change type and so consolidates and compounds the impasse . . .

Two other examples, mentioned elsewhere, fall into the same category and shall be repeated here briefly: The constitution of an imaginary country provides for unlimited parliamentary debate. This rule can be used to paralyze democratic procedure completely—the opposition party only has to engage in endless speeches to make impossible any decision that is not to its liking. To escape this impasse, a change of the rule is absolutely necessary, but can be made impossible precisely by what is to be changed, i.e. by endless filibuster. That this example is not merely intellectual exercise, but has very practical analogies in the world of international relations, is shown by the other example, a quotation from Osgood: 'Our political and military leaders have been virtually unanimous in public assertions that we must go ahead and stay ahead in the armament race; they have been equally unanimous in saying nothing about what happens then. Suppose we achieve the state of ideal mutual deterrence . . . what then? Surely no sane man can envisage our planet spinning on into eternity, divided into two armed camps poised to destroy each other, and call it peace and security! *The point is that the policy of mutual deterrence includes no provision for its own resolution.*'

This last sentence points very clearly to the invariance factor which prevents a system (this term is being used here as equivalent to *group* in the mathematical sense) from generating within itself the conditions for second-order change. It can, as we have seen, run through many first-order change phenomena, but as its structure remains invariant, there is no second-order change.

(b) Group property *b*, it will be remembered, has to do with the fact that a sequence of operations, performed on the group members in accordance with the combination rule of that group, may be changed without changing the result of the operations. A rather abstract example has been given above. More directly related to our subject matter are examples which can be found in the functioning of complex homeostatic systems. These systems may run through long sequences of internal states—and even over long periods of observation no two such sequences need to be exactly alike—but eventually reach the same result, i.e., their steady state. Ashby's homeostat is a model of this. In the realm of human interaction, a pattern frequently observed is that involving two partners, e.g., two spouses, who for one reason or another maintain a certain emotional distance between each other. In this system it does not matter if either tries to establish more contact, for every advance by one partner is predictably and observably followed by a withdrawal of the other, so that the overall pattern is at all times preserved. A somewhat more complex pattern of essentially the same structure is often found when a drinker provokes criticism and surveillance of his drinking by his wife. As she complains and attempts to 'protect' him from alcohol, his drinking increases, which, in turn, brings about an increase in her criticism, etc. Similarly, when a juvenile delinquent's behavior improves, his parents may 'discover' delinquent behavior in a child previously regarded as the 'good one'. This is not just their fantasy; clinical experience shows that, indeed, this so-called counter-delinquent's behavior can often be seen to undergo marked changes as soon as his sibling 'goes straight'. Instead of being critical of his sibling's badness, as before, he may now taunt him for his goodness and thereby either re-establish the original situation or engage in delinquency himself. Similar patterns can be observed in the decision-making of certain families. When they are trying to plan something together, it does not matter who proposes something, the others are bound to dismiss the idea. A particularly interesting clinical example was mentioned to us recently by Professor Selvini Palazzoli from her work with numerous Italian families with anorectic daughters. Almost all these girls, although abhorring food themselves, showed an inordinate interest in cooking and in supplying food to the rest of their family. The overall impression, as Selvini puts it, is that in these families there is an extreme, almost caricaturing reversal of the function of feeder and fed. Such sequences of behaviors, maintaining what Jackson called family homeostasis, are not just role reversals, as the sociologist may conceptualize them, but true first-order change phenomena, whereby different behaviors out of a finite repertory of possible behaviors are combined into different sequences, but leading to identical outcomes.

In general, the persistence phenomena inherent in group property *b* can be observed most frequently wherever the causality of a sequence is circular rather than linear, which is usual in ongoing systems of interacting elements. Armaments races and escalations, like that between the Arab countries and Israel, are good examples. Assuming for simplicity's sake that there are only two parties involved, the circularity of their interaction makes it undecidable for all practical purposes whether a given action is the cause or the effect of an action by the other party. Individually, of course, either party sees its actions as determined and provoked by the other's actions; but seen from the outside, as a whole, any action by either partner is a stimulus, provoking a reaction, which reaction is then itself again a stimulus for what the other part considers 'merely' a reaction . . . Discrepancies in the way the participants in an interaction 'punctuate' the sequence of events can become the cause of serious conflict.

(c) The identity member, which is the basis of group property *c*, means, in essence, *zero first-order change* when combined with any other member. This complicates exemplification, for it is difficult to show that which is *not* the case, or trivial to emphasize that anything that does not produce change leaves things as they are. But this is only apparently so; it ceases to be trivial the moment we realize that zero change refers to necessity to both levels of change. However, for the moment it may be simplest to proceed to exemplifications of the last group property, for in the course of this it will become easier to appreciate that the identity member is not just a *nothing*, but has substance of its own.

(d) Group property *d,* as we have seen, refers to the fact that the combination of any group member with its reciprocal or opposite gives the identity member. What are the practical implications of this postulate? On the surface it would be difficult to imagine a more drastic and radical change than the replacement of something by its opposite. But in a somewhat less superficial perspective it quickly becomes apparent that the world of our experience (which is all we can talk about) is made up of pairs of opposites and that, strictly speaking, any aspect of reality derives its substance or concreteness from the existence of its opposite. Examples are numerous and commonplace: light and dark, figure and ground, good and evil, past and future, and many, many other such pairs are merely the two complementary aspect of one and the same reality or frame of reference, their seemingly incompatible and mutually exclusive nature notwithstanding. To exemplify:

One of the changes effected by the Red Guards during the early stages of the Chinese cultural revolution was the destruction of all public signs (of streets, shops, buildings, etc.) which contained any reference to the reactionary, 'bourgeois' past, and their replacement by revolutionary names. Could there be a more radical break with the past? But in the wider context of Chinese culture this break is fully in keeping with that basic rule which Confucius called the *rectification of names* and which is based on the belief that from the 'right' name the 'right' reality should follow—rather than assuming, as we do in the West, that names *reflect* reality. In effect, therefore, the renaming imposed by the Red Guards was of the first-order change type; it not only left an age-old feature of Chinese culture intact, but actually re-emphasized it. Thus there was no second-order change involved, a fact that the Red Guards would probably have had difficulty appreciating.

Things may be 'as different as day and night' and the change from the one to the other appear to be extreme and ultimate, and yet, paradoxically, in the wider context (within the group in the mathematical sense) nothing may have changed at all. 'In order to save the town we had to destroy it,' an American field commander in Vietnam is supposed to have said, presumably unaware of both the dreadful absurdity and the deeper meaning of his report. One of the most common fallacies about change is the conclusion that if something is bad, its opposite must of necessity be good. The woman who divorces a 'weak' man in order to marry a 'strong' one often discovers to her dismay that while her second marriage should be the exact opposite of the first, nothing much has actually changed. The invocation of stark contrast has always been a favorite propaganda technique of politicians and dictators. 'National Socialism or Bolshevik chaos?' pompously asked a nazi poster, implying that there were only these two alternatives and that all men of good will should make the obvious choice. 'Erdäpfel oder Kartoffel?' (Spuds or Potatoes?) read a little sticker which an underground group affixed to hundreds of these posters, triggering off a huge Gestapo investigation.

The strange interdependence of opposites was already known to Heraclitus, the great philosopher of change, who called it *enantiodromia*. The concept was taken up by C. G. Jung, who saw in it a fundamental psychic mechanism: 'Every psychological extreme secretly contains its own opposite or stands in some sort of intimate and essential relation to it. . . . There is no hallowed custom that cannot on occasion turn into its opposite and the more extreme a position is, the more easily may we expect an enantiodromia, a conversion of something into its opposite'. Our history is certainly rich in enantiodromic patterns. For instance, the romantic idealization of women in the troubadour era of the eleventh to thirteenth centuries and its religious counterpart, the fervent cult of the Virgin Mary from the eleventh century onwards, had a strange, terrifying fellow traveler through history: the outbreak and the horrible crescendo of the witch hunts. Mary and the witch—two aspects of femininity which could hardly be more antithetical and apart; and yet they are 'only' a pair of opposites. And, to cast a brief glance into the future, it is a fairly safe bet that the offspring of our contemporary hippie generation will want to become bank managers and will despise communes, leaving their well-meaning but bewildered parents with the nagging question: Where did we fail our children?

With these examples in mind, the concept of the identity member should become a little less elusive. As pointed out under (c) above, combined with a group member it preserves the identity of *that member* (i.e., produces zero first-order change), while the combination of a group member with its opposite preserves the identity of the *group* (i.e., produces the identity member and therefore zero second-order change). For example: It is in the nature of tradition to ensure persistence, if necessary through corrective action. As a basis for action, tradition can, therefore, be considered as having the function of an identity member. On the other hand, it is in the nature of revolution to bring about change. But as the Red Guard example shows, there can be revolutionary action which is itself a traditional way of attempting change. This type of action has thus the function of a reciprocal or opposite and, as we have seen, preserves the identity of a social system. In fact, history offers an embarrassingly long list of revolutions whose end results were, by and large, more of the same conditions which the revolu-

tion had set out to overthrow and replace by a brave new world. In everyday human affairs, the eventual recognition of this zero change may then lead cooler heads to the sad conclusion: We would probably have been better off not bothering with the situation in the first place. But this realization is by no means the rule; more often than not the peculiar 'zero' effect of the identity member is all the greater because of its 'invisibility'. It is one thing to notice, take into account, or argue about something as patent as a change of something into its opposite, but it is very difficult, especially in human relationships, to be aware that this change actually is no change in the overall pattern. Much human conflict and many conflict-engendering 'solutions' are due to this unawareness.

So much for our exemplifications of the four group properties. They show us that any one, or any combination, of these properties cannot produce second-order change. A system which may run through all its possible internal changes (no matter how many there are) without effecting a systemic change, i.e., second-order change, is said to be caught in a *Game Without End*. It cannot generate from within itself the conditions for its own change; it cannot produce the rules for the change of its own rules. Admittedly, there are games which have their end point built into their structure, and they will reach it sooner or later. Whether these outcomes are happy or painful, such games do not lead into the vicious circles which are almost invariably found at the roots of human conflict. Games without end are precisely what the name implies; they are endless in the sense that they contain no provisions for their own termination. Termination (like waking up, in our nightmare example) is not part of the game, is not a member of that group; termination is *meta* to the game, is of a different logical type than any move (any first-order change) within the game.

Yet there is the undeniable fact that far from being impossible, second-order change is an everyday phenomenon: people *do* find new solutions, social organisms *are* capable of self-correction, nature finds ever-new adaptations, and the whole process of scientific discovery or artistic creation is based precisely on the stepping out of an old into a new framework—in fact, the most useful criterion for judging the viability or 'health' of a system is exactly this puzzling, uncommonsense ability which Baron Münchausen demonstrated when he pulled himself from the quagmire by his own pigtail.

But the occurrence of second-order change is ordinarily viewed as something uncontrollable, even incomprehensible, a quantum jump, a sudden illumination which unpredictably comes at the end of long, often frustrating mental and emotional labor, sometimes in a dream, sometimes almost as an act of grace in the theological sense. Koestler, in his *Act of Creation,* has collected an encyclopedic array of examples of this phenomenon, and has introduced the concept of *bisociation.* According to him, bisociation is 'the perceiving of a situation or idea in two self-consistent but habitually incompatible frames of reference', and 'the sudden bisociation of a mental event with two habitually incompatible matrices results in an abrupt transfer of the train of thought from one associative context to another'. In a brilliant paper, Bronowski deals with the same problem and also assigns to the decisive leap an unpredictable, almost random nature: we do not know how this event occurs, and there is no way in which we can know it. 'It is a free play of the mind, an invention outside the logical processes. This is the central act of imagination in science, and it is in all respects like any similar act in literature. In this respect, science and literature are alike: in both of them, the mind decides to enrich the system as it stands by an addition which is made by an unmechanical act of free choice.'

Despite such combined weight of authority and common perception, it is our experience that second-order change appears unpredictable, abrupt, illogical etc. only in terms of first-order change, that is, from within the system. Indeed, this must be so, because, as we have seen, second-order change is introduced into the system from the outside and therefore is not something familiar or something understandable in terms of the vicissitudes of first-order change. Hence its puzzling, seemingly capricious nature. But seen from outside the system, it merely amounts to a change of the premises (the combination rules in terms of group theory) governing the system *as a whole.* No doubt this group of premises may itself again be subject to group invariance, and any change of these premises would then have to be introduced from a yet higher level (i.e., one that is *meta-meta* to the original system and *meta* to the premises governing that system as a whole). However—and this is an eminently practical and crucial point—to effect change within the original system it is sufficient to go only as far as the metalevel.

A somewhat abstract but very simple example will make this clearer. The nine dots shown in Figure 4.1 are to be connected by four straight lines without lifting the pencil from the paper. The reader who is not familiar with this problem is advised to stop at this point and to try the solution on a piece of paper before reading on, and especially before turning to the solution (Figure 4.2).

Figure 4.1

Almost everybody who first tries to solve this problem introduces as part of his problem-solving an assumption which make the solution impossible. The assumption is that the dots compose a square and that the solution must be found *within* that square, a self-imposed condition which the instructions do not contain. His failure, therefore, does not lie in the impossibility of the task, but in his attempted solution. Having now created the problem, it does not matter in the least which combination of four lines he now tries, and in what order; he always finishes with at least one unconnected dot. This means that he can run through the totality of the first-order change possibilities existing within the square but will never solve the task. The solution is a second-order change which consists in leaving the field and which cannot be contained within itself because, in the language of *Principia Mathematica,* it involves all of a collection and cannot, therefore, be part of it.

Very few people manage to solve the nine-dot problem by themselves. Those who fail and give up are usually surprised at the unexpected simplicity of the solution (see Figure 4.2). The analogy between this and many a real-life situation is obvious. We have all found ourselves caught in comparable boxes, and it did not matter whether we tried to find the solution calmly and logically or, as is more likely, ended up running frantically around in circles. But, as mentioned already, it is only from inside the box, in the first-order change perspective, that the solution appears as a surprising flash of enlightenment beyond our control. In the second-order change perspective it is a simple change from one set of premises to another of the same logical type. The one set includes the rule that the task must be solved within the (assumed) square; the other does not. In other words, the solution is found as a result of examining the assumptions *about* the dots, not the dots themselves. Or, to make the same statement in more philosophical terms, it obviously makes a difference whether we consider ourselves as pawns in a game whose rules we call reality or as players of the game who know that the rules are 'real' only to the extend that we have created or accepted them, and that we can change them.

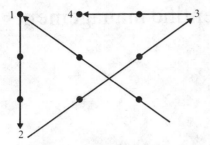

Figure 4.2   The solution of the nine-dot problem

But all of this presupposes awareness of the logical structure of our universe and of the need to keep the levels of logical discourse neatly separated. The theory of logical types makes it clear that we must not talk about the class in the language appropriate for its members. This would be an error in logical typing and would lead to the very perplexing impasses of logical paradox. Such errors of typing can occur in two ways: either by incorrectly ascribing a particular property to the class instead of to the member (or vice versa), or by neglecting the paramount distinction between class and member and by treating the two as if they were of the same level of abstraction. It will be remembered that second-order change is of the next-higher logical level, the (n + 1)th level, than first-order change. It cannot, therefore, be expressed in the language appropriate to first-order change or achieved by the methods applicable to the first-order change level without causing the most perplexing, paradoxical consequences. For instance, some of the tragicomic controversies between experimental psychologists and psychiatrists could be avoided if they realized that when the former talk about change, they usually mean first-order change (i.e., a change from one

behavior to another within a given way of behaving), while psychiatrists, though often not aware of this, are predominantly concerned with second-order change (i.e., the change from one way of behaving to another).

References

Ashby, W. R. (1956) *An introduction to cybernetics,* Chapman and Hall.

Bateson, G. and Jackson, D. D. (1964) 'Some varieties of pathenogenic organization', in *Disorders of communication,* ed. D. Rioch, Vol. 42, Research Publications, Association for Research in Nervous and Mental Disease.

Bronowski, J. (1966) 'The logic of the mind', *American Scientist,* 54: 1–14.

Dostoevsky, F. M. (1936) *The Possessed,* New York: Modern Library.

Fry, W. F. (1963) *Sweet madness: a study of humour,* Pacific Books.

Jackson, D. D. (1957) 'The question of family homeostasis', *Psychiatric Quarterly Supplement,* 31: 79–90, part 1.

Jackson, D. D. (1959) 'Family interaction, family homeostasis, and some implications for conjoint family psychotherapy', in Masserman, J. (ed.) *Individual and familial dynamics,* Grune and Stratton.

Jung, C. G. (1952) *Symbols of transformation,* Bollingen Foundation.

Keyser, C. J. (1922) *Mathematical philosophy: a study of fate and freedom,* Dutton.

Koestler, A. (1964) *The act of creation,* Macmillan.

Laing, R. D., Phillipson, H. and Lee, A. R. (1966) *Interpersonal perception,* Springer.

Lao Tsu *Tao Te Ching* trans. Gia-Fu Feng and English, J. (1972) Vintage Books.

Osgood, C. E. (1962) 'Reciprocal initiative', in Roosevelt, J. (ed.) *The liberal papers,* Quadrangle Books.

Watzlawick, P., Beavin, J. H. and Jackson, D. *Pragmatics of human communication,* W. W. Norton.

Whitehead, A. N. and Russell, B. (1910–13) *Principia Mathematica,* 2nd ed. Vol. 3, Cambridge University Press.

5 A socio-technical critique of scientific management
E. Trist

The term 'scientific management' begs two questions—what is 'science' and what is 'management'. If, philosophically, the answers are plural and ambiguous, historically the answer is singular and clear. Scientific management refers to the movement concerned with work measurement, inaugurated by Frederick Taylor at the end of the first century of the first industrial revolution (Taylor 1911). Since then it has become the vast enterprise known as production or industrial engineering. Since then has also begun the second industrial revolution based on an information technology rather than simply an energy technology. 'Management science', growing out of operational research, is becoming as intimately associated with this second industrial revolution as scientific management has been with the first.

Along with a number of others, I hold the view that the more complex, fast-changing, interdependent but uncertain world growing up in the wake of the second industrial revolution is rapidly rendering obsolete and maladaptive many of the values, organizational structures, and work practices brought about by the first. In fact, something like their opposite seems to be required. Nowhere is this more apparent than in the efforts of some of the most sophisticated firms in the advanced science-based industries to de-centralize their operations, to de-bureaucratize their organizational form, and to secure the involvement and commitment of their personnel at all levels by developing forms of participatory democracy.

Nevertheless, the classic efficiency cult, which Taylorism has come to symbolize, remains the prevailing value of contemporary industry. The majority of those pursuing the second industrial revolution are as much obsessed with it as those who pursued the first, and this includes many operational research workers who treat systems in much the same way as most industrial engineers treat jobs.[1] It will take some time before the minority who have already learned to think in much wider terms secure an extensive hearing. By then much will have happened in the way of violence, alienation, and poor performance that could have been avoided—if the world

were a more rational place.

What then are the characteristics of the philosophy of work called scientific management? It has been summarized by my colleague Louis E. Davis as follows:

1 The man and his job are the essential building blocks of an organization; if the analyst gets these 'right' (in some particular but unspecified way), then the organization will be correctly defined.

2 Man is an extension of the machine, useful only for doing things that the machine cannot do.

3 The men and their jobs—the individual building blocks—are to be glued together by supervisors who will absorb the uncertainties and variabilities that arise in the work situation. Furthermore, these supervisors need supervisors, and so on *ad infinitum*, until the enterprise is organized in a many-layered hierarchy. In bureaucratic organizations, the latter notion ultimately leads to situations in which a man can be called a 'manager' solely on the grounds that he supervises a certain number of people, and without regard to the degree of judgment or decision-making responsibility such supervision requires.

4 The organization is free to use any available social mechanisms to enforce compliance and ensure its own stability.

5 Job fractionation is a way of reducing the costs of carrying on the work by reducing the skill contribution of the individual who performs it. Man is simply an extension of the machine, and, obviously, the more you simplify the machine (whether its living part or its non-living part), the more you lower costs.

This whole conception is now often referred to by social scientists as the 'machine theory of organization'.

Industrial organizations built on these principles had their heyday in the mass production plants of the interwar period. Daniel Bell (1956), in his essay *Work and its discontents,* sums up the patterns as follows;

These three logics of size, time, and hierarchy converge in that great achievement of industrial technology, the assembly line: the long parallel lines require huge shed space; the detailed breakdown of work imposes a set of mechanically paced and specified motions; the degree of coordination creates new technical, as well as social, hierarchies.

There is less need in the present context to elaborate on the extent to which the concentration, atomization, and control of work was carried than to point to the nature of the penalty paid for the benefits gained. If the latter brought more productivity at less cost in the short run within the enterprise itself, the former brought more alienation in the longer run, which spread into the larger society only to react back on the more immediate economic sphere. For some time this was masked in the classic forms of industrial struggle as organized labour sought better conditions for the mass of semi-skilled and un-skilled workers—more pay, shorter hours, improved amenities, etc. After a period of initial resistance unions began to learn how to use work-study as a bargaining method in their own interest. Nor was the question inherently related to ownership of the means of production. Lenin admired Taylor and entertained high hopes of what scientific management might do for industry in the Soviet Union.

But as the first signs of the affluent society began to appear, as the Great Depression faded into the background and a new level of economic well-being established itself after the Second World War, it became evident that something of another kind was wrong, whatever the amount of take-home pay or even security of employment. A first glimpse of what this might be had been obtained in the Hawthorne Experiments carried out by Elton Mayo's followers in Western Electric's plants in the Chicago area at the height of the scientific management wave (Roethlisberger & Dickson 1939). These were the first extensive studies made in industry by social scientists, as distinct from psychologists concerned with more limited psycho-physical problems. They led to the curious and belated discovery that the worker was human even in the work place, and that he responded to being treated as such. This led to the rise of the human relations movement, which in sophistication of theory and method has reached a degree of elaboration as great as scientific management, though it has never matched it in extensiveness of application.

The direction of development taken by the human relations movement was one that concentrated exclusively on the enterprise as a social system. The technology was not considered. The worker was to be treated better but his job would remain the same. Similarly with the supervisor—or, for that matter, the manager himself. As Peter Drucker (1952) put it:

It has been fashionable of late, particularly in the 'human relations' school, to assume that the actual job, its technology, and its mechanical and physical requirements are relatively unimportant compared to the social and psychological situation of men at work.'

What this statement means is that nobody thought the job itself could be changed. It was regarded as invariant. The technological imperative was taken for granted. It was logical, therefore, to concentrate attention on what were considered, however mistakenly, the only variable aspects.

The need to pay attention to the social and psychological aspects as a matter of practical personnel policy was generally recognized when full employment conditions were established after the Second World War in countries such as Britain. Full employment more than anything else gave rise to personnel management. The stick was unavailable. The carrots on offer were often indigestible and always limited. The game of economic rewards continued to be played according to the rules of wage-bargaining between management and labour, where expectations of a fair deal were based on the power balance between the two parties. But wage matters apart, attempts were made to set up good relations between all groups and types of personnel in the company, most especially between management and workers. So far as greater loyalty and trust could be established labour turnover would be reduced and industrial disputes made less likely.

As the management–worker interface was mediated by the foreman, a massive movement took place in supervisory training. How far was person-centred better than task-centred supervision, two-way better than one-way communication, persuasion better than coercion, a democratic better than an authoritarian style of leadership? How could one change supervisors from one way of behaving to the other? It was soon shown that it was of no avail to change the attitudes of foremen if those of management did not change as well (Likert 1958). So began a far-reaching movement in management training, which later broadened first into management and then into organizational 'development' as more of the complex interdependencies and dimensions of the enterprise as a social system were taken into account (Bennis 1966a).

Certain beliefs about the nature of man and his basic needs and motivations in the work setting began to gain currency, beliefs that were the opposite of those held in the scientific management school. Abram Maslow introduced his need-hierarchy which postulated that as the more primitive needs for food, sex, and security became satisfied higher needs concerned with group belongingness, self-esteem, and self-fulfilment would become more salient (Maslow 1954). Emphasizing that this would be so even in the work place, Douglas McGregor contrasted two models of industrial man which he called Theory X and Theory Y (McGregor 1960). The first represented the traditional management view of the worker that had grown up with the first industrial revolution. He was fundamentally 'a no-good'—lazy, irresponsible, selfish, etc. He therefore required external control. The second represented an emergent view: that industrial man was an ordinary, good human being at work as much as at home or as a citizen. He had a need for achievement, to take responsibility, and both to be creative himself and to take cognizance of others, etc. He was therefore capable of internal control. Basically, he was self-motivating and self-supervising.

Later we shall return to a fact of utmost significance—these views made their impact at a time when advanced industrial societies, especially the United States, were becoming not only more affluent but were already well into the second industrial revolution, with the very different tasks and roles that the newer technologies were beginning to create. These demand involvement and commitment, initiative and the good use of discretion at the bottom of the enterprise, no less than in the middle and at the top. This connection was not made by anyone within the human relations approach.[2] Nevertheless, a view of the human side of enterprise developed that was incompatible with the machine theory of organization. But no one attempted to alter the character of the jobs themselves, which continued to be designed according to the principles of scientific management. In the United States social science attention shifted to the problems of higher management with its increasing needs for flexibility and adaptability in facing change and uncertainty (Trist 1968). While at this level democratic social climates with transactional forms of relationship between superior and subordinate were tried out, as being best suited to the ends of the enterprise; for the same economic reasons the shop-floor continued to be set up and operated in terms of the values and concepts of the first industrial revolution, elaborated and refined by the principles of scientific management.

Quite early in the post-Second-World-War period, 1948–51, the Tavistock Institute undertook an intensive action-research study at the London factories of the Glacier Metal Company (Jaques 1951). Concerned with group relations at all levels, it led to the establishment of a new type of representative structure. Enlightened personnel policies and wage practices were implemented with unusual thoroughness. Yet the underlying alienation of the ordinary worker persisted. The 'split at the bottom of the executive chain' remained. The only major factor that had not undergone change was the task or work organization deriving from the technology. This had remained in the old modality. What would happen if this modality itself were changed?

An opportunity to begin finding out arose at this same time in the then recently nationalized coal industry, where strikes, labour turnover, and absenteeism were persisting unabated, despite the change over to public ownership and the introduction of many improvements in pay and working conditions. In the first of what turned out to be a very long series of researches, I was able, with a colleague who was a former miner, to observe at a pit in the Yorkshire coalfield what happened when the method of work organization was changed from the traditional form of job-breakdown to one in which autonomous groups interchanged tasks and took responsibility for the production cycle as a whole. The new groups were formed by the men themselves (Trist & Bamforth 1951). More extensive experiments using what became known as the composite method were made in East Midland Division between 1951 and 1953, initiated by V. W. Sheppard, who was later to become NCBs Director-General for Production (Sheppard 1951). The gains in productivity and job satisfaction were both substantial, the former being up between 20 and 30 per cent for less cost and the latter, apart from expressions of opinion, manifesting itself in decreased absenteeism, negligible labour turnover, and an improved health record (Wilson & Trist 1951). During further studies in Durham Division, 1954–8, an opportunity arose to carry out a crucial experiment in which the performance of two identical coal-faces using an identical longwall technology, one organized in the conventional, the other in the composite, way, were monitored over a period of two years. The composite face was superior in all respects (Trist et al. 1963).

Meanwhile, another Tavistock research worker, A. K. Rice, had applied composite principles in another industry in another country—the textile industry in Ahmedabad, India (Rice 1958). As soon as the idea of a group of workers becoming responsible for a group of looms was mentioned in discussions of the experimental reorganization of an automatic loom-shed, the workers spontaneously took up the idea, returning next day with a scheme that was accepted and immediately tried out. Early success was followed by vicissitudes due to many factors, which were investigated, but thereafter a steady state of significantly improved performance was attained. Higher wages were earned and the internally led loom groups, which carried out their own maintenance, offered 'careers' from less to more skilled roles, while Hindus and Moslems worked together. The system spread to ordinary looms. Though supported by the local trade union, the system came under political attack. Agitators from all parts of the country were brought into Ahmedabad by the Indian Communist Party, which like communist parties elsewhere opposed innovation that it could not fit into its 'operational model'—though Marx might have been more appreciative, judging from his neglected observations on machines and their relations to men. Members of the work-teams and their families were threatened with physical violence if they continued the new system. Attempts were made to set the Hindu and Moslem workers against each other. The attack failed. The workers stuck to a system that was very largely their own creation and that enabled them to enjoy a quality of work-life as well as a level of income that they had not previously known.

While their own change experiments were proceeding the Tavistock workers were able to ascertain that sporadic developments along the same lines had taken place in the telephone industry in Sweden, in the building industry in Holland, and in appliance manufacture and chemicals in the United States. There was another way to organizing productive work than the prevailing way. There was *organizational choice*.

In the United States recognition grew that quantified external control and job fractionation had been carried too far, and job enlargement received extensive trials (Walker & Guest 1952). A distinction was made between extrinsic job satisfaction (which included the pay packet) and intrinsic satisfaction deriving from the quality of the job itself. This was recognized as a major factor affecting motivation (Herzberg *et al.* 1959). But such recognition implied altering the way jobs were *designed* (Davis 1955, 1957). This meant changing the technological organization, the system that the human relations school had left intact and the scientific management school had continued to design according to the atomistic ideology that had characterized 19th-century science.

From the beginning the Tavistock workers had felt that a new unit of analysis was required. This led me to introduce the concept of the *socio-technical system* (Trist 1950). The problem was neither that of simply 'adjusting' people to technology nor technol-ogy to people but organizing the interface so that the best match could be obtained between both. Only the socio-technical whole could be effectively 'optimized'. In the limit, the socio-technical whole comprised the enterprise as a whole—in relation to its environment—as well as its primary work-groups and intervening subsystems (Emery and Trist 1960). It was necessary to change the basic model in which organization theory had been conceived.

Using Sommerhoff's theory of directive correlation (Sommerhoff 1950, 1969) Emery has formulated the matching process in terms of *joint optimization* (Emery 1966):

> Where the achievement of an objective is dependent upon *independent* but *correlative* systems, then it is impossible to optimize for overall performance without seeking to *jointly optimize* these correlative systems.
>
> Any attempts to optimize for one without due regard to the other will lead to sub-optimal overall performance, so even if an effort is made in an industrial situation to follow the traditional pattern, i.e. to optimize the technical system and hope the social system will somehow sort itself out, then sub-optimization is certain to result. This is also the case when attempting to optimize each system, but independently, ignoring interaction effects.
>
> It is important to remember that this principle applies where the systems are *independent but correlative*. . . . It does not necessarily apply where one system is, in fact, a *part of another*, i.e. a sales section of a company is part of a social system governed by the same laws as the rest of the social system. Where this is the case . . . the chain may be seized by the key link and the rest follows. Socio-technical systems, however, are composed of two distinct systems which, although correlative, are governed by different laws.

Pulling together the findings of a number of investigations, he has offered a set of general socio-technical principles for job-design (Emery 1963). As these go to the heart of the matter they will be quoted in full:

> The judgement that it is possible to redesign jobs in this way rests upon the evidence that men have requirements of their work other than those usually specified in a contract of employment (i.e. other than wages, hours, safety, security of tenure, etc.). The following list represents at least some of the general psychological requirements that pertain to the content of a job (to what a person is called upon to carry out in his job from hour to hour and from year to year):
>
> 1 The need for the content of a job to be reasonably demanding in terms other than sheer endurance and yet providing a minimum of variety (not necessarily novelty);
>
> 2 the need for being able to learn on the job and go on learning: again it is a question of neither too much nor too little;
>
> 3 the need for some minimal area of decision-making that the individual can call his own;

4   the need for some minimal degree of social support and recognition in the workplace;

5   the need to be able to relate what he does and what he produces to his social life;

6   the need to feel that the job leads to some sort of desirable future (not necessarily promotion).

These requirements are obviously not confined to any one level of employment. Nor is it possible to meet these requirements in the same way in all work settings or for all kinds of people. Complicating matters further is the fact that these needs cannot always be judged from conscious expression. Like *any* general psychological requirements they are subject to a wide range of vicissitudes. Thus, where there is no expectation that any of the jobs open to a person will offer much change of learning, that person will soon learn to 'forget' such requirements.

As already indicated, these requirements, however true they may be, are too general to serve as principles for job redesign. For this purpose they need to be linked to the objective characteristics of industrial jobs. The following is the preliminary set of such principles with which these studies started. They represent the best we were able to achieve by way of generalizing upon existing findings. They are not, we hope, final.

At the level of the individual:
(a) *Optimum variety of tasks within the job.* Too much variety can be inefficient for training and production as well as frustrating for the worker. However, too little can be conducive to boredom or fatigue. The optimum level would be that which allows the operator to take rest from a high level of attention or effort or a demanding activity while working at another and, conversely, allow him to stretch himself and his capacities after a period of routine activity.

(b) *A meaningful pattern of tasks that gives to each job a semblance of a single overall task.* The tasks should be such that, although involving different levels of attention, degrees of effort, or kinds of skill, they are interdependent: that is, carrying out one task makes it easier to get on with the next or gives a better end result to the overall task. Given such a pattern, the worker can help to find a method of working suitable to his requirements and can more easily relate his job to that of others.

(c) *Optimum length of work cycle.* Too short a cycle means too much finishing and starting; too long a cycle makes it difficult to build up a rhythm of work.

(d) *Some scope for setting standards of quantity and quality of production and a suitable feedback of knowledge of results.* Minimum standards generally have to be set by management to determine whether a worker is sufficiently trained, skilled or careful to hold the job. Workers are more likely to accept responsibility for higher standards if they have some freedom in setting them and are more likely to learn from the job if there is feedback. They can neither effectively set standards nor learn if there is not a quick enough feedback of knowledge of results.

(e) *The inclusion in the job of some of the auxiliary and preparatory tasks.* The worker cannot and will not accept responsibility for matters outside his control. In so far as the preceding criteria are met then the inclusion of such 'boundary tasks' will extend the scope of the worker's responsibility and make for involvement in the job.

(f) *The tasks included in the job should include some degree of care, skill, knowledge or effort that is worthy of respect in the community.*

(g) *The job should make some perceivable contribution to the unity of the product for the consumer.*

At group level:
(h) *Providing for 'interlocking' tasks, job rotation or physical proximity where there is a necessary interdependence of jobs (for technical or psychological reasons).* At a minimum this helps to sustain communication and to create mutual understanding between workers whose tasks are interdependent, and thus lessens friction, recriminations and 'scape-goating'. At best, this procedure will help to create work groups that enforce standards of co-operation and mutual help.

(i) *Providing for interlocking tasks, job rotation or physical proximity where the individual jobs entail a relatively high degree of stress.* Stress can arise from apparently simple things such as physical activity, concentration, noise or isolation if these persist for long periods. Left to their own devices, people will become habituated but the effects of the stress will tend to be reflected in more mistakes, accidents and the like. Communication with others in a similar plight tends to lessen the strain.

(j) *Providing for interlocking tasks, job rotation or physical proximity where the individual jobs do not make an obvious perceivable contribution to the utility of the end product.*

(k) *Where a number of jobs are linked together by interlocking tasks or job rotation they should as a group:*
(i) have some semblance of an overall task which makes a contribution to the utility of the product;
(ii) have some scope for setting standards and receiving knowledge of results;
(iii) have some control over the 'boundary tasks'.

Over extended social and temporal units:
1   *Providing for channels of communication so that the minimum requirements of the workers can be fed into the design of new jobs at an early stage.*

2   *Providing for channels of promotion to foreman rank which are sanctioned by the workers.*

It is clearly implied in this list of principles that the redesigning of jobs may lead beyond the individual jobs to the organization of groups of workers and beyond into at least the organization of support services (such as maintenance). There is reason to believe that the implications are even wider and that they will in any organization be judged to be much wider and reacted to accordingly.

Since these principles were formulated, a good deal of experience has been gained with more advanced technologies that depend on processes of continuous production and a high level of automation and computerization. As a result, a nine-step analytical model for socio-technical inquiry has been gradually taking shape (Emery 1967). Though never formalized, this may be summarized as follows:

1 An initial scanning is made of all the main aspects—technical and social—of the *selected target system,* i.e. department or plant to be studied.

2 The *unit operations* are then identified, i.e. the transformations (changes of state) of the material or product that take place in the target system, whether carried out by men or machines.

3 An attempt is then made to discover the *key process variances* and their interrelations. A variance is any deviation from a standard or specification. A variance is key if it significantly affects (i) either the quantity of production or its quality, (ii) either its operating or its *social* costs.

4 A table of variance control is then drawn up to ascertain *how far the key variances are controlled by the social system*—the workers, supervisors, and managers concerned. Some of the most important variances may be imported or exported. Investigation of this is one of the most critical steps. Another is to check *how far existing work roles satisfy the six basic psychological requirements.* Attention is then paid to ancillary activities, spatio-temporal relationships, the flexibility of job boundaries, and the payment system.

5 A separate inquiry is made into the *men's perception of their roles*—and of role possibilities as well as constraining factors. Here is a mine of unsuspected knowledge as much as of unsuspected feeling.

6 So far concern has focused on the target system. It now changes to *neighbouring systems,* beginning with the support or *maintenance system*;

7 and continuing with the boundary-crossing systems on the input and the output side, i.e. the *supplier* and *user systems,* which comprise adjacent departments. How do the structures of these units affect the target system and in what state are relations across these interfaces?

8 The target system and its immediate neighbours must now be considered in the context of the *general management system* of the plant or enterprise, particularly as regards the effects of *general policies* or *development plans either technical or social.*

9 Suggestions for change may arise at any point in the analysis, which proceeds by a re-cycling rather than a strictly sequential procedure, but only when all stages have been completed does it become possible to formulate *redesign proposals* for the target system, or to take up wider implications.

This analytical model, which uses an open systems approach similar to that of Katz and Kahn (1966), is not intended as a procedure for the sole use of research workers. It is intended also for operating people in plants where management and workers together have decided to undertake change in which explicit use will be made of socio-technical principles. It has therefore been prepared as a training method. Recently, Dr. Davis and I, along with other colleagues, held the first university course in the method at the Graduate School of Business Administration of the University of California, Los Angeles. Some 20 managers, industrial engineers, and personnel people attended for an intensive period of three weeks. They were drawn from Alcan's smelting plants in Quebec Province, Canada, where socio-technical experiments have been in progress for some two and a half years with the operators and the union now thoroughly involved (Davis & Trist 1969).

Though towards the end of the 1950s the Tavistock research group had extended its enquiries to examples of the more advanced technologies, these had remained descriptive studies. No further opportunities to conduct operational field experiments arose in a British setting. The next major developments took place in Norway, in conjunction with what has become known as the Norwegian Industrial Democracy Project (Emery & Thorsrud 1969). This has given a new dimension to socio-technical studies, relating them to central questions of value change as the era of the postindustrial society is brought nearer by the technologies of the second industrial revolution.

The project began in 1961 and grew out of a crisis between the Norwegian Confederation of Employers and the Norwegian Confederation of Labour over a sudden increase in the demand for workers' representation on boards of management, proposed as a way of reducing alienation and increasing productivity. What is remarkable is that the two Confederations (later joined by the government) should have requested the assistance of social scientists in order to gain a better understanding of what ordinarily would have been treated as a political problem. But, having helped establish a group, directed by Einar Thorsrud, that had earned their trust, they requested it to undertake research relevant to their problem. Through the ramifications of the project the group concerned has had to move from Trondheim to Oslo, where it now comprises the Institutes of Work Psychology. From the beginning it drew on the Tavistock's Human Resources Centre as a collaborating organization. Another remarkable feature of the project has been the extent to which research plans have been drawn up in conjunction with representatives of the sponsoring Confederations. This was a necessary condition for success, since the objective could not be limited to undertaking isolated socio-technical experiments. It was, first, to secure an understanding in the leadership of both sides of Norwegian industry of the relevance of a socio-technical philosophy of work to problems at the national level; and, thence, to establish the conditions that would allow this philosophy to diffuse through Norwegian industry at large.

The first phase of the project consisted of a field study of what actually happened in the five major concerns where workers were represented on the boards. These were either government-owned or part-owned enterprises obliged by law to have workers' representatives. The results showed that very little happened except at the symbolic and ceremonial level. There was no increase in participation by the rank and file, no decrease in work alienation, no increase in productivity. The overall state of industrial relations being stable within a stable framework of political democracy, little was added simply by adding a workers' representative to the board of directors. These results, which were compared with experiences in other countries, were widely discussed in both Confederations and in the press; and these discussions opened the way for the second phase of the project, which was to search out ways for securing improved conditions for personal participation in a man's immediate setting as constituting 'a different and perhaps more important basis for the democratization of the work place than the formal systems of representation'. This led to the idea of socio-technical experiments in selected plants in key industries, which, if successful, could serve as demonstration models for diffusion purposes. The selections were made by the members of the two Confederations serving on the research committee in consultation with sector committees of the industries concerned. No pains were spared in developing at all levels an understanding of, and in securing an acceptance of, the experiments in the plants proposed, which had to be respected organizations carrying weight, and which, moreover, had also to be seen as foreshadowing the future direction of Norwegian industrial development without being 'too far out'. It was regarded as essential to obtain this breadth and depth of sanctioning and centrality of societal positioning. Its absence in other contexts had prevented the spreading of proven innovations.

The first experiment was carried out in the metal-working industry, a sector regarded as critical but requiring considerable rehabilitation. A rather dilapidated wire-drawing plant in a large engineering concern was chosen on the grounds that if improvements could be brought about here they could be brought about anywhere. Productivity increased so much that the experiment was suspended; the workers concerned had begun to take home pay-packets in excess of the most skilled workers in the plant; a very large problem had now to be sorted out. If this experiment confirmed earlier findings regarding what could be accomplished when alienation is reduced, it shows up for the first time the magnitude of the constraining forces lying in wage structures and agreements negotiated according to the norms of the prevailing work culture, and accumulating historically. The difficulty of changing such structures accounted in considerable measure for the failure of earlier pilot experiments to spread.

The second experiment was in the pulp and paper industry, also regarded as a critical sector, but where the problem was not so much to upgrade performance with old technologies as to gain control over new. A sophisticated chemical plant was selected, where the basic work was information-handling—the core task in the technologies of the second industrial revolution. The requisite skills are perceptual and conceptual; the requisite work organization is one capable of handling the complex information flows on which controlling the process depends. To do this requires immense flexibility and capability for self-regulation. In the experimental plant a number of the key process-variances were not controlled by the social system nor had some of the most important been identified. The research team had to engage those concerned in evolving a form of organization that brought as many of them as possible under the control of the primary work-groups. After much resistance and many setbacks a process of continuous learning began to establish and to maintain itself as improvements were effected first in one area, then in another.

The model was established of an 'action-group'. This involved the operators concerned actively using supervisors, specialists, and managers as resources (rather than passively responding to them simply as bosses) in order to fashion an optimum work organization for a new technology as they were learning the know-how of its operation. This model was now taken up by Norskhydro, the largest enterprise in Norway, which manufactures fertilizers and other chemicals for the world market. The model was first used to re-fashion an old plant, then to develop the entire organization and operating procedure for a new one (Thorsrud 1968).

The success of the Norskhydro experiments has been widely publicized throughout Scandinavia. It marked the beginning of the third phase of the project, concerned with the diffusion process itself. In Norway the Joint Committee that originally sponsored the project was transformed into a National Participation Council and a new Parliamentary Commission on Industrial Democracy was formed. In Sweden similar developments have recently taken place at the national level, but it will be some time before a critical mass of concrete experience with the new methods can build up; similarly in Denmark. Meanwhile in Norway the most significant recent developments have taken place in the shipping industry in the manning of bulk carriers (Herbst 1969).

Undoubtedly there are features in the culture of the Scandinavian countries and in their situation, Norway most particularly, that have enabled them to act as the laboratory of the world in developing a new concept of industrial democracy based on socio-technical theory. In larger countries which are more authoritarian, where the first industrial revolution has left a deeper imprint, or where the culture is more fragmented, much greater difficulties are to be expected.

In Britain there are signs of the trial being taken up again by specific, important firms. The refining side of Shell, for example, some five years ago invited the Tavistock Institute to assist it in developing a new management philosophy based on the principle of joint optimization (Shell Refining 1966). In Ireland the national transport undertaking (CIE) undertook an extensive project (van Beinum 1966). Sporadic developments continue here and there in the US (Seashore & Bowers 1963; Myers 1967).

The underlying change that has taken place is that in the science-based industries of the second industrial revolution the worker is not a worker in the sense of the first industrial revolution. He is no longer embedded in the technology, contributing his energy to it or even his manipulative skill, but outside it, handling information from it and himself becoming a source of information critical for its management. This change of position and role makes him in fact a manager, different in degree but not in kind from those who traditionally have carried

this title. For the task of management is the regulation of systems and the function of managerial intervention (decision) to establish control over the boundaries conditions. Such is the type of activity in which the worker now primarily engages, as fact-finder, interpreter, diagnostician, judge, adjuster, and change-agent; whatever else he does is secondary. In Jaques's terms (1956, 1960), the *prescribed* part of his role has become minimal, for the 'programme' is in the machine; the *discretionary* part has become maximal, since the reason for his presence is to assess the performance of the programme and, if necessary, to change it—either by himself, or in conjunction with others at higher levels. No longer is there 'a split at the bottom of the executive chain' that separates managers and managed. Everyone is now on the same side of 'the great divide' and whatever fences there may still be on the common side would seem best kept low. A general change is in consequence taking place in all role-relations in the enterprise. This is the underlying reason for the bureaucratic model being experienced as obsolete and maladaptive, and also for a possible new role beginning to emerge for trade unions (van Beinum 1966).

To maintain in a steady state the intricate interdependencies on which the science-based industries rely requires commitment to, and involvement in, their work from the men on the shop-floor (those who are left) as much as from anyone higher up (and there are fewer of these at intermediate levels). External supervision may correct errors that have been made, but only internal supervision can prevent their occurrence. The amount of error that capital-intensive continuous-production plants can tolerate is small compared with plants based on technologies that are labour-intensive and discontinuous. There is a straight economic reason for this: work-stoppages have become too costly, whether they result from machine breakdowns due to incompetence or carelessness, or from labour trouble due to bad internal relations or external pressures. But if anything at all has become clear about automated plants it is that they do not work automatically. They are the creation of those who man them as much as of those who build them; design continues as operation commences and operational experience informs further design, which from the beginning has to be developed as a socio-technical process. Moreover, this socio-technical creativeness must be maintained because the change-rate is both rapid and continuous. The autonomous work-group setting out on an expedition of learning and innovation from which there is no return would appear to be the organizational paradigm that matches, and is 'directively cor-related' with, the information technology. The advance of technology itself has reversed the world of Frederick Taylor.

Though a great deal of industry does not yet belong to the information technology, and though some of it will never belong, the part that does has already become the 'leading part'. Its influence on the rest may be expected to increase. Moreover, in all contexts there is organizational choice. This is likely to be more frequently exercised in the direction of the new paradigm now that the old paradigm is no longer taken to be a law of nature. Marshall McLuhan (1964) seems to be right in thinking that automation means 'learning a living'.

The transition to a new concept of the world of work may be slow, unpleasant, and difficult, but into-lerance (whether in the form of rebellion or drop-ping out) of narrow and over-prescribed jobs is mounting. The contemporary malaise deplored by the 'silent majority' may itself be a main force that will hasten beneficial change, for the technological excuse for any job to be inhuman rather than human is rapidly diminishing. Those who wish to be human will have more of a chance in the future than many have had in the past. It is disconcerting, however, to think of industry as being the place where one will find out who one is.

Notes

[1] Among industrial engineers who thought along very different lines were James Gillespie in Britain and Adam Abruzzi in the United States.

[2] Among British social scientists, however, the connection bet-ween technology and organization was central for such writers as Woodward (1958) and Burns & Stalker (1961).

References

Ackoff, R. L. 1970, 'The evolution of management systems,' *Canadian Operational Research Society Journal* **8** (3).

Bell, D. 1956, *Work and its discontents,* Boston: Beacon Press.

Bennis, W. G. 1966a, *Changing organizations,* New York: McGraw-Hill.

—1966b, *Theory and method in applying behavioural change,* in J. R. Lawrence (ed.), *Operational research and the social sciences.* London: Tavistock Publications.

Burns, T. & Stalker, G. 1961, *The management of innovation,* London: Tavistock Publications.

Davis, L. E. 1955, 'Job design', *Journal of Industrial Engineering,* January.

—1957, 'Job design research', *Journal of Industrial Engineering,* November–December.

Davies, L. E. & Trist, E. L. 1969, *The socio-technical project in Alcan.* Unpublished.

Drucker, P. F. 1952, 'The employee society', *American Sociological Review* **58**.

Emery, F. E. 1963, *Some hypotheses about the ways in which tasks may be more effectively put together to make jobs,* London: Tavistock Institute, Doc. No. T.176.

—1966, *The democratization of the work place,* London: Tavistock Institute, Doc. No. T.813.

—1967. *Statement on socio-technical analysis,* unpublished paper presented to the International Conference on Socio-technical Systems, Lincoln.

Emery, F. E. & Thorsrud, E. 1969, *Form and content in industrial democracy,* London: Tavistock Publications; Oslo: Oslo University Press, 1964.

Emery, F. E. & Trist, E. L. 1960, *Socio-technical systems,* in C. W. Churchman & M. Verhulst (eds.), *Management science: models and techniques,* vol. 2. Oxford & London: Pergamon Press.

Herbst, P. G. 1969, *Socio-technical design in ships,* unpublished. Oslo: Institutes of Work Psychology.

Herzberg, F., Mausner, B. & Snyderman, B. 1959, *The motivation to work,* New York: John Wiley.

Jaques, E. 1951, *The changing culture of a factory,* London: Tavistock Publications.

—1956, *The measurement of responsibility,* London: Tavistock Publications.

—1960, *Equitable payment,* London: Heinemann.

Katz, D. & Kahn, R. L. 1966, *The social psychology of organizations,* New York: John Wiley.

Likert, R. 1958, Effective supervision: an adaptive and relative process, *Personnel Psychology* **11**.

McGregor, D. 1960, *The human side of enterprise,* New York: McGraw-Hill.

McLuhan, B. 1964, *Understanding media,* London: Routledge & Kegan Paul; New York: McGraw-Hill.

Maslow, A. 1954, *Motivation and personality,* New York: Harper.

Myers, M. S. 1964, 'Who are your motivated workers?', *Harvard Business Review* **42** (1).

Rice, A. K. 1958, *Productivity and social organization: the Ahmedabad experiment,* London: Tavistock Publications.

Roethlisberger, F. J. & Dickson, W. J. 1939, *Management and the worker,* Cambridge, Mass.: Harvard University Press.

Seashore, S. E. & Bowers, D. G. 1963, *Changing the structure and functioning of an organisation,* Ann Arbor: University of Michigan Institute for Social Research, Monograph 33.

Shell Refining 1966, *Statement on company objectives and management philosophy,* London: Shell Centre.

Sheppard, V. W. 1951, 'Continuous longwall mining: experiment at Bolsover Colliery', *Colliery Guardian* **182.**

Sommerhoff, G. 1950, *Analytical biology,* London: Oxford University Press.

—1969, 'The abstract characteristics of living systems', in F. E. Emery (ed.), *Systems thinking.* Harmondsworth: Penguin.

Taylor, F. W. 1911, *The principles and methods of scientific management,* New York: Harper.

Thorsrud, E. 1968, *Papers on the project at Norskhydro,* unpublished. Oslo: Institutes of Work Psychology.

Trist, E. L. 1950, *The concept of culture as a psycho-social process.* Paper presented to the Anthropological Section, British Association for the Advancement of Science.

—1968, 'The professional facilitation of planned change in organisations: review paper,' *Proceedings,* International Association of Applied Psychology, Sixteenth International Congress.

Trist, E. L. & Bamforth, K. W. 1951, 'Some social and psychological consequences of the longwall method of coal-getting,' *Human Relations* **4** (3).

Trist, E. L., Higgin, G. W., Murray, H., & Pollock, A. B. 1963, *Organizational choice: capabilities of groups at the coal face under changing technologies*, London: Tavistock Publications.

Van Beinum, H. 1966, *The morale of Dublin busmen*, Dublin: Mount Salus Press.

Walker, C. R. & Guest, H. 1952, *The man on the assembly line*, Cambridge, Mass.: Harvard University Press.

Wilson, A. T. M. & Trist, E. L. 1951, *The Bolsover system of continuous mining*, London: Tavistock Institute, Doc. No. 290.

Woodward, J. 1958, *Management and technology*, London: HMSO.

6   Socio-technical systems

D. Silverman

The somewhat varied group of writers dealt with under the title of 'technological implications' share a concern with elaborating the consequences of different types of technology (given certain assumed personality needs of those studied) for job satisfaction and workgroup behaviour. While this illustrates the demands of one structure on another, it is not fully satisfactory from a systems point of view. This is because such an approach need not ask questions about the nature and causes of system stability and goal-attainment or take account of the resources provided and demands made by the environment in which an organization is located. The view of organizations as socio-technical systems, on the other hand, stresses the inter-relationships of technology, environment, the sentiments of the participants and organizational form. Since the nature of these relationships will determine the stability and even the survival of any economic organization, all the variables must be taken into account in empirical analysis and in prescribing change.

Socio-technical system theorists have usually been satisfied that the assumptions of the organizational psychologists, together with certain propositions derived from psycho-analytic theory, provide an appropriate way to deal with the purposes and orientations of the members of organizations (sentiments). At the same time, they are agreed that the value of much early work was vitiated by a concentration on 'informal' behaviour and its consequent failure to develop a view of an organization as a system, with inter-related formal and informal structures, which is shaped by and shapes the environment. Two psychologists, Schein (1965) and Bennis (1966), are concerned with the processes whereby the psychological problems of systems can be met and with assessing their relative success in doing so: to meet these problems as Bennis points out, is a 'healthy' response, while not to do so implies a pathological organism. Socio-technicists, as will be seen, are equally committed to this organic view of organizations. Yet there are certain differences between their approach and that of the functionalists.

Structural-functionalism is a well-developed mode of analysis which has been taken from the realms of sociological grand theory and applied to the substantive study of organizations. The socio-technical system approach, on the other hand, grew out of observation of behaviour in economic organizations and was only later codified into a set of related propositions. Many of its proponents have been prescriptive in their orientation and much of the work in this tradition has arisen out of attempts to make greater sense of material gathered during consultancy. Finally, socio-technicists have sought to develop an inter-disciplinary perspective, which has drawn on economics, psychology, and even psycho-analysis, rather than to make use of the more strictly sociological frame of reference of the functionalists. It is possible, however, to exaggerate the differences between the two approaches. Both adhere to a systems position and in so doing manage to ask much the same questions and to derive similar answers.

An organization may be viewed as a socio-technical system in the sense that, while the technology, the formal role-structure and the sentiments of the members are systematically connected, none is of prime importance or necessarily the first target of analysis. All may be seen as inter-related with each other and with the environment in which the organization is located. Thus the technology, together with the formal structure, is thought to limit the amount of human satisfaction that may be derived from participation and to shape the nature of the output to the outside world. In turn, both are shaped by the demands which the environment makes on the organization. The problem of this type of analysis then becomes: what kind of formal structure can most effectively relate to one another the varied demands of the environment, of the technology and of the members? Effectiveness is here usually defined as the attainment of the goal or 'primary task' of the organization.

There is no one most efficient form of organization; even bureaucracy, the attractions of which were so vigorously presented at the beginning of the century and then equally vehemently denied as knowledge was obtained of the 'vicious circle' (Gouldner,

1954)—an appeal to formal rules can add to instability—and the 'displacement of goals' (Merton, 1949)—a means to a goal may become the goal itself—is, by itself, neither an efficient nor inefficient instrument. It all depends on the nature of the organizational goal and on the demands made by subsystems (e.g. the members) and by other systems (e.g. the economy) on the organization. Different organizational forms are, therefore, appropriate to different combinations of demands.

We shall now turn to various discussions of the nature and consequences of the demands made, respectively, by the technology employed, the sentiments of the participants, and the environment.

Joan Woodward: Technology, decision-making and organizational structure

Joan Woodward's (1958 and 1965) study of industrial firms in S.E. Essex suggested to her that production systems could be placed somewhere on a continuum based on degree of technical complexity. At one end would be found the relatively non-complex unit (or small-batch) production; highly complex process production would come at the other end, while mass (or large-batch) production would be located somewhere in the middle. She went on to examine the range of organizational forms that she encountered and found that firms with similar production systems were organized in a similar manner. The levels of authority in management increased with technical complexity, as did the proportion of managers and supervisors to non-supervisory staff. However, there were also certain similarities between firms using unit and process production—the least and the most complex technologies. In the first place, although staff (experts) and line (administrators) were sharply distinguished in mass production firms, there was very little specialization among the functions of management in the other technical forms. In unit production firms, this was because a smaller number of specialists tended to be employed and line management, therefore, had to be technically competent. On the other hand, the status of expert positions was so high in the process production enterprises that it was often impossible to distinguish between the specialist's role of advice-giving and the administrator's role of decision-taking. Moreover, in such organizations, even those most directly concerned with administration require a level of technical expertise in order to grasp the complexities of the production process.

A second similarity between the extremes of technical complexity was that the organizations concerned tended to have relatively non-bureaucratic structures as opposed to the more rigid bureaucratic form often found in mass production. This arose, Woodward suggests, because the 'central problem' of unit and process technologies (respectively, product development and marketing) involves the need to innovate; and decisions made through a formal hierarchy might be slow and unoriginal. On the other hand, in mass production the central problem is the efficient administration of production and bureaucracy is clearly appropriate.

The number and nature of policy decisions arising in each technical system also have an influence on the organizational form that is most efficient. In unit production, while a relatively large number of decisions needs to be taken, these tend to have only short-term consequences which commit the firm for the period during which an article is produced. It is most appropriate, therefore, to have decisions made on the spot by those with the most competence for the problem at issue, instead of having to work up through a bureaucratic hierarchy. In mass production, fewer decisions are taken but these tend to commit the firm further into the future (for instance, compare the limited consequences of a decision made by an haute couture dressmaker with the long-term consequences of a motor firm deciding to produce a new car). However, Woodward argues, these decisions often affect only one function of management (e.g. production, sales or research) and can be taken by the senior executive responsible for that function through the normal bureaucratic channels. In process technologies, however, while the fewest policy decisions of all are made, these tend to commit the firm furthest into the future and cannot be taken by one individual. Instead, they require the pooling of all the expert knowledge on the topic at hand—irrespective of the formal position of the expert in an authority hierarchy. In this situation the limitations of bureaucracy are further revealed as decision-making becomes far less dependent on 'hunches'; it is therefore difficult to establish a separate administrative function for the non-expert.

E. Trist: Technology and the needs of workgroups

Woodward's work points out the limitations of the view that there are principles of management valid for all situations by showing the different demands that technical systems made on organizations. An organizational form may be right for the technology and economic tasks of the enterprise, yet fail to satisfy other important demands. This was the conclusion of a study of the process of mechanization in the coalmines of N.W. Durham conducted by Eric Trist and others (1963). Their research convinced the writers of the intimate relationship between the technical, economic and social aspects of organizations. The traditional technology of the mines ('single-place working'), where small teams of men worked their own part of the coal-seam, had facilitated the formation of multi-skilled, self-selected, largely autonomous workgroups. This allowed a great deal of independence within the workgroup and generated a relatively high level of job satisfaction. Since the workgroups did not compete with one another, their relations were normally harmonious.

This technology was, however, being replaced by mechanical coal-cutting and specialization of workers by shift: one shift cut the coal with a mechanical coal-cutter, the next loaded the coal on to a conveyor, and the third shift propped up the roof and moved the conveyor and the cutter for the next shift. This 'conventional longwall method' was technically efficient but had dysfunctional social consequences. It broke up the self-selected workgroup and destroyed some of the loyalties and cohesion necessary in dangerous work, especially since the members of each shift were not always able to get along with each other. Moreover, the specialization by shift necessitated greater co-ordination from the surface to ensure that each shift completed its part of the cycle. Supervision became closer and the men reacted strongly against having to forgo still more of the independence which they had traditionally enjoyed. The end product of the change was technical and economic inefficiency and social disturbance.

However, a different form of work organization, Trist argues, could maximize the benefits of technical advance and minimize the dangers of unrest and conflict. According to the 'composite longwall method', the three-shift cycle remains but there is no sharp division of tasks between shifts; miners are allowed to make use of their multiple skills. At the same time, supervision is lessened and the workgroup retains its autonomy by being given the responsibility for the deployment of men to each shift. Thus it permitted, Trist would suggest, an optimum relationship between the often opposed claims of technical, economic and social systems.

Woodward and Trist deal with the demands which technology and the social ties of the participants make upon organizations. Other socio-technical theorists have concentrated on the ways in which the characteristics of an organization's environment (especially those associated with the nature of the market in which it operates) shape what would be the most appropriate organizational structure. This problem has been taken up notably by Burns and Stalker (1961) and by Emery and Trist (1965).

Environment and organizational structure

In the course of a study of twenty British firms, Burns and Stalker became convinced that management systems could usefully be seen in two ideal-typical forms. The mechanistic model approaches Weber's bureaucratic type and is characterized by a clear hierarchy of offices involving strict specialization, vertical communication, and the implicit assumption that 'somebody at the top' is responsible for making sure that everybody's specialism is relevant to organizational goals. The organic model, on the other hand, has no clearly defined hierarchy and involves a continual re-definition of roles and hence a lack of formal job titles. Functions are co-ordinated by frequent meetings between managers, and communications are lateral and regarded as providing information and advice rather than instructions. There is no longer an omniscient person at the top to whom consideration of action in terms of organizational objectives can safely be left. Instead, individuals are expected to perform their tasks in the light of their knowledge of the overall aims of the enterprise.

Burns and Stalker now go on to note that *neither* model is necessarily efficient or inefficient; it all depends on the nature of the environment in which the firm is located. The mechanistic type is most appropriate for enterprises operating under relatively stable market conditions and using an unchanging technology. In these situations, the routinization of behaviour which it generates is functional for the unchanging tasks which must be dealt with. An organic structure, on the other hand, mobilizes expert knowledge without too much regard for the formal place of the expert in the hierarchy. By not freezing at a certain point of time the amount of authority given to different tasks, it is appropriate to an unstable situation in which the organization is continually experiencing relatively unpredictable new tasks and problems.

The open system perspective, which Burns and Stalker's study implies, seeks to take account of the full range of inputs into an organization. In the same manner (but influenced by the general system theory of von Bertalanffy, 1967, and his use of concepts drawn from the natural sciences), Emery and Trist (1965) advocate an open systems model and consider various types of environment, each of which makes different demands on organizational structure.

In a 'placid, randomized' environment, there is no causal connection between the unchanging and separate parts, and relatively small, undifferentiated organizations can flourish. In a 'placid, clustered' environment, organizations must develop a measure of specialization and adopt strategies, as distinct from tactics, in order to meet a setting where aspects of their environment are causally related. In a 'disturbed-reactive' environment there are organizations pursuing similar goals and each one must decide between competition, co-optation and co-operation with the others. Finally, in 'turbulent fields', where the environment itself is changing in addition to the changes deriving from the interaction of organizations, organizations must adopt non-bureaucratic structures and attempt to develop a consensus of values about their forms of relationship. Such a consensus provides an 'organizational matrix'.

Underlying what Emery and Trist are doing, and perhaps confused by the terms that they bring in from the physical sciences, is an assumption that the situations which organizations were originally designed to meet may no longer exist. As technical and economic change accelerates, an attempt must be made to make the unpredictable predictable, or at least to create structures which will be prepared to deal with rapidly changing conditions. This point of view has its parallel in the work of Bennis, and in the studies of Burns and Stalker and of Woodward. It is interesting to note that the 'open-system' concept, when based on an organic analogy and concerned with the way in which environments serve to meet the 'needs' of organizations (which in turn perform 'functions' for other systems) becomes indistinguishable from structural-functional analysis. This is particularly clear in the emphasis of Emery and Trist on an evolutionary process of differentiation in social systems which bears striking resemblances to the views of Parsons.

Miller and Rice: Task systems and sentient systems

Rice (1963) has also been explicitly concerned with the analysis of organizations as open systems which 'can only exist by the exchange of materials with their environment' (p. 184). However, unlike the other writers so far discussed, he considers together the impact of the various components of the system on each other and provides a means of assessing the relative success of an enterprise in adapting to the demands made upon it. An organization is successful to the extent that it manages to attain its 'primary task'. This concept is central to the development of Rice's approach.

Miller and Rice (1967) define primary task as 'the task it [the organization] must perform if it is to survive' (p. 25). If this seems somewhat tautological, they add that it is a descriptive rather than normative category and hence is not to be identified with the commonsense view within the society about what the primary task of an organization should be. A better way of establishing the nature of the primary task is to examine the statements which the leaders of an enterprise make about the goals of their organization. However, these views can be 'wrong', 'if through inadequate appraisal of internal resources and external forces, the leaders of an enterprise define the primary task in an *inappropriate* way' (p. 27, my italics). If this is so, then the very survival of the organization may be jeopardized. Thus one is only left with inferring the primary task from observation of the behaviour within the organization and of the criteria by which it is judged by those taking part. This allows us to argue that 'This enterprise is behaving as if its primary task were . . .', or that 'This part of the enterprise is behaving as if the primary task of the whole were . . .' (p. 28).

The means by which organizations attain their primary task are embodied in the formal structure, or what Miller and Rice call the task system. This is distinguished from the informal structure, or sentient system, which directly commands the loyalty of the members. Sentient systems derive from the personality needs which motivate the human participants. Following the Hawthorne approach, individuals are assumed to need to belong to small face-to-face groups at work: in return for the security provided, loyalty must be shown towards group norms. Hence, in a view not unreminiscent of a much older analysis, it follows that, unlike task systems, sentient systems are non-rational: 'At the level of task performance', they suggest, 'members take part as rational, mature human beings; at the level of assumptions they make about each and the group, they go into collusion with each other to support or to hinder what they have met to do' (p. 18).

The concept of a socio-technical system is arrived at by suggesting that the task system operates directly upon the sentient system. Thus Miller and Rice write: '. . . the nature of the task and of the activities involved in its performance can provide the individual with *overt* satisfactions . . . or . . . deprivations . . . it can also provide satisfaction and deprivation by reciprocation with the *inner* world of *unconscious drives* and needs for defence against *anxiety*' (p. 31, my italics). So the personality needs of the workforce provide a limiting factor on the type of organization used to achieve the primary task; that is why we must talk about socio-technical systems. The goal of analysis must, therefore, be that set down by Trist in his development of '. . . solutions that [take account of] . . . the technical requirements of the task and the human needs of those performing it. The assumption was made that the "right" organization would satisfy the *task* and *social* needs' (pp. xi–xii).

Thus an organization needs a structure to 'ensure the commitment of its members to enterprise objects and . . . to regulate relations between task and sentient systems' (p. xiii), so that, as far as possible, human needs and the task system coincide. Three situations are possible: the tasks performed may preclude a coincidence with the sentient system, as in the case where people have commitments to task systems outside the organization (for instance 'cosmopolitan' professionals); a 'natural coincidence' may occur, as in the case of a family business where task and sentient groups coincide; or there may be a 'contrived coincidence' such as Trist claims is provided by the composite longwall method of mining. Such a contrived co-incidence will need to ensure that the method of work allows 'internally led, quasi-autonomous, primary work groups' (p. 255) to survive and flourish.

An evaluation of socio-technical systems
This brief treatment of the literature has had to impose a false measure of unity on a range of different positions. As with structural-functionalism, therefore, it is difficult to evaluate an approach which has no clear orthodoxy. Nevertheless, the socio-technical theorists do share certain views in common, not least because of their situation on the eastern side of the Atlantic and their commitment to abstracted empiricism in preference to grand theory.

The advantages of the approach, while they are by no means insubstantial, can be speedily dealt with. They can be seen most clearly by a comparison with the perspectives that historically preceded it. Unlike them, it has taken account of the inter-relatedness of formal and informal, and of organizational and extra-organizational. Unlike them, it does not imply that there is one most efficient form of organization which is appropriate for all situations. Finally, unlike them it has been able to offer fairly convincing explanations of the differences between organizations which comparative studies have revealed.

The limitations of the socio-technical system approach arise, firstly, in the orientation which it suggests towards what are taken to be the problems

of systems. Its usefulness depends on how far one is prepared to concede that social institutions are similar to biological organisms and that their functioning is best understood in terms of a series of adaptations to an often hostile environment.

The connection of their system with organic analogy is found most clearly in the work of Rice: 'This book', he states in a recent work, 'seeks to establish a series of concepts and a theory of organization that treats enterprises . . . as living organisms' (1963, p. 179). The organism has demands made upon it by other systems and reacts by seeking to stabilize itself. The concept of 'primary task' provides a referent by which to judge the health or disease of the organism: where the primary task is secured, the system has made a healthy response to the demands which it experiences; where it is failing in performing adequately (in terms of the primary task), the system must be restructured so as to bring the parts into a better balance.[1]

The deficiencies of the organic analogy as applied to social life have been discussed elsewhere, and it is only necessary to raise the more obvious questions. Does patterned social interaction depend upon a primary task? Is social action best understood as a response to demands perceived by the observer but not necessarily by the participants? Is it useful to conceive of social forms in terms of health and pathology?

Of more practical importance than these issues, is the problem of whether the systems perspective can deal adequately with 'why' questions concerning the origins and causes of social phenomena. While, if you accept its assumptions, it can explain rather neatly the manner in which social systems adapt to one another and, thereby, maintain social order (both 'how' questions), it has considerably more difficulty in explaining *why* systems have their present characteristics and why they react in different ways, and to a varied extent, to external and internal threats to their stability. Although it can, for instance, suggest the means by which an organization can be more successful or adaptive, it provides very little in the way of an explanation of the causes of this initial non-adaptiveness. Thus Parsons's view that organizations become inefficient when too much attention is paid to integration and 'latency' rather than to adaptation and goal-attainment is more a definition of inefficiency than an explanation of its causes. Without reference to human motivation it is arguable that one cannot explain why social life has the characteristics that it does.

This is tacitly recognized by many system theorists. Burns and Stalker (1961), for example, while they begin by stressing the objective demands of the environment, ultimately resort to the definitions of the situation which are held by the participants in order to explain why organizations respond in different ways to the same market conditions. Thus, the political and status commitments of the actors influence the way they interpret the situation, while the response to a given rate of technical or market change is shaped by the orientations of top management—or what Burns and Stalker call, 'their capacity to lead'.[2] This is because each organizational form is not only 'objectively' better for a certain set of economic conditions but is also assessed from the point of view of the ends of the members.[3] The action which they take will be governed by their definition of the situation rather than that of the observer.

If the objections to a systems perspective are put on one side, serious limitations to the work carried out in the tradition of socio-technical systems remain. These arise from a failure to distinguish 'is' and 'ought' propositions; from a commitment to a primarily prescriptive frame of reference; from an insufficient attention to the different types of attachment to economic organizations; and from a consideration of environment in almost exclusively economic terms. Each of these four criticisms are briefly discussed below.

1 *Is or ought:* It is one thing to say that technology, market pressures, and the needs of the participants ought to be important in organizations, it is quite another thing to maintain that these factors actually do determine organizational form. A limitation of socio-technical analysis is that one is never quite sure whether it is being argued that such factors are the causes of an organizational structure or merely variables that require attention in any attempt to change the organization. While each of these factors is supposed to be given equal weight in analysis, it becomes apparent on reading the literature that an implicit distinction is made between what may be called 'operational' variables which shape an organization *if left to itself*, and 'evaluative' variables which are used to judge the efficiency of an existing structure. Technology and the pressures of the market, it seems, determine organizational form (e.g. Woodward, Trist *et al.*). But since this may mean that insufficient attention is paid to the personality needs of the participants (Miller and Rice, Trist), or to the rate of environmental change (Burns and Stalker, Emery and Trist), a certain amount of planned organizational change is necessary.

Distinctions between 'is' and 'ought' propositions

are clearly essential if one is to come to grips fully with the nature of what is being studied or to predict how it is likely to change. Yet, as with Parsons, one is never quite sure whether what is being attempted is a description of how organizations actually work or an abstract discussion of the conditions necessary for their stable functioning. The notion of a socio-technical system thus requires a more conscious distinction between those factors which determine organizational form and those which can be used to judge its efficiency.

2 *Prescription.* Part of the confusion over 'is' and 'ought' no doubt arises out of the dual role of many socio-technicists as academic analysts and as consultants to business organizations. Consultancy, despite the solution it provides to the problem of access, by its nature involves a prior orientation to the question of how an efficient organization can be constructed. While this clearly does not imply that the consultant cannot pay attention to the highest standards of rigorousness in the collection of his data, it does mean that he is likely to be immediately concerned with social rather than sociological problems, and that theories and empirical material which do not have a direct bearing on the task at hand may not be taken up. This impression is supported by the tendency of their works to refer almost entirely to other socio-technical writers, to the exclusion of much that one might have thought was common ground in the literature.[4]

Consultancy necessarily implies a commitment (if only temporarily) to the problems of those who are paying one's salary, the concerns of other members of the organization being important only in so far as they affect the task at hand. This is not meant to suggest that consultants deviate in any way from the highest ethical standards; indeed many of them are quite aware of the limitations of their position and admit to it freely.[5] It reminds one, however, as R. K. Brown (1967) has pointed out, that observation depends upon the spectacles being used and that the difficulties of an organization may well be a polite name for the difficulties of those in positions of authority.

Two further consequences of the consultancy posture should be noted. First, it is no coincidence that the theory that has been developed is specifically applicable to economic organizations, since it is in these that most consulting has occurred. Certainly it would be rather difficult to incorporate the emphasis on technology into an approach to all organizations. Secondly, a commitment to problem-solving as a first priority is usually associated with an attempt to mobilize all perspectives that might be useful. Socio-technical theorists thus tend to make use of a wide range of disciplines.

Opinions vary as to the fruitfulness of an inter-disciplinary approach. What is gained by the collapse of artificial boundaries is balanced and sometimes outweighed by the failure to make use of the full insights of any of the constituent disciplines: a good partial approach is to be preferred to any number of hastily constructed general theories. Nevertheless, even as a general theory, one is struck by the absence of a sociological perspective or of due atten-tion to the sociological literature in the work of some socio-technical theorists. Instead, their primary orientation often seems to be towards psycho-analysis in the understanding of motivation, and economics and sometimes biology in the study of organization-environment relations.

3 *Attachments.* The weakest part of the socio-technical system approach is the regular failure of its proponents to discuss adequately the sources of the orientations of members of organizations. Sentient systems are supposed to derive from what is often a hotch-potch collection of human needs which group together in equal measure the social man of classical human relations, the theory of self-actualization of the organizational psychologists and Melanie Klein's psycho-analytic object-relations theory. Instead of examining the different types of involvement in organizations, they argue that men are (or should be) morally attached to their work and that organ-izational form is only satisfactory (from the point of view of efficiency as much as of the men themselves) when it provides for such an attachment. Trist (1963), for instance, suggests that, by showing how large autonomous workgroups can function effec-tively in a modern technology, his study has a gen-eral relevance for industry. Yet this is to assume that the type of attachment to work of a Durham miner is repeated among other workers and that all would be satisfied in the same work-setting. In a similar way, with similar objections, Woodward (1958) argues that assembly-line production has a poorer record of industrial relations because, as a mass production industry, it limits the amount of job satisfaction and frustrates the workers' desire to belong to stable workgroups.

4 *Environment.* Adequate analysis of the orienta-tions of members of organizations would require attention to the specific ways of perceiving situations which they bring from their extra-organizational experiences. However, the socio-technicists have generally considered the environment in purely economic terms as a series of market demands upon organizational structures. While sufficient for some

purposes, this gives no means of explaining the dif-ferent reaction of those in authority to the same objective set of demands or of predicting the pattern of social interaction that will develop.

The four limitations are not inherent in socio-technical system analysis. If attention is paid to them, then there is no reason why an adequate analytic theory, as opposed to a series of prescrip-tions, could not be constructed. Such a theory, it seems likely, will be much more intimately related to structural-functionalism with which it will share the same conceptual apparatus.

Notes and references

[1] The difficulty in this, as R. K. Brown has noted, is that, 'though a biological system has an obvious "primary task" in relation to its environment, the same is not true of a social system' (Brown, 1967, p. 45).

[2] They explain that 'to lead' is 'to interpret the requirements of the external situation and to prescribe the extent of the per-sonal commitments of individuals to the purposes and activities of the working organizations' (Burns and Stalker, 1961, p. 96).

[3] 'As soon as the span of considerations we bring into play widens beyond that of organizational analysis, it is clear that "dysfunctional" types of management system are developed . . . [and] are seen to be entirely effective in appropriate parts of the social organization in which they serve rationally as means to specific ends' (Burns and Stalker, 1961, preface). I am grateful to Prof. Burns for drawing my attention to this statement.

[4] There is, for instance, no mention of Dalton, Crozier, Gould-ner or Selznick in the text or in the bibliography of Miller and Rice (1967).

[5] 'The elaboration of theories about organizations and the col-lection of data to support [sic] hypotheses', Rice notes about their work, 'have usually had the severely practical objective of attempting to clarify the difficulties that my clients and I were meeting' (1963, p. 4).

Bennis, W. G., 1966, *Changing Organisations, Essays on the Development and Evolution of Human Organisation*, McGraw-Hill.

Brown, R. K., 1967, 'Research and Consultancy in Industrial Enterprises', *Sociology*, 1, pp. 33–60.

Burns, T. and Stalker, G. M., 1961, *The Management of Innova-tion*, Tavistock.

Emery, F. E. and Trist, E. L., 1965, 'The Causal Texture of Organisational Environments', *Human Relations*, 18, pp. 21–32.

Gouldner, A. W., 1954, *Patterns of Industrial Bureaucracy*, Free Press, Glencoe, Ill.

Merton, R. K., 1949, *Social Theory and Social Structure*, Free Press, Glencoe, Ill.

Miller, E. J. and Rice, A. K., 1967, *Systems of Organisation: The control of Task and Sentient Boundaries*, Tavistock.

Rice, A. K., 1963, *The Enterprise and its Environment: A System Theory of Management Organisation*, Tavistock.

Schein, E. H., 1965, *Organisational Psychology*, Prentice-Hall.

Trist, E. L. *et al.*, 1963, *Organisational Choice*, Tavistock.

Woodward, J., 1958, *Management and Technology*, HMSO.

Woodward, J., 1965, *Industrial Organisation: Theory and Prac-tice*, Oxford University Press.

Section III   Organizations

Introduction

The introduction to this book emphasized the importance of organizations in advanced societies. So in many ways this is the core section of the book, as it looks at the organizational level of analysis. However, it would be wrong to assume that this is the major, or even the most important, level at which one should look, for one must see organizations in the context both of small groups and of society as a whole—and, as some would extend the argument, the social system of the world as a whole. Thus, although organization theorists and many systems theorists have placed a priority on organizational analysis such an approach is questionable in terms of theoretical adequacy—but perhaps is more of a reflection on the level at which the concerns of managers are centred, for much organization theory has been developed along with consultancy in areas of managerially defined 'problems'. Thus the concern of organization theorists is far more likely to be to develop frameworks for analysing the potential organization of enterprises from the 'top down' rather than posing 'bottom up' concerns such as the supply and choice of reasonable jobs in a particular location.

Given these reservations, the organizational level is clearly an important one, provided it is not seen in isolation. Angela Bowey in Reading 7 summarizes some of the main approaches to organizational analysis which she sees as:

1 *systems theory*
2 *contingency theory*
3 *action theory*
4 *goal-oriented behaviour theories*

Although these categories do give a reasonable general picture it would be misleading to consider the only real 'systems' approaches to be those within Bowey's categories. For, as she states, it is becoming increasingly difficult to decide precisely who is and isn't a systems theorist, and this is also a rather pointless exercise which tends to obscure rather than illuminate issues for those interested in the area. Thus this section has in general selected from theorists who, whilst they might not consider themselves

to be advocates of a systems approach, have concerns relevant to the application of systems ideas to organizations.

Goals are one of the key systems concepts used in analysing organizations and are introduced by Hall (Reading 8). Whilst goals are the creations of people, it is clear that organizations may be seen *as if* they have been created to pursue particular goals which are not merely the 'sum' of the members' individual or subgroup goals. Thus a basic question is who has the power to determine goals and how is this exercised? Hall does not concentrate on this area (discussed by Ruth Elliott in a later reading) as much as he might although it does underly his discussion of how overall 'official' goals are converted into the 'operative' goals pursued in the day-to-day running of the organization, particularly as different subgroups have different potential influence over this process. One other important aspect of Hall's presentation is his emphasis on relations with the organization's environment in modifying goals—and the need to look at the multi-organization level and the use of strategies such as 'co-optation' to achieve goals and maintain the power of the organization.

To achieve goals, a management or, in more democratic organizations, the membership will have to use its power to create and maintain some form of organizational structure, as the quote at the start of the reading by John Child (Reading 9) states. Child discusses some of the structural options—or 'organizational choices'—open to designers of organizations. Such choices involve both the organization of subgroups and the co-ordination and control mechanisms under which they work. In this area there has been a major debate between 'universalist' and 'contingency' theories of the appropriate structure for organizations. Universalist theories stress the existence of relatively timeless principles of management for all organizations, such as the 'one best way' advocated in 'scientific management'. Contingency theories on the other hand see appropriate organizational structures as dependent upon both the goals and the environment of the organization. This approach is now dominant and it implies that a much wider range of organizational choice exists than that admitted by universalist theories—and, it should be added, by many of those who call themselves contingency theorists.

However appropriate a particular structure is to the goals of those running an organization, it cannot be seen as a way of resolving underlying conflicts of interest, such as those which many argue exist between workers and management.

Galbraith in Reading 10 emphasizes the role of information in complex organization and the need for structures which can both cope with it and respond well to the stimuli information provides, particularly in situations in which uncertainty is important. In this the co-ordination of varied activities is crucial, and hence the question of organizing the work of subgroups. Three strategies of co-ordination are outlined, which he argues are appropriate to increasing levels of uncertainty affecting the tasks people do:

1 rules, programmes and procedures
2 hierarchy
3 goal or target setting

Such a framework clearly assumes both a contingency and a top-down approach to overall strategies of organizational design, even though Galbraith advocates more participative structures, notably that of 'matrix organization' in which one person can be responsible to, say, both product-based and functional managers. In overall terms Galbraith sees organizations being able to try to decrease information processing needs or to increase their information processing capacity, again indicating the extent to which organizations have a potential choice over forms of organization, within market and other constraints. However, in his analysis he does tend to consider information in isolation from problems of managerial control.

Den Hertog (Reading 11) uses some similar ideas, particularly that of uncertainty, to look at the role of information and control systems together in organizational change. Arguing that many approaches to change have tended to consider different aspects of management in isolation, he discusses some of the ways in which such systems must fit in with other organizational changes if they are not to become 'roadblocks' to organizational renewal.

Argyris and Schön (Reading 12) put a rather different focus upon related areas, concentrating on how and what organizations can 'learn'. In talking about organizational learning, they first discuss the nature of organizations and the dangers of personification—making them appear as if it were

people learning. Their solution to this paradox is rather similar to that used in the issue of organizational goals (see Hall in Reading 8), that organizational learning is a powerful metaphor, despite the impossibility of the organization literally learning separately from its members. This learning can be seen as *single-loop,* in which changes in actions to achieve certain ends within organizational norms are learnt. This is essentially a question of detecting and measuring deviations from a desired end state, a process of feedback and error correction. However there may be contradictions within the organization's norms—making such a process inappropriate because a resolution of the problems created requires modification of the norms themselves. This requires *double-loop* learning in which the norms which define measures of effectiveness (and hence of deviation from a desired state) are themselves open to change. Finally, *deutero-learning* is of a rather different level, for it involves 'learning about how to learn' and thus is concerned with the need to continually promote single- and double-loop learning. These ideas are developed in more detail in the rest of Argyris and Schön's book, but we should note how these ideas are similar in structure to those of Buckley (Reading 3) on morphostasis and morphogenesis and of Watzlawick *et al.* (Reading 4) on first- and second-order change. All of them emphasize not only the need to look at changes in the state of a system but the necessity of seeing structural changes in the system as a possibility, and sometimes a necessity, if contradictions are to be resolved.

In Reading 13 Ruth Elliott outlines some of the main theoretical issues concerning power in organizations. In particular, she sees value consensus in society, which is assumed by many systems theorists, to be questionable, just as ideas that power can only be achieved by one person or group at the expense of another are inadequate. She goes on to point out that in organizations some of the most pervasive exercises of power are largely invisible—keeping issues off an agenda of discussions, blocking decisions, and shaping others' views of both the organization and the legitimacy of the orders of those who run it. Its highest form is that of 'manipulation' in which those being manipulated are unaware of the exercise of power. Such a framework is necessary if we are to form an adequate picture of how organizations work and to assess the adequacy of other theories.

Benson (Reading 14) puts forward a critical view of much organization theory and outlines an alternative, based largely on marxist lines, which he labels 'dialectical'. In another article (Benson, 1976) he sees the dominant views of organization as inadequate in their conceptualization of

1 *power* (which they tend to play down)
2 *process*
3 *levels* (in which the organizational one is predominant)
4 *action* (the meaningful nature of which has often been played down or ignored).

His alternative view stresses the process of the production of social structure and its reproduction, within the existing set of social relations, and the need for a holistic approach—the 'principle of totality'—which is central to much systems thinking. He also stresses the nature of contradictions in society which may lead to the undermining of the system itself, and hence lead to a radical 'second-order change' (in Watzlawick *et al.*'s terminology), and the idea of 'praxis' or meaningful human action based on analysis of the existing system. In his view the type of dialectical analysis he advocates is a powerful means of seeing both the limitations of existing structures and relationships and making clear that they have been created and can be re-created by people's actions. In the second part of the reading he applies these general ideas to organizations. The reading is not a particularly easy one, in part because it tries to go outside the normal framework of organization theory, but it does contain important ideas that are seldom related to the study of organizations. It also demonstrates that systems concepts and ideas are not necessarily confined to managerially-biased theories of organizations, despite the fact that their origins are largely in such a tradition. Perhaps the most important question it poses but does not tackle is the degree to which the 'radical transformation of organizations' Benson would like to see can be realized. Many writers (including Hedberg *et al.*—see Further Reading) show a similar interest in change, but at a more restricted level.

Their emphasis is on the need for organizations to be able to adapt structurally to new conditions, hence the use of the term 'self-designing organization'. The view that in future there will be a much greater need to live with uncertainty and contradiction seems a reasonable one, although it does not bring out the ways in which large corporations will increasingly attempt to control and dominate their environment, as suggested by Bonis (Reading 15), and the concentrations of power in such corporations. This of course raises the whole question of organization and environment, which Section IV on multiorganizations examines.

Further reading

The organizational level is one where masses of publications abound—the difficulty being the selection of interesting and relevant presentations of suitable approaches. For general clarity and coverage John Child's *Organization: a guide to problems and practice* is recommended, provided its emphasis on managerial problems is accepted. Other general books in the area include Hall *Organizations: structure and process* and Pradip Khandwalla *Design of organisation,* although the latter tends to put too much weight on sometimes rather questionable generalizations. Khandwalla has an interesting chapter on goals, to which can be added Charles Perrow's own views in 'The analysis of goals in complex organizations' and H. A. Simon's 'On the concept of organizational goals'.

The politics of organizational decision-making are well illustrated in Andrew Pettigrew's book, whilst more general questions of power are analysed in Steven Lukes' *Power: a radical view.* Power also plays an important role in the work of Michel Crozier whose book *Bureaucratic phenomenon* is a classic. His latest work is contained in a book currently available only in French, *L'acteur et le système* (The actor and the system) by M. Crozier and E. Friedberg, which is highly recommended when it appears in an English translation. The reading by Crozier (Reading 17) reflects some of this work, and is printed together with a selection of other theoretical approaches, including Luhmann's influential approach to systems theory and organizations (which is mainly available only in German), in Hofstede and Kassem.

On questions of structure, Child's article 'What determines organizational performance?' contrasts universalist and contingency views concisely. Contingency views are outlined in more detail by Lorsch and subject to criticism by Crozier and Friedberg in terms of their neglect of wider power relations. On the more historical side Chandler's *Strategy and structure* looks at the development of large U.S. corporations.

Information problems are linked to the practice of management information systems, to which Cloot provides a readable introduction. Ackoff's 'Management misinformation systems' provides a cynical view of some experiences in the area.

On a more critical note, Benson's collection *Organizational analysis* provides a range of views dissatisfied with current organization theory, as does Clegg and Dunkerley's *Critical issues in organizations,* although some papers in these collections manage to obscure their arguments with complex jargon, a fault shared with other branches of organization theory and systems. On the practicalities of alternative forms of organization, Part 2 of Vanek, ed., *Self-management* gives examples of co-operative forms of organization and Bettelheim *Cultural revolution and industrial organization in China* looks rather uncritically at the interesting innovations in China in the early 1970s.

Ackoff, R. (December 1967) 'Management misinformation systems' *Management Science,* No. 14.
Benson, J. K. (ed.) (1976) *Organizational analysis,* Sage.
Bettelheim, C. (1975) *Cultural revolution and industrial organization in China,* Monthly Review Press.
Chandler, A. D. (1962) *Strategy and structure,* MIT Press.
Child, J. (1977) *Organization: a guide to problems and practice,* Harper-Row.

Child, J. (1974) 'What determines organization performance?', *Organizational Dynamics,* Vol. 3, No. 1.

Clegg, S. and Dunkerley, D. (1977) *Critical issues in organizations,* Routledge and Kegan Paul.

Cloot, P. L. (1974) *Management information: a systematic approach.* Administrative Staff College.

Crozier, M. (1964) *The bureaucratic phenomenon,* University of Chicago Press.

Crozier, M. and Friedberg, E. (1977) *L'acteur et le système,* Editions du Seuil.

Hall, A. D. (1972) *Organizations: structure and process,* Prentice-Hall.

Hedberg, B. L. T., Nystrom, P. C. and Starbuck, W. H. (1977) 'Designing organizations to match tomorrow', from *Studies in the Management Sciences,* 5, pp. 171–181, North-Holland Publishing Company.

Hofstede, G. and Kassem, M. S. (1975) *European contributions to organization theory,* Assen.

Khandwalla, P. N. (1977) *Design of organizations,* Harcourt Brace Jovanovich, Inc.

Lorsch, J. W. and Mark, J. J. (1974) *Organizations and their members: a contingency approach,* Harper and Row.

Lukes, S. (1964) *Power: radical view,* Macmillan.

Perrow, C. (December 1961) 'The analysis of goals in complex organizations', *Administrative Science Quarterly,* Vol. 6, No. 6.

Pettigrew, A. (1973) *Politics of organizational decision making,* Tavistock Publications.

Simon, H. A. (June 1964) 'On the concept of organizational goals', *Administrative Science Quarterly,* Vol. 9, No. 1.

Vanek, J. (ed.) (1975) *Self-management,* Penguin.

7 Approaches to organization theory
A. M. Bowey

Current trends in a number of different branches of organization theory indicate an impending convergence of views. At the same time, lack of liaison and sterile arguments between specialists in the different branches is producing duplication of effort and hindering progress.

In this paper I have attempted to outline the major concepts and the most recent trends which have occurred under the headings of systems theory, contingency theory, subjective-interaction theory or the action approach (which I have referred to as action theory), and studies of goal-oriented behaviour. The direction of change in systems theory and action theory has direct significance for the work done by contingency theorists and goal-orientation theorists, much of whose work has been based on models of human behaviour which are shown to be inadequate. At the same time, the work of contingency theorists and goal-orientation theorists may help the 'systems' and 'action' sociologists to solve some of their problems in interpreting macro-social phenomena.

Other writers have attempted to give accounts of all the contributions to organization theory, usually classifying them into categories to impose some kind of order on the confused situation. Unfortunately, very few writers use the same categories and the result is more confusion. Table 1 shows some recent classifications of contributions to organization theory. Many of these writers have confessed that the categories they have used are not easily differentiable because they overlap and because writers in the field of organization theory have progressed from one category to another. Whyte (1969, p. 19), for example, acknowledged that the groupings which he has used only delineate people in terms of problem interests and styles of research, and that even this preliminary sorting will not stand close scrutiny because writers change their views.

I would go further than Whyte and suggest that the application of labels to some recent work could be a hindrance to the development of organization theory.

Table 1 *Recent classifications of contributions to organization theory*

Author	Categories
Hodge et al. (1970)	1 Classical school and scientific management 2 Neo-classical school and human relations management 3 Modern doctrine and mathematical management
Whyte (1969)	1 Event-process analysis 2 Social structuralists 3 Organizational surveyors 4 Group dynamicists 5 Decision-making theorists 6 Psychiatric analysts 7 Technological structuralists
Litterer (1965)	1 The classical school 2 The naturalistic school 3 The systems concept
George (1968)	1 The traditional school: scientific management 2 Behavioural school 3 Management process school 4 Quantitative school
Silverman (1970)	1 Human relations 2 Organizational psychology 3 Socio-technical systems 4 Structural-functionalism 5 Decision-making theory 6 Action approach

Hutchinson (1967)	1 Scientific management
	2 Environmental and human relations schools
	3 Man as a decision-maker
	4 Current theories, subdivided into
	  (a) Operational school
	  (b) Empirical school
	  (c) Human behaviour school
	  (d) Social systems school
	  (e) Decision theory school
	  (f) Mathematical school

P.A. (1970)	1 The classical approach 2 The human relations approach 3 The systems approach
Price (1968)	1 The economic system 2 The political system 3 The control system 4 The population ecology

Action theory, systems theory, and contingency theory are not entirely incompatible approaches to the understanding of behaviour in organizations. Recent work from each of them appears to be converging. For example, the systems theory approach propounded by Walter Buckley (1967) departs from the traditional 'systems theory' type of interpretation and proposes a model of human behaviour which is very similar to and quite consistent with the model proposed by recent 'action theorists' such as David Silverman (1970). The superiority of this kind of approach, in which the best of each theory is combined, is illustrated in a recent article by Reuben Hill (1971). Although Hill has not entirely accepted the model of the family as a morphogenic system, he has presented some interesting evidence which suggests that families very often do operate as structure-evolving systems. This concept of the continual evolution of structures (morphogenesis) is precisely what distinguishes Buckley's approach from more traditional 'systems' theories, and which also makes systems theory consistent with the axioms of action theory.

In the next section I will summarize the key concepts and outline the development of the three or four major perspectives of organization theory which are currently prominent, before suggesting some implications of these trends. More detailed accounts of these different approaches have been published elsewhere[1], but in the discussion below I have tried to include some more recent contributions, and to restrict the account to the most significant contributions and the major concepts of each approach.

Systems theory

The title 'systems theory' or 'systems analysis' has been applied to a range of theories which have in common a number of assumptions about the nature of organizations (or other social entities). Silverman has named three 'main assumptions underlying the view of organizations as systems'. These were 'that organizations are composed of a set of interdependent parts: organizations have needs for survival; and organizations, as systems, behave and take actions' (1970, p. 27).

These assumptions belong to those sociologists who based their work on what Runciman has called 'the discredited analogy of society as an organism' (1969).

But there are many writers who have called themselves 'systems' theorists and who have not tried to draw analogies between societies or organizations and organisms. Taken to the limit, there is even a sense in which all attempts to interpret human behaviour scientifically use a 'systems' approach. As Runciman stated '[. . .] the injunction "look at it as a system" is uncomfortably like the injunction "talk prose".

All inter-related variables constitute a system by definition' (1969, p. 256).

We can trace the enthusiasm for a 'systems' approach in sociology to a definite source, namely to the 'logic of systems' which philosophers and psychologists deduced from the scientific methods of biology. In psychology this approach gave rise to the 'Gestalt' school of psychology, and provided many insights and advances in that subject. Basically it states that any entity or 'whole' is composed of other entities or parts at a lower, less complex, level of organization. These parts are arranged in a system and it is from the arrangement of its parts that the 'whole' derives its characteristics not from the mere aggregation of these parts. The 'whole' is in turn a part of some higher order system constituting another whole at some more complex level of organization. To the 'Gestalt' psychologists, a 'whole' can only be fully understood if it is viewed as an entity, and not from the process of aggregating its parts.

This work, which was developed largely in the 1920s and 1930s gave rise to two schools of thought which have had major impacts on sociology. One was 'functionalism' (and structural functionalism) in sociology itself, and the other was 'general systems theory'—or the study of the general dynamic principles of organization.

L. von Bertalanffy, a theoretical biologist, wrote two papers in 1950 which had a major impact on systems thinking. In this work he outlined with greater rigour than had previously been achieved some of the concepts of systems theory. The distinction between open and closed systems became a central interest in sociology and social organizations were viewed as open systems existing in an environment, with self-regulating mechanisms maintaining the state or structure of the system within definite limits (homeostasis). In order to survive in its environment the system had needs which its parts fulfilled as their 'function'. According to a functionalist view of sociology, every part of a social system should be interpreted or analysed from the point of view of the contribution which it makes to the survival or adaptation of the system as a whole.

Functionalism has been widely criticized because it leads to a conservative bias (if all existing institutions contribute towards the needs for survival of a society, then they are valuable to that society for that reason); it cannot adequately include in its model phenomena such as conflict, delinquency and rebellion, which are dysfunctional for the persistence of the existing structure; and it reifies the social system and imputes 'actions' to it.

From the second of these criticisms there arose a debate in the late 1950s and 1960s amongst sociologists about 'consensus' models and 'conflict' models of social behaviour. As Silverman stated, 'at one time, it seemed that the alternative to systems theory and its sociological offshoot, structural-functionalism, should centre around their alleged concentration on consensus and order and their apparent incapacity to explain conflict situations' (1970, p. 5). But this proved to be a sterile debate when Coser (1965), and others, showed that functionalism could cope adequately with interpreting conflict within a system.

Many of the shortcomings of functionalism arise from the analogies which have been drawn. Systems approaches which are based on biological analogies, (such as structural-functionalism and open system theory) have frequently confused an analogy with an organism and an analogy with a species[2]. The analogy between an organism and a society is most misleading, since it suggests that the various parts of a society co-operate as do the parts of a body, rather than compete in a struggle for survival. It is, unfortunately, this analogy which underlies much of the work that is termed 'systems theory' today. As Buckley (1967, p. 14) pointed out, mature organisms cannot change their given structure beyond very narrow limits and still remain viable, whereas this capacity is precisely what distinguishes sociocultural systems. Any useful model of social organization must take account of the ability of a social system to modify its structure.

One of the major concepts derived from the analogy with an organism and used by systems theorists recently, has been the concept of homeostasis. A system is maintained in a state of homeostasis when its structure is maintained within fairly definite limits by processes known as 'homeostatic mechanisms'. But as Karl Deutsch pointed out (1956, pp. 161–162), homeostasis is not a broad enough concept to describe the internal restructuring of learning systems. Buckley (1967, pp. 15–16) also points out the major shortcomings of this kind of 'systems' approach.

We can summarize the criticisms of the functionalist approach as follows. In the search for the social equivalents of the organism's relatively fixed structure, the functionalist tends to over-emphasize the stable normatively supported aspects of the social system, at the expense of the equally significant minority group activities, including delinquency and rebellion. He is also drawn into searching for homeostatic maintenance mechanisms which preserve this dominant, institutionalized part of the social structure which, for him, is virtually synonymous with the social system. As Buckley has pointed out, 'Parsons has fallen into this trap of defining the structure of the social system as the "institutionalized" patterns of normative culture' (Parsons, 1961). If the structure of the system is comprised only of those activities and beliefs which are engaged in, or approved of, by the majority of participants in the system, (or perhaps as Buckley suggests, defined by the official establishment), then we have no place in our model for the variant, deviant or alternative subcultures which exist in a complex social system. And very often, it is the interaction of these alternative subcultures with each other, or with the dominant culture, which leads to changes in a social system.

The major alternative to systems theory, is the action frame of reference, which will be discussed below. Writers on 'action theory' have generally rejected the system model entirely. Silverman, for example, suggests 'that the time is right for the presentation of a clear-cut alternative to what is fast becoming a systems orthodoxy' (1970, p. 4). But I suspect that the 'action' theorists may be in danger of 'throwing out the baby with the bath water' if they insist on rejecting the concept of a system entirely. It is a conceptual tool which has been much abused but which, nevertheless, can be very useful.

Walter Buckley (1967) has likened a social organization to a totally different kind of system from the homeostatic 'open systems model' or the functionalists model. Taking his model from general systems theory, which has developed a long way since the days when it spawned the homeostatic open-system model, Buckley likens social system to complex adaptive systems which 'are distinguished precisely by the fact that, rather than minimize organization, or preserve a given fixed structure, they typically create, elaborate, or change structure as a prerequisite to remaining viable, as ongoing systems' (1967, p. 5).

To Buckley, an organization is a system of meanings and alternative responses to information. These give rise to patterned interactions, 'that are more or less temporary adjustments always open to redefinition and rearrangement' (1967, p. 205). As Buckley points out, causal relationships within an organization do not usually arise from direct physical contact. One person influences the behaviour of another by the transmission of information, either verbally or via their actions: the second person assigns a meaning to the information received and selects an appropriate orientation in response. Unless the participants share similar interpretations of particular words or actions, the response elicited will not correspond with the expectations of the person providing the stimulus; this may lead to an adjustment in the meanings attached to this particular action or expression for future reference. In this way, and also from changes induced by stimuli from the non-social environment, the structure of the organization is continually being changed or elaborated (the process of morphogenesis).

Buckley takes the view that structure arises from the process of interaction. This puts his work squarely in the 'action' camp, if we regard sociology after Dawe as divided into two, 'a sociology of social systems and a sociology of social action' in which 'the first asserts the paramount necessity [. . .] of external constraint; hence the notion of a social system ontologically and methodologically prior to its participants. The key notion of the second, is that of autonomous man [. . .] Society is thus the creation of its members; the product of their construction of meaning and of the action and relationships through which they attempt to impose that meaning on their historical situations' (Dawe, 1970).

We might conclude that Buckley is mistaken in calling himself a systems theorist, since in his model, the 'system' is subordinated to the processes of symbolic interaction. Or we might conclude that when the nature of the sociocultural system is more accurately understood, a sociologist who begins by trying to understand the system, arrives at much the same conclusions as the sociologist who starts by analysing interaction between individuals.

The second perspective in organization theory which I wish to outline, has been described as the 'contingency approach' and has generally been regarded as a type of systems analysis.

Contingency theory

In the late 1950s and the early 1960s, a number of books were published which reported research findings indicating that particular states of particular aspects of organizations (e.g. a wide span of control, or a rigidly adhered to communications network), were either more prevalent, or more 'successful', in one type of environment than in others. Some of these writers suggested that the structure of the organization is contingent upon the environment in which it exists (see for example Udy, 1959); others suggested that the 'success' of an organization is contingent upon its utilizing the most appropriate structure for its environment (see in particular Woodward, 1965; Burns and Stalker, 1961).

In either case, this approach cast doubt on the work of many previous writers on organization design, who had suggested that there was one optimum state for the components of an organization (e.g. Currie, 1961 and for the alternative panacea, Brown, 1962).

Burns and Stalker (1961), whose work together with that of Woodward and possibly Udy, inspired most of today's contingency theorists, began their research with an investigation into the behaviour of people working in a rayon mill, hoping to make use of a concept of the industrial concern as a 'community'. This project was ended when they realized that the local village would have to be included in this 'community' if they were to make sense of their data. But, by this time, they had observed that this contented, successful factory, was operating with the kind of management style which, according to many contemporary authorities on management practice, should have led to discontent and inefficiency. Later, Burns and Stalker studied an engineering factory which was highly successful, but which utilized an entirely different style from the rayon mill. This led them to initiate a large scale investigation into the relationship between management systems and the organization's tasks and, in particular, into the ways in which management systems changed when the technical and commercial tasks of the firm changed.

They found that there were two identifiable systems of management practice, which they called 'mechanistic' and 'organic'. The mechanistic system was appropriate to a firm in a stable environment and the organic system appropriate to a changing environment.

Recent work by Aiken and Hage (1971) has supported Burns and Stalker's findings. This work indicates that an 'organic' system of organization has characteristics which facilitate innovation.

At approximately the same time as Burns and Stalker were investigating 'organic' and 'mechanistic' systems of management, Joan Woodward (1958, 1965) was studying the relationship between types of technology and types of management structure. She analysed the production systems of the firms she studied on a continuum of technological complexity, with three main categories: small-batch production, mass or large-batch production and continuous process production (in increasing order of complexity). On investigating the forms of organization in a large number of firms from each category, she found marked correlations between aspects of the organization's structure and its type of production process.

The number of levels of authority was higher the more complex the technology; the relative proportions of supervisory (including managers) to non-supervisory staff was also higher the more complex the technology; the distinction between 'staff' and 'line' managers was sharpest at the two extremes of the complexity scale; and the use of bureaucratic procedures was less prevalent at the two extremes than in the middle of the scale. Clearly Woodward's findings, like those of Burns and Stalker, indicate the shortcomings of panaceas for organization design. If there is a correlation between technological complexity and features of organization structure, then those authors who recommend one structure as the optimum for all circumstances, are recommending practices which are at odds with observed facts.

Recent work by Pugh and his colleagues (Hickson et al., 1969), suggests that the relationship between technological complexity and organization structure is more complex than Woodward had suggested.

Another early 'contingency' theorist was Udy (1959) who investigated the relationship between the structures of production organizations used by non-industrial peoples and both the technological processes which these organizations employed and the social context of the organizations. He found strong correlations between these variables and went on to investigate the specific aspects of the structure which were related to aspects of the technology and social context. He then focussed on the reward systems of such organizations, investigating their relationship to the production organization, the social context and the technological process; and once again, Udy found correlations, indicating that the reward system was dependent upon the organizational, social and technological contexts.

Since these early writers suggested that different types of management systems (or structures or policies) were 'successful' under different circumstances, there have been a number of attempts to get away from panaceas and develop management practices which were contingent to the situation of the organization concerned[3].

Most of these writers and the earlier contingency theorists, based their work on an 'open system' model of an organization, using the analogy between a social system and an organism. Many have discussed the 'needs' of the system in order that it should 'survive' and its 'success' in 'adapting to its environment'. Burns and Stalker (1961, p. 36) for example, suggested that the survival of industrial concerns is 'a matter of intense and widespread concern' and they propose ways of improving their chances of survival.

Lawrence and Lorsch (1969) quite directly use the analogy with the human body: 'As an analogy (to the organization as a system), the human body is differentiated into a number of vital organs, which are integrated through the nervous system and the brain. Second, an important function of any system is adaptation to what goes on in the world outside' (p. 7).

As discussed in the sections above and below, recent developments in organization theory indicate that this kind of analogy between a social system and an organism, is unsound and misleading. The conclusions arrived at by a 'contingency–structural–functionalist' approach, are not useful, nor enlightening, because they have assumed the organization has a particular goal (meeting needs for survival).

In a recent paper on hospital administration, E. J. Cooper (1971) applied Lawrence and Lorsch's theories of differentiation and integration to the problem of the administration of a hospital. His conclusions were that the hospital management structure should be reorganized into divisions containing departments with similar orientations (in terms of time scales, degree of uncertainty in tasks, etc.). But, as Cooper himself acknowledged, a previous planned management structure for hospitals in Britain (the tripartite system) had failed to be realized in practice, because the interactions between the participants themselves had given rise to a different structure. Insufficient attention had, apparently, been paid to the power and motivations of the people involved and to the consistency or degree of conflict involved in the role-relationships required to operate the proposed tripartite system. By concentrating on the system and its structure, Cooper, following Lawrence and Lorsch, was again suggesting the imposition of a structure, without paying adequate attention to the inter-actions between individuals from which the structure is created. This is an example of one kind of error which arises from a contingency-systems view of an organization.

Recent and forthcoming publication by contingency theorists[4], indicate an increasing concern with the part played by the motivation of individuals and the interactions between individuals in generating the structure of an organization.

If contingency theory were to be based on an approach which combined the most useful concepts from the 'systems' approach with an 'action theory' approach (discussed below), then the conclusions reached would be more pertinent to the actual behaviour of people in organizations. If we regard the family as a type of organization, Hill's paper on the family (1971) demonstrates some of the potentialities of this kind of approach when it is applied to practical problems.

Action theory

According to Alan Dawe (1970) there are two distinctive disciplines in sociology—the sociology of social systems and the sociology of social action. The former derives from a concern with the 'problem of order' and the latter from concern with the 'problem of control'. He argues convincingly that the social action perspective owes its origin to the concern about man's control over his situation which was generated by the 'enlightenment'. . . .

Dawe is probably right in his theory about the intellectual origins of 'action theory'. But as a recognisable approach to sociology action theory can be traced back quite directly to the work of Max Weber and of Georg Simmel. There would be no particular value in replicating the accounts of the origins of action theory which other writers have covered adequately (Wagner, 1964; Rex, 1961; Silverman, 1970, pp. 126–143). I will concentrate instead on defining what is meant by action theory as proposed by modern sociologists.

David Silverman (1970) has summarized the main points of action theory, or as he and many others call it, the action frame of reference, in a very useful chapter of this recent book.

He lists seven propositions of action approach, one of which he later rejects as inappropriate. Of the other six, I consider that three are essential principles of this perspective whilst the other three are derivatives from it (pp. 126–127).

I have summarized these three essential principles in the following basic axioms of action theory: (a) sociology is concerned with 'meaningful action' and not just behaviour, (b) particular meanings persist through their reaffirmation in actions, (c) actions can also lead to changes in meanings.

The claim that sociology is more correctly concerned with 'meaningful action' than with behaviour comes from the realization that by concentrating on behaviour alone, the sociologist is not able to make accurate predictions of the way in which people will respond to one another in an interaction situation.

Many social scientists have argued that behaviour is concrete and quantifiable, but that the mental processes which associate meanings with particular behaviours are intangible and not amenable to direct observation.

Nevertheless, social relationships develop through the interpretations which each person puts on the behaviour of the other, and these interpretations are not fixed. The differences which may be found in interpretations of identical behaviour are most evident when we compare different cultures. Belching at the meal table is a good-mannered way of expressing approval to one's host in some Arab countries; but in many parts of Western European society it is interpreted in an entirely different way, as indicating 'bad manners' and possibly as an expression of disrespect for others present. When people from different cultures interact, confusion and irritation can arise from differences in interpretations of behaviour. An illustration of this kind of misunderstanding is contained in the following account of an incident which occurred on a visit I made to Bulgaria in 1969.

A coach of holidaymakers were returning from a day-trip to a farming community. None of the visitors spoke Bulgarian, and an accordianist who had sung and played for the party all day did not speak a word of English and communicated with them by signs. On the return journey he conducted a sign conversation with a member of the party. He took a £1 note from his own pocket, tucked it into one of the folds in the top of the accordian, started to play and proffered the top of the accordian to the tourist.

As an observer I interpreted this behaviour as a request for a tip in payment for his services as entertainer.

The tourist looked puzzled and the entertainer repeated the series of actions. The other passengers had now interpreted this behaviour as I had done, and exhorted the tourist to offer some money. This he did and looking at the entertainer for approval of his action he placed his note on top of the accordian. The Bulgarian shook his head from side to side and the tourist, interpreting this to mean 'no' retrieved his money. I was now frankly puzzled particularly when the whole series was then repeated from the placing in the accordian of the entertainer's £1 note to the shaking of the head and retrieval of the tourist's note. Whatever meaning the entertainer intended by his actions and signs could not be understood by myself as observer; in fact according to the meanings which I assigned to his actions he was contradicting himself. The explanation was that in Bulgaria shaking the head from side to side means 'yes' and nodding the head means 'no'. To understand the scene between the tourist and the entertainer the observer would need to know both the meanings which the entertainer intended by his actions and the meanings which the tourist interpreted from these actions.

In cross-cultural examples such as those above, it is easy to see that different people may assign different meanings to the same behaviour. But it is equally true that within the same culture, even within subcultures, differences in interpretations of behaviour are quite common.

An individual learns or invents a set of meanings

which he attaches to the behaviour of himself and others and which enable him to predict the responses which others will show to his actions. If they respond in the way he expects, then he is well satisfied that the way he acted conveyed the desired message. This is the second basic axiom of action theory listed above, namely that particular meanings persist through their reaffirmation in actions.

But if the response is not as expected, then he will doubt his interpretation of this piece of behaviour and readjust the meaning he assigns to it for future reference. New situations (which may arise from technological innovations, economic changes, etc.) or contacts with persons from different subcultures can produce occasions for adjusting the meanings which the individual assigns to patterns of behaviour. But such adjustments can also occur from misunderstanding, unintended nuances, or even clarification, between long-standing acquaintances. This is the third axiom of action theory—that actions can lead to changes in meanings.

When applied to an organization, an 'action' theory interpretation leads us to conclude that 'an organization is itself the outcome of the interaction of motivated people attempting to resolve their own problems' (Silverman, 1970, p. 126). This is a major difference in emphasis from a 'systems' theory approach, where the behaviour of individuals is seen to arise from the constraints imposed by the organization.

In the previous section I referred to E. J. Cooper's application of Lawrence and Lorsch's 'contingency' theories to hospital administration. In a recent paper (Bowey, 1971), I have pointed out that this kind of approach in which the organization is seen as an entity with a 'need' to adapt to its environment leads to prescriptions which would not achieve the desired effect. The reason for this is that the structure of the organization arises from the meaningful interactions of its members; and if these members are powerful and if they have objectives which would not be met by some organizational structure designed with the 'needs of the system' in mind, then they will evolve a structure more in keeping with their own objectives whilst paying lip-service to the supposed structure. This is in fact what had happened in the British hospital service to a previous design for the management structure.

The discussion above indicates that human behaviour in organizations can most usefully be interpreted from the 'action' perspective. But one of the difficulties involved in the use of this approach is that it does not lend itself easily to the interpretation of large-scale phenomena (Wagner, 1964). It needs

to be augmented by the addition of concepts to account for facts such as the patterned behaviour which may occur in an organization; the identifiable groups of people who perform similar actions in organizations; and the evolution and change of patterns of action. The concepts which may be borrowed from systems theory which apply to these phenomena are role, relationship, structure, and process respectively. But their current systems theory definitions are inconsistent with the basic axioms of action theory.

The following definitions of role, relationship, structure, and process, are consistent with an action approach, and should therefore make it possible for action theory to be used to analyse macro-social behaviour such as behaviour in organizations.

1   *Role:* Actors perceive the behaviours of themselves and others in coherent patterns of action (with related meanings and objectives) termed roles, in the light of which they devise their own action.

The observing behavioural scientist may usefully impose similar classifications on the individuals he observes in an organization, bearing in mind that as meanings and objectives change, so he must modify his interpretation of the roles.

2   *Relationship:* A relationship between two actors consists of the roles each perceives for the other and themselves. For as long as a given set of perceptions persist, a pattern may be observed in the behaviours performed by the actors towards one another.

3   *Structure:* The patterned behaviour resulting from the relationships between members of an organization may be in flux and unstable; or it may be sufficiently stable to be identifiable as a structure which persists so long as the current objectives and perceptions of the members of the organization persist.

4   *Process:* Continuous, interdependent sequences of actions which are significant either because they account for a change of organizational structure, or for the derivation of the present structure, or for how a particular set of events came about, may be identified and defined as 'processes'.

Augmented by these additional concepts, an action approach is similar to the modern systems theory suggested by Buckley. The major difference is one of emphasis and not a major methodological split.

Studies of goals with respect to organizations

The first three sections of this paper have been concerned with theories of organization. In this section I wish to consider what Merton (1967, p. 39) would call a 'theory of the middle range', namely, studies of goals in organizations.

Many prominent writers on organizations have concentrated on the goals of the organization. Early writers, particularly the economists, identified the goals of the organization with the goals of its owner or the entrepreneur. This was noted by Simon (1967, p. 58): 'In the classical economic theory of the firm, where no distinction is made between an organization and a single entrepreneur, the organization's goal—the goal of the firm—is simply identical with the goal of the real or hypothetical entrepreneur.'

This perspective derives from an excessive concern with the very small, privately-owned enterprise, a type of organization which was perhaps more common at the time such theories were first propounded than it is today.

Contemporary work on organizational goals can be subdivided into three types of approach each bearing a distinctive relationship to the perspectives on organizations described above. These are:

1   Those who take a 'systems' perspective of the organization and, as Hill and Egan (1967, p. 3) put it 'envision the business enterprise as a unified acting entity'. These theorists, apart from reifying the organization, assume that this entity acts via the co-operative efforts of its component members in order to achieve some specified goals. They also specify an external environment that creates the need for action.

An example of this kind of approach to the study of goals is found in Edward Gross's paper, 'The definition of organizational goals' (1969). Gross's perspective leads him to flounder over questions to which the answers would be simple if he used an 'action' model of the organization. For example, he wonders about the nature 'of the process whereby persons might be led to substitute means for ends. Assuming that such persons do in fact exist in organizations, an important question is whether organizations make persons behave in this manner or whether organizations attract persons who feel comfortable in the presence of strict rules?' (p. 281).

Gross is here referring to the phenomenon which Merton described of the individual in an organization for whom the rules and procedures laid down for his job became his goals, even though from the point of view of the achievement of an overall objective of the organization these rules and procedures are only means to an end. Implicit in Gross's treatment of goals is the notion that if the goals of the individual differ from the stated objectives of the organization then this is some form of perversion, something dysfunctional for the organization.

The shortcomings of this kind of holistic approach have been discussed under 'systems theory' above. When reference is made to organizational goals there is the added difficulty of recognizing which are the organizational goals in any particular situation. Are they the goals of the firm's owners, or of its top management, or of those who hold the authority to direct the organization? What, then, is the status of alternative goals within the same organization, such as the goals of the trade union officials or the goals of the welfare officer? Empirical evidence suggests that the greater part of the activities performed by members of an organization cannot be explained by reference to the organizational goals (Perrow, 1967, p. 131).

Many contingency theories have used this kind of over-simplified model of organizational goals. For example, Lawrence and Lorsch (1969, p. 39) tried to assess the success of an organization from its success in achieving the following three objectives: (a) increase in profits, (b) increase in sales volume, (c) the introduction of new products.

These are clearly organizational goals and are based on a view of the organization as an entity with its own objectives.

2   The second type of approach to the study of goals in organizations is typified by the work of Herbert Simon. Simon's descriptions of goal-oriented behaviour take account of the individual and his motivations, his meaningful actions, his role and his decision-making processes. He considers the way organizational goals are related to the behaviour of individuals and concludes that 'it might be well to give up the idea that the decision situation can be described in terms of a simple goal. Instead it would be more reasonable to speak of a whole set of goals [...] that the decision-maker is trying to attain' (1967, p. 61).

Clearly Simon's model of goal-oriented behaviour in organizations more closely approximates to observed behaviour. But, unfortunately he places his 'behavioural' approach to goals within a 'systems' framework and treats the system as an entity with its own goals which are distinguishable from these of its members: 'In motivational theory postulated by Barnard and me [Simon], it is postulated that the motives of each group of participants can be divided into *inducements* (aspects of participation that are desired by the participants) and *contributions* (aspects of participation that are inputs to the organization's production function but that generally have negative utility to the participants)' (p. 65).

Simon interprets decision-making as a process of the pursuit of a goal within limits imposed by numerous side constraints. As Dawe (1970, p. 209) pointed out, many systems theorists have attempted to subsume the concept of meaningful action in their systems scheme by postulating constraints which are internalized by the individuals through the process of socialization and which produce the 'order' in the system. Simon has taken a similar perspective. His distinction between inducements and contributions would be meaningless from an 'action' perspective of the organization since from that perspective activity is not derived from the constraints of the system but from the meaningful actions of individuals. As a basis for planning management policies in an organization a model which contains an erroneous distinction between two types of motivation must lead to misinterpretations and faulty predictions.

3   The third type of approach to organizational goals is the 'action theory' interpretation. There are very few sociological action theorists who have applied themselves to the problem of organizational goals, partly because from an action perspective goal-orientated behaviour in an organization is less problematic than a systems perspective, and partly because until recently 'action' sociologists had not focussed to any extent on organizations as their subject area. Amongst the organization theorists who concern themselves with relationships between organizational structures, goals, and environments (contingency theorists), only Perrow stands out as having treated the problem of goals with the respect it deserves. In his paper 'The analysis of goals in complex organizations' (1967), Perrow makes a distinction between 'official goals', statements of intent for the organization as a whole, and 'operative goals', the ends sought through the actual operating policies of the organization. Perrow's comments on 'unofficial operative goals' come very close to an 'action' perspective of organizational behaviour: 'Unofficial operative goals, on the other hand, are tied more directly to group interests and while they may support, be irrelevant to or subvert official goals, they bear no necessary connection with them. An interest in a major supplier may dictate the policies of a corporation executive. The prestige that attaches to utilizing elaborate high speed computers may dictate the re-organization of inventory and accounting departments. Racial prejudice may influence the selection procedures of an employment agency. On the other hand, while the use of interns and residents as 'cheap labour' may subvert the official goal of medical education, it may substantially further the official goal of providing a high quality of patient care' (p. 131).

Unfortunately in his later book Perrow does not pursue this perspective, and adopts instead a systems perspective in which he states: 'For our purpose we shall use the concept of an organizational goal as if there were no question concerning its legitimacy, even though we recognize that there are legitimate objection to doing so' (1970, p. 134).

An action perspective combined with observations of empirical behaviour lead to the conclusion that the relationship between members of an organization and the organizational goals (or statements of intent) varies between organizations. In some cases the members may be totally committed to the stated aims of the organization and have no other interests in the organization. In other cases the members may accept the goals as belonging to the organization and feel an obligation to contribute towards these goals even though thay have other aims which they wish to achieve by means of their membership. Very often in these cases the organization's goals are used as legitimating criteria by individuals in the organization to justify their plans and actions to others, even though these plans and actions may have been devised originally with a view to their significance for the individual's own goals. In other cases the goals of the organization may be nebulous and/or flexible, and the members may spend much time discussing what they ought to be. In these situations the members' own personal objectives in belonging to the organization may enter more openly into discussions about organizational goals than in either of the two previous types of organization. And fourthly, the members of an organization may totally disagree with its stated aims, but have no option but to remain as members (prisons, for example). There are probably also other types of relationships which an organization's members may hold towards its goals.

It appears to me that this kind of analysis of behaviour in relationship to 'organizational goals' affords a model which more closely approximates to reality than the earlier interpretations discussed above. From this more accurate model it should be possible to interpret, predict, and plan for human behaviour more successfully.

Conclusions
Although on the surface there appears to be little in common between the theories of organization put

forward by systems theorists, contingency theorists, action theorists and those who focus on goal orientations, it is possible to detect a convergence in the recent work of some writers from these different schools. Systems theorists such as Walter Buckley propose that their model of a social system must emphasize that patterned interactions arise from meanings and alternative responses to information and are temporary adjustments open to redefinition. Action theorists such as David Silverman see the need for action theory to develop concepts to cope with large scale phenomena. Studies of goals in organizations have progressed a little way towards interpretations which are consistent with the trends in these two schools. But there is clearly scope for detailed study from an action perspective of the 'official organizational goals' in different types of organization. For example, to what extent do arguments about 'what the organization's goals are' occur more frequently in 'organic' organizations than in 'bureaucratic' organizations, and why? And when the 'official organizational goals' are not clearly defined or are in dispute, how does the behaviour of the members differ from those in organizations with clearly stated goals (such as the British hospital's 'patient care' goal)?

But it is contingency theory which is at present least integrated with the other approaches discussed in this paper. Contingency theorists have conducted a great deal of sound empirical research and produced many exciting findings about the relationships between organizational structures and the environments and contexts in which they exist. If these data were to be interpreted from the perspective of a more accurate model of human interaction, and further contingency research based on this model, it seems reasonable to expect that organization theory would advance considerably. I hope that the ideas presented in this paper may contribute towards this end, and towards the greater integration and cross fertilization of ideas between the different branches of organization theory.

Notes

[1] For an account of the development of systems theory, see W. Buckley, 1967, chap. 2 and 3. Also, F. E. Emery (ed.), 1969. For an account of contingency theory, see T. Lupton, 1970, pp. 98–113. Also P. R. Lawrence and J. W. Lorsch, 1969, pp. 185–210. For an account of the action approach, see D. Silverman, 1970, chap. 6 and 7.

[2] For a discussion of this, see W. Buckley, 1967, pp. 15–16.

[3] For example, Lawrence and Lorsch, 1969. Also F. F. Fiedler, 1967, and P.A. Management Consultants, 1970, and T. Lupton and D. Gowler, 1969.

[4] For example, J. Child, 'Organisation structure environment and performance: The role of strategic choice'. Also a forthcoming book by Lorsch and Morse on the subject of organization structure and motivation.

References

Aiken, M. and Hage, G., 1971, 'The organic organisation and innovation', *Sociology* 5 (1), Jan.: 63–82.

Bertalanffy, L. von, 1950, 'The theory of open systems in physics and biology', *Science* 111: 23–29. 1950, 'An outlined general system theory', *British Journal of Philosophical Science* 1: 134–165.

Bowey, A. M., 1971, 'Organisation theory and hospital administration', *The Hospital* 67 (11).

Brown, W., 1962, *Piecework abandoned,* London, Heinemann.

Buckley, W., 1967, *Sociology and modern systems theory,* Englewood Cliffs, NJ, Prentice-Hall.

Burns, T. and Stalker, G. M., 1961, *The management of innovation,* London, Tavistock.

Cooper, I. J., 1971, 'Beyond functional management', *The Hospital* 67 (5).

Coser, L. A., 1965, *The functions of social conflict,* London, Routledge and Kegan Paul.

Currie, R. M., 1961, *Financial incentives based on work measurement,* London, BIM.

Dawe, A., 1970, 'The two sociologies', *British Journal of Sociology* 21 (2).

Deutsch, K., 1956, pp. 161–162 in: R. Grinker (ed.), *Toward a unified theory of human behavior,* New York, Basic Books.

Emery, F. E. (ed.), 1969, *Systems thinking: Selected readings,* Harmondsworth, Penguin Books.

Fiedler, F. F., 1967, *A theory of leadership effectiveness,* New York, McGraw-Hill.

George, C. S., Jr., 1968, *The history of management thought,* Chapter 10, Englewood Cliffs, NJ, Prentice-Hall.

Gross, E., 1969, 'The definition of organisational goals', *British Journal of Sociology* 20 (3): 277–294.

Hickson, D. J., Pugh, D. S. and Pheysey, D. C., 1969, 'Operations technology and organization structure: An empirical appraisal', *Administrative Science Quarterly* 14 (3).

Hill, R., 1971, 'Modern systems theory and the family: A confrontation', *Social Science Information* 10 (5): 7–26.

Hill, W. A. and Egan, D. (eds.), 1967, *Readings in organization theory: A behavioral approach,* Boston, Mass., Allyn and Bacon.

Hodge, B. J. and Johnson, H. J., 1970, *Management and organizational behavior,* New York, Wiley, pp. 18–34,

Hutchinson, J. G., 1967, *Organizations: Theory and classical concepts,* New York, Holt, Rinehart and Winston, pp. 6–11.

Lawrence, P. R. and Lorsch, J. W., 1969, *Organization and environment: Managing differentiation and integration,* Homewood, Ill., R. D. Irwin.

Litterer, J. A., 1965, *Organizations: Structure and behavior,* New York, Wiley, pp. 3–5.

Lupton, T., 1970, *Management and the social sciences: An essay,* Bella Vista, The Administrative Staff College.

Lupton, T. and Gowler, D., 1969, *Selecting a wage payment system,* London, Engineering Employers Federation. (Research Paper 111.)

Merton, R. K., 1967, *On theoretical sociology: Five essays, old and new,* New York, Free Press of Glencoe.

P.A. Management Consultants, Ltd., 1970, *Company organisation: Theory and practice,* chapter 2, London, Allen and Unwin.

Parsons, T., 1961, 'Some considerations on the theory of social change', *Rural sociology* 26: 219–239.

Perrow, C., 1967, 'The analysis of goals in complex organisations', in: Hill and Egan (eds.). *op. cit.,* 1970, *Organisational analysis: A sociological view,* London, Tavistock.

Price, J. L., 1968, *Organizational effectiveness: An inventory of propositions,* Homewood, Ill., R. D. Irwin, p. 14.

Rex, J., 1961, *Key problems in sociological theory,* London, Routledge and Kegan Paul, pp. 78–79.

Runciman, W. G., 1969, 'What is structuralism?', *British Journal of Sociology,* 20 (3).

Silverman, D., 1970, *The theory of organisations: A sociological framework,* London, Heinemann, p. 217.

Simon, H. A., 1967, 'On the concept of organizational goal', in: Hill and Egan (eds.), *op. cit.*

Udy, S. H., Jr., 1959, *Organisation of work: A comparative analysis of production among non-industrial people,* New Haven, Conn., HRAI Press.

Wagner, H. R., 1964, 'Displacement of scope: A problem of the relationship between small-scale and large-scale sociological theories', *American Journal of Sociology,* 69 (6).

Whyte, W. F., 1969, *Organizational behavior: Theory and application,* Homewood, Ill., Irwin and Dorsey, pp. 11–20.

Woodward, J., 1958, *Management and technology,* London, HMSO. 1965, *Industrial organisation: Theory and practice,* London, Oxford University Press.

8 Organizational goals
R. H. Hall

[Much discussion] has made use of the concept of organizational goals either explicitly or implicitly. From the original definitions to the major models of organizations in the literature, the goal concept has ranged from the status of primary importance to that of whipping boy for those who believe that organizations are basically not goal-seeking entities. In either case, attention is paid to goals. The plan of this reading is to examine the nature of organizational goals, as abstractions and as practical and research issues.

'An organizational goal is a desired state of affairs which the organization attempts to realize.'[1] This desired state of affairs is by definition many things to many people. In a large organization, top executives may see the organization seeking one kind of state while those in the middle and lower echelons may have drastically different goals for the organization and for themselves personally. Even in an organization in which there is high participation in decision making and strong membership commitment, it is unlikely that there will be a totally unanimous consensus on what the organization should attempt to do, let alone on the means of achieving these ends.

The goal idea at first glance seems most simple in the case of profit-making organizations. The readily quantifiable profit goal is not such a simple matter, however. It is confounded by such issues as the time perspective (long-run or short-run profits); the rate of profit (in terms of return to investors); the important issue of survival and growth in a turbulent and unpredictable environment that might in the short run preclude profit making; the intrusion of other values, such as providing quality products or services, or benefiting mankind; and the firm's comparative position vis-à-vis others in the same industry. Leaving aside for the moment the question of *whose* goals these alternative values might represent, the difficulties apparent in the straightforward profit-making firm are indicative of the difficulties inherent in determining what the goals of an organization really are. When the situation is shifted to a consideration of the goals of a government agency, university, or church, the determination of the organization's goals becomes almost impossible.

Take, for example, the case of a governmental regulative agency charged with administering the public utilities laws and regulations of a state. A casual view suggests that this is a unitary goal, assuming that the laws and regulations are clearly stated. However, this assumption is seldom met, given the large number of lawyers and other technical experts employed by the agency for the purpose of developing and defending interpretations of the existing laws. Administration in such a case is not a simple matter either, since the choice between active and passive administration is a political and organizational football. The well-known distinction between the letter and the intent of the law becomes an issue for such agencies as they develop their operating procedures. What is the goal for the agency? If it is staffed by personnel who have values above and beyond simply administering the existing laws (every organization contains personnel with differing values), their own values toward social action or inaction can clearly modify the stated goals of the organization. In the case of the public utilities agency, beliefs in such diverse areas as air and water pollution, the nature of the publics served by the agency (the public, segments of the public, or the organizations involved), the desirability of maintaining certain public services despite their unprofitability (as in the case of railroad passenger service), and competition versus monopoly in public services—these merely exemplify the range of alternatives available as goals for this organization aside from those found in its formal charter.

The three commonly stated goals of colleges and universities—teaching, research, and public service—are almost by definition too vague to serve as much of a guide for organizational analysis or practice. In the light of contemporary reality, it can also be seen that they have become essentially incompatible in practice. Universities and colleges tend to concentrate on one of the three goals to the exclusion of the others. While emphases change, the basic issue of deciding among these goals remains. And also, since each contains vast uncertainties—exactly what is meant by good teaching, research, or service?—the use of the goal concept in this setting becomes excruciatingly difficult.

With an understanding of some of the difficulties in the utilization of the goal concept, let us examine the concept more systematically.

The meaning of organizational goals

Organizational goals can be approached from a variety of perspectives. Parsons has cogently pointed out that organizational goals are intimately intertwined with important and basic societal functions, such as integration, pattern maintenance, and so on.[2] From this point of view, organizational goals are really an extension of what the society needs for its own survival. At the other extreme is the position that organizational goals are nothing more than the goals of the individual members of the organization. Both positions disguise more than they illuminate. If the level of analysis is kept in the broad societal-function framework, the variations in goals and activities among organizations performing the same basic functions are ignored. If the level of analysis focuses on just the variety of individual goals, the whole point of organizations is missed—if there were only individual goals, there would be no point in organizing. Clearly, many individuals may have the same goal, such as making a profit, furthering a cause, or destroying an enemy. Clearly also, however, when these people come together in the form of an organization, the profit, cause, or destruction becomes an abstraction toward which they work together.

Organizational goals by definition are creations of individuals, singly or collectively. At the same time, the determination of a goal for collective action becomes a standard by which the collective action is judged. As we will see, the collectively determined, commonly based goal seldom remains constant over time. New considerations imposed from without or within deflect the organization from its original goal, not only changing the activities of the organization, but also becoming part of the overall goal structure. The important point is that the goal of any organization is an abstraction distilled from the desires of members and pressures from the environment and internal system. While there is never 100 per cent agreement among members as to what organizational goals are or should be, members can articulate a goal that is a desired state for the organization at some future point in time.

This approach is in some ways similar to that of Herbert Simon. Simon's major focus is on decision making within the organization. He notes that:

'When we are interested in the internal structure of an organization, however, the problem cannot be avoided. . . . Either we must explain organizational behavior in terms of the goals of the individual members of the organization, or we must postulate the existence of one or more organizational goals, over and above the goals of the individuals.'[3]

Simon then goes on to differentiate between the goals or value premises that serve as inputs to decisions and motives, and the causes that lead individuals to select some goals over others as the basis for their decision making. He keeps the goal idea at the individual level, but offers the important notion that the goals of an organization at any point in time are the result of the interaction among the members of the organization.

To this we would add that external conditions also affect the nature of an organization's goals. An example is the case of many current military organizations. The official goal is typically to protect the state and its people from external threats. The leaders of the military organization may come to believe, for any number of reasons, that the goal is to be victorious over a wide variety of enemies (this is not necessarily the same as protecting the state). This then becomes the goal until it is modified by interactions or conflicts with lower-level personnel, or with external forces in the form of some type of civilian control, with the goal again becoming altered to engagement in limited wars without winning or protecting the state. In this hypothetical and oversimplified example, the goals of individual organization members, particularly those in high positions, are crucial in goal setting. These goals are modified in the course of internal and external interactions.

In Simon's approach, goals become constraints on the decision-making process. The constraints are based on abstract values around which the organization operates. Decisions are made within the framework of a set of constraints (goals), and organizations attempt to make decisions that are optimal in terms of the sets of constraints they face. While the approach taken here is not based solely on the decision-making framework, the perspective is the same. Organizational actions are constrained not only by goals, but also by the external and internal factors that have been discussed. In probably the great majority of cases, goals are one, if not the only, relevant constraint.

Operative goals

Treating goals as abstract values has the merit of showing that organizational actions are guided by more than the day-to-day whims of individual members. At the same time, abstract values are just that—abstract. They must be converted to specific guides for the actual operations of an organization. Perrow takes this position when he distinguishes between 'official' and 'operative' organizational goals.[4] Official goals are 'the general purposes of the organization as put forth in the charter, annual reports, public statements by key executives and other authoritative pronouncements'. Operative goals, on the other hand, 'designate the ends sought through the actual operating policies of the organization; they tell us what the organization actually is trying to do, regardless of what the official goals say are the aims'.

This distinction is grounded in reality. Two organizations, both with the official goal of profit making, may differ drastically in the amount of emphasis they place on making profits. Blau's examination of two employment agencies with the same official goals shows wide variations between the agencies in what they were actually trying to accomplish.[5] In his discussion of this point, Perrow states:

'Where operative goals provide the specific content of official goals, they reflect choices among competing values. They may be justified on the basis of an official goal, even though they may subvert another official goal. In one sense they are means to official goals, but since the latter are vague or of high abstraction, the "means" become ends in themselves when the organization is the object of analysis. For example, where profit making is the announced goal, operative goals will specify whether quality or quantity is to be emphasized, whether profits are to be short run and risky or long run and stable, and will indicate the relative priority of diverse and somewhat conflicting ends of customer service, employee morale, competitive pricing, diversification, or liquidity. Decisions on all these factors influence the nature of the organization, and distinguish it from another with an identical official goal.'[6]

From this perspective, operative goals become the standards by which the organization's actions are judged and around which decisions are made. In many cases these operative goals reflect the official goals, in that they are abstractions made more concrete. However, operative goals can evolve that are basically unrelated to the official goals. In this regard, Perrow notes:

'Unofficial operative goals, on the other hand, are tied more directly to group interests, and while they may support, be irrelevant to, or subvert official goals, they bear no necessary connection with them. An interest in a major supplier may dictate the policies of a corporation executive. The prestige that attaches to utilizing elaborate high-speed computers may dictate the reorganization of inventory and accounting departments. Racial prejudice may influence the selection procedures of an employment agency. The personal ambition of a hospital administrator may lead to community alliances and activities which bind the organization without enhancing its goal achievement. On the other hand, while the use of interns and residents as 'cheap labor' may subvert the official goal of medical education, it may substantially further the official goal of providing a high quality of patient care.'[7]

Operative goals thus reflect the derivation and distillation of a set of goals from both official and unofficial sources. These operative goals are developed through interaction patterns within the organization, but persist after the interactions are completed. They reflect the 'desired state of affairs', or abstract official goals, the modifications and subversions of these by personnel in decision-making positions, and the force of pressures from the external environment. It is the combination of official goals with internal and external factors that leads to an existing set of operative goals.

If the use of unofficial goals is carried too far, of course, every organization could be viewed as having a huge, perhaps infinite, number of such goals. The distinction must be made, therefore, between goals and operating policies and procedures. The latter are the exact specifications, formally or informally stated, of what individual actors at all levels are to do in their daily activities. Goals, on the other hand, remain at the abstract level, serving as constraining or guiding principles from which policies and procedures can be derived. Operative goals are abstractions in the same way as official goals. They are a set of ideas about where the organization should be going, which is operationalized into specific plans and procedures.

The determination of organizational goals

How does one find out exactly what the goals of an organization are? From the research point of view, this is a vital step if there is to be any concern with issues such as effectiveness, personnel and resource allocation, or optimal structuring. In a very real sense, organizational research must be concerned with goals if it is to be anything more than simply descriptive. For the member of the organization at any level, goal determination is similarly vital. If he misses what the goals really are, his own actions may not only not contribute to the organization, they may contribute to his own organizational demise. Members of organizations must know the 'system' if they are to operate within it or to change it. From the discussion above, it should be clear that the 'system' is much more than official statements.

The vital importance of understanding operative goals can perhaps best be exemplified by an actual case.[8] The case in point is the familiar one of the goals of a university. The University of Minnesota

Faculty Information booklet contains the following statements:

TEACHING
The University emphasizes excellence in teaching. The first duty of every faculty member engaged in instruction is the communication of knowledge and values to students, and the stimulation of their intellectual ability, curiosity, and imagination.

RESEARCH
Research is the second strong arm of the University. The faculty member is aided in obtaining funds and facilities for research, and is encouraged to contribute to the ever-expanding realms of human knowledge.
PUBLIC SERVICE AND PROFESSIONAL COMMITMENTS
. . . .
UNIVERSITY SERVICE
. . . .
COMMUNITY SERVICE
. . . . [9]

As everyone must know, these goals are not equally stressed, even though the official pronouncement would lead one to believe otherwise. If a new (or old) faculty member actually believed what he read, he would probably soon find himself at a distinct disadvantage. One of the questions asked of the faculty, in at least one department, when salary increases for the coming year were being considered was the number of offers from other universities that each had received. The larger number of offers, apparently, the greater the likelihood of receiving a substantial raise, and vice versa. But the vast majority of such offers are forthcoming to those who are active in the research side of the goal equation, since the other factors cannot be readily visible to other institutions. This is not an unusual case, nor is the meaning of it limited to colleges and universities. Knowledge of operative goals is imperative for effective functioning and for the effective implementation of one's own ideas. At the extreme, such knowledge is necessary for individual survival in organizations.

Operative-goal determination for the individual is obviously important. It is plainly part of the ongoing organizational system, also, and thus central to organizational functioning. It is equally important for the organizational analyst. The significance of operative goals forces the analyst to go beyond the more easily determined official goals. The key to finding out what the operative goals are lies in the actual decisions of the top decision-makers in the organization. The kinds of decisions they make about allocation of resources (money, personnel, equipment etc.) are a major indicator. In a study of juvenile correctional organizations, Mayer Zald found that resources were consistently allocated to the custodial and traditional aspects of the institutions rather than to professional treatment personnel, despite official pronouncements that rehabilitation was the goal.[10] Although lower-level personnel influence the decisions made in the organization, it is the people near or at the top who have the major and sometimes final say in organizational matters.

The determination of these operative goals is more easily said than done. Organizations may be reluctant to allow the researcher or member access to the kinds of records that show the nature of resource allocation. In interviews they may tend to repeat the official goal as a form of rhetoric. However, the analyst or member can determine operative goals through the use of multiple methods of data collection from a variety of goal indicators, such as the deployment of personnel, growth patterns among departments, examination of available records, and so on.

Since operative goals reflect what the major decision-makers believe to be the critical areas and issues for the organization, it follows that the operative goals will shift as internal and external conditions impinge upon the organization. It was argued in the last chapter that these conditions can deflect the organization from a pursuit of its goals. In a real sense, the operative goals are deflected by these threats or conditions during periods of severe stress. At the same time, *the operative goals will usually reflect some variation on the theme of the official goal*. That is, operative goals are generally based on the official goals, even though there is not perfect correspondence. Profit-making organizations vary in their emphases, colleges and universities pay more or less attention to teaching, research, and so on, and hospitals are concerned to varying degree with teaching, patient care, and research. If the official goals remain the same when pressures, conditions, and priorities change, the shift in operative goals will be mainly in emphasis.

Changes in organizational goals
Organizational goals change for three major reasons. The first is direct pressure from external forces, which leads to a deflection from the original goals. Second is pressure from internal sources. This may lead the organization to emphasize quite different activities than those originally intended. The third factor is changed environmental and technological demands that lead the organization to redefine its goals. While this is similar to the first reason, the factors here occur in *indirect* interaction with the organization, whereas in the first case the organiza-

tion is in direct interaction with the relevant environmental factors.

The impact of external relationships on goals is best seen in Thompson and McEwan's analysis of organization–environmental interactions.[11] They note that organizational goal setting is affected by competitive, bargaining, co-optative, and coalitional relationships with the environment. In the competitive situation—'that form of rivalry between two or more organizations which is mediated by a third party'—organizations must devote their efforts toward gaining support for their continued existence. Competition is most easily seen among business firms that compete for the customer's dollar, but it is also very evident among government agencies as they compete for a share of the tax dollar or among religious organizations as they compete for members and their support. (Religious and other voluntary organizations must also compete with alternative organizations for membership and money.) Competition partially controls the organization's 'choice of goals' in that its energies must be turned to the competitive activity. Continuous support is vital for continued survival as an organization.

Bargaining also involves resources, but in this case the organization is in direct interaction with supplier, consumer, and other organizations. In the bargaining situation, the organization must 'give' a little to get what it desires. Bargaining takes place in standard relationships between two organizations, as in the case where a routine supplier is asked to alter its goods for the organization. This 'custom' order will cost the supplier more money and hence he bargains for a better price, with the organization bargaining to get its custom equipment at the old price. Thompson and McEwan note that universities will often bargain away the name of a building for a substantial gift. Government agencies may bargain by not enforcing certain regulations in order to maintain support for the seeking of other goals. The impact of bargaining is more subtle than that of competition, but it has a similar impact on goal setting.

Co-optation is 'the process of absorbing new elements into the leadership or policy-determining structure of an organization as a means of averting threats to its stability or existence'.[12] The classic study of co-optation is Selznick's *TVA and the Grass Roots,* in which he documents the impact of bringing new societal elements into the governing structure of the TVA.[13] The organization shifted its emphases partially as a result of the new pressures brought to bear in the decision-making system. It is no accident that boards of directors or trustees contain members from pressure groups important to the organizations involved. If a member of a group that is antipathetic to the organization can be brought into the organization, the antipathy can be minimized. At the same time, the presence of person on a controlling board has an influence on decisions made, even though the hostility rate may be down. The recent movement toward 'student power' among high school and college students is interesting to observe in this regard. It is predicted that student members of college and university governing bodies and boards of trustees will be co-opted—that is, the students will become part of the power structure and take its view—but also that the organizations involved will find their goal setting at least minimally influenced by the presence of the students. Cooptation is thus a two-way street. Both those co-opted and those doing the co-opting are influenced.

The final type of external relationship is coalition, or the 'combination of two or more organizations for a common purpose. Coalition appears to be the ultimate or extreme form of environmental conditioning of organizational goals'.[14] While seeking common purposes, coalitions place strong constraints on the organizations involved, since they cannot set goals in a unilateral fashion.

Although it is clear that other environmental factors also affect the nature of organizational goals, Thompson and McEwen's analysis centers around transactions with other organizations. They suggest a very important consideration in the determination of the operative goals of an organization: Organizations operate in a 'field' of other organizations,[15] and these affect what the local organization does. While this has been amply demonstrated in economic analysis of market competition, the impact goes beyond this type of relationship. The interactions we have described are direct evidence that the use of official-goal statements would be misleading, since the transactions with other organizations by definition would deflect an organization from its official goal.

Operative goals are also affected by what goes on inside an organization. A given set of goals may be altered drastically by changes in the power system of the organization, new types of personnel, as in the case of a sudden influx of professionals, and the development of new standards that supersede those of the past. Etzioni has called this phenomenon 'goal displacement'.[16]

Goal displacement is clearly evident in Robert Michels' analysis of Socialist parties and labor unions in Europe in the early twentieth century.[17] In this study he developed the idea of the 'iron law of oligarchy'. Michels pointed out that these revolutionary groups began as democratic organizations. The need for organization to accomplish the revolutionary purposes (operative goals) led to the establishment of leaders of the organizations. The leaders, tasting power, did not want to relinquish it, and therefore devoted much of their energies to maintain their positions. Since members of most voluntary organizations, even revolutionary parties, are politically indifferent, and since the skills necessary for leading the parties are not universally distributed, the leaders could rather easily perpetuate themselves in power—in part by co-opting or purging the young potential leaders. The emphasis in the parties shifted to organizational maintenance, at the expense of militancy and revolutionary zeal. Close parallels to this situation exist in contemporary revolutionary and militant movements of every political and social persuasion.

A different form of goal displacement can be seen in Robert Scott's analysis of the 'sheltered workshop for the blind'.[18] When these workshops were formed in the early twentieth century, the overall goal was to integrate the blind into the industrial community. However, it was recognized that many blind people could not work in regular factories, and so the sheltered workshops were developed to provide the blind with work (making brooms and mops, weaving, chair caning, etc.) as a social service. Owing to a series of events, the workshops began to define themselves as factories in competition with nonblind producers of goods. The emphasis shifted from helping the blind to employing competent workers (not necessarily mutually exclusive categories), and the social-service function largely fell by the wayside. Part of the reason for the shift in emphasis lay in changed environmental conditions, with an increased demand for the workshops' products. But it appears that these demands could have been resisted and the original intent of the workshops maintained intact. The internal decision-making process led to the development of clearly different goals from those professed at the outset.

Still another type of displacement can be seen in what Etzioni calls 'over-measurement' and Bertram Gross labels 'number magic.'[19] Both refer to the tendency for organizations of all types to organize their energies (goals) around activities that are easily quantified. Easy quantification leads to counting publications of university faculty rather than evaluating classroom performance, looking at output per worker rather than 'diligence, cooperation, punctuality, loyalty, and responsibility,'[20] and counting

parishioners in a church rather than assessing the spiritual guidance of the parishioners.[21] These examples could be multiplied many times for many organizations. The obvious solution to this problem is to use multiple indicators for determining the extent to which organizations are achieving their goals. When this is not done and the easily quantifiable measure is stressed, organizational goals become deflected toward the achievement of the easily measured aspect.[22] This may in turn actually defeat the purpose for which the organization was designed. These internal sources of goals change can be found in any organization and are a basic part of the determination of the operative goals. In the extreme cases discussed here, the changes are rather clearly dysfunctional in terms of the official and original operative goals; but the processes inherent in these changes are a normal part of the goal-setting process.

The final source of goal change is a more generalized environmental pressure—generalized, that is, in terms of falling within abstract categories such as technological development, cultural changes, and economic conditions; however, the impact on the organization is direct. Several studies are available that provide direct evidence for this basis of goal change. Perhaps the most dramatic evidence comes from David L. Sills' analysis of the national Foundation for Infantile Paralysis.[23] Although the study was completed before the transition to be discussed was accomplished, the change in operative goals is very evident. The foundation was formed to assist in the prevention and treatment of polio through research, coordinating, and fund-raising activities. At the time the foundation was organized, polio was a major health problem, highlighted by Franklin D. Roosevelt's crippled condition as a result of the disease. Roosevelt himself founded the organization in 1938 at the height of his own popularity and the seriousness of the polio problem. The organization grew rapidly, and its March of Dimes became a very successful volunteer fund-raising effort.

In less than two decades, the organization accomplished its primary goal. Through the development of the Salk and Sabine vaccines, polio has largely been eliminated as a serious health hazard. Rehabilitation facilities have been consistently improved to assist those who suffer from the effects of polio contracted in the past (the number of new cases at present is insignificant). For the organization, these events presented a clear dilemma. The choice was between going out of business and developing a new goal. The latter alternative was chosen, as the organization decided to concentrate on 'other crippling diseases,' with particular emphasis on birth defects. Sills suggests that the presence of a strong national headquarters together with committed volunteers should maintain the organization over time. The historical evidence seems to confirm this, although the organization does not appear to be as strong as it was during the polio epidemics.

The volunteer and nonvolunteer members of this organization had a vested interest in its maintenance. At the same time, technological developments outside the organization made its continuation questionable because of its operative goals at that time. The focus of the organization shifted to adapt to the changed technology. While some of the operative goals remained the same, others shifted to meet the new concerns.

The impact of technological shifts can also be seen in Lawrence and Lorsch's analysis of firms in the plastics industry. In this case, technological change, in the form of a rapidly changing 'state of the art', is an ever-present and pressing factor of the environment. In discussing the performance of organizations in this industry, Lawrence and Lorsch comment:

'The low-performing organizations were both characterized by their top administrators as having serious difficulty in dealing with this environment. They had not been successful in introducing and marketing new products. In fact, their attempts to do so had met with repeated failures. This record, plus other measures of performance available to top management, left them with a feeling of disquiet and a sense of urgency to find ways of improving their performance.[24]

This sense of urgency would be translated into altered operative goals for the organization as it seeks to cope more effectively with the rapidly changing technological system.

Technology is not the only environmental factor impinging upon the organization, despite its apparent centrality. The general values in the environment surrounding an organization also affect its operation. Burton Clark's analysis of the adult education system in California indicates clearly that an organization is vitally affected by the values of those whom it serves and whose support it seeks.[25]

The adult education system's official goals are concerned with relatively lofty matters, such as awareness of civic responsibilities, economic uplift, personal adjustment in the family, health and physical fitness, cultural development, broadened educational background, and the development of vocational interests. This educational system suffers from a number of handicaps. It is part of the public educational system but not part of the normal sequence. It is a 'peripheral, non-mandatory' part; and this mar-

ginality is heightened by the fact that the system operates on an 'enrollment economy.' That is, school income is determined largely by attendance (paid) in classes. If attendance declines, support for the program from tax revenues is likely also to decline. Course enrollments become 'the criterion by which courses are initiated and continued.'[26]

Courses are offered only if they are popular. It is not surprising, therefore, to find classes in cake decorating, rug making, and square dancing. While these are legitimate avocational activities, the pressure for courses such as these precludes much attention being paid to the other official goals and increases the criticisms of the adult education program from other segments of the educational enterprise. The adult education administrators are thus caught in the bind of trying to maintain attendance in the face of competing demands for the potential student's time and trying to satisfy the pertinent criticism of other educators and members of the legislature. The values of the clientele are inconsistent with those of the system itself. The organization adapts to their demands, but then finds itself out of phase with another part of its relevant environment.

Organizations in the service area are constantly confronted with changed values that make their services in greater or lesser demands. Colleges and universities were unprepared for the rise in enrollments caused by the increased valuation placed on education during most of the 1960s. While demographic conditions would have led to a prediction of some increase, more than the expected proportions of high school graduates opted for college as opposed to other endeavors (for whatever reason). These changed values have obviously affected the goals of the organizations as they are forced to 'process' students at the expense of some of the traditional goals.[27]

Shifts in cultural values and their impact on the goals of organizations are obvious in the profit-making sector also. While the goals of profit may remain, the operative goals shift as more energies are put into market research and as organizations redefine themselves as 'young' organizations for the 'now' generation. These are often more than advertising slogans, in that internal transformations have occurred to refocus the organizations' activities.

Shifts in the economic and political systems surrounding an organization would have similar influences on the goals of the organization involved. While much more than goals are affected by these interactions with the environment, it should be clear that organizational goals, like the organizations for which they serve as constraints and guides for action, are not static. Internal and external factors affect them. The relative strength of the various factors affecting goals, which would include the decision-making and power processes within the organization, have not been determined. We do know that these factors are operative, but we cannot specify the conditions under which the importance of these factors varies.

The utility of the goal concept

The factors that affect goals, and the fact that the meaningful goals for an organization are not those officially pronounced, might lead us to reject the goal concept altogether. But there is still the simple but basic fact that the organization would not exist if it were not for some common purpose. Except in the case of conscription, as in the military system or the public schools, members come to the organization willingly, if not enthusiastically. In all cases, the organization engages in some activity. This activity is not simply random behavior; it is based on some notion of what the purpose of the action is.

This purpose or goal is the basis for organizational activities. It is true that means can come to be emphasized more heavily than the goal itself, that members of the organization may have no idea of why they are doing what they are doing, and that ritualistic adherence to outmoded norms may become the norm; but these behaviors would be impossible without the presence of a goal. Even when forgotten or ignored, the goal is still the basis for the organization, since the means would not have developed without it in the first place.

From the discussion above, it is clear that most organizations have more than one goal. These multiple goals may be in conflict with one another; even then, they are still a basis for action. The action itself may or may not conflict with conflicting goals. The relative importance of the goals can be determined by the way the organization allocates its resources to them. Since both external and internal pressures affect goals, along with the more rational process of goal setting, goals cannot be viewed as static. They change, sometimes dramatically, over time. These changes, it should be stressed, can occur because of decision making within the organization. This decision making is almost by definition a consequence of internal or external forces. Goal alterations decided within the organization are a consequence of the interactions of members who participate in the goal-setting process. This can be done by an oligarchic elite or through democratic processes (in very few organizations would a total democracy prevail).

Shifts in goals can also occur without a conscious decision on the part of organization members—that is, as a reaction to the external or internal pressures without a conscious reference to an abstract model of where the organization is going. While this is not goal-related behavior, the persistence of such activities leads to their becoming operative goals for the organization, as where the organization focuses its efforts on achieving easily measured objectives at the expense of more central but less easily measured goals.

It is at this point, of course, that the goal concept is most fuzzy. If an organization is oriented toward some easily quantifiable objective for the sake of measuring its achievements, the analyst can stand back and say, 'Aha, this organization isn't doing what it is supposed to do!' At the same time, the easily quantified goal is an abstraction despite its easy quantification, just as is the possibly more lofty objective that serves as the analyst's point of departure. The analyst can also point out the deflections that occur as a result of the external and internal pressures discussed. Concentration upon deflections from official goals, whether they are due to quantification or external and internal pressures, can lead to the decision that goals are really not relevant for organizational analysis. It is at this point that the work of Perrow and Simon is most pertinent. Perrow's emphasis on the operative goals, however they are developed, and Simon's notion that goals place constraints on decision making both suggest that goals are relevant, even central, for organizational analysis. It does not matter what the source of operative goals might be; what does matter is that they come into the decision-making and action processes of the organization. They are still abstractions around which the organization and its members behave.

The goal concept, with the modifications we have discussed, is vital in organizational analysis. The dynamics of goal setting and goal change do not alter the fact that goals still serve as guides for what happens in an organization. If the concept of goals is not used, organizational behavior becomes a random occurrence, subject to whatever pressures and forces exist at any point in time. Since organizations have continuity and do accomplish things, the notion of goals as abstractions around which behavior is organized remains viable.

Notes and references

[1] Amitai Etzioni, *Modern Organizations,* Englewood Cliffs, N.J.: Prentice-Hall Inc., 1964, p. 6.

[2] Talcott Parsons, *Structure and Process in Modern Societies*, New York: The Free Press, 1960, pp. 17–22 and 44–47.

[3] Herbert A. Simon, 'On the Concept of Organizational Goal,' *Administrative Science Quarterly*, Vol. 9, No. 1, June 1964, 2.

[4] Charles Perrow, 'The Analysis of Goals in Complex Organizations,' *American Sociological Review*, Vol. 26, No. 6, December 1961, 855.

[5] Peter M. Blau, *The Dynamics of Bureaucracy*, Chicago: University of Chicago Press, 1955.

[6] Perrow, *Analysis of Goals*, pp. 855–56.

[7] *Ibid.*, 6. 856.

[8] Cases and case studies are useful as examples, but they cannot be used as bases for generalizations concerning other organizations, even of a very similar type.

[9] *Faculty Information*, Minneapolis: University of Minnesota, 1966, pp. 7–8.

[10] Mayer N. Zald, 'Comparative Analysis and Measurement of Organizational Goals: The Case of Correctional Institutions for Delinquents,' *The Sociological Quarterly*, Vol. 4, No. 2, Spring 1963, 206–30.

[11] James D. Thompson and William J. McEwen, 'Organizational Goals and Environment: Goal Setting as an Interaction Process.' *Administrative Science Quarterly*, Vol 23, No. 1, February 1958.

[12] *Ibid.*, p. 27.

[13] Phillip Selznick, *TVA and the Grass Roots*, New York: Harper Torchbook Edition, 1966.

[14] Thompson and McEwen, *Organizational Goals and Environment*, p. 28.

[15] For a further discussion of this point, see Roland L. Warren, 'The Interorganizational Field as a Focus for Investigation', *Administrative Science Quarterly*, Vol. 12, No. 3, December 1967, 396–419.

[16] Etzioni, *Modern Organizations*, p. 10.

[17] Robert Michels, *Political Parties*, New York: The Free Press, 1949.

[18] Robert A. Scott, 'The Factory as a Social Service Organization: Goal Displacement in Workshops for the Blind.' *Social Problems*, Vol. 15, No. 2, Fall 1967, 160–75.

[19] Etzioni, *Modern Organizations*, pp. 8–10; and Bertram M. Gross, *Organizations and Their Managing*, New York: The Free Press, 1968, p. 293.

[20] Gross, *op. cit.*, p. 295.

[21] Etzioni, *op. cit.*, p. 10.

[22] For an extended discussion of this point, see W. Keith Warner and A. Eugene Havens, 'Goal Displacement and the Intangibility of Organizational Goals,' *Administrative Science Quarterly*, Vol. 12, No. 4, March 1968, 539–55.

[23] David L. Sills, *The Volunteers*, New York: The Free Press, 1957.

[24] Paul R. Lawrence and Jay W. Lorsch, *Organization and Environment: Managing Differentiation and Integration*, Cambridge: Harvard Graduate School of Business Administration, 1967, p. 42.

[25] Burton R. Clark, 'Organizational Adaptation and Precarious Values,' *American Sociological Review*, Vol. 21, No. 3, June 1956, 327–36.

[26] *Ibid.*, p. 333.

[27] The case of the WCTU, discussed earlier, illustrates what happens when an organization *does not* adapt to changed values. The current shifts in college enrollment illustrate still another shift of values.

9 The contribution of organization structure

J. Child

'Structure is a means for attaining the objectives and goals of an institution.' Peter F. Drucker, 'New Templates for Today's Organization', *Harvard Business Review,* Jan-Feb 1974, p. 52.

The design of its organization is one of management's major priorities. This entails creating a structure which suits the need of the particular enterprise or institution, achieving consistency between the various aspects of the structure, and adapting it over time to changing circumstances. As Drucker points out, the function of an organizational structure is to assist the attainment of objectives, and it can do this in three main respects.

First, structure contributes to the successful implementation of plans by formally allocating people and resources to the tasks which have to be done, and by providing mechanisms for their co-ordination. This is sometimes called the *basic structure*. It takes the form of job descriptions, organization charts and the constitution of boards, committees and working parties.

Second, it is possible to indicate to the members of an organization more clearly what is expected of them by means of various structural *operating mechanisms*. For example, devices such as standing orders or operating procedures can set out the ways in which tasks are to be performed. In addition, or perhaps as an alternative when the manner of doing tasks cannot be closely defined, standards of performance can be established incorporating criteria such as output or quality of achievement. These would be accompanied by procedures for performance review. As well as control procedures such as these, other operating mechanisms include reward and appraisal systems, planning schedules and systems for communication.

Third, the ambit of structure encompasses provisions for assisting decision-making and its associated information processing requirements. These may be called *decision mechanisms*. They include arrangements for relevant intelligence to be collected from outside the organization, partly through specifying these among the duties of specialist jobs. Procedures can be established whereby information is collated, evaluated and made available to decision-makers on a regular basis and/or in response to some new development outside of the organization. The process of decision-making itself can be assisted, where appropriate, through programming, specification of stages in the process, indication of decision rules and provision of procedures for post-audit.

The allocation of responsibilities, the grouping of functions, decision-making, co-ordination and control—all these are fundamental requirements for the continued operation of an organization. The quality of an organization's structure will affect how well these requirements are met.

Components of structure

The structure of an organization is often taken to comprise all the tangible and regularly occurring features which help to shape its members' behaviour. This encompasses what used misleadingly to be called formal and informal organization. The way in which those terms have generally been used is misleading because it fails to distinguish between the degree of formality in a structure and the separate dimension of whether it is officially sanctioned or not. The degree of formality in structure is a dimension of design. On the other hand, a book like this naturally lays emphasis on structural arrangements which managers can design and which are therefore official by definition. Unofficial practices have to be recognized as part of the context of organizational design, and they often point to a deficiency in the official structure. But organizational designers do not implement unofficial structures.

There has also been a long standing confusion as to whether the term 'organization' refers to the structure of an organized body, institution or enterprise, or whether it describes the total entity *per se*. I shall use the term 'structure' whenever the sense of 'organization' would be ambiguous. Otherwise, I have conformed with popular expression and used organization to refer to structural attributes (as in 're-organization' or 'the organization of a company'), and the term 'an organization' or similar to refer to institutions or units as a whole.

Some idea of the components of an organization structure has already emerged. Major dimensions are:

1   The allocation of tasks and responsibilities to individuals, including discretion over the use of resources and methods of working. Structural features concerned here are the degree of job specialization and definition.

2   The designation of formal reporting relationships, determining the number of levels in hierarchies and the spans of control of managers and supervisors.

3   The grouping together of individuals in sections or departments, the grouping of departments into divisions and larger units, and the overall grouping of units into the total organization.

4   The delegation of authority together with associated procedures whereby the use of discretion is monitored and evaluated.

5   The design of systems to ensure effective communication of information, integration of effort, and participation in the decision-making process.

6   The provision of systems for performance appraisal and reward which help to motivate rather than to alienate employees.

If any of these structural components is deficient, there can be serious consequences for the performance of an organization.

Consequences of structural deficiencies

Among the features which so often mark the struggling organization are low motivation and morale, late and inappropriate decisions, conflict and lack of co-ordination, rising costs and a generally poor response to new opportunities and external change. Structural deficiencies can play a part in exacerbating all these problems.

1   Motivation and morale may be depressed because:

(a) Decisions appear to be inconsistent and arbitrary in the absence of standardized rules.

(b) People perceive that they have little responsibility, opportunity for achievement and recognition of their worth because there is insufficient delegation of decision-making. This may be connected with narrow spans of control.

(c) There is a lack of clarity as to what is expected of people and how their performance is assessed. This is due to inadequate job definition.

(d) People are subject to competing pressures from different parts of the organization due to the absence of clearly defined priorities, decision rules or work programmes.

(e) People are overloaded because their support systems are not adequate. Supervisors, for instance, have to leave the job to chase up materials, parts and tools as there is no adequate system for communicating forthcoming requirements to stores and tool room.

2   Decision-making may be delayed and lacking in quality because:

(a) Necessary information is not transmitted on time to the appropriate people. This may be due to an over-extended hierarchy.

(b) Decision-makers are too segmented into spearate units and there is inadequate provision to co-ordinate them.

(c) Decision-makers are overloaded due to insufficient delegation on their part.

(d) There are no adequate procedures for evaluating the results of similar decisions made in the past.

3   There may be conflict and a lack of co-ordination because:

(a) There are conflicting goals which have not been structured into a single set of objectives and priorities. People are acting at cross purposes. They may, for example, be put under pressure to follow departmental priorities at the expense of product or project goals.

(b) People are working out of step with each other because they are not brought together into teams or because mechanisms for liaison have not been laid down.

(c) The people who are actually carrying out operational work and who are in touch with changing contingencies are not permitted to participate in the planning of the work. There is therefore a breakdown between planning and operations.

4   An organization may not respond innovatively to changing circumstances because:

(a) It has not established specialized jobs concerned with forecasting and scanning the environment.

(b) There is a failure to ensure that innovation and planning of change are mainstream activities backed up by top management through appropriate procedures.

(c) There is inadequate co-ordination between the part of an organization identifying changing market needs and the research area working on possible technological solutions.

5 Costs may be rising rapidly, particularly in the administrative area because:

(a) The organization has a long hierarchy with a high ratio of 'chiefs' to 'indians'.

(b) There is an excess of procedure and paperwork distracting people's attention away from productive work and requiring additional staff personnel to administer.

(c) Some or all of the other organization problems are present.

Organizational choices

All the components of organization structure can be designed to take different forms, and they in fact vary considerably in practice. As Jay W. Lorsch of the Harvard Business School has put it, 'the structure of an organization is not an immutable given, but rather a set of complex variables about which managers can exercise considerable choice' (G. W. Dalton, P. R. Lawrence and J. W. Lorsch, *Organizational Structure and Design* 1970, p. 1). There is no single way of organizing and therein lies the dilemma facing managers, or indeed anyone else participating in organizational design decisions.

The one model of organization with which we are most familiar is bureaucracy. Bureaucracy not only has a long history, its genesis reaching back to the administration of ancient civilizations, but it is in a more advanced form the type of structure commonly adopted by large organizations today. For several thousand years, bureaucracy has been widely accepted as the most efficient, equitable and least corruptable basis for administration. Despite some early social criticism by novelists such as Balzac and sociologists like Max Weber, it is only during the past few decades that bureaucracy has been attacked as an inefficient model of organization in the conditions of unprecedented change, complex technology and an ethos of personal individuality which prevail today.

Bureaucratic structures are characterized by an advanced degree of specialization between jobs and departments, by a reliance on formal procedures and paperwork, and by extended managerial hierarchies with clearly marked status distinctions. In bureaucracies there tends to be a strictly delimited system of delegation down these hierarchies whereby an employee is expected to use his discretion only within what the rules allow.

The bureaucratic approach is intended to provide organizational control through ensuring a high degree of predictability in people's behaviour. It is also a means of trying to ensure that different clients or employees are treated fairly through the applica-

tion of general rules and procedures. The problem is that rules are inflexible instruments of administration which enshrine experience of past rather than present conditions, which cannot be readily adapted to suit individual needs, and which can become barriers behind which it is always tempting for the administrator to hide. This is why bureaucracy today has come under increasing attack on the grounds of its inability to innovate, its demotivating effects on employees and its secrecy. The search for alternative forms of organization serves to remind us that bureaucracy is only one organizational design and that other choices are available. The fundamental question is what form of organization should be selected and on what basis? The following are some of the decisions that have to be made.

1 Should jobs be broken down into narrow areas of work and responsibility, so as to secure the benefits of specialization? Or should the degree of specialization be kept to a minimum in order to simplify communication, and to offer members of the organization greater scope and responsibility in their work? Another choice arising in the design of jobs concerns the extent to which the responsibilities and methods attaching to them should be precisely defined.

2 Should the overall structure of an organization be 'tall' rather than 'flat' in terms of its levels of management and spans of control? What are the implications for communication, motivation and overhead costs of moving towards one of these alternatives rather than the other?

3 Should jobs and departments be grouped together in a 'functional' way according to the specialist expertise and interests that they share? Or should they be grouped according to the different services and products which are being offered, or the different geographical areas being served, or according to yet another criterion?

4 Is it appropriate to aim for an intensive form of integration between the different segments of an organization or not? What kind of integrative mechanisms are there to choose from?

5 What approach should a management take towards maintaining adequate control over work done? Should it centralize or delegate decisions, and all or only some decisions? Should a policy of extensive formalization be adopted in which standing orders and written records are used for control purposes? Should work be subject to close supervision?

When thinking about these organizational choices, there are certain more general questions which help to place one's analysis in a more dynamic context. These are:

6   What are the structural requirements posed by the growth and development of an organization? What practical conclusions can be drawn from research into the association between structure and performance in general?

7   What are the pressures which force managements to change organization structures, and what problems commonly arise with re-organization? How can these be tackled?

8   Finally, in the light of contemporary changes in social and industrial circumstances, what kinds of structural arrangements are we likely to see in the future? In what ways are our present approaches to organization going to become inadequate or unacceptable?

These are the main issues which a manager faces when thinking about the design of his organization. They constitute the subject matter of this book. It is not possible to offer any precise answers to problems of organization structure in abstraction from the particular institution we are talking about, and from the conditions it is facing. As Drucker has also said in the article cited, 'organization is organic and unique to each individual business or institution'. What one can do, however, is to provide the reader with a constructive way of analysing his organizational problems and to alert him to the kind of alternatives he has available when designing a structure.

A full consideration of structural design has to be informed by the objectives which are selected for the organization. It is in this respect a political rather than a purely technical question. If the members of an organization value its present culture and way of doing things, then the preservation of these features will enter into the range of objectives of that organization. I wish to stress this point at an early stage because most of the literature on organizational design treats it as a purely technical matter, a question of adjusting structures to suit prevailing contingencies. These contingencies are, of course, significant and they will be discussed shortly. A recognition that organizational design should have regard to contingencies is important in drawing attention to the need to select an appropriate structure and to avoid the fallacy of thinking that there is any 'best' general model of administration. My point is, however, that in reality this choice goes even further. It incorporates the preferences of decision-makers for a particular approach to management, preferences which are ultimately derived

from their philosophies of man. Consensus over such preferences and its embodiment in an accepted culture can itself have a powerful positive motivating effect, and goes some way towards explaining a phenomenon whereby successful enterprises operating under similar contingencies are found to utilize different types of organizational design.

The objectives selected for an organization are embodied in a strategy. Strategy refers to the policies and plans through which a management attempts to realize the objectives it has set (or has been given) for its organization. The implementation of strategies over the course of time will determine the tasks an organization performs, its areas of location, the diversity of its activities and the kind of people it seeks to employ. The degree of success it attains will influence its growth and its latitude to pursue policies of its management's own choosing, as will also the decisions of external bodies to which it may be responsible. If factors such as these bring about contingencies for the design of organization structure, they do so largely as a product of strategy and its degree of realization against external constraint. Decisions on the type of structure to be adopted themselves represent major items of policy which may in practice be weighed against other strategic considerations. This is increasingly likely to be the case as in contemporary societies the design of organization has to satisfy political expectations such as those embodied in demands for the extension of participation. Nevertheless, the impact of existing contingencies upon structure is substantial enough, and warrants some consideration at this point.

Structural contingencies
Decisions to follow a particular policy will usually have some direct implications for organizational design. For example, if primacy is given in a business company to a policy of growth via acquisition then the experience of American firms indicates that the establishment of specialized acquisition teams is normally required to carry out a thorough search for and evaluation of opportunities. If greater emphasis comes to be placed upon cost reduction and cash budgeting in order to improve profitability and use of funds, then an elaboration of financial control procedures and an expansion of financial departments may logically follow. The success with which policies have been achieved will contribute to the amount of surplus resources ('slack') available to an institution, or conversely to the degree of pressure its management feels itself to be under. A pressure situation almost invariably leads to a greater central-

ization of decision-making, as well as to reductions in the scale of some activities which may in turn reduce numbers of departments and the level of specialization within the organization.

The overall size of an organization has been shown in many research surveys to be closely associated with the type of structure adopted, particularly in the range from about 100 to about 5,000 employees.

Institutions in many fields of business, public service, trade unionism and so forth have grown steadily larger, with the aim of expanding their fields of activity, taking advantage of economies of large-scale operation and supporting the overheads of advanced research and development or a wider range of specialist support services. As the numbers employed in an organization grow so does its complexity. The number of levels of management increases, bringing additional problems of delegation and control at each level. The increase in size makes it economically possible to utilize specialist support services which must be slotted in to the organization structure. The spread of separate groups and departments across the organization also increases with growth. Additional procedures are then required for co-ordination and communication between these different units, while the contribution of new specialists has to be integrated with the activities of line management.

Size in these ways has very significant implications for organizational design, a theme which will be illustrated at many points later on. It creates so many administrative and behavioural problems that many organizations are divided into semi-autonomous units upon reaching a certain scale, especially if this coincides with diversification into different fields of activity. Hence, the relative impact of size on an organization's structure may in practice be progressively reduced beyond this stage in its development.

Many large organizations, business companies in particular, have diversified their activities into a number of distinct fields or industries. Large companies will also quite often be selling and manufacturing in several different regions of the world. Diversification is an important means of growth, through which firms move into expanding fields and avoid the constraint of legislation which discourages overconcentration in any one industry. When an organization's operations in a new field have attained a certain maturity and scale, it is normally appropriate for its structure to be divisionalized. This permits suitable personnel and resources to be allocated specifically to what is now a distinctive field of operation and for their activities to be integrated closely around it. If the proportion of a company's business in a particular geographical area reaches a significant scale, then a similar logic may justify the establishment of area divisions. Depending on the balance between product and area diversification, area divisions may be an alternative to product divisions or may be established concomitantly with them. Divisionalization is an organizational response to diversification, though it is also encouraged by the growing administrative problems of large scale. As divisions themselves grow large, and possibly diversified, pressures towards further sub-division are activated both to achieve smaller units of management and to reflect the distinctiveness of separate business areas.

Diversification extends the range of different environments in which an organization operates. These environments may also vary in their characteristics, especially the rate of change experienced in market and technological features, the rate at which they are expanding, types of competitive pressure and the degree of dependence on other institutions. These factors will serve to generate different levels of managerial uncertainty regarding new developments to which the organization has to adapt. The greater its dependence on other organizations for custom, supplies, governmental sanction or other necessary support, the more that uncertainty will be reinforced because management's ability to ignore new developments or to control them will be correspondingly reduced. Uncertainty and dependence together place a premium upon an organization's capacity to secure and rapidly disseminate intelligence about the outside world, and to operate in a flexible manner which permits any necessary reactions to new developments that have been forecast. The conglomerate ITT, which had been operating in a climate of chronic uncertainty about the future of its telephone business in countries such as Chile, felt it necessary to build up a highly developed system of political intelligence in order to provide this capacity to anticipate and adapt. Environmental conditions have important implications for the type of organization structure to be adopted.

The kinds of environment in which an organization is operating determine the tasks and production it undertakes, and these have implications for its structural design and choice of personnel. For example, a firm may be operating in a high-technology science-based industry. It will have to give special attention to organizing its research and development activities so as to encourage inventiveness while also retaining control over expenditures and commercial relevance. Seeking to utilize advanced technical knowledge, it will probably employ a broad range of occupational specialists who must be adequately co-ordinated. If a company can place its operations onto a mass-produced basis, this will speak for a different form of production organization than if it happens to be producing for a small batch or one-off market. Much attention was paid in pioneering studies of organization to the physical technology of production as a contingent influence on effective organization, and the practical implications of these studies will be considered later on. By and large, the technology of an organization reflects the kind of environment in which its management has chosen to operate. Some complex technological processes may also only be available on an economic basis to organizations which have attained a given size.

The purpose of some institutions will reflect the nature of their membership. This is obviously true of a voluntary association like a trade union. The character of other institutions such as hospitals or universities will attract certain types of employees, most notably in these cases staff who expect to work to their own professional standards free from close administrative control. A science-based company will employ a significant body of scientists who similarly are likely to have strong preferences about how they wish to work. The proportion of the total working population accounted for by professional and highly trained personnel such as these is steadily rising. In contrast, a mass-production car assembly plant will tend to attract semi-skilled workers who place more emphasis on relatively high pay than conditions of work. These instances go to show that the kind of job design and working environment which is in tune with the expectations of an organization's members will vary according to who they are and why they have joined the institution. Both from a managerial viewpoint of securing motivation and a social viewpoint of raising people's quality of working life, the type of membership and workforce an institution has provides a further important contingency to be satisfied in the design of jobs, operating procedures, career opportunities and so forth.

The brief discussion of structural contingencies permits three further points to be made at the outset of this book. The first point is that the attainment of an organization's objectives will be facilitated if two conditions are satisfied:

(a) the policies it adopts are realistic in the light of prevailing conditions, and (b) its structure is designed to satisfy these policies. A simple example can illustrate this point.

The management of a small company producing good quality and rather expensive confectionery wished to expand out of its limited markets by supplying a new low-price quality line to a chain store. This line would consist of simply produced and wrapped sweets which were made from standard ingredients and varied only in flavouring. The company proved unable to supply the store at a sufficiently high rate of production, and it lost the contract.

Its structure was such that it had a director in charge of quality control ('Technical Director') as well as a director of production. Quality control was rigorously applied at various stages of production and to wrapping. The company was sufficiently small to mean that initial production of the new line used existing mixing, boiling and other plant. Also no change was made to quality control procedures or to the system of production control. Considerable conflict arose between production management and quality control who attempted to apply the normal procedures to the new line, including rules such as the placing of trays at certain distances from walls. (The higher level of volume generated pressures on storage space.) Production was seriously disrupted by batches being rejected or delayed, and by batches of traditional products holding up those of the new. At this stage, then, the company had not modified its structure to suit its new growth-oriented policies.

At a later date the company was successful in securing and fulfilling another high volume contract. This time it revised its quality requirements for the new line, held discussions between quality control and production about the new operation, and after a short while placed inspectors under the day-to-day control of production management. It also set up a formal procedure whereby decisions on conflicting batch priorities were referred to the sales manager as opposed to merely following traditional practice on the sequencing of batches. The structure had now been amended to support the shift in objectives.

The second point is that contingencies such as environment, size, type of work, and personnel employed are not the same in different divisions and departments within an organization. Accounting tasks and the kind of personalities carrying them out are not very similar to research tasks and personnel. An electronics division of a conglomerate like ITT operates in quite different conditions to its hotel chain. This means that within an institution one should expect to find variations in structure to suit its different parts. There is no merit in imposing a common form of structure on the diverse sections of an organization. That would merely represent a misplaced sense of administrative tidiness. Structural diversity, however, does mean that the integration of sections is a problem. The more an organization is internally differentiated, the more its management will have to pay special regard to integrative mechanisms.

Thirdly, structural contingencies are themselves interrelated; for instance, larger companies are generally the more diversified. The particular combination of objectives and contingencies found in an organization gives it a unique character. The set of contingencies which are peculiar to that organization may also in some degree conflict, which poses a policy and structural dilemma for its management. For instance, the firm which has based its commercial success on low cost mass-production technology may today be beginning to reap severe costs of employee alienation in the form of disruption to production, high absenteeism and turnover. Local authorities in Britain have been amalgamated in pursuit of scale economies but this is at the expense of their ability to maintain close involvement with local people.

The implication of this is not that we should give up any hope of designing structures which will cope, or even forget about considering any general guidelines at all. The unique character of an institution can be identified in terms of component dimensions which can be compared with the experience of other organizations along the same dimensions. Managers in practice have to take account of a multiplicity of details and attempt to reconcile the pressures of conflicting contingencies. This really means that improvements in organizational design can only proceed through a process of organizational development, which entails a painstaking working through of details with the managers and employees concerned. As I wrote a few years ago, the guidelines which can be derived from our present knowledge will assist managers in working through their organizational problems. 'But, in the present state of knowledge, this working through is necessary. Particular cases have to be assessed, that is researched, virtually from scratch.' This is, of course, what managers often attempt to do by trial and error. In many organizations today, structures are constantly being adjusted, partly as operating conditions and contingencies change, partly in response to the changing balance of managerial politics.

Limitations to the contribution of structure

I have so far put forward the view that the design of organization structure must make reference to a complexity of different requirements, and that it cannot proceed on an *a priori* basis. At certain times one of those requirements may be given priority over the others, but it will not be fruitful to ignore them completely. In this section, I shall mention some of the reasons why structure, however well designed, can only be expected to make a limited, though nonetheless significant, contribution to an organization's effectiveness. Effectiveness is first discussed in economic terms from the standpoint of the whole organization, and then from the standpoint of the individual employee.

The performance of an organization is influenced by many factors apart from its structure. For instance, an organization structure may be quite effective in guiding people to perform the right tasks, in co-ordinating their efforts and in processing information, but this will not be reflected in overall performance if strategies are being followed that are not in tune with desired objectives or prevailing circumstances. Nor can a mere structure of organization support an appropriate pattern of behaviour if there is not the will or competence among managers and employees to perform in that manner. If skills are lacking or the climate of morale is bad, then an otherwise appropriate structure will have relatively little effect.

Certain structural features can come to be regarded as ends in themselves, whether or not they contribute to a higher level of performance. Provisions to allow employees or their representatives to have a greater say in decision-making are today under serious discussion in Europe. The argument for these lies not so much in their possible contribution to economic efficiency (which could nevertheless be quite real) as in the way they can satisfy other aspirations. Family-controlled firms have often been known to persevere with a centralized system of decision-making long beyond the stage of growth at which delegation to non-family members came to be required on grounds of effectiveness. Some organizations may temper their pursuit of economic goals with social policies which cause their organization structures to be other than the most efficient. I know of one large group of companies in which a policy of plant rationalization coupled with one of declaring few managerial redundancies has led to extended hierarchies within which surplus managers are lodged. These not only embody excess manpower costs but give rise to communication problems.

Organization structure cannot be expected to resolve political problems within an institution. There are deep-seated conflicts in many fields about the legitimate objectives of institutions, and concerning the correctness of the methods by which they are run. If objectives are in dispute between managers and employees, managers and groups outside the organization or between managers themselves, a formal structure cannot of itself resolve these differences in a way that integrates people's actions in an effective manner. At best, it can be designed to provide mechanisms, such as discussion meetings, which bring conflicts into the open and so offer some chance of reconciling them.

Structure itself often becomes victim to politics, and indeed it will not be allowed to operate effectively if it does not reflect political forces within the organization. A department, for instance, will tend to ignore a restrictive procedure if it has the power to do so. Political ambitions are frequently a driving force behind structural changes. Recently a major programme of organizational development was initiated in the division of a large British company partly because a newly appointed production manager felt he was not occupying a viable job and wished to make his mark in time to succeed the divisional director due to retire in 18 months hence. The development involved the re-grouping of various functional support activities under his command.

Structure cannot resolve conflicts over objectives. It can, however, be shaped in a way that more closely accords with changing views on the correct manner of conducting relationships at work. Traditional norms of authority are being challenged from many quarters today and effective structures of organization have to change accordingly. Whether in fact the organization of any units above the primary group size can be designed in such a way as completely to eliminate formal authority relationships is a moot point. Therein probably lies an inevitable source of conflict between managers and others which is heightened by contemporary notions of the freedom and responsibility necessary to the achievement of personal fulfilment. Organization structure in this respect will always appear potentially coercive to the employee. In business firms and other institutions where there is a cash nexus with their members, this coercion of formalized authority will be reinforced by economic conflicts of interest. Organizational design and development can only help to resolve this conflict with the individual to a limited extent, by exploring more satisfactory means of reconciling the different interests involved.

10 Organization design: an information processing view
J. R. Galbraith

The Information Processing Model
A basic proposition is that the greater the uncertainty of the task, the greater the amount of information that has to be processed between decision makers during the execution of the task. If the task is well understood prior to performing it, much of the activity can be preplanned. If it is not understood, then during the actual task execution more knowledge is acquired which leads to changes in resource allocations, schedules, and priorities. All these changes require information processing *during* task performance. Therefore *the greater the task uncertainty, the greater the amount of information that must be processed among decision makers during task execution in order to achieve a given level of performance.* The basic effect of uncertainty is to limit the ability of the organization to preplan or to make decisions about activities in advance of their execution. Therefore it is hypothesized that the observed variations in organizational forms are variations in the strategies of organizations to (1) increase their ability to preplan, (2) increase their flexibility to adapt to their inability to preplan, or, (3) to decrease the level of performance required for continued viability. Which strategy is chosen depends on the relative costs of the strategies. The function of the framework is to identify these strategies and their costs.

The Mechanistic Model
This framework is best developed by keeping in mind a hypothetical organization. Assume it is large and employs a number of specialist groups and resources in providing the output. After the task has been divided into specialist subtasks, the problem is to integrate the subtasks around the completion of the global task. This is the problem of organization design. The behaviors that occur in one subtask cannot be judged as good or bad *per se*. The behaviors are more effective or ineffective depending upon the behaviors of the other subtask performers. There is a design problem because the executors of the behaviors cannot communicate with all the roles with whom they are interdependent. Therefore the design problem is to create mechanisms that permit coordinated action across large numbers of interdependent roles. Each of these mechanisms, however, has a limited range over which it is effective at handling the information requirements necessary to coordinate the interdependent roles. As the amount of uncertainty increases, and therefore information processing increases, the organization must adopt integrating mechanisms which increase its information processing capabilities.

1 *Coordination by Rules or Programs*
For routine predictable tasks March and Simon have identified the use of rules or programs to coordinate behavior between interdependent subtasks [March and Simon, 1958, Chap. 6]. To the extent that job related situations can be predicted in advance, and behaviors specified for these situations, programs allow an interdependent set of activities to be performed without the need for inter-unit communication. Each role occupant simply executes the behavior which is appropriate for the task related situation with which he is faced.

2 *Hierarchy*
As the organization faces greater uncertainty its participants face situations for which they have no rules. At this point the hierarchy is employed on an exception basis. The recurring job situations are programmed with rules while infrequent situations are referred to that level in the hierarchy where a global perspective exists for all affected subunits. However, the hierarchy also has a limited range. As uncertainty increases the number of exceptions increases until the hierarchy becomes overloaded.

3 *Coordination by Targets or Goals*
As the uncertainty of the organization's task increases, coordination increasingly takes place by specifying outputs, goals or targets [March and Simon, 1958, p. 145]. Instead of specifying specific behaviors to be enacted, the organization undertakes processes to set goals to be achieved and the employees select the behaviors which lead to goal

accomplishment. Planning reduces the amount of information processing in the hierarchy by increasing the amount of discretion exercised at lower levels. Like the use of rules, planning achieves integrated action and also eliminates the need for continuous communication among interdependent subunits as long as task performance stays within the planned task specifications, budget limits and within targeted completion dates. If it does not, the hierarchy is again employed on an exception basis.

The ability of an organization to coordinate interdependent tasks depends on its ability to compute meaningful subgoals to guide subunit action. When uncertainty increases because of introducing new products, entering new markets, or employing new technologies these subgoals are incorrect. The result is more exceptions, more information processing, and an overloaded hierarchy.

Design Strategies

The ability of an organization to successfully utilize coordination by goal setting, hierarchy, and rules depends on the combination of the frequency of exceptions and the capacity of the hierarchy to handle them. As the task uncertainty increases the organization must again take organization design action. It can proceed in either of two general ways. First, it can act in two ways to reduce the amount of information that is processed. And second, the organization can act in two ways to increase its capacity to handle more information. The two methods for reducing the need for information and the two methods for increasing processing capacity are shown schematically in Figure 10.1. The effect of all these actions is to reduce the number of exceptional cases referred upward into the organization through hierarchical channels. The assumption is that the critical limiting factor of an organizational form is its ability to handle the non-routine, consequential events that cannot be anticipated and planned for in advance. The non-programmed events

place the greatest communication load on the organization.

1 *Creation of Slack Resources*

As the number of exceptions begin to overload the hierarchy, one response is to increase the planning targets so that fewer exceptions occur. For example, completion dates can be extended until the number of exceptions that occur are within the existing information processing capacity of the organization. This has been the practice in solving job shop scheduling problems [Pounds, 1963]. Job shops quote delivery times that are long enough to keep the scheduling problem within the computational and information processing limits of the organization. Since every job shop has the same problem standard lead times evolve in the industry. Similarly budget targets could be raised, buffer inventories employed, etc. The greater the uncertainty, the greater the magnitude of the inventory, lead time or budget needed to reduce an overload.

All of these examples have a similar effect. They represent the use of slack resources to reduce the amount of interdependence between subunits [March and Simon, 1958, Cyert and March, 1963]. This keeps the required amount of information within the capacity of the organization to process it. Information processing is reduced because an exception is less likely to occur and réduced interdependence means that fewer factors need to be considered simultaneously when an exception does occur.

The strategy of using slack resources has its costs. Relaxing budget targets has the obvious cost of requiring more budget. Increasing the time to completion date has the effect of delaying the customer. Inventories require the investment of capital funds which could be used elsewhere. Reduction of design optimization reduces the performance of the article being designed. Whether slack resources are used to reduce information or not depends on the relative cost of the other alternatives.

The design choices are: (1) among which factors to change (lead time, overtime, machine utilization, etc.) to create the slack, and (2) by what amount should the factor be changed. Many operations research models are useful in choosing factors and amounts. The time-cost trade off problem in project networks is a good example.

2 *Creation of Self-Contained Tasks*

The second method of reducing the amount of information processed is to change the subtask groupings from source (input) based to output based categories and give each group the resources it needs

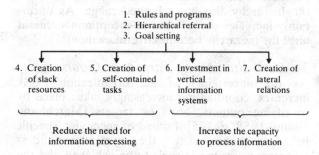

        1. Rules and programs
        2. Hierarchical referral
        3. Goal setting

| 4. Creation of slack resources | 5. Creation of self-contained tasks | 6. Investment in vertical information systems | 7. Creation of lateral relations |

Reduce the need for information processing   Increase the capacity to process information

Figure 10.1 Organization design strategies

to supply the output. For example, the functional organization could be changed to product groups. Each group would have its own product engineers, process engineers, fabricating and assembly operations, and marketing activities. In other situations, groups can be created around product lines, geographical areas, projects, client groups, markets, etc., each of which would contain the input resources necessary for creation of the output.

The strategy of self-containment shifts the basis of the authority structure from one based on input, resource, skill, or occupational categories to one based on output or geographical categories. The shift reduces the amount of information processing through several mechanisms. First, it reduces the amount of output diversity faced by a single collection of resources. For example, a professional organization with multiple skill specialties providing service to three different client groups must schedule the use of these specialties across three demands for their services and determine priorities when conflicts occur. But, if the organization changed to three groups, one for each client category, each with its own full complement of specialties, the schedule conflicts across client groups disappears and there is no need to process information to determine priorities.

The second source of information reduction occurs through a reduced division of labor. The functional or resource specialized structure pools the demand for skills across all output categories. In the example above each client generates approximately one-third of the demand for each skill. Since the division of labor is limited by the extent of the market, the division of labor must decrease as the demand decreases. In the professional organization, each client group may have generated a need for one-third of a computer programmer. The functional organization would have hired one programmer and shared him across the groups. In the self-contained structure there is insufficient demand in each group for a programmer so the professionals must do their own programming. Specialization is reduced but there is no problem of scheduling the programmer's time across the three possible uses for it.

The cost of the self-containment strategy is the loss of resource specialization. In the example, the organization forgoes the benefit of a specialist in computer programming. If there is physical equipment, there is a loss of economies of scale. The professional organization would require three machines in the self-contained form but only a large time-shared machine in the functional form. But those resources which have large economies of scale or for which specialization is necessary may remain centralized. Thus, it is the degree of self-containment that is the variable. The greater the degree of uncertainty, other things equal, the greater the degree of self-containment.

The design choices are the basis for the self-containment structure and the number of resources to be contained in the groups. No groups are completely self-contained or they would not be part of the same organization. But one product divisionalized firm may have eight of fifteen functions in the division while another may have 12 of 15 in the divisions. Usually accounting, finance, and legal services are centralized and shared. Those functions which have economies of scale, require specialization or are necessary for control remain centralized and not part of the self-contained group.

The first two strategies reduced the amount of information by lower performance standards and creating small autonomous groups to provide the output. Information is reduced because an exception is less likely to occur and fewer factors need to be considered when an exception does occur. The next two strategies accept the performance standards and division of labor as given and adapt the organization so as to process the new information which is created during task performance.

3   Investment in Vertical Information Systems

The organization can invest in mechanisms which allow it to process information acquired during task performance without overloading the hierarchical communication channels. The investment occurs according to the following logic. After the organization has created its plan or set of targets for inventories, labor utilization, budgets, and schedules, unanticipated events occur which generate exceptions requiring adjustments to the original plan. At some point when the number of exceptions becomes substantial, it is preferable to generate a new plan rather than make incremental changes with each exception. The issue is then how frequently should plans be revised—yearly, quarterly, or monthly? The greater the frequency of replanning the greater the resources, such as clerks, computer time, input–output devices, etc., required to process information about relevant factors.

The cost of information processing resources can be minimized if the language is formalized. Formalization of a decision-making language simply means that more information is transmitted with the same number of symbols. It is assumed that information processing resources are consumed in proportion to the number of symbols transmitted. The accounting system is an example of a formalized language.

Providing more information, more often, may simply overload the decision maker. Investment may be required to increase the capacity of the decision maker by employing computers, various man–machine combinations, assistants-to, etc. The cost of this strategy is the cost of the information processing resources consumed in transmitting and processing the data.

The design variables of this strategy are the decision frequency, the degree of formalization of language, and the type of decision mechanism which will make the choice. This strategy is usually operationalized by creating redundant information channels which transmit data from the point of origination upward in the hierarchy where the point of decision rests. If data is formalized and quantifiable, this strategy is effective. If the relevant data are qualitative and ambiguous, then it may prove easier to bring the decisions down to where the information exists.

4   Creation of Lateral Relationships

The last strategy is to employ selectively joint decision processes which cut across lines of authority. This strategy moves the level of decision making down in the organization to where the information exists but does so without reorganizing around self-contained groups. There are several types of lateral decision processes. Some processes are usually referred to as the informal organization. However, these informal processes do not always arise spontaneously out of the needs of the task. This is particularly true in multi-national organizations in which participants are separated by physical barriers, language differences, and cultural differences. Under these circumstances lateral processes need to be designed. The lateral processes evolve as follows with increases in uncertainty.

4.1   *Direct Contact* between managers who share a problem. If a problem arises on the shop floor, the foreman can simply call the design engineer, and they can jointly agree upon a solution. From an information processing view, the joint decision prevents an upward referral and unloads the hierarchy.

4.2   *Liaison Roles*—when the volume of contacts between any two departments grows, it becomes economical to set up a specialized role to handle this communication. Liaison men are typical examples of specialized roles designed to facilitate communication between two interdependent departments and to bypass the long lines of communication involved in upward referral. Liaison roles arise at lower and middle levels of management.

4.3   *Task Forces*. Direct contact and liaison roles, like the integration mechanisms before them, have a limited range of usefulness. They work when two managers or functions are involved. When problems arise involving seven or eight departments, the decision making capacity of direct contacts is exceeded. Then these problems must be referred upward. For uncertain, interdependent tasks such situations arise frequently. Task forces are a form of horizontal contact which is designed for problems of multiple departments.

The task force is made up of representatives from each of the affected departments. Some are full-time members, others may be part-time. The task force is a temporary group. It exists only as long as the problem remains. When a solution is reached, each participant returns to his normal tasks.

To the extent that they are successful, task forces remove problems from higher levels of the hierarchy. The decisions are made at lower levels in the organization. In order to guarantee integration, a group problem solving approach is taken. Each affected subunit contributes a member and therefore provides the information necessary to judge the impact on all units.

4.4   *Teams*. The next extension is to incorporate the group decision process into the permanent decision processes. That is, as certain decisions consistently arise, the task forces become permanent. These groups are labeled teams. There are many design issues concerned in team decision making such as at what level do they operate, who participates, etc. [Galbraith, 1973, Chapters 6 and 7]. One design decision is particularly critical. This is the choice of leadership. Sometimes a problem exists largely in one department so that the department manager is the leader. Sometimes the leadership passes from one manager to another. As a new product moves to the market place, the leader of the new product team is first the technical manager followed by the production and then the marketing manager. The result is that if the team cannot reach a consensus decision and the leader decides, the goals of the leader are consistent with the goals of the organization for the decision in question. But quite often obvious leaders cannot be found. Another mechanism must be introduced.

4.5   *Integrating Roles*. The leadership issue is solved by creating a new role—an integrating role [Lawrence and Lorsch, 1967, Chapter 3]. These roles carry the labels of product managers, program managers, project managers, unit managers (hospitals), materials managers, etc. After the role is created, the design problem is to create enough power in the role to influence the decision process. These roles have power even when no one reports directly to them. They have some power because they report to the general manager. But if they are selected so as to be unbiased with respect to the groups they integrate and to have technical competence, they have expert power. They collect information and equalize power differences due to preferential access to knowledge and information. The power equalization increases trust and the quality of the joint decision process. But power equalization occurs only if the integrating role is staffed with someone who can exercise expert power in the form of persuasion and informal influences rather than exert the power of rank or authority.

4.6 *Managerial Linking Roles.* As tasks become more uncertain, it is more difficult to exercise expert power. The role must get more power of the formal authority type in order to be effective at coordinating the joint decisions which occur at lower levels of the organization. This position power changes the nature of the role which for lack of a better name is labeled a managerial linking role. It is not like the integrating role because it possesses formal position power but is different from line managerial roles in that participants do not report to the linking manager. The power is added by the following successive changes:

(a) The integrator receives approval power of budgets formulated in the departments to be integrated.

(b) The planning and budgeting process starts with the integrator making his initiation in budgeting legitimate.

(c) Linking manager receives the budget for the area of responsibility and buys resources from the specialist groups.

These mechanisms permit the managers to exercise influence even though no one works directly for him. The role is concerned with integration but exercises power through the formal power of the position. If this power is insufficient to integrate the subtasks and creation of self-contained groups is not feasible, there is one last step.

4.7 *Matrix Organization.* The last step is to create the dual authority relationship and the matrix organization [Galbraith, 1971]. At some point in the

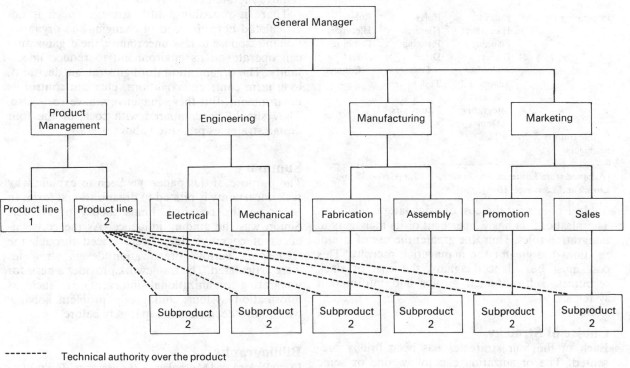

-------- Technical authority over the product

———— Formal authority over the product (in product organization these relationships may be reversed)

Figure 10.2   A pure matrix organization

organization some roles have two superiors. The design issue is to select the locus of these roles. The result is a balance of power between the managerial linking roles and the normal line organization roles. Figure 10.2 depicts the pure matrix design.

The work of Lawrence and Lorsch is highly consistent with the assertions concerning lateral relations [Lawrence and Lorsch, 1967, Lorsch and Lawrence, 1968]. They compared the types of lateral relations undertaken by the most successful firm in three different industries. Their data are summarized in Table 1. The plastics firm has the greatest rate of new product introduction (uncertainty) and the greatest utilization of lateral processes. The container firm was also very successful but utilized only standard practices because its information processing task is much less formidable. Thus, the greater the uncertainty the lower the level of decision making and the integration is maintained by lateral relations.

Table 1

	Plastics	Food	Container
% new products in last ten years	35%	20%	0%
Integrating Devices	Rules	Rules	Rules
	Hierarchy	Hierarchy	Hierarchy
	Planning	Planning	Planning
	Direct Contact	Direct Contact	Direct Contact
	Teams at 3 levels	Task forces	
	Integrating Dept.	Integrators	
% Integrators/ Managers	22%	17%	0%

[Adopted from Lawrence and Lorsch, 1967, pp. 86–138 and Lorsch and Lawrence, 1968].

Table 1 points out the cost of using lateral relations. The plastics firm has 22 per cent of its managers in integration roles. Thus, the greater the use of lateral relations the greater the managerial intensity. This cost must be balanced against the cost of slack resources, self-contained groups and information systems.

Choice of Strategy

Each of the four strategies has been briefly presented. The organization can follow one or some combination of several if it chooses. It will choose that strategy which has the least cost in its environmental context. [For an example, see Galbraith,

1970.] However, what may be lost in all of the explanations is that the four strategies are hypothesized to be an exhaustive set of alternatives. That is, if the organization is faced with greater uncertainty due to technological change, higher performance standards due to increased competition, or diversifies its product line to reduce dependence, the amount of information processing is increased. *The organization must adopt at least one of the four strategies when faced with greater uncertainty*. If it does not consciously choose one of the four, then the first, reduced performance standards, will happen automatically. The task information requirements and the capacity of the organization to process information are always matched. If the organization does not consciously match them, reduced performance through budget overruns, schedule overruns will occur in order to bring about equality. Thus the organization should be planned and designed simultaneously with the planning of the strategy and resource allocations. But if the strategy involves introducing new products, entering new markets, etc., then some provision for increased information must be made. Not to decide is to decide, and it is to decide upon slack resources as the strategy to remove hierarchical overload.

There is probably a fifth strategy which is not articulated here. Instead of changing the organization in response to task uncertainty, the organization can operate on its environment to reduce uncertainty. The organization through strategic decisions, long term contracts, coalitions, etc., can control its environment. But these maneuvers have costs also. They should be compared with costs of the four design strategies presented above.

Summary

The purpose of this paper has been to explain why task uncertainty is related to organizational form. In so doing the cognitive limits theory of Herbert Simon was the guiding influence. As the consequences of cognitive limits were traced through the framework various organization design strategies were articulated. The framework provides a basis for integrating organizational interventions, such as information systems and group problem solving, which have been treated separately before.

Bibliography

Cyert, Richard, and March, James, *The Behavioral Theory of the Firm*, Prentice-Hall, Englewood Cliffs, N. J., 1963.
Galbraith, Jay, 'Environmental and Technological Determinants of Organization Design: A Case Study' in Lawrence and Lorsch

(ed.) *Studies in Organization Design,* Richard D. Irwin Inc., Homewood, Ill., 1970.

Galbraith, Jay, 'Designing Matrix Organizations' *Business Horizons,* (Feb. 1971), pp 29–40.

Galbraith, Jay, *Organization Design,* Addison-Wesley Pub. Co., Reading, Mass., 1973.

Lawrence, Paul, and Lorsch, Jay, *Organization and Environment,* Division of Research, Harvard Business School, Boston, Mass., 1967.

Lorsch, Jay, and Lawrence, Paul, 'Environmental Factors and Organization Integration', Paper read at the Annual Meeting of the American Sociological Association, August 27, 1968, Boston, Mass.

March, James, and Simon, Herbert, *Organizations,* John Wiley & Sons, New York, N.Y., 1958.

Pounds, William, 'The Scheduling Environment' in Muth and Thompson (eds.) *Industrial Scheduling,* Prentice-Hall, Inc., Englewood Cliffs, N. J., 1963.

Simon, Herbert, *Models of Man,* John Wiley & Sons, New York, N.Y., 1957.

11 The role of information and control systems in the process of organizational renewal

J. F. den Hertog

If there is one characteristic that gives production organizations the chance to survive it is their capacity to deal with uncertainty. The organizational environment changes continuously and with an increasing pace. Changes in technologies, the economic climate and especially in the labour factor forces the organizations to adapt. Many of them, however, are playing a lost game. They have become what Skinner (1970, p. 61) calls 'anachronisms', because '. . . conventional methods of management and decision making are equally out of touch with the times'. The effects says Skinner, get different labels: 'blue collar blues', 'The productivity problem', or 'can we stay competitive?'. But the disease remains the same— poor adaptation to new values and expectations.

Organizational changes and renovations are so difficult and painful, because manufacturing executives in many industries permit themselves the luxury of what Skinner calls 'the piecemeal syndrome'. In his opinion a renovation and planning of the entire factory has to take place. Instead however, management tackles the organizational subsystems one by one.

Practical examples abound. For instance a production department is making large annual losses and not meeting its planning standards (Moors & Vansina, 1976). One staff department after the other tackles the problem. Successively the department is analyzed by quality controllers, machine and tool designers, planners and efficiency experts. Each defines the situation in his own terms. The effect is that after two years of staff interference productivity remains below the critical level and production targets still are not met. The man responsible for the department, the production head, thought that the situation was growing out of his control. 'He constantly had to attend meetings with the one or other staff group to discuss the problems. In the meantime he had no chance to find out for himself what was going wrong in his department' (Moors & Vansina, 1976, p. 19). The piecemeal syndrome creates inconsistencies or a lack of congruence in the subsystems, which damage the performance and utility of the whole. Changes in subsystems become, to use

Rhenman's (1973) terminology, *dissonant* (disturbing and wearing each other down) instead of *consonant* (reinforcing each other).

Two basic trends

Two basic tendencies may be distinguished in the way organizations try to adapt to growing environment turbulence (Emery, 1967).

The first approach is aimed at the reduction of uncertainty by extension and refinement of the information and control systems. Dealing with uncertainty in this respect means knowing more, knowing it faster and knowing it better. Economists, operation researchers have provided a growing number of new and refined accountancy and control techniques (Caplan, 1973, p. 21). The enormous possibilities of data processing technologies make this structuring of unstructured decision processes (Mintzberg *et al.*, 1976) a very powerful one.

The second tendency is quite different in appearance. It is aimed at the reduction of the necessity for control and information by making peripheral parts of the organization more flexible and autonomous. To get back the advantages of the small workshop in the factory, is one of the objectives of organizational renewal projects. The factory in the factory ('Job reform in Sweden', 1975) is the name given to this movement in Sweden. It represents a search for 'the human size', self-regulation of subsystems and a break with past traditions as they have developed since Weber, Taylor & Fayol. Important aspects of this tendency are: (1) the creation of lateral relations, (2) self regulation for peripheral units, (3) reduction of scale and (4) improvement of the quality of working life.

Placing the two trends alongside one another raises the question of consonance or dissonance. How far are the development of information and control systems and the search for more organic organizational structures reinforcing or defeating each other? From the point of view of the change agent this question can be translated into a consideration of the conditions under which information and control systems act as roadblocks or as roadbridges in the process of organizational renewal. That is the central question that is discussed in this article.

Time lags

The interface between information and control systems and the organizational environment becomes visible in two situations. In situation A (Figure 11.1) a new information system is being introduced. The organization (i.e. the rest of the subsystems) remains unchanged at the outset. So whilst the information and control system is moving, the organization stays behind. And the result of this time lag is dissonance.

For example in the spare-parts department of a large international manufacturer of scientific instruments a new computerized planning system was implemented in order to reduce delivery times. At the same time however, the employees were still being appraised on the basis of the service given to customers in cases of emergency. The effect was that the employees tried to beat the new system and the delivery times remained as long as before.

Situation B on the other hand, represents the renewal of a number of organizational subsystems, while the 'nervous system' stays behind. Rhenman

(1973, p. 25) shows how dissonance originates from such a situation: 'In 1966 the construction and building company (ABAB) reorganized production along divisional lines. In this way the company achieved better consonance with the market, which was making greater demands on specialized knowledge of the different products. During the first year, however, the company had big internal problems, partly because of difficulty in adapting the budget and cost accounting systems sufficiently quickly to the demands of the new organization'.

Unintended consequences

In both situations unintended consequences of new systems and procedures were overlooked. In the development of formal control systems, as in situation A, most attention is given to the direct measurement purposes of the system. 'These systems are intended to enhance an organization's ability to co-ordinate the actions of its members. Often, however, instead of increasing organizational control these systems reduce the amount of effective control that the organization exercises' (Cammann & Nadler, 1976, p. 65).

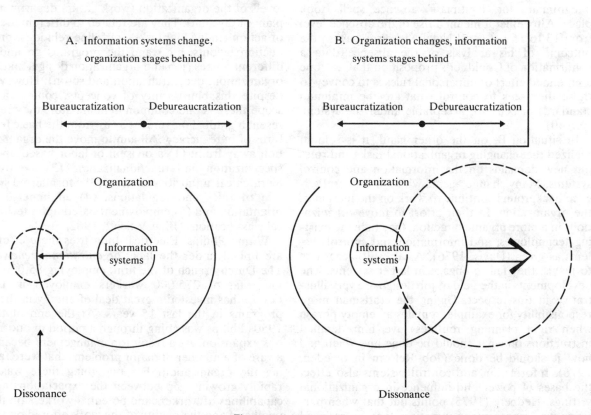

Figure 11.1 Time lags

Cammann & Nadler indicate that the problem often stems from the way in which managers *use* control systems. In the case where the control approach is very tightly structured, for instance, subordinates may begin to develop an attitude to performance in which 'doing well' means doing well on the performance measures rather than necessarily performing their jobs more effectively. This phenomenon is well illustrated by Nicholson's (1976) research in the field of absenteeism control. Some years ago the management of a large British factory became anxious about the rising cost of the company's sick-pay scheme and its increasing wage bill. The firm's average annual time lost due to absenteeism was running at about 13 per cent. In full agreement with the trade unions, management decided to tighten the control system. The objective was both to reduce the amount of absence time lost and the prevalence of absence spells. The 'clamp down' consisted of a systematic retrospective check on employee absence records. The procedure comprised a sequence of verbal warnings, then written warnings and finally dismissal. What was the effect? From an analysis of absence data it became very clear that a 'trade-off' of short for longer and of 'illegitimate' for 'legitimate' absence spells took place. Altogether it meant a rise of the absence level from 13 to 15 per cent! Nigel Nicholson saw in the outcome of his analysis of the absence data a confirmation of Gouldner's proposition that '. . . one unintended effect of impersonal rules is to convey to those they seek to control what are the minimum standards of behavior acceptable under the system' (p. 140).

In situation B, on the other hand, it is seldom realized that changing organizational tasks and roles put new demands on the information and control systems. Many change agents with a behavioral science background continue to work on the margin of the organization. In their effort to move organizations in a more organic direction, they take the existing technologies, and information and control systems as given (Davis, 1976). As a result, according to Davis, they fail to engage in larger systems. The developments in the field of job design are very illustrative in this respect. Giving the craftsman more responsibility for example, remains an empty phrase when rigid planning routines give him detailed instructions on what should be done and when and how it should be done (Job Reform in Sweden, 1976). Information and control systems also effect the bases of power and influence in organizational settings. Hedberg (1975) points out that when participative management practices are introduced without the replacement of the traditional management information systems the workers soon discover that instead of sharing the power of management, they share the lack of power in the traditional decision centres. The aim of this article is to illustrate the consequences of organizational renewal for the design of information and control systems. The illustrations will be taken from the experiences with organizational renewal programs of a large Dutch multi-national company.

Organizational renewal

Bureaucracy is, according to writers such as Perrow (1970), Galbraith (1973) and Blau & Scott (1962), the more predominant model on which our production organizations are built. Bureaucracies (Perrow, 1970, Galbraith, 1973) are well equipped to deal with routine problems in stable environments. Facing however, growing task uncertainty they have to invest in new strategies. As stated before, one of the main strategies is directed toward more flexible, organic and decentralized structures. In organized practice a diversity of programs aimed at the renewal of traditional structures and procedures can be observed. These programs take place at different levels of the organization (work group, department, plant or division). They are related to different areas of action (individual tasks, staff–line relations, production layouts, etc.) and the programs go under different names (job and organization design, matrix organization, decentralization and so on). However despite this pluriformity of concepts, content and scope there is one common denominator: they represent a gradual movement away from the basic features of bureaucracy. All aim to move the organization away from: (1) a division of labor based upon specialization and functionalization, (2) a strong hierarchical authority structure, (3) a formalized system of rules and regulations, (4) an impersonal orientation and (5) employment based upon technical classifications (Blau & Scott, 1962, p. 32).

Within Philips' Electrical Industries these efforts are linked under the label *organizational renewal*. The Dutch branch of the firm, employing 85,000 of the total of 375,000 workers employed in the Group, has invested a great deal of energy in these programs in the last 15 years. At the end of the 1950s Philips was going through a period of enormous expansion. As a result top management became aware of a number of major problems that were facing the organization. For one thing there was a rapidly growing gap between the expectations and capabilities of workers and potential workers on the one hand and the quality of the work offered on the other. This created a problem in attracting and retaining workers (Van der Graaf, 1964). At the same time, however, it became clear that the traditional production systems, and hierarchical and staff–line relations were too rigid to cope with the accelerating succession of new processes and products. As a result an increasing number of experimental field projects were started, of which those in the field of job design (or *work structuring* as it is called in the company) have the longest history. Most of the approximately 60 projects undertaken to date have been situated at the shop floor level. They have involved a number of different elements such as job enrichment, job enlargement, job rotation, the creation of small relatively autonomous product groups, shortening of the hierarchy and work consultation between workers and supervisors.

A good illustration of the content of such a project is provided by the production of 'special miniatures', small bulbs made for special purposes (dashboards, telephones, etc.) in fairly small batches. The production process is partly automated, but the finishing process is done manually by female workers. The department had a lot of problems. The precalculated

production norms were not being achieved, the proportion of rejects was high and the production process as a whole was very hard to control. The women showed very little interest in the (short-cycled) work itself and in the results of their units. In consultation with representatives of the female workers and the supervisors the decision was made to experiment with a new work design. The most important elements of the new work systems were the formation of small groups (four instead of 14 workers) with every woman performing four operations instead of one, job rotation, a short line with no foreman or 'assistant fore(wo)man' and a consequent delegation of the foreman's duties, group consultation and quick feedback. Both in the economic and the social sense this program was a success.

The proportion of rejects dropped from 9 to 5 per cent and productivity rose to 10 per cent above the precalculated norms. None of the workers was willing to go back to the old lines, and women working a short distance from the experimental groups asked management if they could be allowed to join the experiment.

Another stream of projects were located at higher

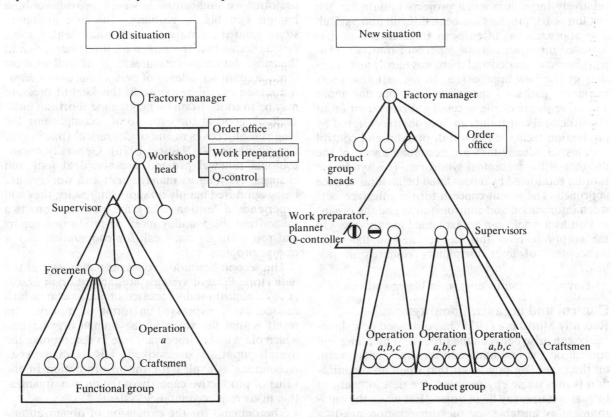

Figure 11.2 Towards a new organizational shop structure

levels in the organization. They concern the development of more or less selfsustaining production units. The basic idea was that the staff and the line functions should be integrated in such a way that production management can maintain the operation of a unit within a time span of about two months. Staff structures were decentralized and the organization changed from a process to a product basis. For example in one large tool factory, employing more than 600 workers, the differentiation on the basis of operations was left but a number of product-groups were created, each having its own management team composed of supervisors and staff specialists (Figure 11.2).

On the corporate level a very general policy concerning organizational renewal has been formulated and stimulated. Local management however remains responsible for the initiation, steering and elaboration of the concept of projects. Corporate staff departments play a supportive role by offering research and consultancy capacity.

From time to time an assessment is made of the state of the art. Recent studies (Den Hertog 1975, Den Hertog & DeVries, 1977) show that despite the relatively large number of projects initiated in the last ten years, progress has been difficult and painful. The approach has often been fragmented and has focussed on rather narrow aspects of the task. Projects became isolated and there was hardly any diffusion of the new approaches. In the last few years managers and staff specialists have become more and more aware of the necessity to pay attention to the structural constraints and possibilities offered by production technology and information and control systems. Gradually they are becoming aware of the dangers of the piecemeal syndrome. This syndrome is often reinforced by a one-sided behavioral science approach. The recent concern for the interface between information and control system and the organization as a whole can be explained in this way. On the corporate level this has resulted in the commencement of inter-disciplinary research in this field.

Control and organizational renewal

Recently Mintzberg (1976) has discussed how dissonance can arise between the process of planning and control on the one hand and creative management on the other. He points out that when an organization is in a stable environment, the development of formal systems may be in order. 'But when the environment is unstable, or the organization needs a creative strategy, then strategic planning may not be the best approach to strategy formulation, and planners have no business pushing the organization to use it' (p. 58). Similarly Lawler & Rhode (1976) illustrate how formal control systems can reinforce rigid bureaucratic behavior.

In examining the latent or manifest dissonance between information and control systems and creative management effort which strives to go beyond the bureaucratic model, three topics will be considered: (1) the role of the information and control systems in performance appraisal, (2) the information and control technology and (3) the control of the design and use of the information and control systems.

The role of information and control systems in performance appraisal

Control systems strongly influence the way members of organizations direct their energy on the job. The performance indicators provide organizational visibility: they make clear which kind of behavior is reinforced or is to be avoided. Members are more likely to put time and effort into those areas covered by the system (Cammann & Nadler, 1976). Most performance indicators however provide only a limited and biased visibility. The first limitation stems from the time span of measurement. Caplan (1973) states that the return on investment, one of the most dominant measures, '. . . as well as most other accounting indexes of performance—are *short run* measures, the response of this kind of pressure may be to concentrate on making the short run indexes look good at the expense of accomplishing the long run objectives of the organization' (p. 29) (see also Cammann & Nadler, 1976). Generally organizational renewal projects are aimed at long run changes. As long as management and workers are being appraised mainly on short run results, they will experience a tension. They are pushed from two sides: from the Monday morning production report and top management's call for cooperation in the change projects.

The second limitation concerns the *content* of the indicators. Present systems are, according to Likert (1967), almost totally focussed on parameters which can be easily expressed in terms of money. The result is that the value of the human organization which plays a very important role in determining the overall input, is overlooked. His Human Asset Accounting is a plea for the incorporation of the value of productive capacity of the human organization in current accountancy systems.

The demand for the expansion of organizational visibility also originates from the social environment.

More and more societal groups have come to the unpleasant realization that material progress (or economical well-being) does not necessarily trigger improvement in individual well-being (Strumpel, 1976). Accordingly they try to influence the goals of the organization, trying to place greater emphasis on the Quality as well as the Quantity of Working Life. The growth of the social indicators school is a result of this development. Social indicators are statistics, statistical series and all other forms of evidence that enable us to assess where we stand and where we are going with respect to our values and goals and to evaluate specific programs and determine their impact (Bauer, 1966). At this moment a number of researchers are trying to operationalize 'those vague social variables' in terms of money. Most recent studies deal with the more tangible variables such as absenteeism, days lost by strikes (Macy & Mirvis, 1967), labor turnover and test scores (Arends, 1974), and employee attitudes (Mirvis & Lawler, 1976). As a start for the development of social indicators these studies are very important. However, they are restricted to the obvious variables. What is needed right now is a set of indicators telling us how flexible the organization is in adapting to new environmental values, new technologies and the new categories of employees. Organizational change has to be appraised according to the goals of change.

Information and control technology

The refinement and extension of information and control systems has become a very powerful tendency in our organizations. It is very obvious that this process has been heavily reinforced by the pervasive development of computer technology. New information technologies seem to offer almost unlimited possibilities: (1) a fast growing number of applications, (2) a growing storage capacity of memories, which continue to fall in price, (3) the possibilities offered by data communication, (4) increased speed of processing and (5) the opportunities created by the integration of data bases.

Bureaucratization

However the technological optimism, which seems characteristic of the first phase in each technological renewal (Hedberg & Mumford, 1975), is now fading. In a technological sense, opportunities may be unlimited, but in a human sense, more and more constraints appear above the surface.

In this respect Tomeski and Lazarus (1975) talk of the *computer crisis* created by neglecting the human consequences of the system. They suggest that the problems of introducing automated information systems can be traced to what they call *Hardware Hypnosis*. This, they say, is what you have when people gaze blindly at technological opportunities and do not consider the social or organizational consequences which in real life strictly limit the effectiveness of a system.

'Human not technical problems are the major obstacles to more effective computer applications. Yet, it is the human problems that tend to be neglected. Because the computer, one of the foremost technological developments of our time, has often been used with little sensitivity to its impacts on people, it has been resisted by many whose cooperation is needed to realize the full benefits that computerizing can bring' (Tomeski & Lazarus, 1975). Hedberg & Mumford (1975) come to the same conclusion. It is their opinion that in most cases, systems are not built upon the organizational worlds of the workers and management who use the system, but upon the organizational world of the computer specialist. The result can be, in their terms, a non viable system, a system which cannot survive or which will only survive in a state of instability (1975, p. 35). In the discussion of this subject (see Hedberg & Mumford, 1975; Mumford, 1976; Tomeski & Lazarus, 1975; Withington, 1969; Galbraith, 1973) a number of common trends connected with the implementation of computerized information and control systems can be observed: (1) centralization of authority, (2) formalization and standardization of procedures and rules and (3) specialization and division of labor along functional lines. They represent a move in the direction of bureaucratization. Or in Hedberg's words (1975, p. 214) the accentuation of the trend: '. . . to separate the moment in time, when decisions are made about how decisions should be made, and the later moments when decisions are made in accordance with pre-determined rules'.

Illustrative of the phenomenon of hardware hypnosis is the fact that empirical research into the social and organization consequences of information and control systems is almost lacking. One of the few exceptions is the work of Whisler (1970). His research in 23 insurance companies seems to confirm the basic options mentioned above—these systems help to lubricate the salience of power of the vertical dimensions of the organization. They move in the opposite direction to organizational renewal programs which aim at decentralization, deverticalization and despecialization.

A number of writers (Van Berkel, 1976; Burnett & Nolan, 1975) point out that the degree of possible decentralization depends to a large extent upon the chosen computer configuration (Figure 11.3). Large

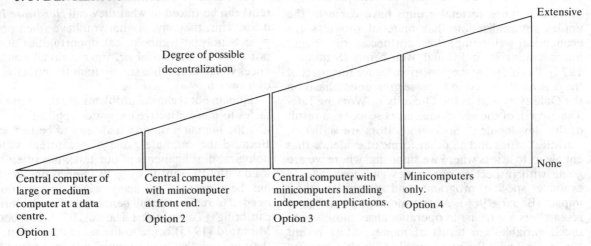

Figure 11.3   Computer configuration and decentralization (Burnett and Nolan, 1975)

central computers offer the least opportunity for decentralization and mini-computers the greatest opportunity. Indeed small computers are becoming popular because they seem to leave more room for self-regulation by peripheral units and do not demand such rigid procedures (Van Berkel, 1976; Burnett & Nolan, 1975). Producers of small computers, like Philips and Data SAAB, even use these issues in their advertisements as sales arguments (den Hertog, 1977).

Decision control

Information and control systems are outcomes of organizational choices: choices with regard to form and content and the way they are used. The question therefore arises as to upon which implicit or explicit organizational and behavioral models these choices are based. Caplan (1973) states that the fact that management accountants have been paying little attention to the behavioral consequences of accountancy originates from the implicit model of human behavior they have adopted.

This behavioral model seems to have been strongly influenced by behavioral assumptions from related fields, primarily the economic theory of the firm, scientific management and 'early principles of management' (p. 24).

We find the same conclusion in Mumford (1974), writing about designers of computerized systems. She argues that systems are designed in terms of a vision of man and of man's needs and abilities which is derived from the systems designer's own values, training and experience. On the basis of a survey,

she concludes: '. . . that systems designers use a restricted Theory X type model of man when designing computer systems' (p. 48) . . . 'they see their principle work activities as increasing efficiency through streamlining of procedures and providing better information. They do not appear to appreciate the potential of the computer technology for improving the overall quality of working life. They do not design their systems to facilitate good human relationships' (p. 46).

At the same time it is becoming clear that one of the most essential conditions for participative decision-making is that the right information reaches the right places. The fact of being badly informed proved to be one of the biggest handicaps in the development of work consultation (Van der Bruggen & Den Hertog, 1976; Koopman & Drenth, 1977). Besides, most representative studies in the field of job design stress the need for adequate feed back systems for the self-regulating units (Herzberg, 1974: Job Reform in Sweden, 1975; Den Hertog, 1975; Thorsrud, 1972). In organizational renewal programs the organizational participants need information for self control rather than for control by others. However in the light of the foregoing it is not surprising that a researcher such as Hedberg (1975) found only very few cases in which computerized information and control systems were used to facilitate participative management practices. The main problem seems to be the balancing of values of different groups and disciplines within the organization in order to foster overall organizational health, or in Skinner's words, to escape the piecemeal syndrome.

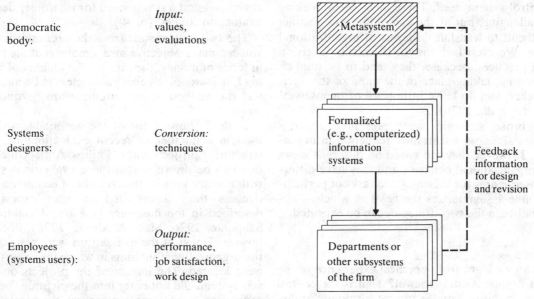

Figure 11.4   A metasystem—a system for systems design (Hedberg, 1975)

Hedberg & Mumford (1975) point out that for this purpose we have to concentrate on the design process. However, they state, that user participation in the design phase is not enough. They have evidence that much effort in this field has not been successful, because of the greater expert power on the side of the system designers. Hedberg & Mum-ford stress that the balancing of values and the evaluations of what has been achieved has to take place at the *meta-level*. Different groups in the organization have to participate in the design of the meta-system, which controls the design and use of the system (Figure 11.4). Mintzberg *et al.* (1976) call this process *decision control*: decision making about

Table 1   Fields of dissonance

Field	Organization renewal	Informational and control systems
Model of man	Theory Y	Theory X
Objective	Dealing with uncertainty	Dealing with uncertainty
Strategy	Investment in intra-organizational flexibility	Investment in extension and refinement of control systems
Indicators	Incorporation of environmental values; social and economic, qualitative and quantitative; long-run objectives	Economic, in quantitative terms only; short-run measures
Base decision making	Consensus (effectiveness)	Programmed (efficiency)
Target groups' information systems	Broad (management and workers)	Professionals and management
Change strategy	Participative, learning	Directive, appraising
Organizational implications	Decentralization Self-regulation Product/client orientation Despecialization Delegation Reduction in scale Shift of staff functions to the line organization	Centralization Regulation Functional orientation Specialization Upward allocation of control Scale enlargement Strengthening of staff functions

the control system itself. These ideas seem evoking and challenging, but at the same time too abstract and difficult to translate in terms of organizational practice. We even lack insight of existing decision control practices, because 'they tend to be implicit and informal, taking place in the mind of the decision maker, and do leave little trace of themselves' (Mintzberg et al., 1976).

Two broad strategies were presented above—strategies aimed at uncertainty reduction in organization. However they are based on different views about organizational behavior and they have different consequences for the roles and tasks of participants. Table 1 summarizes the fields in which dissonance between the two strategies can be expected.

Practice

What can we learn from practical experience in the field or organizational renewal? That is the central question in this section. Searching for points of dissonance and consonance, we have collated a number of examples of projects in which information and accountancy systems played a specific role.

Assessing QWL experiments

Cummings & Salipante (1976) point out that the improvement of working life will depend solely on intuition and chance if we do not develop 'research-based strategies'. They continue: 'The poor design of most field experimental studies in the review suggest a strong need for rigorously designed evaluation studies' (p. 40).

The two writers start from the premise that once you can make objective measurements of the pay off in terms of money, the case for the Quality of Working Life is won. However parameters to be measured and the method of measurement are beyond their scope.

Table 2 shows a list of the economic yardsticks used in a number of recent evaluations of work-structuring projects within Philips. A first conclusion that can be drawn is that these evaluations started with a wider view of the concept of economic effectiveness than is reflected in most experiments described in the literature (see also Cummings & Salipante, 1976; Macy & Mirvis, 1976). Secondly, however, most of the evaluations were restricted to the organizational subunits in which the experiments were located. The impact of the projects on other sub-systems did not enter into the picture. The third conclusion is that most measures were related to those short-run parameters that are used in the daily practice of performance appraisal. In one plant, for instance, a work structuring project was evaluated using popular economic criteria such as absenteeism, labor turnover, performance level, reject rate, and waiting time. While the results of an attitude survey were quite positive, it was shown that, economically speaking, the project was neither a success nor a failure. The enthusiasm of the department head, who was under heavy pressure to reduce the factory

Table 2 Economic evaluation of work-structuring projects

Project	A	B	C	D	E	F	G	H
Labour turnover	X	X	X	X	X		X	
Absenteeism	X	X	X	X				
Intial training	X				X	X	X	
Balancing	X		X					
Waiting time			X	X		X		
Pre/post calculation of hours		X		X				
Underutilization			X					
Productivity (units/hour)	X				X	X	X	
Delivery times		X			X			
Cost supervisory personnel	X		X					X
Floorspace	X		X	X				X
Machines and tools	X	X	X			X		
Procurement			X					
Stocks			X					X
Reject rate	X	X	X		X		X	X
Repair of rejects		X	X					X
Tool maintenance		X						
Hours consultation			X	X				

Design group		Order office		Supervisor	Work groups	Q control	Client
Design of tools and machines	Drawing	Settles priority, price and scheduling	Work prepa-ration	Task allocation	Operations	Check	Implementation of product

Figure 11.5 Traditional flow in a workshop

price of the product, slowly faded away. Two years later however, it appeared that the economic pay off was not to be found within the production center itself, but in the central sales office (located 200 km from the plant). Sales management were very positive about the flexible way in which production was reacting to changes in planning and in technical specifications of the product. It enabled them to reduce stock and more adequately meet the specific demands of their customers. This example illustrates the restricted scope of many evaluations or organizational change projects. And, as a result, often very little is assessed about the final goals of the project.

Production control

The development of a 'professional industry' and the mechanization of the production process have given the mechanical workshops an important position within Philips. About 7,000–8,000 craftsmen work in this sector in the Dutch organization. However the management of these workshops, which are located in the various divisions, is facing a range of problems. The workshops are generally the last link in the chain of a development process, which means that they have to cope with cumulative delays in the preceding phases. Flexibility and short delivery times are therefore of primary importance. Other problems are related to the traditional culture in the workshops. On the one hand they are characterized by ingenious systems for optimizing the use of labour and machine capacity. On the other hand they employ very well-trained and critical craftsmen—craftsmen who feel undervalued having no real 'say' (Den Hertog, 1975). In the hope of solving those problems a number of organizational renewal projects have been started in this sector with the aim of improving the work situation and creating greater organizational flexibility. Elements of these projects are: (1) an integration of function (such as drilling, milling and fitting), (2) a delegation of tasks (work preparation, allocation of tasks, quality control), and (3) the creation of autonomous workgroups.

However practically at the same time new computerized production control systems are being introduced with the aim of optimizing the use of labor and machine capacity on the basis of product specifications and the priorities of the client. Figure 11.5 illustrates the traditional workflow in a workshop. The new systems are now trying to plan the operations of the workshops, control the progress of work and provide a basis for performance appraisal. It should be noted that the computerized control systems differ between workshops. Some operate on a real-time basis; others via periodic reviews. The planning can be based on products, projects or on operations and a system can aim to regulate the workflow of a single workshop or a group of workshops. Also there are remarkable differences in the way in which the systems are being used. In one workshop the system is used as a direct basis for programmed decision making: it states who has to do what and when. In another workshop however, the system is seen as only giving rough guidelines for emergencies often create a need for overruling the planning.

In Table 3 we have tried to give an impression of the impact of the production control systems on the organization in those workshops where organizational change programs were in progress. It is based on a number of unstructured interviews with supervisors, planners, craftsmen and, in some cases, with customers.

Although we realize that it is dangerous to make generalizations on the basis of a small explorative study, we shall try nevertheless to extract the most important observations:

planning on the basis of operations reinforces functional specialization and reduces the room for handling a larger and more meaningful part of the product;
calculation of the efficiency of individual craftsmen can be an important barrier to group formation: workers remain each other's competitors;
planning on the basis of operations and a strictly

Table 3 Production control: five cases

The system	A	B	C	D	E
Scope	Workshop (N=80)	Workshop (N=40)	Workshop (N=250)	Three autonomous groups (N=30)	Four workshops (N=400)
Planning per	Operation	Operation	Operation and product	Product	Operation
Pre/postcalculation of Hours	Individual	Individual	Group	Individual	Individual
Procedures	Work preparator within the workshop settles with the client price and priority and does scheduling	As in A	Each product group has its own work preparator, who together with the supervisor settles price and priority with the client. Scheduling is also done by him. Planning and scheduling are regularly discussed in work consultation	Scheduling, pricing and settlement of priority is done by the order office outside the workshop. One of the craftsmen in every group acts as a liaison	Before the supervisors had an important say in the planning procedure. This task has shifted for an important part to the central workshop planners and work preparators
Participants in design process	Management and Specialists	Management and a representative group	Management and representative groups	Management and specialists	(Top) management and specialists
Effects	The workshop works for a large R & D department. The workers reacted negatively: they had less direct contacts with clients and designers and other specialists; they had to deal with more paperwork and the system reinforced specialization	The introduction of the new system and the forming of autonomous groups take place at the same time. It was decided to place the system in the cupboard; it did not fit in with the new organization	Before the change project was started, workers made it very clear that for them the system of individual efficiency calculation was an important roadblock to work as a group. When a new specially designed group calculation was introduced efficiency showed a remarkable drop. At first supervisors were complaining that they had lost a control tool. Later on when the groups became more cohesive and group norms developed, efficiency exceeded the original level	In the workshop (N = 250) 3 autonomous groups were formed, aimed at the production of complete products. The centralized systems did not fit in with this change. Together with the planning office an interface was created to make it possible to plan on products instead of on operations and to give the group an adequate feed back system. It stayed unclear for the workers what the function was of the individual calculations in the new set up	Order intake and scheduling in the new system shifted from the supervisors task to a central function in each workshop. Task allocation too was no longer their responsibility but was derived from computer lists. The supervisors experienced this change as a hollowing out of their jobs. The workers reacted positively to the replacement of personal control by remote control in task allocation. The reinforcement of specialization however was seen as a negative aspect

formal division between order intake and work preparation on the one hand and the work itself on the other hand isolates the craftsman from the designer, the customer and other specialists;

the scope of the system (covering one or more than one workshop) has a fairly considerable influence on the scope for self-regulation within groups;

it is not just the system itself that plays an important role; it is also how it is used, e.g. the way in which workers and supervisors can participate in decision-making with regard to the input and output of the system and the way control tasks are allocated;

in some situations the workers prefer remote control of the system to personal control by supervisors when tasks are allocated or progress reviewed;

the most elaborated and detailed systems are to be found in areas where time, cost and performance are most easily measured; as a result these areas are given most of the attention in times of pressure. For instance, one of the workshops heads told us: 'In our workshop almost everything can be expressed in terms of 1/10 of per cents. In periods when planning and budgets of the organization as a whole are becoming tight, everybody is looking to my department, because our figures are the most detailed and reliable. The design groups, which account for 50 per cent of the total budget and which determine about 60 per cent of the schedules receive far less attention'.

So far this pilot study has illustrated the danger of dissonance between ongoing organizational renewal programs and the development of formal information and control systems. The basic observation however is that in the design of these systems there are areas of choice, the exercising of which have more or less room for the development of more organic production organizations. Workers *can* participate in the planning process, a system *can* be designed for autonomous groups, individual performance appraisal *can* be replaced by group appraisal and bureaucratic procedures *can* be resimplified. If these latter choices are exercised the organization is no longer viewed as a set of separate sub-systems, but as an organic whole.

The product team

In the consumer sector of the business life cycles of products and processes are becoming shorter and shorter. Management has to respond to these rapid changes and one form of response is the introduction of *product teams*. Within the plants of a division one manager is given the responsibility for the design of the product and the process and also for the production of a specific product family. His product team is composed of people from different staff and line departments: product design, engineering, production materials management, quality control and so on. The product team thus operates as a matrix structure. The coordination problem is solved by creating, using Galbraith's (1973) terms, self sustaining units and lateral relations. Almost at the same time, however, decisions have been made at the division level to introduce new and complex materials management systems. For the control of the material flow is one of the basic conditions for a good overall performance and high priority has therefore been given to the development of materials management systems by the central information and automation department. Emphasis is placed on the design of global systems which regulate the flow of raw materials, parts and finished products from a central point in the product division.

Like most multinational companies Philips uses pilot plants to try out new technologies, control systems and procedures. As a result dissonance between the information and control systems and the new organizational approaches became clearly visible at an earlier moment than it otherwise might. In the case of the product teams and the computerized materials management systems, there were two important consequences. First the team loses much of its autonomy with regard to its purchase and stock policy. A large number of decisions shift to a higher level in the organization. In some cases the position of materials manager is created on a central level and this manager reports directly to division management rather than to plant management. As a result the product team becomes more dependent upon other production centers and upon central staff departments. Second, staff functions become more influential in the development and maintenance of the system. Thereby the product group becomes burdened with more and more complex new procedures and rules.

Discussion

Information and control systems can form difficult roadblocks in organizational renewal projects. One of the sources of dissonance stems from their role as appraisal systems. Change projects aimed at long-run goals are often evaluated by short-run yardsticks. The less available social indicators (and often too the less readily available economic indicators) are not considered in the decision-making process.

A second source of dissonance results from the unintended consequences which the information and control systems can have for the tasks and the roles of participants or groups of participants. Frequently the information and control systems move the organization in the direction of further bureaucratization, by evoking centralization, specialization, standardization and formalization both on plant and departmental as well as on individual level. Finally dissonance can arise from the bad fit between the information offered and the information which is needed for groups and individuals to steer their own operations.

Roadbridge

At the same time however, it has become clear that it does not make sense to talk about a *technological determinism* in this context. 'They can be designed in a manner which successfully meets the needs of groups which will operate them and use the data outputs from them' (Mumford, 1974, p. 40).

Presently few attempts have been made to relate information and control systems to efforts to design more organic organizational forms. In Table 2 we referred to two cases in which such systems were influenced by an overall redesign of the organization. Hedberg (1975) provided another example by describing an on line real time system that had been implemented in Volvo's Kalmar Plant. This system had been designed to facilitate self-regulation by autonomous production groups.

Recent publications stress that the redesign of information and control systems is in fact one of the basic conditions for changes towards deverticalization and group autonomy. Gordon & Miller (1976), and also Reimann & Negandhi (1975), point out that administrative control systems, which make it possible for top management to monitor the performance of subunits, are prerequisite for decentralization: 'Decentralized firms must carefully consider how they will allocate and control their resources among the divisions so that the maximum return is achieved without negating the potential motivational benefits to be derived from decentralization' (Gordon & Miller, 1976, p. 62). To reach this condition, Gordon and Miller continue, the accountancy system itself must become decentralized. The report on the 500 Swedish job reform projects (Job Reform in Sweden, 1975) make a similar point with regard to formal planning systems: '. . . a large part of the actual detailed planning has by itself become decentralized to a level near the actual manufacturing' (p. 107). The same study shows that this process calls for a *resimplification* of the control apparatus. 'The

central idea is that the less important administrative tasks are pushed down in the organization and taken care on the level where they belong. The rest of the administrative resources can be used to propel the operation ahead—that is, concentrated on important strategic and economic factors rather than being dissipated in handling small matters. But a resimplification of the administrative system does not mean a return to a more primitive level. It means that we agree to learn from our mistakes, that there is a better understanding of the need to adapt the models to reality, that there is a recognized limit to our ability to administer, and, finally, that it is better to concentrate our energy in areas where administrative efforts can produce the best results'. (Job Reform in Sweden, 1975, p. 111).

The choice and allocation of computer configurations also plays an important role. Burnett & Nolan (1975) point to the fact that the degree of autonomy of peripheral units is strongly dependent upon the room they have to control the computer system itself. In their opinion networks of mini computers provide a better basis for decentralization than large or medium-sized central systems. The relevance of the allocation of computer systems is also stressed in a recent study by Blau *et al.* (1976).

Strategy of change

Starting from the observation that dissonance and consonance are outcomes or organizational choices emphasizes the issue of strategy. In other words how do organizations escape from the piecemeal syndrome in the design and use of information and control systems? Cammann & Nadler (1976) point out that this effort requires an *informed choice*: 'A control system and the way that it is used constitutes a powerful tool for influencing the behavior of individuals in organizations. Just as the manager needs to make a careful and informed choice among control strategies the organization needs to be conscious of the alternative approaches to designing and using control systems. Becoming aware of the potential effect of control systems and of the great importance of the process of control—as opposed to technology of control—is central to making an organization and its people more productive and effective'.

However at the present time we have very little empirical data on which such informed choices can be based. Most studies in the field of organizational renewal and job design have given little attention to information and control systems and studies of information and control systems have tended to ignore their social and organizational implications.

Hence if we cannot, as yet, base our choices on

Table 4 Checklist for an informed choice

1.	*What effects do the systems have on the decision structure of the organization?*
1.1	Which decisions shift to a higher level and which to a lower?
1.2	Can decision procedures be made more visible and more discussible by the system?
1.3	To what level (upwards and downwards) in the organization is the information accessible and intelligible?
1.4	Is the period within which decisions are made shortened or lengthened?
1.5	Does the system increase or reduce ability to test policy (and does it reduce top management's room to manoeuvre)?
2.	*What consequences do the systems have to the job structure of employees?*
2.1	What room does the system leave for the division and/or integration of jobs at the bottom?
2.2	What consequences has the system for the jobs within data-processing groups (accounting, production office)?
2.3	Does automation impoverish or enrich the pattern of contacts between operatives on one hand and customers and ancillary services on the other?
2.4	To what extent does the system lead to streamlining or extension of formal procedures and the associated paperwork?
2.5	In organization renewal the aim is generally to create new organizational units (product or article groups, autonomous groups, project groups). Good feedback to the independent operation of these groups is of primary importance. Does the system satisfy the specific needs of these new units with regard to information?
3.	*How do the relations between line and staff services alter under the influence of the system?*
3.1	Does the system create a need for a new staff function within or outside the line organization?
3.2	To what extent do control functions which formerly came under the staff shift to the line (and vice versa)?
3.3	Can underlying conflicts between departments be expected to emerge into the daylight?
4.	*What are the consequences for present and future staffing?*
4.1	Will the requirements which the performance of most employees involved has to satisfy be stiffened or slackened?
4.2	Are there employees who will simply not fit into the new set-up?
4.3	Will its introduction create a need to bring in employees with clearly different capacities and experience?
4.4	Will career prospects change for many employees?
4.5	Will introduction of the system give rise to new questions of training?
5.	*How is the project set up?*
5.1	Is there a key manager responsible for the assignment and authorization of the final proposal?
5.2	Is there a special project structure, involving a steering group and task forces?
5.3	How are these groups composed?
5.4	Is the project planned in clear phases (from problem recognition to implementation and up-dating?).
5.5	How and to what extent do workers of different levels and functions participate in the design process?
5.6	How are workers informed about the project?
5.7	What is the role of representative bodies like workers councils and unions?
5.8	Are special training courses set up?
5.9	Will the project be evaluated?

empirical evidence, it is necessary to ensure that a number of important questions are at least considered. Such questions should focus attention on the most relevant differences between design alternatives, emphasizing in the process, both the choices available and their consequences for organizational functioning. The checklist presented in Table 4 can be a useful tool in this respect.

The last section of the checklist focuses on planning the design and implementation of systems. It deals with what Starbuck (1975) has called 'playing the metagame'. A recent evaluation study (Betlem, 1977) of the implementation of an on-line production steering system within one Philips' division has demonstrated that this is one of the most crucial areas on which future research has to focus. How should the consultation process between designers and users be conducted? How should users, management and system specialists be involved in the design process? And how should this involvement be structured? Also it needs to be realised that the fostering of informed choice and more participative approaches to design is not a matter of structure alone. It also calls for cultural changes, changes in attitudes and patterns of reasoning.

One of the big challenges is the abandonment of the *billiards model* which is so pervasive in thinking about organizational control. Do we have a problem with absenteeism? Then build a registration system and punish the offenders! Are employees arriving late every morning? Then buy yourself a time clock! Is your planning in a mess? Then get a computerized system! 'Push your cue in the right direction, give the right siding and you're sure to score a cannon'. Or are you? So many system designers are blind to the unintended consequences of such strategies. They ignore the fact that subordinates may themselves devote a great deal of effort to 'game playing' or 'beating the system'. They forget that the transfer of information and the implementation of new systems are forms of behavior—behavior on a bumpy billiard table with an indefinite number of cushions and balls of living material.

The creation of multidisciplinary design teams and the use of the behavioral sciences in the training of accountants, system analysts and industrial engineers may be ways of making designers more sensitive to unintended behavioral consequences. But many users also lack the relevant sensitivity. Mumford (1974, p. 49) found that 'the system designers in our sample saw their users as narrow and conservative, perhaps because these users were too passive and noninitiating'. This is an area in which experiences and theories about planned organizational change and organizational development can be very useful (see also Galbraith, 1973). The organization has to learn to renovate itself, by learning from its own actions. One precondition, however, is a climate in which successes and failures can be openly discussed.

References

Arends, G., *Labour Turnover, Summary of Findings in the Philips-Concern* (Eindhoven: Philips, 1974).

Bauer, R. A., *Social Indicators* (Cambridge: The M.I.T. Press, 1966).

Berkel, P. L. M. van, Computers leiden niet alleen tot verhoogde Efficiency, maar eveneens tot Taakverrijking, *Financieel Dagblad*, (1976).

Betlem, H. Q., *De Beteueis van Database met Online-Faciliteiten voor de Organisatie van de Productie Besturing* (Eindhoven: Philips, 1977).

Blau, P. M. & Scott, W. R., *Formal Organizations* (San Francisco: Chandler, 1962).

Blau, P. M., McHugh Falbe, C., McKinley, W. & Tracy, Ph. K., Technology and Organization in manufacturing, *Administrative Science Quarterly* (Vol. 21, no. 1, 1976), pp. 20–40.

Bruggen, A. L. A. van der & Den Hertog, J. F., Werkoverleg op Afdelingsnivo, *Mens en Onderneming* (Vol. 30, no. 4, 1976), pp. 334–353.

Burnett, G. J. & Nolan, R. L., At Last, Major Roles for Minicomputers, *Harvard Business Review* (Vol. 53, no. 2, 1975), pp. 148–156.

Cammann, C. & Nadler, D. A., Fit Control Systems to your Managerial Style, *Harvard Business Review* (Vol. 54, no. 1, 1976), pp. 65–72.

Caplan, E. H., The Behavioral Implications of Management Accounting, *Management International Review* (nos. 2–3, 1973), pp. 21–49.

Cummings, T. G. & Salipante, P. F., The Development of Research based Strategies for Improving the Quality of Working Life. In: Warr, P., (ed.) *Personal Goals and Work Design* (London: Wiley & Sons, 1976).

Davis, L. E., Current Developments in Job Design. In: Warr, P. (ed.), *Personal Goals and Work Design* (London: Wiley & Sons, 1976).

Emery, F. E., The Next Thirty Years: Concepts, Methods and Anticipations, *Human Relations* (Vol. 20, no. 3, 1967), pp. 199–237.

Galbraith, J., *Designing Complex Organizations* (London: Addison-Wesley Publ. Co., 1973).

Gordon, L. A. & Miller, D., A Contingency Framework for the Design of Accounting Information Systems, *Accounting Organizations and Society* (Vol. 1, no. 1, 1976), pp. 56–59.

Graaf, M. H. K. van der, *Attracting and Holding Staff* (Eindhoven: Philips, 1964).

Hedberg, B., Computer Systems to support Industrial Democracy. In: Mumford, E. and Sackmann, H. (eds.), *Human Choice and Computers* (Amsterdam: North Holland, 1975).

Hedberg, B. & Mumford, E., The Design of Computer Systems, Man's Vision of Man as an Integral Part of the System Design Process. In: Mumford, E. and Sackmann, H. (eds.), *Human Choice and Computers* (Amsterdam, North Holland, 1975).

Hertog, J. F. den, *Work, Work System, Work System Design* (Eindhoven: Philips, 1975).

Hertog, J. F. den, Work Structuring. In: Warr, P. (ed.), *Personal Goals and Work Design* (London: Wiley & Sons, 1976).

Hertog, J. F, den, *Information and Control vs Renewal* (Eindhoven: Philips, 1977).

Hertog, J. F. den & De Vries, H. J. J., *Breaking the Deadlock* (Eindhoven: Philips, 1977).

Herzberg, F., The Wise Old Turk, *Harvard Business Review* (Vol. 52, no. 5, 1974), pp. 70–81.

Job Reform in Sweden (Stockholm: S.A.F., 1975).

Koopman, P. L. & Drenth, P. J. D., Werkoverleg, Experiments in Participative Decision Making on the Shop Floor. *Paper presented at the Second International Conference on Participation, Workers' Control and Self Management* (Paris, 1977).

Lawler, E. E. & Rhodes, J. G., *Information and Control in Organizations* (Pacific Palisades: Goodyear, 1976).

Likert, R., *The Human Organization: its Management and Value* (London: McGraw-Hill, 1967).

Macy, B. A. & Mirvis, P. H., A Methodology for Assessment of Quality of Work Life and Organizational Effectiveness in Behavioral–Economic Terms, *Administrative Science Quarterly* (Vol. 21, no. 2, 1976), pp. 212–216.

Mirvis, P. H. & Lawler, E. E. III, Measuring the Financial Impact of Employee Attitudes, *Journal of Applied Psychology* (Vol. 62, No. 1), pp. 1–8.

Mintzberg, H., Planning on the left side and managing on the right side, *Harvard Business Review* (Vol. 54, no. 2, 1976), pp. 49–58.

Mintzberg, H., Raisinghandi, D. & Théorêt, A., The Structure of

"Unstructured" Decision Processes, *Administrative Science Quarterly* (Vol. 21, no. 2, 1976), pp. 246–275.

Moors, S. & Vansina L., *Werkstrukturering en Gemechaniseerde Arbeid* (Brussels: Belgian Productivity Center, 1976).

Mumford, E., Computer Systems and Work Design: Problems of Philosophy and Vision, *Personnel Review* (Vol. 3, no. 2, 1974), pp. 40–49.

Nicholson, N., Management Sanctions and Absence Control, *Human Relations* (Vol. 29, no. 2, 1976), pp. 139–151.

Perrow, C., *Organizational Analysis* (London: Tavistock Publications, 1970).

Reimann, B. C. & Negandhi, A. R., Strategies of Administrative Control and Organizational Effectiveness, *Human Relations* (Vol. 28, no. 5, 1976), pp. 475–486.

Rhenman, E., *Organizational Theory for Long-Range Planning* (London: John Wiley & Sons, 1973).

Skinner, W., The Anachronistic Factory, *Harvard Business Review* (Vol. 49, no. 1, 1971), pp. 61–70.

Starbuck, W. H., Information Systems and Organizations in the Future. In: Grochla, E. & Szyperski, N. (eds.), *Information Systems and Organizational Structure* (New York: De Gruyter, 1975).

Strumpel, B. (eds.), *Economic Means for Human Needs, Social Indicators of Well-Being and Discontent* (Ann Arbor: Institute for Social Research, 1976).

Thorsrud, E. L., Job Design in the Wider Context. In: Davis, L. E. and Taylor, J. C., (eds.) *Design of Jobs* (Harmondsworth: Penguin Books, 1972).

Tomeski, E. A. & Lazarus, H., *People-oriented Computer Systems, the Computer in Crisis* (New York: Van Nostrand Reinhold, 1975).

Withington, F. G., *The Real Computer: its Influence, Uses and Effects* (Reading: Addison-Wesley, 1969).

Whisler, T. L., *Information Technology and Organizational Change* (Belmont: Wadsworth, 1970).

12   What is an organization that it may learn?
C. Argyris and D. Schön

The Question

There has probably never been a time in our history when members, managers, and students of organizations were so united on the importance of organizational learning. Costs of health care, sanitation, police, housing, education, and welfare have risen precipitously, and we urge agencies concerned with these services to learn to increase their productivity and efficiency. Governments are torn by the conflicting demands of full employment, free collective bargaining, social welfare, and the control of inflation; we conclude that governments must learn to understand and accommodate these demands. Corporations have found themselves constrained by a web of increasingly stringent regulations for environmental protection and consumer safety, at the same time that we are most sensitive to the need for jobs and for economic growth. Government and business must learn, we say, to work together to solve these problems.

Sometimes our demands for learning turn back on our history, as when politicians and planners ask, 'What have we learned from the last 20 years of housing policy?' 'What have we learned from the Great Depression?' 'What have we learned from Vietnam?' In a bicentennial article on 'The American Experiment,' Daniel Moynihan begins by asking, 'What have we learned?' (Glazer and Kristol 1976).

It is not only that we are poignantly aware of our dilemmas and of the need for learning. We are also beginning to notice that there is nothing more problematic than solutions. Some of our most agonizing problems have been triggered by our solutions to slum eradication and urban renewal, by the success of the labour movement in achieving income security for workers, by rising expectations consequent to our economic growth, by the unwanted consequences of technological innovations. We begin to suspect that there is no stable state awaiting us over the horizon. On the contrary, our very power to solve problems seems to multiply problems. As a result, our organizations live in economic, political, and technological environments which are predictably unstable. The requirement for organizational learning is not an occasional, sporadic phenomenon, but is continuous and endemic to our society.

Nevertheless, it is not all clear what it means for an organization to learn. Nor is it clear how we can enhance the capacity of organizations to learn.

The difficulty has first to do with the notion of learning itself. When we call for learning or change, we seem to be calling for something good. But there are kinds of change which are not good, such as deterioration, regression and stagnation. And there are kinds of learning, such as government's learning to deceive and manipulate society, which are no better. So we need to spell out both the kinds of change we have in mind when we speak of learning, and the kinds of learning we have in mind when we call for more of it.

Further, it is clear that organizational learning is not the same thing as individual learning, even when the individuals who learn are members of the organization. There are too many cases in which organizations know *less* than their members. There are even cases in which the organization cannot seem to learn what every member knows. Nor does it help to think of organizational learning as the prerogative of a man at the top who learns *for* the organization; in large and complex organizations bosses succeed one another while the organization remains very much itself, and learns or fails to learn in ways that often have little to do with the boss.

There is something paradoxical here. Organizations are not merely collections of individuals, yet there is no organization without such collections. Similarly, organizational learning is not merely individual learning, yet organizations learn only through the experience and actions of individuals.

What, then, are we to make of organizational learning? What is an organization that it may learn?

Theory of action

In our earlier book, *Theory in Practice* (Argyris and Schön 1974), we set out to understand how practitioners of management, consultation, and intervention might learn to become more competent and effective. Our concern was especially directed to learning about interpersonal interaction. In that context, we found it useful to look at professional practice as informed by *theories of action:*

'All human beings—not only professional practitioners—need to become competent in taking action and simultaneously reflecting on this action to learn from it. The following pages provide a conceptual framework for this task by analyzing theories of action that determine all deliberate human behavior, how these theories are formed, how they come to change, and in what senses they may be considered adequate or inadequate'. (p. 4)

When we attributed theories of action to human beings, we argued that all deliberate action had a cognitive basis, that it reflected norms, strategies, and assumptions or models of the world which had claims to general validity. As a consequence, human learning, we said, need not be understood in terms of the 'reinforcement' or 'extinction' of patterns of behavior but as the construction, testing, and restructuring of a certain kind of knowledge. Human action and human learning could be placed in the larger context of knowing.

We found it necessary to connect theories of action to other kinds of theory:

' . . . whatever else a theory of action may be, it is first a theory. Its most general properties are properties that all theories share, and the most general criteria that apply to it—such as generality, centrality, and simplicity—are criteria that apply to all theories.' (p. 4)

And we also found it necessary to differentiate theories of action from theories of explanation, prediction, and control:

'A full schema for a theory of action, then, would be as follows: in situation S, if you want to achieve consequence C, under assumptions a . . . n, do A . . . A theory of action is a theory of deliberate human behavior which is for the agent a theory of control but which, when attributed to the agent, also serves to explain or predict his behavior.' (p. 6)

Because we wished to do empirical research into human learning in situations of interpersonal interaction, we distinguished espoused theory from theory-in-use:

'When someone is asked how he would behave under certain circumstances, the answer he usually gives is his espoused theory of action for that situation. This is the theory of action to which he gives allegiance and which, upon request, he communicates to others. However, the theory that actually governs his actions is his theory-in-use, which may or may not be compatible with his espoused theory; furthermore, the

individual may or may not be aware of the incompatibility of the two theories.' (p. 7)

From the directly observable data of behavior, we could then ground our construction of the models of action theories which guided interpersonal behavior. And we could relate these models to the capacity for types of learning in professional practice.

It is tempting to apply this line of thought to the problem of understanding organizational learning. Perhaps organizations also have theories of action which inform their actions, espoused theories which they announce to the world and theories-in-use which may be inferred from their directly observable behavior. If so, then organizational learning might be understood as the testing and restructuring of organizational theories of action and, in the organizational context as in the individual one, we might examine the impact of models of action theories upon the capacity for kinds of learning.

But this path is full of obstacles. It is true that we do apply to organizations many of the terms we also apply to individuals. We speak of organizational action and organizational behavior. We speak also of organizational intelligence and memory. We say that organizations learn, or fail to learn. Nevertheless, a closer examination of these ways of speaking suggests that such terms are metaphors. Organizations do not literally remember, think, or learn. At least, it is not initially clear how we might go about testing whether or not they do so.

It is even puzzling to consider what it means for an organization to act or behave—notions which are essential to the construction of organizational theories of action. Does an organization act whenever one of its members acts? If so, there would appear to be little difference between an organization and a collection of individuals. Yet it is clear that some collections of people are organizations and others are not. Furthermore, even when a collection of people is clearly an organization, individual members of the organization do many things (such as breathe, sleep, gossip with their friends) which do not seem, in some important sense, to be examples of organizational action.

If we are to speak of organizational theories of action, we must dispel some of the confusion surrounding terms like organizational intelligence, memory, and action. We must say what it means for an organization to act, and we must show how organizational action is both different from and conceptually connected to individual action. We must say what it means for an organization to know something, and we must spell out the metaphors of organizational memory, intelligence, and learning.

Perspectives on Organization

Let us begin by exploring several different ways of looking at an organization. An organization is:

a government, or *polis;*
an agency;
a task system.

Each of these perspectives will illuminate the sense in which an organization may be said to act. Further, an organization is:

a theory of action;
a cognitive enterprise undertaken by individual members;
a cognitive artifact made up of individual images and public maps.

Each of these descriptions will reveal the sense in which an organization may be said to know something, and to learn.

Consider a mob of students protesting against their university's policy. At what point do they cease to be a mob and begin to be an organization?

The mob is a collectivity. It is a collection of people who may run, shout, and mill about together. But it is a collectivity which cannot make a decision or take an action in its own name, and its boundaries are vague and diffuse.

As the mob begins to meet three sorts of conditions, it becomes more nearly an organization. Members must devise procedures for: (1) making decisions in the name of the collectivity, (2) delegating to individuals the authority to act for the collectivity, and (3) setting boundaries between the collectivity and the rest of the world. As these conditions are met, members of the collectivity begin to be able to say 'we' about themselves; they can say, 'We have decided,' 'We have made our position clear,' 'We have limited our membership.' There is now an organizational 'we' that can decide and act.

When the members of the mob become an identifiable vehicle for collective decision and action, they become, in the ancient Greek sense of the term, *a polis,* a political entity. Before an organization can be anything else, it must be in this sense political, because it is as a political entity that the collectivity can take organizational action. It is individuals who decide and act, but they do these things *for* the collectivity by virtue of the rules for decision, delegation, and membership. When the members of the collectivity have created such rules, they have organized.

Rule making need not be a conscious, formal process. What is important is that members' behavior be rule-governed in the crucial respects. The rules themselves may remain tacit, unless for some reason they are called into question. So long as there is continuity in the rules which govern the behavior of individuals, the organization will persist, even though members come and go. And what is most important for our purposes, it now becomes possible to set up criteria of relevance for constructing organizational theory-in-use. Organizational theory-in-use is to be inferred from observation of organizational behavior—that is, from organizational decisions and actions. The decisions and actions carried out by individuals are organizational insofar as they are governed by collective rules for decision and delegation. These alone are the decisions and actions taken in the name of the organization.

Through such a process, a mob becomes an organization. But if we are interested in organizational theory of action, we must ask what *kind* of an organization it becomes.

If a collection of people begins to decide and to act on a continuing basis, it becomes an instrument for continuing collective action, an *agency*. In this sense, the collections of workers involved in the labor movement organized from time to time to form unions, and collections of individual investors organized to form limited liability corporations. Such agencies have functions to fulfill, work to do. Their theories-in-use may be inferred from the ways in which they go about doing their work.

Generally speaking, an agency's work is a complex task, continually performed. The agency—an industrial corporation, a labor union, a government bureau, or even a household—embodies a strategy for decomposing that complex task into simpler components which are regularly delegated to individuals. Organizational roles—president, lathe-operator, shop steward—are the names given to the clusters of component tasks which the agency has decided to delegate to individual members. The organization's *task system,* its pattern of interconnected roles, is at once a design for work and a division of labor.

An agency is thus the solution to a problem. It is a strategy for performing a complex task which might have been carried out in other ways. This is true not only for the design of the task system, the division of labor, but also for the selection of strategies for performing component tasks.

We can view a sugar-refining company, for example, as an answer to questions such as these: What is the best way to grow and harvest cane? How should it be refined? How is it best distributed and marketed? For each subquestion the organization is an answer. The company's way of growing cane reflects certain strategies (for the cultivation of land, for harvesting and fertilizing), certain norms (for productivity and quality, for the use of labor), and certain assumptions (about the yields to be expected from various patterns of cultivation). The norms, strategies, and assumptions embedded in the company's cane-growing practices constitute its *theory of action* for cane-growing. There are comparable theories of action implicit in the company's ways of distributing and marketing its products. Taken together, these component theories of action represent a theory of action for achieving corporate objectives. This global theory of action we call 'instrumental'. It includes norms for corporate performance (for example, norms for margin of profit and for return on investment), strategies for achieving norms (for example, strategies for plant location and for process technology), and assumptions which bind strategies and norms together (for example, the assumption that maintenance of a high rate of return on investment depends on the continual introduction of new technologies).

The company's instrumental theory of action is a complex system of norms, strategies, and assumptions. It includes in its scope the organization's patterns of communication and control, its ways of allocating resources to goals, and its provisions for self-maintenance—that is, for rewarding and punishing individual performance, for constructing career ladders and regulating the rate at which individuals climb them, and for recruiting new members and instructing them in the ways of the organization.

Like the rules for collective decision and action, organizational theories of action need not be explicit. Indeed, formal corporate documents such as organization charts, policy statements, and job descriptions often reflect a theory of action (the *espoused theory*) which conflicts with the organization's *theory-in-use* (the theory of action constructed from observation of actual behavior)—and the theory-in-use is often tacit. Organizational theory-in-use may remain tacit, as we will see later on, because its incongruity with espoused theory is *undiscussable*. Or it may remain tacit because individual members of the organization know more than they say—because the theory-in-use is *inaccessible* to them. Whatever the reason for tacitness, the largely tacit theory-in-use accounts for organizational identity and continuity.

Consider a large, enduring organization such as the U.S. Army. Over 50 years or so, its personnel may turn over completely, yet we still speak of it as 'the Army'. It is no longer the same collection of people, so in what sense is it still the same? Suppose we wanted to discover whether it was in fact the same organization. How would we proceed? We might examine uniforms and weapons, but in 50 years these might have changed entirely. We might then study the 50-year evolution of military practices—that is, the norms for military behavior, the strategies for military action, the assumptions about military functioning. We would then be studying the evolution of the Army's theory-in-use. And we might learn that certain features of it—for example, the pattern of command, the methods of training, the division into regiments and platoons—had remained essentially unchanged, while other features of it—battle strategies, norms for performance—had evolved continuously from earlier forms. We might conclude that we were dealing with a single organization, self-identical, whose theory-in-use had evolved considerably over time.

It is this theory-in-use, an apparently abstract thing, which is most distinctively real about the Army. It is what old soldiers know and new ones learn through a continuing process of socialization. And it is the history of change in theory-in-use which we would need to consult in order to inquire into the Army's organizational learning.

In order to discover an organization's theory-in-use, we must examine its practice, that is, the continuing performance of its task system as exhibited in the rule-governed behavior of its members. This is, however, an outside view. When members carry out the practices appropriate to their organization, they are also manifesting a kind of knowledge. And this knowledge represents the organization's theory-in-use as seen from the inside.

Images and maps

Each member of the organization constructs his or her own representation, or image, of the theory-in-use of the whole. That picture is always incomplete. The organization members strive continually to complete it, and to understand themselves in the context of the organization. They try to describe themselves and their own performance insofar as they interact with others. As conditions change, they test and modify that description. Moreover, others are continually engaged in similar inquiry. It is this continual, concerted meshing of individual images of self and others, of one's activity in the context of collective interaction, which constitutes an organization's knowledge of its theory-in-use.

An organization is like an organism each of whose cells contains a particular, partial, changing image of itself in relation to the whole. And like such an organism, the organization's practice stems from those very images. Organization is an artifact of individual ways of representing organization.

Hence, our inquiry into organizational learning must concern itself not with static entities called organizations, but with an active process of organizing which is, at root, a cognitive enterprise, Individual members are continually engaged in attempting to know the organization, and to know themselves in the context of the organization. At the same time, their continuing efforts to know and to test their knowledge represent the object of their inquiry. Organizing is reflexive enquiry.

From this perspective, organizational continuity is a considerable achievement. But we could not account for organizational continuity if the cognitive enterprise of organizing were limited to the private inquiry of individuals. Even when individuals are in face-to-face contact, private images of organization erode and diverge from one another. When the task system is large and complex, most members are unable to use face-to-face contact in order to compare and adjust their several images of organizational theory-in-use. They require external references. There must be public representations of organizational theory-in-use to which individuals can refer.

This is the function of organizational maps. These are the shared descriptions of organization which individuals jointly construct and use to guide their own inquiry. They include, for example, diagrams of work flow, compensation charts, statements of procedure, even the schematic drawings of office space. A building itself may function as a kind of map, revealing patterns of communication and control. Whatever their form, maps have a dual function. They describe actual patterns of activity, and they are guides to future action. As musicians perform their scores, members of an organization perform their maps.

Organizational theory-in-use, continually constructed through individual inquiry, is encoded in private images and in public maps. These are the media of organizational learning.

Organizational Learning

As individual members continually modify their maps and images of the organization, they also bring about changes in organizational theory-in-use.

Not all of these changes qualify as learning. Members may lose enthusiasm, become sloppy in task performance, or lose touch with one another. They may leave the organization, carrying with them important information which becomes lost to the organization. Or changes in the organization's environment (a slackening of demand for product, for example) may trigger new patterns of response which undermine organizational norms. These are kinds of deterioration, sometimes called organizational entropy.

But individual members frequently serve as agents of changes in organizational theory-in-use which run counter to organizational entropy. They act on their images and on their shared maps with expectations of patterned outcomes, which their subsequent experience confirms or disconfirms. When there is a mismatch of outcome to expectation (error), members may respond by modifying their images, maps, and activities so as to bring expectations and outcomes back into line. They detect an error in organizational theory-in-use, and they correct it. This fundamental learning loop is one in which individuals act from organizational theory-in-use, which leads to match or mismatch of expectations with outcome, and thence to confirmation or disconfirmation of organizational theory-in-use.

Quality control inspectors detect a defect in product, for example; they feed that information back to production engineers, who then change production specifications to correct that defect. Marketing managers observe that monthly sales have fallen below expectations; they inquire into the shortfall, seeking an interpretation which they can use to devise new marketing strategies which will bring the sales curve back on target. When organizational turnover of personnel increases to the point where it threatens the steady performance of the task system, managers may respond by investigating the sources of worker dissatisfaction; they look for factors they can influence—salary levels, fringe benefits, job design—so as to reestablish the stability of their work force.

Single-loop learning

In these examples, *members of the organization respond to changes in the internal and external environments of the organization by detecting errors which they then correct so as to maintain the central features of organizational theory-in-use.* These are learning episodes which function to preserve a certain kind of constancy. As Gregory Bateson has pointed out (Bateson 1972), the organization's ability to remain stable in a changing context denotes a kind of learning. Following his usage, we call this learning single-loop. (Bateson 1960) There is a single feed-back loop which connects detected outcomes of action to organizational strategies and assumptions which are modified so as to keep organizational performance within the range set by organizational norms. The norms themselves—for product quality, sales, or task performance—remain unchanged.

These examples also help to make clear the relationship between individual and organizational learning. The key to this distinction is the notion of *agency. Just as individuals are the agents of organizational action, so they are the agents for organizational learning.* Organizational learning occurs when individuals, acting from their images and maps, detect a match or mismatch of outcome to expectation which confirms or disconfirms organizational theory-in-use. In the case of disconfirmation, individuals move from error detection to error correction. Error correction takes the form of inquiry. The learning agents must discover the sources of error—that is, they must attribute error to strategies and assumptions in existing theory-in-use. They must invent new strategies, based on new assumptions, in order to correct error. They must produce those strategies. And they must evaluate and generalize the results of that new action. 'Error correction' is shorthand for a complex learning cycle.

But in order for *organizational* learning to occur, learning agents' discoveries, inventions, and evaluations must be embedded in organizational memory. They must be encoded in the individual images and the shared maps of organizational theory-in-use from which individual members will subsequently act. If this encoding does not occur, individuals will have learned but the organization will not have done so.

Suppose, for example, that the quality control inspectors find a product defect which they then decide to keep to themselves, perhaps because they are afraid to make the information public. Or suppose that they try to communicate this information to the production engineers, but the production engineers do not wish to listen to them. Or suppose that the interpretation of error requires collaborative inquiry on the part of several different members of the organization who are unwilling or unable to carry out such a collaboration. (Indeed, because organizations are strategies for decomposing complex tasks into task/role systems, error correction normally requires collaborative inquiry.) In all of these instances, individual learning may or may not have occurred, but individuals do not function as agents of organizational learning. What individuals may have learned remains as an unrealized potential for organizational learning.

From this it follows both that there is no organizational learning without individual learning, and that individual learning is a necessary but insufficient condition for organizational learning. We can think of organizational learning as a process mediated by the collaborative inquiry of individual members. In their capacity as agents of organizational learning, individuals restructure the continually changing artifact called organizational theory-in-use. Their work as learning agents is unfinished until the results of their inquiry—their discoveries, inventions, and evaluations—are recorded in the media of organizational memory, the images and maps which encode organizational theory-in-use.

If we should wish to test whether organizational learning has occurred, we must ask questions such as these: Did individuals detect an outcome which matched or mismatched the expectations derived from their images and maps of organizational theory-in-use? Did they carry out an inquiry which yielded discoveries, inventions, and evaluations pertaining to organizational strategies and assumptions? Did these results become embodied in the images and maps employed for purposes such as control, decision, and instruction? Did members subsequently act from these images and maps so as to carry out new organizational practices? Were these changes in images, maps, and organizational practices regularized so that they were unaffected by some individual's departure? Do new members learn these new features of the organizational theory of action as part of their socialization to the organization?

Each of these questions points to a possible source of failure in organizational learning, as well as to the sources of organizational learning capacity. So far, however, we have limited ourselves to the kind of learning called single-loop. Let us now consider learning of another kind.

Double-loop learning

Organizations are continually engaged in transactions with their internal and external environments. Industrial corporations, for example, continually respond to the changing pattern of external competition, regulation and demand, and to the changing internal environment of workers' attitudes and aspirations. These responses take the form of error detection and error correction. Single-loop learning is sufficient where error correction can proceed by changing organizational strategies and assumptions within a constant framework of norms for performance. It is concerned primarily with effectiveness—that is, with how best to achieve existing goals and objectives and how best to keep organizational performance within the range specified by existing norms. In some cases, however, error correction requires an organizational learning cycle in which organizational norms themselves are modified.

Consider an industrial firm which has set up a research and development division charged with the discovery and development of new technologies. This has been a response to the perceived imperative for growth in sales and earnings and the belief that these are to be generated through internally managed technological innovation. But the new division generates technologies which do not fit the corporation's familiar pattern of operations. In order to exploit some of these technologies, for example, the corporation may have to turn from the production of intermediate materials with which it is familiar to the manufacture and distribution of consumer products with which it is unfamiliar. But this, in turn, requires that members of the corporation adopt new approaches to marketing, managing, and advertising; that they become accustomed to a much shorter product life cycle and to a more rapid cycle of changes in their pattern of activities; that they, in fact, change the very image of the business they are in. And these requirements for change come into conflict with another sort of corporate norm, one that requires predictability in the management of corporate affairs.

.Hence, the corporate managers find themselves confronted with conflicting requirements. If they conform to the imperative for growth, they must give up on the imperative for predictability. If they decide to keep their patterns of operations constant, they must give up on the imperative for growth, at least insofar as that imperative is to be realized through internally generated technology. A process of change initiated with an eye to effectiveness under existing norms turns out to yield a conflict in the norms themselves.

If corporate managers are to engage this conflict, they must undertake a process of inquiry which is significantly different from the inquiry characteristic of single-loop learning. They must, to begin with, recognize the conflict itself. They have set up a new division which has yielded unexpected outcomes; this is an error, in the sense earlier described. They must reflect upon this error to the point where they become aware that they cannot correct it by doing better what they already know how to do. They must become aware, for example, that they cannot correct the error by getting the new division to perform more effectively under existing norms; indeed, the more effective the new division is, the more its results will plunge the managers into conflict. The managers must discover that it is the norm for predictable management which they hold, perhaps tacitly, that conflicts with their wish to achieve corporate growth through technological innovation.

Then the managers must undertake an inquiry which resolves the conflicting requirements. The results of their inquiry will take the form of a restructuring of organizational norms, and very likely a restructuring of strategies and assumptions associated with those norms, which must then be embedded in the images and maps which encode organizational theory-in-use.

We call this sort of learning *double-loop*. There is in this sort of episode a double feedback loop which connects the detection of error not only to strategies and assumptions for effective performance but to the very norms which define effective performance.

Single-loop learning, as we have defined it, consists not only of a change in organizational strategies and assumptions but of the particular sort of change appropriately described as learning. In single-loop learning, members of the organization carry out a collaborative inquiry through which they discover sources of error, invent new strategies designed to correct error, produce those strategies, and evaluate and generalize the results. Similarly, double-loop learning consists not only of a change in organizational norms but of the particular sort of inquiry into norms which is appropriately described as learning.

In organizational double-loop learning, incompatible requirements in organizational theory-in-use are characteristically expressed through a conflict among members and groups within the organization. In the industrial organization, for example, some managers may become partisans of growth through research and of a new image of the business based upon research, while others may become opponents of research through their allegiance to familiar and predictable patterns of corporate operation. Double-loop learning, if it occurs, will consist of the process of inquiry by which these groups of managers confront and resolve their conflict.

In this sense, the organization is a medium for translating incompatible requirements into interpersonal and intergroup conflict.

Members of the organization may respond to such a conflict in several ways, not all of which meet the criteria for organizational double-loop learning. First, the members may treat the conflict as a fight in which choices are to be made among competing requirements, and weightings and priorities are to be set on the basis of prevailing power. The 'R & D faction,' for example, may include the chief executive who wins out over the 'old guard' through being more powerful. Or the two factions may fight it out to a draw, settling their differences in the end by a compromise which reflects nothing more than the inability of either faction to prevail over the other.

In both of these cases, the conflict is settled for the time being, but not by a process that could be appropriately described as learning. The conflict is settled not by inquiry but by fighting it out. Neither side emerges from the settlement with a new sense of the nature of the conflict, of its causes and consequences, or of its meaning for organizational theory-in-use.

On the other hand, parties to the conflict may engage the conflict through inquiry of the following kinds:

They may invent new strategies of performance which circumvent the perceived incompatibility of requirements. They may, for example, succeed in defining a kind of research and development addressed solely to the existing pattern of business, which offers the likelihood of achieving existing norms for growth. They will then have succeeded in finding a single-loop solution to what at first appeared as a double-loop problem.

They may carry out a 'trade-off analysis' which enables them to conclude jointly that so many units of achievement of one norm are balanced by so many units of achievement of another. On this basis, they may decide that the prospects for R & D payoff are so slim that the R & D option should be abandoned, and with that abandonment there should be a lowering of corporate expectations for growth. Or they may decide to limit R & D targets so that the disruptions of patterns of business operation generated by R & D are limited to particular segments of the corporation.

Here there is a compromise among competing requirements, but it is achieved through inquiry into the probabilities and values associated with the options for action.

In the context of the conflict, the incompatible requirements may not lend themselves to trade-off analysis. They may be perceived as incommensurable. In such a case, the conflict may still be resolved through inquiry which gets underneath the members' starting perceptions of the incompatible requirements. Participants must then ask why they hold the positions they do, and what they mean by them. They may ask, what factors have led them to adopt these particular standards for growth in sales and earnings, what their rationale is, and what are likely to be the consequences of attempting to achieve them, through any means whatever? Similarly, they may ask what kinds of predictability in operations are of greatest importance, to whom they are most important, and what conditions make them important.

Such inquiry may lead to a significant restructuring of the configuration of corporate norms. Or it may lead to the invention of new patterns of incentives, budgeting, and control which take greater account of requirements for both growth and predictability.

We will give the name 'double-loop learning' to those sorts of organizational inquiry which resolve incompatible organizational norms by setting new priorities and weightings of norms, or by restructuring the norms themselves together with associated strategies and assumptions.

In these cases, individual members resolve the interpersonal and intergroup conflicts which express incompatible requirements by creating new understandings of the conflicting requirements, their sources, conditions, and consequences— understandings which then become embedded in the images and maps of organization. By doing so, they make the new, more nearly compatible requirements susceptible to effective realization.

There are three observations we wish to make about distinction between single- and double-loop organizational learning.

First, it is often impossible, in the real-world context of organizational life, to find inquiry cleanly separated from the uses of power. Inquiry and power-play are often combined. Given such mixtures, we will want to differentiate the two kinds of processes which are often mixed in practice so that we may speak of those aspects of interpersonal and intergroup conflict which involve organizational learning and those which do not.

Second, while we have described the *kinds* of inquiry which are essential to single- and double-loop learning, we have not yet dwelt on the *quality* of inquiry. Two different examples of double-loop-learning, both of which exhibit detection of error and correction of error through the restructuring or organizational norms, may be of unequal quality. The same is true of single-loop learning. Organizations may learn more or less well, yet their inquiries may still qualify as learning of the single- or double-loop kind.

Finally, we must point out that the distinction between single- and double-loop learning is less a binary one than might first appear. Organizational theories-in-use are systemic structures composed of many interconnected parts. We can examine these structures from the point of view of a particular, local theory of action, such as the industrial firm's theory of action for quality control, or we can attend to more global aspects of the structure, such as the firm's theory of action for achieving targeted return on investment. Furthermore, certain elements are more fundamental to the structure and others are more peripheral. For example, the industrial firm's norms for growth and for predictability of management are fundamental to its theory of action—in the sense that if they were changed, a great deal of the rest of the theory of action would also have to change—and it is their fundamental status which gives a special poignancy to their conflict. On the other hand, a particular norm for product quality may be quite peripheral to the organization's theory of action; it could change without affecting much of the rest of the theory of action.

Now, an inquiry into a *strategy* fundamental to the firm's theory of action, such as the strategy of measuring divisional performance by monthly profit-and-loss statements, will be likely to involve much of the rest of the organization's theory of action, including its norms. But an inquiry into a *norm* peripheral to the organization's theory of action may involve very little of the rest of its theory of action. From this, two conclusions may be drawn. First, in judging whether learning is single- or double-loop, it is important to notice where inquiry goes as well as where it begins. Second, it is possible to speak of organizational learning as *more or less* double-loop. In place of the binary distinction we have a more continuous concept of depth of learning.

It is possible, we think, to make clear distinctions between relatively deep and relatively peripheral examples of organizational learning. We will continue to call the former double- and the latter, single-loop learning. Our examples of double-loop learning will involve norms fundamental to organizational theories of action, for these are the examples we believe to be of greatest importance. The reader should keep in mind, however, that we speak of these categories as discrete when they are actually parts of a continuum.

With these *caveats,* we can return to our main line of argument.

Deutero-learning

Since World War II, it has gradually become apparent not only to business firms but to all sorts of organizations that the requirements of organizational learning, especially for double-loop learning, are not one-shot but continuing. There has been a sequence of ideas in good currency—such as 'creativ-ity,' 'innovation,' 'the management of change'—which reflect this awareness.

In our earlier example, to take one instance, managers of the industrial firm might conclude that their organization needs to learn how to restructure itself, at regular intervals, so as to exploit the new technologies generated by research and development. That is, the organization needs to learn how to carry out single- and double-loop learning.

This sort of learning to learn Gregory Bateson has called *deutero-learning* (that is, second-order learning). Bateson illustrates the idea through the following story:

> 'A female porpoise . . . is trained to accept the sound of the trainer's whistle as a "secondary reinforcement." The whistle is expectably followed by food, and if she later repeats what she was doing when the whistle blew, she will expect again to hear the whistle and receive food.
>
> The porpoise is now used by the trainers to demonstrate "operant conditioning" to the public. When she enters the exhibition tank, she raises her head above the surface, hears the whistle and is fed . . .
>
> But this pattern is (suitable) only for a single episode in the exhibition tank. She must break that pattern to deal with the *class* of such episodes. There is a larger context of contexts which will put her in the wrong . . .
>
> When the porpoise comes on stage, she again raises her head. But she gets no whistle. The trainer waits for the next piece of conspicuous behavior, likely a tail flip, which is a common expression of annoyance. This behavior is then reinforced and repeated (by giving her food).
>
> But the tail flip was, of course, not rewarded in the third performance.
>
> Finally the porpoise learned to deal with the context of contexts—by offering a different or new piece of conspicuous behavior whenever she came on stage.'

Each time the porpoise learns to deal with a larger class of episodes, she learns *about* the previous contexts for learning. Her creativity reflects deutero-learning.

When an organization engages in deutero-learning, its members learn, too, about previous contexts for learning. They reflect on and inquire into previous contexts for learning. They reflect on and inquire into previous episodes of organizational learning, or failure to learn. They discover what they did that facilitated or inhibited learning, they invent new strategies for learning, they produce these strategies, and they evaluate and generalize what they have produced. The results become encoded in individual images and maps and are reflected in organizational learning practice.

The deutero-learning cycle is relatively familiar in the context of organizational learning curves. Aircraft manufacturers, for example, project the rate at which their organizations will learn to manufacture a new aircraft and base cost estimates on their projections of the rate of organizational learning. In the late 1950s, the Systems Development Corporation undertook the 'cogwheel' experiment, in which members of an aircraft-spotting team were invited to inquire into their own organizational learning and then to produce conditions which would enable them more effectively to learn to improve their performance (Chapman and Kennedy 1956).

In these examples, however, deutero-learning concentrates on single-loop learning; emphasis is on learning for effectiveness rather than on learning to resolve conflicting norms for performance. But the concept of deutero-learning is also relevant to double-loop learning. How, indeed, can organizations learn to become better at double-loop learning? How can members of an organization learn to carry out the kinds of inquiry essential to double-loop learning? What are the conditions which enable members to meet the tests of organizational learning? And how can they learn to produce those conditions?

Organizations are not only theories of action. They are also small societies composed of persons who occupy roles in the task system. What we have called the internal environment of an organization is the society of persons who make up the organization at any given time. These societies have their own characteristic behavioral worlds. These enable us to recognize a person as 'an army man,' 'a government man,' 'a General Electric man.' Within these societies, members tend to share characteristic languages, styles, and models of *individual* theory-in-use for interaction with others. In the light of these behavioral worlds. we can and do describe organizations as more or less 'open,' 'experimental,' 'confronting', 'demanding,' or 'defensive.' These behavioral worlds, with their characteristic models of individual theory-in-use, may be more or less conducive to the kinds of collaborative inquiry required for organizational learning.

Hence, if we wish to learn more about the conditions that facilitate or inhibit organizational learning, we must explore the ways in which the behavioral worlds or organizations affect the capacity for inquiry into organizational theory-in-use.

Summary

Organizational learning is a metaphor whose spelling out requires us to reexamine the very idea of organization. A collection of individuals organizes when its members develop rules for collective decision delegation and membership. In their rule-governed behavior, they act for the collectivity in ways that reflect a task system. Just as individual theories of action may be inferred from individual behavior, so organizational theories of action may be inferred from patterns of organizational action. As individuals have espoused theories which may be incongruent with their (often tacit) theories-in-use, so with organizations.

Organizational learning occurs when members of the organization act as learning agents for the organization, responding to changes in the internal and external environments of the organization by detecting and correcting errors in organizational theory-in-use, and embedding the results of their inquiry in private images and shared maps of organization.

In organizational single-loop learning, the criterion for success is effectiveness. Individuals respond to error by modifying strategies and assumptions within constant organizational norms. In double-loop learning, response to detected error takes the form of joint inquiry into organizational norms themselves, so as to resolve their inconsistency and make the new norms more effectively realizable. In both cases, organizational learning consists of restructuring organizational theory of action.

When an organization engages in deutero-learning, its members learn about organizational learning and encode their results in images and maps. The quest for organizational learning capacity must take the form of deutero-learning; most particularly about the interactions between the organization's behavioral world and its ability to learn.

References

Argyris, Chris, and Donald Schön (1974) *Theory in Practice,* San Francisco: Jossey-Bass.

Bateson, Gregory (1958) *Naven,* Stanford, Calif.: Stanford University Press. Bateson borrows the term from W. R. Ashby's *Design for a Brain,* New York: Wiley, 1960.

Bateson, Gregory (1972) *Steps to an Ecology of Mind,* New York: Ballantine.

Chapman, Robert L., and John L. Kennedy (1956) *Background and Implications of Systems Research Laboratory Studies,* Rand Corporation Report.

Glazer, Nathan, and Irving Kristol (eds.) (1976) Introduction: 'The American Experiment', in *The American Commonwealth— 1976,* New York: Basic Books.

13   Conceptual approaches to power and authority
Ruth Elliott

It seems imperative that any study of power and authority begins by reviewing some conceptual approaches and developing a 'model' of power relations against which people's own perceptions and meaning systems can be assessed and analysed. This is essentially the concern of this reading.

Two approaches to power: 'power to' and 'power over'

In the wealth of writings on power one can distinguish two very different approaches to the concept. One approach is concerned to analyse power as a relationship between individuals or groups which enables one individual or group to impose its will on the other. The emphasis here is on the power of A, as an individual or group, *over* B. The second approach is concerned to analyse power as a 'system property', rather than as a property of individuals or groups, which enables the successful realisation of 'system' goals. The emphasis here is on power *to,* in the sense of a capacity to achieve certain goals or objectives.

This latter approach is very much associated with the name of Parsons, who does not deny that power has its interpersonal manifestations, but the implications of these are subordinated in analysis to a concern with the achievement of collective goals. Hence to Parsons,

'the power of A over B is, in its legitimized form, the "right" of A, as a decision-making unit involved in collective process, to make decisions which take precedence over those of B, in the interests of the effectiveness of the collective operation as a whole'.[1]

By placing emphasis on the 'effectiveness of the collective operation as a whole', Parsons is able to demonstrate that power is not a 'zero-sum' phenomenon which is possessed by one group or person to the impoverishment of another; it is rather a capacity for collective goal realization from which *all* organizational members gain. This capacity may be exerted on *behalf* of the collective by a specific group of 'leaders', but nevertheless, as Giddens put it:

'Everybody gains from this process. Those who have "invested" in their leaders have received back, in the realization of collective goals, an increased return on their investment.'[2]

Although particular individuals in an organization may be vested with the right to exercise power in the name of the collective, this does not mean, according to Parsons' model, that these individuals are exercising power *over* others, in the sense of imposing their own goals or preferences at the expense of the goals or preferences of others; for it is assumed that there is a prior consensus on goals. By emphasizing goal consensus and stressing that the capacity to achieve these common goals is an index of the power of any system or collective, the Parsonian approach to power tends to divert attention from the actual *distribution* of power within an organization and the consequences of this for interpersonal relations and for personal or group goals and aspirations.

It is on his fundamental assumption of goal and value consensus that Parsons has been most criticized, and rightly so. For while, as Giddens points out, Parsons is correct in stressing that 'the creation of a power system does not *necessarily* entail the coercive subordination of the wishes or interests of one party to those of another' and that the existence of defined 'leadership' positions may well in certain situations 'generate power which may be used to achieve aims desired by the majority of the members of the group',[3] to confine one's theoretical definition of power to just such situations is to exclude by definitional fiat a wide range of other possible situations where power is exercised against the preferences and interests of another party. Even where common aims and goals do exist, there may still be clashes of interest insofar as members of the collective may aspire to be more involved in the decision-making and management processes by which these goals are attained. In other words there may be a value consensus over 'goals' but not over 'means'.

To build an assumption of value consensus into a theory of power automatically excludes a number of problem areas—most notably that of the nature and extent of the legitimation of power within industry, with which the present study is concerned. For Parsons, there is no such thing as 'illegitimate power', since power is 'directly derivative of authority; authority is the institutionalized legitimation which underlies power'.[4] While Parsons is correct in seeing authority as an important base of power, he again unnecessarily narrows the field of investigation by seeing it as the *only* base. It is one aim of this study to examine empirically how far power in industry *is* based on authority, how far power *is* regarded as legitimate. Such an investigation is by definition not possible within a Parsonian framework.

The other approach to power, which has been labelled 'power over', and which interprets power essentially as a relationship *between* individuals and groups, stresses the potential for conflict in social relations neglected by Parsons. Power is typically defined in terms of the capacity of A to impose his will on B despite resistance,[5] or in terms of the capacity of A to determine the behaviour of B, or restrict B in his choice of modes of behaviour.[6] Of seminal importance has been Weber's definition of power as 'the probability that one actor within a social relationship will be in a position to carry out his own will despite resistance, regardless of the basis on which this probability rests'.[7] Certainly Weberian conceptualizations of power have been more influential than the Parsonian conceptualization in actual analyses of power relations, both in political science and sociology, and when people talk of 'power' in industry, either on the part of management or workers, they are usually referring to the apparent capacity of one group to 'impose' its own preference on the other, or at least to restrict the other party in their choice of behaviour.

Nevertheless, this approach to power, when applied to industry, is also unsatisfactory and incomplete in some respects as a total conceptualization of the nature of power, although less so than the Parsonian approach.[8] For social relations in industry are not characterized solely by conflicts of will or preference. Industrial organizations can also be viewed in a more Parsonian light as collectivities of people working together to achieve certain goals. To say this need not imply any Parsonian assumption of 'consensus' and common values, and can be quite consonant with a recognition of the fact that 'organization may originate in the imposition of one group's purpose upon another'.[9] It is precisely this tension and ambiguity between conflict and co-operative collective effort that makes any simple definition of the nature of power within industry elusive. As radical Marxist-influenced writers have repeatedly pointed out, the very contradictions inherent in capitalist production derive from the fact that industrial work and the relationships, including power relationships, which it entails, are both 'social' and 'exploitative'. As Beynon has commented:

> 'Because production has a social basis, the factory can obviously be seen, at some level, as a collectivity with management operating in a co-ordinating role. The contradiction of factory production, and the source of contradictory elements within class consciousness, is rooted in the fact that the exploitation of workers is achieved through collective activities within both the factory and society generally'.[10]

That such tensions and contradictions in the nature of industrial production are reflected in people's perceptions of power relations has been amply demonstrated by the complex responses typically evoked by the 'teamwork/conflict' question so popular in empirical research.

In so far as workers and management do co-operate to produce goods, power in industry can be seen in Parsonian terms as 'a generalized medium of mobilizing commitment or obligation for effective collective action',[11] as long as one holds in abeyance the Parsonian notions of value consensus necessarily underlying collective action. Certainly managerial power is only partly related to the obtaining of compliance, willing or otherwise, from the workforce; management also uses power to co-ordinate the use of raw materials and non-human resources to reach managerial goals. The reason why management requires a measure of 'power over' employees is to ensure that it can control their activities, and co-ordinate them with other areas of managerial activity, so as to safeguard the attainment of managerial objectives and goals—which are typically referred to as 'organizational goals'. In other words, management requires 'power over' employees in order to maintain its 'power to' realise system's goals. Insofar as these goals are perceived or interpreted as being in opposition to the interests of employees, or insofar as the attainment of these goals requires employees to behave in ways they would not otherwise choose to behave, then the ultimate emphasis would be on 'power over' rather than 'power to'; but it seems likely that both these conceptualizations of power will be significant in understanding the nature of power relations in industry, and above all, how these power relations are perceived by actors in the system.

Power as a fixed and non-fixed resource

Even if one rejects the value-consensus assumptions behind the Parsonian approach to power, this approach does nevertheless place a valuable emphasis on the fact that power is not necessarily a 'fixed' resource, which is denied to one group to the extent that it is held by another. A major concern of Parsons was to criticize the approach to power typical, he felt, of writers like C. Wright Mills who saw power as 'exclusively . . . a faculty for getting what one group, the power holder, wants by preventing another group, "the outs" from getting what it wants'.[12] The Parsonian approach emphasizes that an increase in the power of superordinates need not mean a decrease in the power of subordinates. An interesting corollary to this has been developed by Lammers in a specifically industrial context. He argues, using the Parsonian concept of power as non-fixed resource, that by increasing the 'power' of subordinates, management is not necessarily decreasing its own power, in the sense of its capacity to achieve organizational goals.[13]

One does not have to subscribe to Parsonian notions of value-consensus for this concept of power as a non-fixed resource to have significance. Such a conceptualization of power is clearly relevant to the current managerial concern with regaining control 'by sharing it'.[14] To acknowledge that power can be a non-fixed resource is to recognize the dangers of simplistic assumptions that an increase in the power of workers *necessarily* means a loss of power to management, and to highlight the possibility that certain increases in worker power might actually *enhance* management's capacity to achieve overall goals and objectives.

There is a danger that Weberian definitions of power tend, by their very semantic structure of '*A* imposing his will on *B*', to suggest that power is exercised in one direction only, and to the extent that it is possessed by A it cannot be possessed by B. But such limitations are by no means inherent in the Weberian model of power. Several developments of this approach to power have emphasized the potential reciprocity of power relations and the fact that both parties in a power relationship can have power based on different sources. For example, Blau's development of the Weberian approach to power, using the concepts of exchange relationships and dependency, emphasizes strongly the elements of reciprocity in power relationships.[15]

That there are elements of reciprocity in the management–employee relationship can easily be demonstrated. Employees 'depend' on management for continued employment and remuneration, and also for the satisfaction of certain aspirations relating to work, social relations at work, work environment, and so on. A workforce may be more dependent on management in a high unemployment area where employee needs cannot easily be satisfied elsewhere. Equally however, employees may be highly dependent on management in a 'good' firm in a full employment area, if the firm offers pay, facilities, or rewarding and satisfying work of a kind that could not be found in other firms in the area.

At the same time, management is also dependent on employees for the continued production of goods, or for the provision of needed expertise and information. Mechanic[16] has demonstrated the power that can be exercised by lower participants in an organization by virtue of their access to information vital to their superiors. The dependence of management on any one group of employees, and hence the power of any one group of employees over management, will again be crucially affected by the substitutability factor, by the 'ability of the organization to obtain alternative performance for the activities of a subunit'.[17] The less easily an individual, work-group or department can be replaced by another from inside or outside the organization, the greater power capacity that unit will possess. Other factors likely to affect the degree of 'dependence' of management on a particular group of employees are, following Hickson *et al.*,[18], workflow pervasiveness, workflow immediacy, and the extent to which a particular group copes with uncertainties.

Of course, the possession of such power capacity does not necessarily mean that a group of employees will actively exercise such power. 'Possible' power will only be translated into 'realized' power if employees are aware both of their power capacity, and of having interests opposed to those of management, which they might use this power capacity to promote. To utilize their power capacity workers must also have a considerable degree of organization and cohesion. As Wrong has commented, 'the achievement of solidarity, common goals, social organization and leadership is necessary to convert possible power into realized power'.[19] Management's ability to 'control' the power of employees by manipulating these perceptual and organizational factors that mediate between possible power and realized power should not be ignored.

Since both parties in a power relationship can have power deriving from different sources of dependence, it follows that an increase or decrease in the power of one party, deriving from one specific basis of dependence, need not entail a corresponding decrease or increase in the power of the other party, if this power derives from an entirely different kind of dependence relationship. Using classifications developed by Martin,[20] if a craftsman's 'expert' power over his employer increases, it by no means follows that his employer's 'reward' power over *him* decreases.

Within the Weberian conceptualization of power, it is therefore possible to envisage a situation where

> 'asymmetry exists in each individual act–response sequence, but the actors continually alternate the roles of power holder and power subject in the total course of their interaction.'[21]

Wrong labels this kind of power relationship 'intercursive power', a term he also applies to a kind of 'institutionalized' reciprocity of power where

> 'the power of each party in a relationship is countervailed by that of the other, with procedures for bargaining or joint-decision-making governing their relations when matters affecting the goals and interests of both are involved.'[22]

This model of 'intercursive power', as Wrong points out, has affinities with pluralist approaches to power. Such an approach to power recognizes the possibility, particularly relevant to industry, that in significant ranges of decision-making, power relationships do not involve A simply imposing his preferences on B, or vice-versa, but rather they involve a kind of bargained compromise; although of course, the compromise may well be more favourable to one group rather than to another. Out of this process of negotiation may arise certain 'collective' goals, but the Weberian approach to power, in contrast to the Parsonian, admits the possibility that:

> 'collective goals or even the values which lie behind them may be the outcome of a "negotiated order" built on conflicts between parties holding differential power'.[23]

The institutional aspects of power

A serious weakness of many Weberian approaches to power, however, has been the tendency to overestimate the degree of symmetry or reciprocity in power relations by concentrating chiefly on the resolution of articulated conflicts in public decision-making processes. Yet, as Fox stresses, power can operate 'not only by determining the outcome of such conflicts as do occur, but also by determining what kinds of conflicts do *not* occur'. [24]

In order to analyse adequately such aspects of power one needs a model of power that recognizes its institutional and structural as well as its interpersonal manifestations. Of crucial importance here is the work of Bachrach and Baratz in developing their essentially Weberian model of power to include a consideration of the role of values and institutions. As these authors remark:

> 'Of course power is exercised when A participates in the making of decisions that affect B. But power is also exercised when A devotes his energies to creating or reinforcing social and political values and institutional practices that limit the scope of the political process to public consideration of only those issues which are comparatively innocuous to A. To the extent that A succeeds in doing this, B is prevented for all practical purposes, from bringing to the fore any issues that might in their resolution be seriously detrimental to A's set of preferences.'[25]

Whereas writers like Wrong suggest that the concept of power be limited to 'intentional effective control by particular agents',[26] Bachrach and Baratz make an important advance in the analysis of power in conceding that such processes *need not be* intentional and conscious:

> 'To the extent that a person or group—consciously or unconsciously—creates or reinforces barriers to the public airing of policy conflicts, that person or group has power. Or as Schattschneider has so admirably put it: All forms of political organization have a bias in favour of the exploitation of some kinds of conflict and the suppression of others because organization is the mobilization of bias. Some issues are organized into politics, while others are organized out'.[27]

Nor need this 'mobilization of bias' be maintained solely by the acts of specifiable individuals or agents, as Lukes has emphasized:

> 'the bias of the system is not sustained simply by a series of individually chosen acts, but also, more importantly, by the socially structured and culturally patterned behaviour of groups and practices of institutions, which may indeed be manifested by individual inaction'.[28]

This valuable emphasis on the structural and institutional bases of power, that serve to suppress or 'organize out' certain issues, is clearly relevant to many important sociological insights as to the nature of power in industrial relations—insights that are not easily accommodated within purely interpersonal models of power.

A major characteristic of the mobilization of bias in industry has been the tendency to narrow the range of 'legitimate' conflict, 'organizing out' key control issues and 'organizing in' economistic issues that offer a less immediate threat to managerial control. Management have reinforced this process, consciously or unconsciously, by being more prepared to concede on 'economic' issues than on 'control' issues. Thus as Michael Mann has commented:

> 'What we call the institutionalization of industrial conflict is nothing more nor less than the narrowing down of conflict to aggressive economism and defensive control'.[29]

This bias of the system, however, is not sustained purely by the acts, intentional or otherwise, of individual managers; it is also sustained by the very institution of collective bargaining which tends to suppress the articulation of certain grievances and 'organize out' certain types of conflict, thereby confining the scope of the bargaining process to relatively 'safe' issues. These institutional manifestations of power tend to prevent certain potential latent grievances from ever developing into publicly debated issues on which divergent preferences are expressed. As Hyman has commented:

'One reason why certain strivings are unverbalized and certain motivations unstated may be that these are unsuited to the language and structure of collective bargaining.'[30]

Since the essence of collective bargaining is that grievances and demands have ultimately to be resolved in some compromise made with the employer, grievances tend inexorably to be channelled into precise quantitative demands that do not challenge the legitimacy of the employment relationship and that make a bargained compromise more feasible:

'Demands framed in terms of hours and wages conveniently define what is at stake. Precise quantitative demands give a concreteness and urgency to the opposition of groups that vaguely felt, but unfocused, dissatisfactions about the quality of life would never do.'[31]

Of course, it is not only institutional practices that maintain the bias of the system and ensure that 'key' issues are organized out of negotiations; also crucial in maintaining the bias is, as Lukes pointed out 'the socially structured and culturally patterned behaviour of groups'.[32] Social conditioning is of the utmost importance in determining the kinds of conflicts that do *not* arise in industry. Working people are socialized into accepting the present structure of industry as 'normal'; insofar as the preferences embodied in existing arrangements are the preferences of management rather than employees, then social conditioning acts in a very real way to bolster the power of management, without management themselves being required to resort to any activity that might openly be identified as an exercise of power. As Fox stresses:

'Power and social conditioning cause the employee interests to accept management's shaping of the main structure long before they reach the negotiating table'.[33]

Consequently 'negotiation' tends to be about marginal adjustments to existing arrangements, and not about the fundamental principles underlying these arrangements.

This narrowing down of the range of conflict has been reinforced in the field of industrial relations by the separation of issues into 'political' issues and 'industrial' issues. This 'organizing out' of certain issues again protects and reinforces the power of those groups whose interests are best served by existing political structures, without such groups having to take any overt action. Indeed, Giddens has argued that the very stability of capitalist society

'depends upon a maintenance of the insulation of economy and polity, such that questions of industrial organization appear as "non-political" '.[34]

Bachrach and Baratz coined the term 'nondecision-making'[35] to describe this process whereby such cultural, structural and institutional manifestations of power limit the scope of decision-making and suppress certain latent grievances that might threaten the interests of a dominant power group.

Unfortunately when Bachrach and Baratz attempt to operationalize this formulation in actual empirical research, they tend to regress to a more 'interpersonal' approach to power. They revise considerably their definition of a 'non-decision', restricting the concept to some kind of actual *decision* made by a specifiable individual or group

'that results in the suppression or thwarting of a latent or manifest challenge to the values or interests of the decision-maker'.[36]

In terms of their study of blacks in Baltimore, this meant studying various decisions taken by the mayor and business leaders that served to deflect and suppress the unarticulated demands and dissatisfaction of blacks, and prevent them from becoming articulated and developed into fully fledged 'issues' that challenged the authority resources of those in power; such decisions included the making of certain 'co-opting' appointments, the initiation of various welfare measures, and the establishing of task forces to defuse the poverty issue. Such non-decisions are clearly important in any study of power. They can be paralleled in the industrial context by the 'co-option' of active shop stewards to managerial committees or to managerial roles such as that of supervisor, by managerial welfare measures, or by managerially-initiated participation and consultation schemes, in as much as these heighten employee perceptions of managerial legitimacy and lessen the likelihood of inarticulated and diffuse dissatisfactions resulting in any real challenge to managerial power. But to restrict the concept of 'non-decision' solely to *actual* decisions made by identifiable people appears to exclude many of the insights about the institutional and structural manifestations of power revealed in Bachrach and Baratz's earlier formulation of the concept of 'non-decision'. It diverts attention from the fact that the exercise of 'power' need not involve any action on the part of a powerful group.

It would be rash to omit from any empirical analysis of power in industry this ability of a powerful group to sustain its power by *inaction*. To do so is to run the risk of underestimating the power of management and overestimating the power of workers, and in consequence to bolster up the pluralist myth of a balance of power in industry. As Fox has aptly pointed out, 'the owners and controllers of resources very rarely need to exert publicly and visibly in open conflict more than a small part of that power that lies at their disposal' because 'society is already in the shape that serves their essential interests and purposes, thanks to the power and influence exerted to this end by past as well as present generations of property owners and their many agents and sympathisers'. They rarely need to *act* or exercise visible power to maintain society in this shape because on the whole 'all the social institutions, mechanisms, and principles which it is crucially important for them to have accepted and legitimized are accepted and legitimized already and come under no serious threat'.[37]

'Invisible' power

This kind of 'invisible power' is highly important—especially if one is considering *perceptions* of power. For as Fox has pointed out:

'unless power is being actively and visibly exercised in terms of sanctions, its effects on behaviour often pass unnoticed'.[38]

While management can to a considerable extent rely on their power being sustained by institutional factors, employees cannot rely on this support; they cannot exercise power through *inaction* but can usually only impose their goals or preferences on management through coercive action. This accounts for the popular illusion that workers are more powerful nowadays than management; for workers are more likely to have to resort to 'visible' power, accompanied by overt conflict, than management. This 'illusion' derives in part from the tendency to assume that because power only really *shows up* when there is overt conflict, then power is only being exercised when there is overt conflict. Hence workers on strike are perceived to be exercising power; management taking decisions in a private boardroom are not. This tendency is not only found in everyday perceptions and conceptions of power; it is also an assumption that has been built in to some theoretical models of power.[39]

Yet it is clearly quite conceivable for an exercise of coercive power to occur without any exercise of sanctions that might be accompanied by overt conflict; or even without any threat of sanctions. As Fox points out, a superordinate

'does not actually have to deprive me of whatever it is I depend on him for—the threat is usually enough. Nor do we mean by "threat" that he continually needs to express it in words and gestures—a belief on my part, derived from experience or hearsay, that he is prepared to exercise his power if necessary is often adequate to ensure that I study his preferences with care'.[40]

Thus even where the stated preferences of groups appear to coincide, or diverge only marginally, there may well be a hidden exercise of power involved; one party may well be consciously or unconsciously tailoring their demands to dimensions deemed to be acceptable to the other party.[41] When one couples these possibilities with the capacity of the powerful, through 'nondecision-making' processes, to suppress certain issues that involve potentially strong conflicts of interest, it becomes clear that to equate 'power' with 'conflict' is superficial.

Nevertheless, this tendency for sociologists and laymen to link the two phenomena and define one in terms of the other does have important implications for the exercise of power. It suggests that possibly 'the most effective and insidious use of power' may be 'to prevent . . . conflict from arising in the first place',[42] since if conflict is absent, the exercise of power may pass unnoticed to the public eye, and the 'authority' of superordinates may be secured from challenge.

Of crucial importance in such processes is that most insidious form of power, manipulation. When power is exercised by means of manipulation, power shifts, as C. Wright Mills points out, 'from the visible to the invisible', since in the process of manipulation 'the one who is influenced is not specifically told what to do but is nevertheless subject to the will of another'.[43] Conflict is much less likely in this kind of social interaction because successful manipulation is hidden—'one cannot locate the enemy and declare war on him'.[44] The manipulated party is *unaware* that he has been subject to an exercise of power, subject to the will of another and 'compliance is forthcoming in the absence of a recognition on the complier's part either of the source or of the exact nature of the demand upon them'.[45] The increasing importance of such 'invisible' or 'insidious' forms of power gives rise to the paradox noted by Blau and Schoenherr that 'we today are freer from coercion through the power of command of superiors than most people have been, yet men in positions of power today probably exercise more control than any tyrant ever has'.[46]

In industry, manipulation might take place through a variety of what Fox calls 'social technologies' which seek 'to order the behaviour and relationships of . . . people in systematic purposive ways, through an elaborate structure of co-ordination, control, motivation and reward systems'.[47] By means of such techniques, worker behaviour can be moulded to fit in with the preferences of management, without workers being subject to direct attempts by management to 'impose' their will on employees. Inasmuch as such indirect forms of control 'are more compatible than army-type submission to commands with our values of human freedom and integrity, they reduce resistance, which makes them more effective means of control'.[48] For the growing importance of increasingly sophisticated motivational techniques in modern management suggests that management and certainly management theorists are becoming increasingly aware of the value of 'hidden' or 'invisible' power at a time when more naked and visible power might give rise to resentment and hostility, and ultimately to a challenge to managerial power and authority.

Authority

Of course, manipulation, or the use of 'insidious' or 'hidden' power, is not the only way in which one group can impose its will on another without encountering resistance. The absence of resistance is also implicit in an authority relationship.

Weber defined authority as

'the probability that certain commands (or all commands) from a given source will be obeyed by a given group of persons'.[49]

What distinguishes authority from manipulation is that in the former there is a 'certain minimum of voluntary submission'[50] whereas responses in the process of manipulation are essentially *involuntary*.

It is important to consider the basis on which this compliance or submission inherent in an authority relationship rests. There has been a tendency to assume that authority relations always imply some element of moral commitment—a sense on the part of subordinates that their superiors have a moral right to exercise power over them. Hence in the industrial context, there has been a strong emphasis on the need to cultivate moral commitment to the firm on the part of employees in order to establish and maintain authority relations. Recent research has demonstrated, however, that this moral commitment is not in fact necessary for stable relationships where employees submit voluntarily to managerial power and control. Goldthorpe[51] and Ingham[52] point out that stable attachment can derive from highly instrumental or calculative orientations on the part of employees.

In the light of these developments, it is worthwhile pointing out that such possibilities are in fact recognized in Weber's original formulation of authority. Weber emphasized that subordinates may be

'bound to obedience to their superior (or superiors) by custom, affectual ties, by a purely material complex of interests, or by ideal (wertrational) motives'.[53]

Weber implies that the *most stable* form of authority relationship will be one endowed with a sense of full moral legitimacy, but it is nevertheless implicit in his analysis that full moral legitimation is not *necessary* for authority relations. Consequently one can incorporate into a Weberian model of authority some relevant contemporary analyses of relationships in industry. For it is increasingly recognized that though authority relations are typically based on some mutually agreed or mutually accepted norms, [54] this acceptance or agreement need not have any moral basis whatsoever.

Such 'agreement' may equally well derive from a recognition on the part of one group that certain norms and practices exhibited by another group are supportive of the material interests of this former group. This is essentially the type of situation described by Goldthorpe *et al.*[55]

Or as Michael Mann has argued, 'agreement' can be essentially pragmatic. Mann distinguishes between

'pragmatic acceptance, where the individual complies because he perceives no realistic alternative, and normative acceptance where the individual internalizes the moral expectations of the ruling class and views his own inferior position as legitimate'. [56]

That pragmatic acceptance of managerial power constitutes the most prevalent kind of authority relations in industry today has been cogently argued by both Mann and Parkin[57] and has been substantiated by some subsequent empirical research.[58] The possibility of such 'pragmatic' authority relations was clearly recognized by Weber when he remarked that

people may submit . . . because there is no acceptable alternative.[59]

Weber also referred to the possibility of 'habit' or 'custom' underpinning authority relations, and this too has been developed in recent thinking on power and authority. Hill[60] has argued that shared norms in industrial relations can usefully be viewed as 'expressions of regularities arising out of interactive behaviour'. He suggests that

> norms serve primarily to codify and formalize these interactions. There is no reason why such norms should necessarily become more than mere statements about the regularity of behaviour, because the internalization of norms as morally binding or desirable is not the necessary consequence of such interaction. Interaction can and does become habitual and can be stable over time without either party attaching moral value to it or treating it as legitimate in terms of social values'.[61]

Although, as Hill points out, such regularities

> 'can become invested with legitimacy and develop a morally binding force if continued over time'.

Weber suggested that this customary or habitual type of authority relationship constitutes 'much the most common type of subjective attitude'.[62]

Undoubtedly authority relations that have a moral basis to them are likely, as Weber suggested, to be most stable. But at the same time it is important to recognize that there is a whole spectrum or continuum of potential authority relationships based on different normative patterns, and endowed with different degrees of stability.

The relationship between power and authority

While Parsons views authority as the essential prerequisite for power relations, the Weberian tradition emphasizes rather that power relations typically *precede* authority. As Blau has commented:

> 'Authority typically has its source in the power of one individual over a group (or of a group over a larger collectivity)'.[63]

If power relations may precede authority relations, then the whole concept of 'authority' as embodying some kind of normative agreement becomes much more problematic. It has to be recognized that power itself can play a crucial role in building such normative agreement and legitimizing the existing power relations. As Fox comments, 'any group which can dominate the promotion and acceptance of values holds the key to legitimacy';[64] indeed 'power may be used to propagate the very system of values through which legitimacy is claimed'.[65]

It follows that the nature of authority relations does not solely rest on the perceptions, values and norms of subordinates, but also on the ability of the powerful to mould and shape these norms. The powerful may well be able to influence subordinates by shaping their 'perceptions, cognitions and preferences in such a way that they accept their role in the existing order of things, either because they can see or imagine no alternative to it, or because they see it as natural and unchangeable, or because they value it as divinely ordained and beneficial'.[66] Subordinates are most likely to be aware of and to resent managerial power, and to mobilise against it building on their own potential power position, if they are conscious of having goals and preferences that conflict with those of management. To the extent that their preferences can be moulded, consciously or unconsciously, to coincide more nearly with those of management, then managerial actions designed to achieve these goals will not be perceived by subordinates as an exercise of power 'over' them, but rather as an exercise of authority.[67]

There is therefore a highly complex interrelationship between power and authority. Authority relations may frequently be moulded by a particular kind of 'invisible' power: the power of a group, not to impose its will upon the less powerful, *but rather to impose its own definition of a situation, its own meaning-system and values.*[68] Such exercises of power are clearly less easy to locate than a coercive imposition by one group of its will on another; but they are none the less crucial in any examination of power and authority and the relationship between them. That such exercises of power are susceptible to analysis has been demonstrated by the work of Mann[69] and Parkin[70]. Both suggest that the contradictory juxtaposition and co-existence, within the meaning systems of groups and individuals, of elements of dominant and deviant or subordinate value systems, is indicative of the partial shaping and moulding of people's perceptions and cognitions through their socialization in the dominant institutions of our society. That deviant values appear to relate more frequently to the concrete experience of individuals, while the dominant values held by individuals tend to be the more abstract type of values propagated by the agencies of socialization, adds further plausibility to this analysis.

The complexity of this relationship between power and authority, which stresses once again the importance of less visible forms of power, highlights the total inadequacy of assumptions that 'the study of power should concentrate on the making and taking of important decisions'.[71] The decision-making process is one *aspect* of power relations, but the implications of what goes on in this arena cannot be understood adequately without an analysis of the other less immediately 'visible' aspects of power, manifested in institutional and organizational practices and arrangements, and in socially-structured behaviour.

References

[1] Talcott Parsons, 'On the Concept of Political Power', in Talcott Parsons, *Sociological Theory and Modern Society*, New York, The Free Press, 1976, p. 318.

[2] Anthony Giddens, 'Power in the Recent Writings of Talcott Parsons', *Sociology*, vol. 2 no. 3, Sept. 1968.

[3] *Ibid.*

[4] Anthony Giddens, 'Power in the Recent Writings of Talcott Parsons', *op. cit.*

[5] Max Weber, *The Theory of Social and Economic Organisation*, Free Press, New York, 1947; Peter M. Blau, *Exchange and Power in Social Life,* John Wiley, 1967.

[6] R. A. Dahl, 'The Concept of Power', *Behavioral Science,* 2, 1957; Dennis Wrong, 'Some Problems in Defining Social Power', *American Journal of Sociology,* 73, 1968; D. J. Hickson, C. R. Hinings, C. A. Lee, R. E. Schneck, J. M. Pennings, 'A Strategic Contingencies' Theory of Intraorganisational Power', *Administrative Science Quarterly,* 16, no. 2, June 1971; H. A. Simon, 'Authority' in Robert Dubin (ed.) *Human Relations in Administration,* New York 1972. J. A. A. van Doorn, 'Sociology and the Problem of Power', *Sociologia Neerlandica,* Winter, 1962–3.

[7] Max Weber, *The Theory of Social and Economic Organisation, op. cit.*

[8] For a useful critique see Roderick Martin, 'The Concept of Power: A Critical Defence', *British Journal of Sociology,* vol. XXII, no. 3, Sept. 1971.

[9] Martin Albrow, 'The Study of Organisations—Objectivity or Bias?' in J. Gould (ed.) *Penguin Social Sciences Survey 1968,* p. 160.

[10] Huw Beynon, *Working for Ford,* Penguin 1973, p. 102.

[11] Talcott Parsons, 'On the Concept of Political Power', *op. cit.*

[12] Talcott Parsons, 'The Distribution of Power in American Society', *World Politics,* 10 October 1957.

[13] C. J. Lammers, 'Power and Participation in Decision-Making in Formal Undertakings', *American Journal of Sociology,* 73, 1967.

[14] A. Flanders, 'Collective Bargaining: Prescription for Change' in *Management and Unions,* Faber and Faber, 1970, p. 172.

[15] Peter M. Blau, *Exchange and Power in Social Life, op. cit.*

[16] D. Mechanic, 'Sources of Power of Lower Participants in Complex Organisations', *Administrative Science Quarterly,* vol. 7, 1962.

[17] D. J. Hickson, *et al.* 'A Strategic Contingencies' Theory of Intraorganisational Power', *op. cit.*

[18] *Ibid.*

[19] Dennis Wrong, 'Some problems in defining social power', *American Journal of Sociology,* 73, 1968.

[20] Roderick Martin, 'The Concept of Power: A Critical Defence', *op. cit.*

[21] D. H. Wrong, 'Some Problems of Defining Social Power', *op. cit.*

[22] *Ibid.*

[23] A. Giddens, 'Power in the Recent Writings of Talcott Parsons', *op. cit.*

[24] A. Fox, *Man Mismanagement,* Hutchinson, 1974, p. 14.

[25] Peter Bachrach and Morton S. Baratz, 'The Two Faces of Power', *American Political Science Review,* 56, 1962.

[26] D. H. Wrong, 'Some Problems of Defining Social Power', *op. cit.*

[27] Peter Bachrach and Morton S. Baratz, 'The Two Faces of Power', *op. cit.*

[28] Steven Lukes, *Power: A Radical View,* Macmillan, 1974, p. 22.

[29] Michael Mann, *Consciousness and Action among the Western Working Class,* Macmillan, 1973, p. 21.

[30] R. Hyman, *Strikes,* Fontana, 1972, p. 123.

[31] D. Lockwood, 'Arbitration and Industrial Conflict', *British Journal of Sociology,* 6, 1955.

[32] Steven Lukes, *Power: A Radical View, op. cit.,* p. 22.

[33] A. Fox, 'Industrial Relations: A Social Critique of Pluralist Ideology', *op. cit.,* p. 219.

[34] A. Giddens, *The Class Structure of Advanced Societies,* Hutchinson, 1973, p. 114.

[35] Peter Bachrach, Morton S. Baratz, 'Decisions and Nondecisions: an Analytical Framework', *American Political Science Review,* 57, 1963.

[36] Peter Bachrach and Morton S. Baratz, *Power and Poverty: Theory and Practice.* New York, Oxford University Press, 1970, p. 44.

[37] A. Fox, 'Industrial relations: A Social Critique of Pluralist Ideology', *op. cit.,* pp. 208, 209.

[38] *Ibid.,* p. 208.

[39] See for example R. A. Dahl, 'A Critique of the Ruling Elite Model', *American Political Science Review,* 52, 1958.

[40] A. Fox, *Man Mismanagement, op. cit.,* p. 38.

[41] Peter Bachrach, Morton S. Baratz, 'Decisions and Nondecisions: An Analytical Framework', *op. cit.*

[42] S. Lukes, *Power: A Radical View, op. cit.,* p. 23.

[43] C. Wright Mills, *White Collar,* Oxford University Press, 1951, p. 109.

[44] *Ibid.,* p. 110.

[45] Peter Bachrach, Morton S. Baratz, *Power and Poverty: Theory and Practice, op. cit.,* p. 28.

[46] Peter M. Blau, Richard M. Schoenherr, *The Structure of Organisations,* New York, Basic Books, p. 347.

[47] A. Fox, *Man Mismanagement, op. cit.,* p. 1.

[48] Peter M. Blau, Richard M. Schoenherr, *The Structure of Organisations, op. cit.,* p. 351.

[49] Max Weber, *The Theory of Social and Economic Organisation, op. cit.,* p. 324.

[50] *Ibid.*

[51] John H. Goldthorpe, David Lockwood, Frank Bechhofer, Jennifer Platt, *The Affluent Worker: Industrial Attitudes and Behaviour,* Cambridge University Press, 1968.

[52] Geoffrey K. Ingham, *Size of Industrial Organisation and Worker Behaviour,* Cambridge University Press, 1970.

[53] Max Weber, *The Theory of Social and Economic Organisations, op. cit.,* p. 324.

[54] A. Fox, *A Sociology of Work in Industry,* Collier Macmillan, 1971, p. 70.

[55] J. Goldthorpe *et al., The Affluent Worker: Industrial Attitudes and Behaviour, op. cit.*

[56] Michael Mann, 'The Social Cohesion of Liberal Democracy', *American Sociological Review,* vol. 35, no. 3, 1970.

[57] Frank Parkin, *Class, Inequality and Political Order,* Paladin, 1972.

[58] R. M. Blackburn, Michael Mann, 'Ideologies in the Nonskilled Working Class', unpublished paper, April 1973.

[59] Max Weber, *The Theory of Social and Economic Organisation, op. cit.,* p. 326.

[60] Stephen Hill, 'Norms, Groups and Power; the Sociology of Workplace Industrial Relations', *British Journal of Industrial Relations,* vol. XII, no. 2, July 1974, p. 230.

[61] *Ibid.,* p. 230.

[62] Max Weber, *The Theory of Social and Economic Organisation, op. cit.,* p. 321.

[63] Peter M. Blau, *Exchange and Power in Social Life, op. cit.,* p. 211.

[64] A. Fox, 'A Sociology of Work in Industry', *op. cit.,* p. 54.

[65] *Ibid.,* p. 69.

[66] Steven Lukes, *Power: A Radical View, op. cit.,* p. 23.

[67] See J. G. March, H. A. Simon, *Organisations,* Wiley, 1958.

[68] This is the definition of power favoured by D. Silverman in *The Theory of Organisations,* Heinemann, 1970.

[69] Michael Mann, 'The Social Cohesion of Liberal Democracy', *op. cit.*

[70] Frank Parkin, *Class, Inequality and Political Order, op. cit.*

[71] David Lockwood, 'The Distribution of Power in Industrial Society', *Sociological Review Monograph no. 8,* Paul Halmos (ed.) Keele University, 1964.

14   Organizations: a dialectical view

J. K. Benson

A dialectical approach to the study of organizations is proposed and contrasted to conventional approaches. Established perspectives fail to deal with the production of organizational arrangements or to analyse the entanglement of theories in those arrangements. The dialectical approach places at the center of analysis the process through which organizational arrangements are produced and maintained. Analysis is guided by four basic principles—social construction, totality, contradiction, and praxis. The organization is seen as a concrete, multi-leveled phenomenon beset by contradictions which continuously undermine its existing features. Its directions depend upon the interests and ideas of people and upon their power to produce and maintain a social formation.

The study of complex organizations has been guided by a succession of rational and functional theories and by positivist methodology. These efforts have proceeded on the basis of an uncritical acceptance of the conceptions of organizational structure shared by participants. The distinctions between divisions, departments, occupations, levels, recruitment and reward strategies, and so forth, through which participants arrange their activities have become scientific categories. Likewise, the participants' explanations for the structure of the organization have been formalized as scientific theories.

As a result of these tendencies the sociology of organizations has failed to develop a critical posture. The theoretical constructs of the field are tied to and tend to affirm the present realities in organizations. Radical transformations of organizations would undermine the corresponding theories.

The basic problem may be seen clearly considering two divergent assessments of the future of organizational life in industrial societies. Howton (1969) envisioned the extension of the core processes of rationalization and functionalization to whole societies; thus, in his view the society would become a large organization with carefully articulated parts contributing to overall objectives. Such a development would permit the continued relevance of rational-functional theories of organizations, indeed would extend the range of those theories. Yet, the process through which this new organizational society emerges would remain outside rational-functional theories, although these theories may describe adequately the operation of such a society.

Simpson (1972) provided an opposing assessment of the future which raises the same theoretical problem. He suggested the possibility of the demise of rationality in organizations and a resurgence of emotional and moralistic bases of decision. The demise of organizational rationality would also spell the end of theories tied to it. As with the Howton example, the process giving rise to and/or undermining the realities to which the theories refer remains outside the theories. Dialectical analysis provides a way of reaching beyond these limits.

Dialectical theory, because it is essentially a processual perspective, focuses on the dimension currently missing in much organizational thought. It offers an explanation of the processes involved in the production, the reproduction, and the destruction of particular organizational forms. It opens analysis to the processes through which actors carve out and stabilize a sphere of rationality and those through which such rationalized spheres dissolve. Thus, dialectical theory can explain the empirical grounding of conventional organization theories because it deals with the social processes which conventional theories ignore.

This article draws upon a general Marxist perspective on social life to develop a dialectical view of organizational theory. This approach to organizational studies has few close parallels. (For related efforts see Heydebrand, 1977; Goldman and Van Houten, 1977.) Marxists have rarely been interested in organizational analysis except to criticize the entire field; and organization scientists, for their part, have made minimal use of Marxist thought.

The dialectical view challenges the theoretical and methodological orthodoxies currently prevalent in the field. The established approaches, although varying in details. share a structure of reasoning or problematic which has been characterized as the 'rational selection model' (Benson, 1971), the 'goal paradigm' (Georgiou, 1973), and the 'tool view' (Perrow, 1972). According to this problematic, much of what occurs in the organization is understood as a result of goal pursuit and/or need fulfillment. This view has been coupled with a methodological stance which accepts the conventionally understood components of the organization as scientific categories. The combination has uncritically accepted existing organizational arrangements and adapted itself to the interests of administrative elites. As a consequence organizational analysis has been dominated by issues of administrative concern. Its primary research questions have been administrative issues one step removed.

Despite this, all existing work will not be categorically rejected. Even work thoroughly within the conventional mode may be valuable. More important, a substantial amount of prior work had remained partially free of the dominant model—focusing on such phenomena as alternative power structures, strategic contingencies, political economy, negotiated order, and co-optative mechanisms—and may be usefully incorporated in a dialectical analysis. Thus, this article builds upon existing work while going beyond it at certain crucial points.

The dialectic as social process

The dialectical view is a general perspective on social life which can be extracted from the Marxist analysis of economic structure and its ramifications. Marx's analysis of the capitalist economy is an application of the general perspective. The general perspective is, then, expressed through Marx's analyses of capitalism but not locked into the specific categories and arguments of that analysis. Rather, a more general perspective running through Marx's work may be discerned.

A dialectical view is fundamentally committed to the concept of process. The social world is in a continuous state of becoming—social arrangements which seem fixed and permanent are temporary, arbitrary patterns and any observed social pattern are regarded as one among many possibilities. Theoretical attention is focused upon the transformation through which one set of arrangements gives way to another. Dialectical analysis involves a search for fundamental principles which account for the emergence and dissolution of specific social orders.

There are four principles of dialectical analysis—social construction/production, totality, contradiction, praxis. These constitute a perspective on the fundamental character of social life. A dialectical view of any particular field of study must be guided by an application of these principles.

Social construction/production

The transformation of the social world is rooted in fundamental characteristics of human social life. People are continually constructing the social world. Through their interactions with each other social patterns are gradually built and eventually a set of institutional arrangements is established. Through continued interactions the arrangements previously constructed are gradually modified or replaced.

The construction of social arrangements is not a wholly rational-purposeful process, although the Marxist vision is that someday it might be. Social arrangements are created from the basically concrete, mundane tasks confronting people in their everyday life. Relationships are formed, roles are constructed, institutions are built from the encounters and confrontations of people in their daily round of life. Their production of social structure is itself guided and constrained by the context.

An important constraint is, of course, the existing social structure itself. People produce a social world which stands over them, constraining their actions. The production of social structure, then, occurs within a social structure. There are powerful forces which tend to occasion the reproduction of the existing social structure. These include, as prominent elements, the interests of particular groups of people and their power to defend their interests within an established order. Nevertheless, the efforts of people to transcend their present limits bring them eventually into conflict with the established arrangements and lead to social change. Sometimes the process is not planned and coherent, for example, where in reaching for higher levels of material productivity people go beyond the limits of present social arrangements. Sometimes, however, people may come to understand the limits of social structure and purposely rearrange it.

Totality

Another important commitment of dialectical thought is that social phenomena should be studied relationally, that is, with attention to their multiple interconnections. Any particular structure is always seen as part of a larger, concrete whole rather than as an isolated, abstract phenomenon.

The basis for this claim lies in the concept of social construction/production itself. People produce social structure, and they do so within a social context. The produced social world always constitutes a context which influences the ongoing process of production.

Components of the social structure then become intertwined in complex ways. Divisions between components are not clear-cut or clean. Analysis must deal with the complex interlocking through which components are built into each other. This involves a search for dominant forces or components without resort to a deterministic argument.

The linkages between components are not complete nor wholly coherent. Rather, the processes of social construction take place in unique, partially autonomous contexts. These varying contexts are not centrally controlled and regulated except in rare cases. Thus, dialectical analysis, while looking at wholes, stresses the partial autonomy of the components. The principle of totality, then, expresses a commitment to study social arrangements as complex, interrelated wholes with partially autonomous parts. Analysis pursues the major breaks or divisions of the social structure which occasion divergent, incompatible productions, and the relations of dominance between sectors or layers of the social structure.

Because social construction is an emergent, partially autonomous process; the realities accepted by participants at any particular time may be continually undermined by ongoing acts of social construction. Even powerful actors may be unable to maintain an orderly, rationalized system of social relations in the face of this ongoing process. The totality, conceived dialectically then, includes newly emerging social arrangements as well as those already in place.

Contradiction

Contradiction in the social order is a third principle of a Marxist dialectical view. The social order produced in the process of social construction contains contradictions, ruptures, inconsistencies, and incompatibilities in the fabric of social life. Radical breaks with the present order are possible because of *contradictions*. Some of these are necessary features of a particular order. For example, an integral part of capitalist social formations is that they are antithetical to the interests of labor, yet the functioning system maintains or reproduces this contradiction.

Other contradictions, by contrast, are system-destructive, that is, their presence undermines the system and destroys it. In classical Marxist analysis, the contradiction between the forces of production and economic relations is of this type. The advancement of the productive forces brings these into contradiction with the established system of economic relations. Economic systems pass from the scene as a consequence of this contradiction. (See Godelier, 1972.)

The ongoing process of social construction produces social formations. Once produced, these develop a seemingly autonomous, determinate structure. The structure may be studied and orderly relations between its components may be observed as if it were not a human product. Hence, conventional, theoretical approaches and positivistic methodologies may contribute to the description of these orderly patterns.

The dialectical approach differs from conventional strategies in treating these orderly patterns as created, produced arrangements with latent possibilities which can be transformed. The dialectical vision of the future is not one of continuous, predictable development through an extension or consolidation of the present order; rather, the future has many possibilities and the final determination depends upon human action or praxis (Marković, 1974: 210).

Social contradictions have important effects upon production. (1) They may occasion dislocations and crises which activate the search for alternative social arrangements; (2) they may combine in ways which facilitate or in ways which thwart social mobilization; (3) they may define the limits of change within a particular period or within a given system. Consciousness of these limits may permit the ultimate negation of the limits; but in the interim the contradictions may be quite constraining.

Praxis

The final principle is praxis or the free and creative reconstruction of social arrangements on the basis of a reasoned analysis of both the limits and the potentials of present social forms.

The commitment to praxis is both a description—that is, that people under some circumstances can become active agents reconstructing their own social relations and ultimately themselves on the basis of rational analysis—and an ethical commitment—that is, that social science should contribute to the process of reconstruction, to the liberation of human potential through the production of new social formations.

Dialectical analysis contributes to this process in part by dereifying established social patterns and structures—points out their arbitrary character, undermines their sense of inevitability, uncovers the contradictions and limits of the present order, and reveals the mechanisms of transformation.

An important dimension of such analysis is the critique of theories which affirm the present order or which deal only with minor adjustments or variations upon that order. From a dialectical perspective, the practice of social science is, like other human activities, a process of production imbedded in a social context. The social scientist uses the tools and raw materials at hand to construct realities.

The next section explores the implications of each of the general principles for the analysis of organizational phenomena. This involves the formulation of a conceptual apparatus and a methodology appropriate to the dialectical study of complex organizations.

The social production of organizational reality

An organization as part of the social world is always in a state of becoming; it is not a fixed and determinate entity. Its major features—goals, structural arrangements, technology, informal relations, and so on—are the outcroppings of the process of social construction. The dialectical perspective focuses attention upon this process through which a specific organizational form has been produced, the mechanisms through which an established form is maintained (or reproduced), and its continuous reconstruction.

The organization is a product of past acts of social construction. As a product, it has some orderly, predictable relationships among its components at any particular point in time. These relationships may be studied scientifically and empirical generalizations may be framed to describe the order. In fact, this is the focus of much sociological research on organizations—for example, Perrow (1967), Woodward (1965; 1970), Zwerman (1970), and others found correlations between the technologies and the power structures of organizations. The demonstration of such relations, however, is not the end of inquiry but the beginning. Rather than treating such relationships as determinate, causal connections, for instance, arguing that technology determines social structure, the dialectician investigates the social process through which the orderly, predictable relations have been produced and reproduced.

There is a tendency in much organizational research to interpret observed correlations in terms of a hypothetical social process. For example, Blau and Schoenherr (1971) formulated some possible processes through which executives decide to increase organizational differentiation. Actual historical research tracing the sequence of events, however, has been rare. (See Chandler, 1962, for an exception.) The usual explanatory strategy, as with Blau and Schoenherr, is to formulate a hypothetical

sequence involving actors who make rational or functional decisions, for example, fitting structure to technology in order to achieve efficiency.

Dialectical explanations observe or reconstruct sequences on the basis of historical evidence. The alternatives conceived by actors are explored; the constraints upon their decisions discovered; and the power bases of various actors uncovered. Once a pattern of organizational life is discovered, the processes through which it is maintained and/or modified are studied. Thus, an orderly pattern is taken to be a crystallized but temporary outcome of the process of social construction whose emergence and maintenance demands explanation. Several principles of social construction may be ventured as tentative guidelines for such investigations.

Ideas and actions

The consciousness of organizational participants is partially autonomous from the contextual situations in which they exist (Murphy, 1971). They are not in any simple sense captives of the roles, official purposes, or established procedures of the organization. The participants fill these 'forms' with unique 'content.' Sometimes they may do so in an automatic, unreflective way; in other periods they may become very purposeful in trying to reach beyond the limits of their present situation, to reconstruct the organization in accord with alternative conceptions of its purposes, structures, technologies, and other features. Zald and McCarthy (1975) and Strauss and others (Strauss *et al.*, 1964; Bucher and Stelling, 1969; Bucher, 1970) have provided examples of this phenomenon.

Interests

The process of social construction proceeds through the mediation of interests in which the participants' perspectives are affected by the present structure of advantages and disadvantages built into the organization. This is not to say that a perfect correspondence between interests and ideas will prevail at all times—rather, over time the structure of interests will gradually influence the formation of ideas. In crisis periods, when thoroughgoing change is possible, participants may see their interests more clearly and conform their ideas and actions closely to them.

Power

The ideas which guide the construction of the organization depend upon the power of various participants, that is, their capacity to control the direction of events. Some parties are in dominant positions permitting the imposition and enforcement of their conceptions of reality. Others are in positions of relative weakness and must act in conformity with the definitions of others. (See Silverman, 1971, for a similar analysis.)

Power in the organization derives to some extent from the official authority structure. Those occupying positions of authority have power to establish and enforce a model. They can design the organization as an instrument in the service of specific purposes. They can articulate its parts, adjust its technology and motivate its participants with certain ends in view. Once the organization is stabilized, they can use their power to maintain it as a rationally articulated structure by resisting interference from outside and opposing sources of resistance inside. (See Bendix, 1956, for a particularly valuable documentation of such processes.)

In most organization theories this state of affairs is assumed and is outside the area of inquiry. The organization is assumed to be an instrument designed for a purpose, and research focuses on the structural consequences flowing from that and on the technical adjustments necessary to enhance goal pursuit. The power base of the leadership is not examined; alternative systems based on different power bases are not considered. Perrow (1972) explicitly recognized that the organization is a tool in the hands of powerful actors; but he did not provide a framework for analysing the struggle to control the tool. Rather, he asserted that organizational analysis should permit us to assess the effectiveness of organizational instruments for reaching specific objectives.

An examination of the power base of authority figures would generally extend beyond the boundaries of the organization itself and this is perhaps why most organization theorists have avoided the problem. The grounding of organizational authority in larger systems—inter-organizational networks, political-economic power blocs, legal systems, and the like—is important to the dialectical approach. Crises in the universities in the late 1960s and the ultimate reliance of university administrators upon military and police forces to maintain order have demonstrated the importance of such investigations.

The sources of power to resist and ultimately to overturn the official authority structure of organizations are also important foci of dialectical analysis. How are some groups better able than others to extract advantages and privileges from the organization? How are some groups better able than others to influence the major decisions affecting the direction of the organization? Analyses of control over uncertainty by Crozier (1964; 1972; 1973); Pfeffer (1972; 1973; Pfeffer and Leblebici, 1973; Pfeffer and Salancik, 1974; Salancik and Pfeffer, 1974; Pfeffer, Salancik, and Leblebici, 1976) and Hickson (Hickson er al., 1971; Hinings et al., 1974) have provided important beginnings on such questions. Yet, these insightful analyses must be placed within a more encompassing framework with a critical-reflexive component, otherwise, this line of investigation breaks down easily into a technocratic effort to reduce irrational bases of resistance to authority. Also, analyses of 'negotiated order' by Strauss, Bucher, and others (Strauss et al., 1963; Bucher, 1970) may provide valuable elements of an explanation, even though their efforts are faulty in giving the impression that everything of importance is currently negotiable. (See Benson and Day, 1976, for a critique.) Likewise, the arguments of Bell (1973), Galbraith (1967), and Touraine (1971) stressing the centrality of occupations to the core technology of the organization as a basis of power should be explored, being careful not to accept the deterministic, functional explanations implicit in some of these analyses (particularly those of Bell and Galbraith).

The mobilization of participants to pursue their interests and to reach out for alternative structural arrangements is also a significant component of a dialectical analysis of power. Occupational groups, racial groups, social classes, and others may envision alternatives and become actively committed to their achievement. Such mobilization of commitment and resources will greatly enhance their power in the organization. It is intriguing that mobilization has been given little thought in organizational theory despite its obvious significance in the labor movement. Although mobilization has been prominent in other fields such as collective behavior, race relations, and politics, it seems to lie outside the paradigm of organizational studies. A few observers with analytical roots in these other fields have analysed mobilization in organizations (Gamson, 1975; Bachrach and Baratz, 1970), as have students of social movement organizations (Zald and Ash, 1966). These efforts, however, are clearly outside the mainstream of organizational studies.

The organization as a totality

In a dialectical analysis the organization must be studied as a whole with multiple, interpenetrating levels and sectors. This means conceptualizing the organization as a concrete total phenomenon and attending to the intricate ways in which its components are tied together. The conventional, taken-for-granted distinctions should be rejected as the boundaries of inquiry. For example, abstracting a 'formal structure' from the flux of ongoing social life is an unacceptable move for the dialectician; for concrete social life consists of an intricate interplay between form and content, between structure and process, and the like. Similarly, abstracting a sphere of 'rational action' from the daily round of events is an equally serious error. Organizational phenomena must be understood as wholes in all of their inter-penetrating complexity.

The principle of totality also directs us to see the intricate ties of organizations to the larger society—not only to macro-structural features such as economic and political systems but also to the every-day activities of people. Again, the arbitrary but conventional boundaries between phenomena must be distrusted. The conventional separation between organization and environment must be critically examined. The essential continuity, the relational character of social life must itself be analysed and not overlooked in a search for analytical boundaries and units of analysis. The processes through which such conventional boundaries are produced and sus-tained must be pursued. The interests and power relations on which the conventional boundaries rest must be examined.

The presently established approaches to organiza-tion theory, by contrast, rely upon abstraction. Their abstractions correspond closely to the conventional administrative view and function as an ideology jus-tifying, rationalizing administrative actions as well as a normative model or goal of administrative actions. That the model corresponds to our experience and seems reasonable is an indicator of our indoctrina-tion with the administrative perspective and of the success of administrators in constructing a world in this image.

The history of organization theory may be seen, in part, as a process in which a series of 'nonrational factors' have been conjured up only to be subdued by the rationalizing core. Thus, in the 1930s human relations theory arose as a champion of the informal structure. The thrust of human relations theory, however, was to harness and control the informal in the interest of rationality. Later, the environment emerged as an important challenge in the work of Selznick (1949) and others. Yet through the years the trend has been toward extending the tentacles of rationalization to this sphere as well. Thus, recent theorists like March and Simon (1958), Lawrence and Lorsch (1967), and the school termed 'neo-Weberians' by Perrow (1972) espouse a refined rationalism in which the sources of irrationality internal and external to the organization can be con-tained. This corresponds, incidentally, with an era of organizational monsters which Perrow (1972) warns

control their environments and in which principles of rationalization and functionalization are being extended to wider spheres of social life (Howton, 1969).

Dialectical analysis is not to be restricted to the narrow, limited, conventional reality promulgated by administrators. Its focus is the total organization from which this limited segment has been wrenched. It analyses the intricate ways in which the organiza-tion as a rationally articulated structure is linked to its unrationalized context; it explores and uncovers the social and political processes through which a segmental view becomes dominant and is enforced; and, it anticipates the emergence of new arrange-ments based on shifting power relations. Thus, the dialectical view takes the rationalized organization as an arbitrary model unevenly imposed upon events and insecure in its hold.

Organizational contradictions

The organizational totality, as conceived dialecti-cally, is characterized by ruptures, breaks, and inconsistencies in the social fabric. To these we apply the general term 'contradiction,' while recognizing that such rifts may be of many different types. Many theorists see the organization as a reasonably coher-ent, integrated system, rationally articulated or func-tionally adjusted. This view, of course, is an abstrac-tion. If one looks at the organization concretely and pays attention to its multiple levels and varied rela-tions to the larger society, contradictions become an obvious and important feature of organizational life. (See Heydebrand, 1977.)

The production of contradictions

Social construction-production is not a rationally guided, centrally controlled process. Despite the efforts of administrations to contain and channel the process, some elements in the organization and out-side of it remain beyond the reach of rationalization. Beyond this, the rationalization process produces structures which then resist further rationalization.

Some contradictions are generated within the organization—growing out of the divisions, reward structures, control structures, and other separation points in the organization. These define distinct, semi-autonomous spheres of social action, which are divergent contexts for social construction-production. The people occupying particular loca-tions will tend to develop models of organizational structure based on their peculiar priorities and problems—from a specific occupational or depart-mental standpoint. Thus, across a range of sectoral divisions or levels the organization generates opposing models or images of organizational morphology. Beyond this, the sub-groups created by sectoral divisions, levels, and the like may be sufficiently autonomous to implement their opposing models to some degree. In any case, a large, complex organization is likely at any given time to harbor a number of structural inconsistencies, for example, some departments organized along professional lines; others, more bureaucratized. Many sociologists have analysed inconsistencies of this kind, but few have recognized their basis as being a fundamental social process.

Beyond this, the ongoing process of social construction in all sectors of the organization will continually generate alternatives to the presently established morphology. This may occur at all stratified levels. Even authorities may frequently generate innovations which are contradictory to the established patterns. Increased use of computers for purposes of coordination and control, new budgeting procedures, and other innovations from above may stand in opposition to previously constructed arrangements. Thus, the organization as established constitutes a structure which may resist its own further development. This should not be seen as a mysterious occurrence, but as a result of the rooting of present arrangements in a concrete structure of advantages, interests, commitments, and the like.

Contradictions may be generated also in the larger society and imposed upon the organization. An organization may be charged with multiple, contradictory functions, for instance, the prison's dual purposes of rehabilitation and protection. This may produce inconsistent moves within the organization yielding contradictory structures, competing interest groups, and occasional periods of crisis. Or, an organization may be made dependent upon support or cooperation from opposing sources. For example, a manpower program might be dependent both upon employers with a conservative ideology regarding work and militant advocacy groups with a radical ideology. The manpower agency may internalize the conflict by developing contradictory components to deal with those opposed publics (Schmidt and Kochan, 1976).

Some contradictions within the organization may directly reflect the fundamental features of the larger economic-political system. Management–labor conflict, for example, is a basis feature of capitalist societies which is reproduced by the workings of those societies. This conflict leads to the production of contradictory arrangements inside all of the work organizations in the society. This sets limits upon structural innovations, ideological formulations, morale levels, and other features within the organizations (Krupp, 1961)

The structure of contradictions

The organization is typically the scene of multiple contradictions. The ongoing processes of social construction internal and external to the organization produce a complex array of interrelated contradictions. The combinations are contingent upon the ways in which components of the organization and the society are engaged. Contradictions become overlaid in unique clusters or patterns depending upon the ways in which different groups become involved in their production. Every organization is, then, a unique case because of the contingencies affecting social construction-production.

Consider, as an example, the knitting together of authority level and racial status as bases of social construction. Where a racial minority is subordinate in the organization's authority structure, the resulting patterns of contradiction may be different from otherwise comparable situations lacking the overlay of race upon authority. Recent crises in some state prisons have reflected the overlay of race and authority. The largely black populations of the prisons have increasingly seen the organization as an instrument of white oppression. Black inmates have created structures based upon racial antagonism, used a racial ideology, and linked their cause to that of racial liberation in the larger society.

Contradictions may be combined in ways which exacerbate conflict or in ways which contain it. Some combinations may constitute what Althusser (1970) terms a 'ruptural unity,' that is, a combination that permits a drastic reorganization of the system. Other combinations may tend to fragment the organization in a series of overlapping, partially competitive interest groups.

Participants may try to reach their objectives by managing or manipulating the combinations of contradictions. It has been argued, for example, that corporate élites have purposely created secondary labor markets for minorities and women as a device for maintaining control over jobs and dividing the labor movement (Gordon, 1972). Of course, combinations produced for one purpose may later produce perverse outcomes. The coincidence of race and occupation produced heightened racial tensions in the 1960s.

The production of change

Contradictions feed into the social construction-production process in several ways. (1) Contradictions provide a continuing source of tensions, conflicts, and the like which may, under some circumstances, shape consciousness and action to change the present order. (2) Contradictions set limits upon and establish possibilities for reconstruction at any given time. (3) Contradictions may produce crises which enhance possibilities for reconstruction. (4) Contradictions are important, finally, as defining limits of a system. Some contradictions may be crucial features of a particular organizational order. Other contradictions of lesser significance may be eroded without changing the fundamental character of the organization. The fundamental contradictions tend to be reproduced in the organization by its normal operation as a system and by its linkages to a larger network. These contradictions define limits which must be exceeded in order to transform an organization.

The most basic, generic contradiction is that between the constructed social world and the ongoing process of social construction. The reification of the organization as a determinate thing standing over against people is contradictory to the ongoing process of production. This contradiction is the essence of social and political alienation. As people become conscious of this contradiction and act to overcome it, they rationally reconstruct the present order and overcome its limitations. Thus, we arrive at praxis.

Toward organizational praxis

Dialectical theory attends to the interplay between practical interests and scholarship. The study of organizations is seen as a product of social construction—that is, theories have been produced by particular groups of people acting within a limited context on the basis of their practical concerns. Theories, then, reflect the social context in which they were created and the practical concerns of their creators (not simply the authors but the larger group of people whose actions produced the theories). In turn, theories are inextricably involved in the construction of organizations. Theories guide actors in their efforts to understand and control the organization. Theories provide models to be implemented, illuminate problems to be solved, reveal controls to be exercised, and so on. There is, then, a dialectical relation between organizational arrangements and organizational theories. The use of theories as guidelines for administrative control and as programs for organizational revolutions should be the object of study. This involves a 'reflexive' moment within dialectical analysis and parallels the kind of analysis proposed by Gouldner (1970), Friedrichs (1970), and others.

The critique of limited perspectives

Many theories of organizations can be understood as formalized solutions of certain actors (usually administrators or other dominant figures) to the technical, practical problems posed by the organization's dialectical character. Such a theory formalizes a way of dealing with (controlling or adjusting to) the multilevel, contradictory complexity of the organization. Devices such as socializing, monitoring, rewarding, adjusting, structuring, and negotiating provide solutions to concrete problems encountered by participants. Theorists pull these devices together into coherent systems which then may be adopted within organizations, sometimes as a result of aggressive social movements. Such theories provide sets of procedures, movements, routines which may be employed to pursue an objective by cancelling, controlling, or capitalizing upon the contradictory complexity of organizational life.

From a dialectical perspective, then, specific theories are not in any simple sense to be set aside. Rather, they are to be superceded in a more encompassing framework. Human relations, structural-functional, decision, and open systems theories may each provide accurate predictive statements about some aspects of organizational structure and process within delimited time periods and institutional locations. The dialectician goes beyond such formulations to inquire into the relationships between organization theories and organizational realities—considering the 'reality-defining' potential of a theory of administration, the linkage between administrator and theoretician, and the connection of social theories to social movements of various kinds. Such issues have been raised regarding human relations theories (see Carey, 1967; Krupp, 1961; Perrow, 1972; Mills, 1970) but, this type of critique must be broadened to include other theories as well. For example, open systems theories appear to be linked in time to the growing prominence in administrative circles of cybernation and its application to the organization structure and not merely to production technology. In this situation, the open systems theories have considerable intuitive appeal and have provided the intellectual foundation for a number of textbooks on management, industrial sociology, and complex organizations. Indeed, such theories may have some predictive power within this new institutional setting. However, it is important from dialectical perspective to recognize that open systems theories and theorists are deeply enmeshed in the social process creating the new administrative situation. The new administrative realities and the new administrative theories have emerged hand-in-hand.

The theories and theorists are, then, part of the reality they describe. Their plausibility and predictive power may be derived from and circumscribed by this historically and institutionally delimited phenomenon. Furthermore, the entire 'package' of events may be linked inextricably to larger and more fundamental processes of societal transformation such as the emergence of dominance patterns within which technology and science serve as legitimating ideologies (cf. Habermas, 1970; Karpik, 1972).

Similarly, theories of 'negotiated order,' which the author finds intuitively more appealing than open systems theory, must be subjected to the same mode of unrelenting critical examination. This perspective has been the creation of analysts working mainly in professional organizations (mostly medical settings). The perspective does seem intuitively to have a high degree of correspondence to events in those settings, particularly to the interactional patterns characterizing everyday life among professional staff members (Strauss *et al.*, 1963; Strauss *et al.*, 1964; Bucher and Stelling, 1969). Some questions that should be pursued about this perspective include the following: Is 'negotiated order' a general theory of order or a theory of a specific kind of order existing within a narrowly delimited class of organizational settings? What issues are generally non-negotiable and thus ignored by or taken as defining boundaries by negotiated order theorists? Are the proponents of negotiated order theory engaged in dispensing its insights to practitioners in professional organizations? Do negotiated order theorists merely articulate and conceptualize the perspectives of insightful actors in the settings under study? (See Benson and Day, 1976.)

The task of the dialectician, then, is neither to reject these theories out of hand nor to accept their accuracy uncritically. Rather, it is to understand the connection between theory and reality by analysing the social context.

The Construction of Alternatives

Dialectical analysis must go beyond reflexivity; it has an active as well as reflexive moment. It must be concerned with the active reconstruction of organizations. This reconstruction is aimed toward the realization of human potentialities by the removal of constraints, limitations upon praxis. This task involves both the critique of existing organizational forms and the search for alternatives. The search for alternatives is based on the view that the future is not necessarily a projection of the present order; rather, the future is full of possibilities and one of them has to be made. This is not an unrealistic or utopian task; rather, it must be tied to an empirically grounded understanding of limits and possibilities in the present.

The commitment to social reconstruction is toward the freeing of the process of social construction from blockages and limitations occasioned by dominance. The larger objective is the realization of a social situation in which people freely and collectively control the direction of change on the basis of a rational understanding of social process (Markovíc, 1974; Habermas, 1971, 1973).

A dialectical analysis of organizations, then, should be concerned with conditions under which people may reconstruct organizations and establish social formations in which continuous reconstruction is possible. This provides guidance regarding the selection of research questions. Some important issues are the humanization of work processes, the development of systems of participation (self-management), the discovery of alternatives to bureaucracy, the removal of systems of dominance, the provision for the utilization of expert knowledge without creating technocratic élites, removing the resistance of organizations to more rational arrangements (for example, overcoming resistance to the development of rationally arranged systems of organization). These are, of course, difficult problems and the task is complicated by the possibility that contradictions will develop between them, for example, creating rational systems may undermine self-management. Thus, the prospect is for a continuous process of reconstruction.

Conclusion

Organizations constitute important instruments of domination in the advanced industrial societies. Any effort to change these societies must deal with the organizational dimension. Likewise, efforts to construct alternative social arrangements within or in the place of the present order must grapple with the problem of organization. (See Schurman, 1968, for an examination of the organizational problems posed in Communist China.)

Despite the central importance of organizations to thoroughgoing social reconstruction, the study of organizations has not developed a capacity to deal with fundamental change. Instead, established approaches tend to affirm present organizational realities and to deal with relatively minor adjustments within the present order.

This article has attempted to begin the process of constructing an emancipatory alternative approach by proposing a dialectical view of organizations committed to the centrality of process. Four basic principles of dialectical analysis—social production, totality, contradiction, and praxis—are developed and applied to organizational studies. The principles of dialectical analysis provide a guiding perspective for organizational studies grounded in a view of human social life. The principles do not constitute a developed substantive theory of organizations nor a conceptual framework to guide research. The dialectical view provides instead a critical-emancipatory stance toward organizational studies. Much work remains to be done in developing the implications of this perspective within substantively based theory and research.

References

Aldrich, Howard 1972 'An organization-environment perspective on cooperation and conflict in the manpower training system.' In A. Negandhi (ed.), *Interorganization Theory: 49–70.* Kent, Ohio: Center for Business and Economic Research. 1976 'Resource dependence and interorganizational relations: local employment service offices and social services sector organizations.' *Administration and Society,* 7:4: 419–454.

Aldrich, Howard, and Jeffrey Pfeffer 1976 'Environments of organizations,' *The Annual Review of Sociology,* 2: 79–106.

Althusser, Louis 1970 *For Marx,* trans. by Ben Brewster, New York: Vintage, a division of Random House.

Althusser, Louis, and Etienne Balibar 1970 *Reading Capital,* trans. by Ben Brewster, New York: Pantheon.

Bachrach, Peter S., and Morton S. Baratz 1970 *Power and Poverty, Theory and Practice,* New York: Oxford University Press.

Bell, Daniel 1973 *The Coming of Post-Industrial Society: A Venture in Social Forecasting,* New York: Basic Books.

Bendix, Reinhard 1956 *Work and Authority in Industry,* New York: Harper and Row.

Benson, J. Kenneth 1971 *Models of Structure Selection in Organizations: On the Limitations of Rational Perspectives.* Paper presented at the Annual Meeting of the American Sociological Association, Denver, Colorado, August. 1973 'The analysis of bureaucratic-professional conflict: functional versus dialectical approaches,' *The Sociological Quarterly,* 14: 376–394. 1975 'The interorganizational network as a political economy,' *The Administrative Science Quarterly,* 20: 229–249.

Benson, J. Kenneth, and Robert A. Day 1976 *On the Limits of Negotiation: a Critique of the Theory of Negotiated Order.* Paper presented at the 71st Annual Meeting of the American Sociological Association, New York, September.

Berger, Peter L., and Thomas Luckman 1966 *The Social Construction of Reality,* Garden City, N.Y.: Doubleday.

Blau, Peter M. 1968 'The hierarchy of authority in organizations,' *The American Journal of Sociology,* 73: 453–467. 1973 *The Organization of Academic Work,* New York: Wiley.

Blau, Peter M., Wolf V. Heydebrand, and Robert E. Stauffer 1966 'The structure of small bureaucracies,' *The American Sociological Review,* 31:2: 179–191.

Blau, Peter M., and Richard A. Schoenherr 1971 *The Structure of Organizations,* New York and London: Basic Books.

Blau, Peter M., and Richard Scott 1962 *Formal Organizations,* San Francisco: Chandler.

Birnbaum, Norman 1969 *The Crisis of Industrial Society,* New York: Oxford University Press. 1971 *Toward a Critical Sociology,* New York: Oxford University Press.

Bucher, Rue 1970 'Social process and power in a medical school,' in Mayer N. Zald (ed), *Power in Organizations: 3–48,* Nashville, Tenn.: Vanderbilt University Press.

Bucher, Rue, and J. Stelling 1969 'Characteristics of professional organizations,' *The Journal of Health and Social Behavior,* 10: 3–15.

Carey, A. 1967 'The Hawthorne studies: a radical criticism,' *The American Sociological Review,* 32:3:403–416.

Chandler, Alfred D., Jr. 1962 *Strategy and Structure: Chapters in the History of the Industrial Enterprise,* Cambridge, MA: MIT Press.

Crozier, Michel 1964 *The Bureaucratic Phenomenon,* Chicago: University of Chicago Press. 1972 'The relationship between micro and macrosociology, a study of organizational systems as an empirical approach to problems of macrosociology,' *Human Relations,* 25:3: 239–251. 1973 *The Stalled Society,* New York: Viking Press.

Etzioni, Amitai 1961 *A Comparative Analysis of Complex Organizations,* New York: Free Press.

Friedrichs, Robert W. 1970 *A Sociology of Sociology,* New York: Free Press.

Galbraith, John Kenneth 1967 *The New Industrial State,* Boston: Houghton-Mifflin.

Gamson, William A. 1975 *The Strategy of Social Protest,* Homewood, IL: Dorsey Press.

Georgiou, Petro 1973 'The goal paradigm and notes towards a counter paradigm,' *The Administrative Science Quarterly,* 18: 291–310.

Godelier, Maurice 1972 'Structure and contradiction in capital,' in Robin Blackburn (ed.), *Ideology in Social Science: 334–368,* New York: Vintage Books.

Goldman, Paul, and Donald R. Van Houten 1977 'Managerial strategies and the worker: a Marxist analysis of bureaucracy,' *The Sociological Quarterly* 18:1.

Goldmann, Lucien 1969 *The Human Sciences and Philosophy,* trans. By Hayden V. White and Robert Anchor, London: Jonathan Cape.

Gordon, David M. 1972 *Theories of Poverty and Underemployment,* Toronto and London: D. C. Heath.

Gouldner, Alvin W. 1970 *The Coming Crisis in Western Sociology,* New York: Basic Books.

Habermas, Jürgen 1970 *Toward a Rational Society,* trans. by Jeremy J. Shapiro, Boston: Beacon Press, 1971 *Knowledge and Human Interests,* trans. by Jeremy J. Shapiro, Boston: Beacon Press.1973 *Theory and Practice,* trans. by John Viertel, Boston: Beacon Press.

Heydebrand, Wolf 1977 'Organizational contradictions in public bureaucracies: toward a Marxian theory of organizations,' *The Sociological Quarterly* 18:1.

Hickson, D. J., C. R. Hinings, C. A. Lee, R. E. Schneck, and J. M. Pennings 1971 'A strategic contingencies' theory of intraorganizational power,' *The Administrative Science Quarterly,* 16: 216–229.

Hinings, C. R., D. J. Hickson, J. M. Pennings, and R. E. Schneck 1974 'Structural conditions of intraorganizational power,' *The Administrative Science Quarterly,* 19: 22–44.

Howton, F. William 1969 *Functionaries,* Chicago: Quadrangle Books.

Karpik, Lucien 1972 *Le Capitalisme. Technologique I:* 2–34.

Krupp, Sherman 1961 *Pattern in Organization Analysis,* New York: Holt, Rinehart and Winston.

Lawrence, Paul R., and Jay W. Lorsch 1967 *Organization and Environment,* Boston: Graduate School of Business Administration, Harvard University.

Lefebvre, Henri 1968 *Dialectical Materialism,* trans. by John Sturrock, London: Jonathan Cape. 1971 *Everyday Life in the Modern World,* trans. by Sacha Rabinovitch, New York: Harper and Row.

Lourenço, Susan V., and John C. Glidewell 1975 'A dialectical analysis of organizational conflict,' *The Adninistrative Science Quarterly,* 20: 489–508.

Lukács, Georg 1971 *History and Class Consciousness. Studies in Marxist Dialectics* trans. by Rodney Livingstone. Cambridge, MA: MIT Press.

March, James, and Herbert Simon 1958 *Organizations,* New York: Wiley.

Markovíc, Mihailo 1974 *From Affluence to Praxis,* Ann Arbor: University of Michigan Press.

Mills, C. Wright 1962 *The Marxists,* New York: Dell. 1970 'The contribution of sociology to studies of industrial relations,' *Berkeley Journal of Sociology,* 15: 11–32.

Murphy, Robert F. 1971 *The Dialectics of Social Life,* New York: Basic Books.

Perrow, Charles 1967 'A framework for the comparative analysis of organizations,' *The American Sociological Review,* 32:3: 194–208. 1972 *Complex Organizations: A Critical Essay,* Glenview, IL: Scott, Foresman.

Pfeffer, Jeffrey 1972 'Size and composition of corporate boards of directors: the organization and its environment,' *The Administrative Science Quarterly,* 17: 218–228. 1973 'Size, composition, and function of hospital boards of directors: a study of organization-environment linkage,' *The Administrative Science Quarterly,* 18: 349–364.

Pfeffer, Jeffrey, and Huseyin Leblebici 1973 'Executive recruitment and the development of interfirm organizations,' *The Administrative Science Quarterly,* 18: 449–461.

Pfeffer, Jeffrey, and Gerald R. Salancik 1974 'Organizational decision-making as a political process: the case of a university budget,' *The Administrative Science Quarterly,* 19: 135–151.

Pfeffer, Jeffrey, Gerald R. Salancik, and Huseyin Leblebici 1976 'The effect of uncertainty on the use of social influence in organizational decision-making,' *The Administrative Science Quarterly,* 21: 227–245.

Salancik, Gerald R., and Jeffrey Pfeffer 1974 'The bases and use of power in organizational decision-making: the case of a university,' *The Administrative Science Quarterly,* 19: 453–473.

Schmidt, Stuart M., and Thomas A. Kochan 1976 'An application of a 'political economy' approach to effectiveness. Employment service–employer exchanges,' *Administration and Society,* 7: 455–474.

Schurman, Franz 1968 *Ideology and Organization in Communist China,* enlarged edition, Berkeley and Los Angeles: University of California Press.

Selznick, Phillip 1949 *TVA and the Grass Roots,* Berkeley, California: University of California Press.

Silverman, David 1971 *The Theory of Organizations, a Sociological Framework,* New York: Basic Books.

Simpson, Richard L. 1972 'Beyond rational bureaucracy: changing values and social integration in post-industrial society,' *Social Forces,* 51: 1–6.

Strauss, Anselm, Leonard Schatzman, Rue Bucher, Danuta Ehrlich, and Melvin Sabshin 1964 *Psychiatric Ideologies and Institutions,* New York: Free Press.

Strauss, Anselm, Leonard Schatzman, Danuta Ehrlich, Rue Bucher, and Melvin Sabshin 1963 'The hospital and its negotiated order,' in Eliot Freidson, ed., *The Hospital in Modern Society:* 147–169, London: Free Press of Glencoe.

Touraine, Alain 1971 *The Post-Industrial Society,* trans. by Leonard F. X. Mayhew, New York: Random House.

Turner, Stephen P. 1977 'Blau's theory of differentiation: is it explanatory?' *The Sociological Quarterly,* 18: in press.

Wamsley, Gary, and Mayer N. Zald 1973 *The Political Economy of Public Organizations,* Lexington, MA: Lexington Books, D C. Heath.

Warren, Roland L., Stephen M. Rose, and Ann F. Bergunder 1974 *The Structure of Urban Reform. Community Decision Organizations in Stability and Change,* Lexington, MA: Lexington Books, D. C. Heath.

Weinstein, Michael, Deena Weinstein, and Peter M. Blau 1972 'Blau's dialectical sociology and dialectical sociology: comments,' *Sociological Inquiry,* 42: 173–189.

Whetten, David, and Howard Aldrich 1975 *Predicting Organization Set Size and Diversity.* Paper presented at the Annual Meeting of the American Sociological Association, San Francisco, California.

Woodward, Joan 1965 *Industrial Organization: Theory and Practice,* London: Oxford University Press. 1970 *Industrial Organization: Behavior and Control,* London: Oxford University Press.

Zald, Mayer N. 1970a 'Political economy: a framework for comparative analysis,' in Mayer N. Zald ed., *Power in Organizations:* 221–261, Nashville, Tenn.: Vanderbilt University Press. 1970b *Organizational Change: The Political Economy of the YMCA,* Chicago: University of Chicago Press.

Zald, Mayer N., and Roberta Ash 1966 'Social movement organizations: growth, decay, and change,' *Social Forces,* 44: 327–341.

Zald, Mayer N. and John D. McCarthy 1975 'Organizational intellectuals and the criticism of society,' *Social Service Review,* 49:3: 344–362.

Zwerman, William L. 1970 *New Perspectives on Organization Theory,* Westport, Connecticut: Greenwood Press.

Section IV Multiorganizations

Introduction

Earlier we commented on the realization by organization theorists that to develop a full understanding of organizational behaviour it was necessary to broaden the focus of attention to include the environment. This is a fairly recent development and theorists began by conceptualizing the environment as a rather amorphous mass that was seen in general terms as, for example, turbulent or stable. Since then the focus has been more specific, studying the way multiorganizational networks operate, how coalitions are built and conflict handled, and so on. The relationship between organization and environment is seen as interactive, that is, the organization attempts certain strategies to deal with the multiorganizational networks, whilst these multiorganizational networks constrain the strategies. Thus intra- and inter-organizational behaviour cannot be separated and are closely related.

The readings in this section look at this relationship. Some readings (particularly Reading 15 by Bonis) are from the perspective of the single organization interacting with the multiorganizational field and others are studies of the multiorganizational field itself. On another dimension, there are some readings which are concerned with the development of prescriptive strategies either for the organization or for an agency (often government) intervening or shaping the interactions of organizations.

From the early realization that organizational behaviour could not be adequately explained except by conceptualizing organizations as open systems within the institutional framework, theory has developed as one would anticipate, along several different lines. Contingency theory, which we met in the organizations section, has correlated the organizational structure and various aspects of the environment. However this has tended to be a rather static, functional approach lacking an emphasis on the interactive processes that lead to a particular configuration of organization and environment. Networks have been studied as a structural concept to help understanding of the patterns of competitive or co-operative strategies of organizations. However there has been only limited study of networks as

embedded in community and social structures and as bridges between different levels. Instead the dominant preoccupation has been with horizontal patterns of linkages and interactions. Reading 20 attempts to fill such a gap.

Exchange theory style analysis of the process of exchange has also been applied to organizational interactions, but here again the emphasis has been on horizontal interactions. Further, the theory has not been adequately related to structural considerations, in particular to the resources available to organizations and the power relationships between interacting organizations. In contrast, another more recent perspective in the field has been based on the analysis of power. Here studies have taken as a starting point the *asymmetric* distribution of opportunities, threats and power bases in the multiorganizational field. The theory has then attempted to show how organizations bargain and negotiate to advance their own interests and how they attempt to modify the rules of interaction, redefine boundaries and change the bases of power (see Reading 17 by Crozier). The game analogy seems to be potentially useful for integrating a number of theoretical ideas, and providing a basis for studying interactions at different levels by looking at a system of games. However it remains to be seen whether or not it leads to useful typologies of interactions, and whether more structural or exchange-based analyses are merely replaced by ideas of a fairly static set of games which in turn neglect many of the important dynamic aspects of multiorganizational systems. Thus the field of theory is marked by diverse themes and approaches. However, there have been significant omissions from most of these approaches in recognising the lessons of political science and economics in such areas of concern as oligopolies, diversification, economics of scale and coalition building. Secondly, there has been a rather limited historical perspective in multiorganizational theories. It may be significant that the growth of multiorganization theory has occurred at a time when growth in many sectors of the industrialized economies is stagnating and where increasing state intervention in market mechanisms is proposed by centre and left political groups, and organizations seek to maintain or improve their position in stagnant or declining markets through control of their environment.

Thirdly, whereas the twin problems of complexity and uncertainty have been recognized, there has been to a certain extent an uncritical acceptance of the system of interactions as a simple understandable reality. In fact the contingency theory problem of matching organizational strategy and structure to environmental variety is compounded when one considers that perception of this multiorganizational reality from within the organization will be partial and only some of the controls needed for effective operation will be 'politically' feasible—hence there are problems of bounded rationality and bounded legitimacy.

The prescriptive change perspectives have paralleled the above theoretical development but perhaps certain governmental norms have been dominant, particularly the perceived need for co-ordination of diverse organizations. Hence consideration of effectiveness of central control as opposed to the problems of pluralist self-coordination has been prominent. Such considerations have given added impetus to the 'game' analogy; for example, much of Crozier's multiorganizational work has been on French local government and other authors who use such analyses (for example, Bardach in *The implementation game*) have been concerned with effective government policy making. Given such a diversity of approaches, the selection of papers has been difficult, if a reasonable coverage is to be given in a limited number of papers. Also, paradoxically, the number of quality papers available has not been great, perhaps because of the relative newness of this field of study.

The first reading (Reading 15), by Bonis, points to the need for the multiorganizational level of analysis, by introducing the ways in which the organization attempts to control its environment; examples are by specialization, by financial control over subcontractors, and supplies, as well as by legitimating its own organizational image.

Next Stern (Reading 16) looks at the way in which interorganizational conflict can be handled in practice. This relates very much to the concerns of organizations attempting to control their environments, whilst widening our field of attention to include several similar organizations attempting to pursue related and potentially conflicting strategies.

Crozier (Reading 17), introduces the game analogy as a way of understanding power, exchange and negotiation, within and outside organizations. He outlines some aspects of different games and suggests the use of the analogy in tying together the different levels of analysis by conceptualizing a 'system of games'.

We then broaden the perspective, with an article by Vickers (Reading 18), examining some broad economic and political considerations such as the public and private sectors and welfare economics versus political choice. He also attempts to put the current kind of multiorganizational system in historical perspective and show how some of the traditional ways of coping with this kind of complexity are now inadequate.

Schön (Reading 19) continues at this macro-level with a paper that addresses the problem of social change by examining how innovation is diffused. He proposes various structures and strategies by which innovation (technological or ideological) has been diffused. These models serve as a basis for establishing a historical perspective in multiorganization theory.

Finally Baumgartner *et al.* (Reading 20) examine the political forces at work in a social and cultural matrix. They argue that it is important to focus on the processes and strategies that are used to structure situations. Only then can a full understanding of power in multiorganizations be achieved. If a system of interactions takes place 'within a social structure, the control attempts to restructure the basis for interaction will take place by operating on three aspects of the system—changing actors' attitudes and orientation towards each other (especially trust dynamics and ideology); changing the interaction payoff or outcome structure (gains and losses); and changing the interaction situation (distribution of rights, resources, etc.).

Further reading

One of the early classics, still very relevant, is Selznick, *TVA and the grass roots*. Also an early work, C. Lindblom, 'The science of muddling through' raises the important centralization/decentralization issue in policymaking. O. Williamson in *Markets and hierarchies* provides an economists' viewpoint of several levels of analysis–group, organization and multiorganization. Benson, *The interorganizational network as a political economy* also attempts to apply some of the lessons from related fields, in a condensed but important paper. Three readers, Karpik, *Organization and environment*, Negandhi, *Interorganizational theory* and Hanf and Scharpf, *Interorganizational policy* provide articles that broadly cover the recent developments in the field, the latter with an emphasis on policy. Vickers' books are all useful in getting a historical and cultural perspective, particularly *Value systems and social process*. Miliband, also at the macro-level, provides a more radical approach in *The state in capitalist society*. Finally a very sophisticated (though difficult) analysis is provided by

Habermas, *Legitimation crisis* where he develops a radical critique of multiorganizational systems and society.

Bardach, E. (1977) *The implementation game,* MIT Press.

Benson, J. K. (June 1975) 'The interorganizational network as a political economy', *Administrative Science Quarterly,* Vol. 20, pp. 229–49.

Habermas, J. (1975) *Legitimation crisis,* Beacon Press.

Hanf, K. and Scharpf, F. W. (1978) *Interorganizational policy: limits to coordination and central control,* Sage.

Karpik, L. (ed.) (1978) *Organization and environment,* Sage.

Lindblom, C. (1959) 'The science of muddling through', *Public Administration Review,* Vol. 1.

Miliband, R. (1969) *The state in capitalist society,* Basic Books.

Negandhi, A. R. (1975) *Interorganizational theory,* Kent State University Press.

Selznick, P. (1949) *TVA and the grass roots,* University of California Press.

Vickers, G. (1968) *Value systems and social process,* Tavistock Publications.

Williamson, O. E. (1975) *Markets and hierarchies,* Free Press.

15 Organization and environment

J. Bonis

The organization can be envisaged from the perspective of the individual or from that of the environment. The first is generally used when studying the workers' behavior—showing man dominated by the organization and bureaucracy. It is also the perspective of the psychologists who are interested in the constraints imposed by the organization on the personality and on the individual's capacity to adapt.[1] The second perspective is that of the economists when considering the totality of firms that, together with their markets, make up an economic system.

In each case, the studies may not be directly concerned with the organization itself, but instead, may be centered around a social group or an aspect of the society. But this is not always the case. The studies can seek information on the organizations themselves, in which case the accent is placed on the relation between the organization and the environment. The relationship between the organization and society can also be considered. Other approaches, on the other hand, consider the logic of the organization's functioning. This is the case, for example, in the work that was developed on bureaucracy after Weber. These approaches emphasize, more or less consciously, the autonomy of the organization.

Without in the least underestimating the value of these approaches, we wish to examine the reasons for, and the consequences of this plurality of perspectives. It seems desirable that they be better integrated into an analytical framework that would underlie the study of organizations. However, the two points of view from which the organization has often been considered are rooted in the nature of the organization. It is no accident that they have generated important work. One cannot deny, however, that these points of view have certain ideological implications. As for approaches that isolate the functioning of the organization and do not emphasize the organization—environment interaction, they are even more suspect in this regard, since the relation to social values has every chance of not being perceived. Better integration of these perspectives is desirable for two reasons: to lessen the role of implicit ideology in the conceptual tools themselves, and to be more capable of taking into account the explicit ideology.

Our goal here is limited to a proposal for a more global grasp of the organization through the use of concepts in the analytic model itself, that can take into account both the relative dependence and autonomy of the organization. In other words, we are seeking to explain the dynamic nature of an organization as the process of resolving a double tension that exists between the organization and its parts, on the one hand, and between the organization and the society on the other. That is, tensions exist between the organization and the individual, or groups of individuals who are parts of the organization, and between the organization and society, of which the organization is only a component, albeit an active one.

The organization's social function is to mobilize individuals and groups towards interactions that conform with the expectations of the environment (or a part of it). We shall call the object of this exchange 'the output [*produit*] of the organization,' even if its forms are varied and nonmaterial.

If the very existence of the organization is related to the exchange of an output with the environment, then the organization can not be entirely explained by its structure and internal workings. It would be necessary for it to produce in a vacuum in order to explain everything from the logic of its organization or from its characteristics of production. Simply stating this proposition shows its incongruity.[2]

This is why we strongly feel that the organization cannot be reduced to its social function. It is neither one part among others, nor an autonomous universe. We must consider the organization as an actor with a certain autonomy. This autonomy permits a certain form of interaction with the environment, which favors the organization's survival and prosperity; and the interaction is realized through the exchange relationship which is the organization's social justification.

The emphasis on the organization as a system of exchanges leads us to see it in two ways: as a collection of means to negotiate its output with the environment, and as a response to its situation in the environment. Thus, this response explains the means used, and the means explain the environment's reaction. The state of the organization at a given moment is the result of this dialectical relationship.

Organization and environment

If the best starting point to study the organization is to consider it as an actor acting in an environment, then the relation between these two elements assumes a primary importance. We have seen that this relation can be viewed as a complex interaction through which the environment influences the form and functioning of the organization, and the organization adapts to the demands and constraints of the environment. This can be envisaged, in a preliminary way, as an exchange in which the organization puts forth a contribution and the environment offers a sanction [rétribution]. But the organization does not only adapt to the environment; it acts upon it as well. In particular, it seeks to extend its control over the closest zones, especially those that include the actors who can affect the realization of the organization's objectives.

The exchange between the organization and the environment is organized essentially around two axes (1) the production, and (2) the integration of the members of the organization. We can study the two subsystems that correspond to these two axes in the organization.[3]

The function of the first is to carry out production and to ensure its exchange with the outside under the best conditions for the organization. Whatever the nature or form of this exchange, it implies a sanction from the environment. In this perspective, the activity of men and groups who in some way contribute to this exchange must be related to the logic of the subsystem.

In an industrial organization, for example, the subsystem's operations concern not only the producers as such, the sellers and the people who are involved in the distribution network, but also the clients. In a hospital, the productive subsystem concerns the doctors, the sanitation personnel, the administrators, and certainly the patients. In a union, it concerns the full time staff and militants, as well as the individuals directly affected by union action and propaganda.

It is possible to distinguish between the 'means' used by the productive subsystem and the 'response' given by those for whom the output is destined in return for some remuneration. We should not forget, however, that the means of the productive subsystem can be interpreted as an institutionalized response to the conditions and constraints of the environment. These notions can only be conceptual tools that freeze the actual situation at any given moment.

The second main axis of interaction with the environment concerns the integration of the members of the organization. Indeed, we can apply the same perspective. In this case, we are concerned about an exchange through which the organization ensures an adequate liaison between itself and the individuals or groups on whom it confers a formal role.

We can simplify this by noting that the exchange mechanism is based on the contribution of the individual: working ability, hours worked, etc., and a sanction from the organization in the form of salaries, social status, prestige, contribution to individual development, etc. This leads to an analysis of a subsystem composed both of an array of means used by the organization to ensure the integration of its personnel, and a response, by the personnel, to these means.

One of the advantages of this outlook is that it centers attention on the fact that the integration of personnel cannot be taken for granted. Integration is the result of a social mechanism. Just as the productive system supposes the adoption of a certain number of means used to carry out production and its exchange, so the integrative system implies an array of means used to establish a particular relationship between the organization and particular individuals or groups.[4]

The disguised imperialism of organizations, or the necessity to control the environment

To carry out their purpose, organizations need to establish stable links with the environment. However, the environment is the source of some major uncertainties. The exchange mechanisms involve men and groups over which the organizations have little control, and this forces organizations to run large risks.[5] A response must be found to this problem. A kind of disguised imperialism results when the organization seeks to control the external elements: customers, suppliers, subcontractors, members of other organizations, politicians and political organizations, the press, public opinion, pressure groups, etc.—not to mention the members of the organization who are not really part of the organization until their integration has been assured. This is why it is not enough to try to understand the organizations by studying their functioning and their internal structure. They must also be seen as externally oriented instruments of control.

This necessity to dominate the immediate environment is reinforced by the fact that, in modern organizations concerned with rationalization, stability or, more accurately, the predictability of change affecting the components of the system becomes a very important factor. One of the forces that characterizes the huge corporations is precisely this ability to mitigate the inevitable instability of the environment through the use of prediction techniques that permit the effective planning of the organization's operations.[6] In a technical, economic, and social universe of rapid change, this capacity is very important. It is in part responsible for the development of organizations in our time. These techniques have given the organizations new methods to control the factors in the environment which most clearly threaten the realization of their project. But whether the responses to this problem are the result of highly sophisticated techniques or empirical practice is not relevant to the fact we wish to emphasize: organizations have a propensity to control their environment.

We can conclude, then, that firms elaborate a strategy towards this end. In the most voluntaristic organizations, this strategy can be embodied in policy and in practices consciously directed towards the accomplishment of this objective. But the most formal and seemingly traditional aspects can respond to this necessity equally well, and can be seen as institutionalized means used to attain this same objective.

To seek isolation is one strategy among many. Obviously, isolation is always relative. The organization seeks operations that imply a limited exchange with a relatively few factors in the environment in order to ensure a certain measure of stability. A 'response' of this type implies the adoption of a relatively unambitious plan, and can be interpreted as an attempt to control the elements of the environment that affect the exchange of the output. But organizations have many other ways to act. A firm, for example, can seek to establish production in a local market, thus avoiding national and international competition by reducing its ambitions to a market where it enjoys an advantageous position which protects it from economic competition. Similarly, some organizations can create a protected market that temporarily ensures almost total control over all the factors of production. But sometimes they elaborate more aggressive strategies that, as we shall see below, demand a diversified arsenal of means.

Control of the environment and production

We shall take the industrial firm in a capitalist regime as an example. The domination of the environment can be exercised in various ways. The firm can seek to ensure its economic superiority either by a massive demand or supply of products or by specialization; these are two strategies among many others to gain an advantage over its economic partners.

Technical dependencies are created as well, for example, between firms with the same technological processes. A particular technological practice can establish an effective community of interests between producers and consumers, which can make it too expensive for the dependent partner to withdraw. These economic and technical bonds are numerous. The dairy industry is just one example. Some dairies provide a rental-sale service of refrigerator tanks to the milk producers. While certainly increasing productivity, which helps the farmers, this service also creates a greater regularity (in quality and in quantity) in the supply to the dairy firm; and, at the same time, it puts the farmer in a more dependent position (contract, depreciation of equipment, etc.). Along the same lines, this subtle dependence is manifested in the links that are formed through various patenting and licensing practices, and by certain governmental bodies that are empowered to set quality or safety norms. In this way, these bodies can eliminate foreign competition and take on the role of the umpire between the small number of competitors that are left.

Financial dependencies can go as far as establishing a quasi-total control over suppliers, subcontractors, customers, etc., either through stock participation or even simple voluntary agreements that sanction, either in legal form or informally, certain common interests, etc. It does not take too much imagination to see that similar means are used in other types of organizations. Besides, in certain cases, actual coercion can play a not insignificant role (police, army, gangs, toughs, etc.).

Psychological means constitute another category; for example, persuasion or the interlocking of personnel between representatives of the organization and those that are formally speaking outside the organization. These psychological links should not be neglected, since they can ensure effective control over persons or groups that are necessary in the productive exchange. To take the example of industrial firms again, we note that commercial agents establish a large number of personal contacts, not always only functional, with people on whom the production process depends. There is no doubt that this is an effective way to establish a situation of dependency between the organization and the environment.

Particular importance should be attached to advertising. Advertising should be interpreted as a form of abstract psychological manipulation, as opposed to the interpersonal links mentioned above, since it does not use face-to-face persuasion. The people who influence and the people being influenced do not know each other. Profiting from knowledge developed in certain social sciences, the industrial firms act on consumer motivations to control some of the uncertainty that affects production. Corporations are not the only ones that seek to control the environment through the manipulation of social symbols. The cultural sphere is becoming increasingly important for many other organizations. It could be shown that even organizations that have not been able consciously to develop methods of this type (e.g., advertising) are still interested in these forms of cultural control (the hospital-patient relationship, for example). Propaganda and public relations stem from these same influencing mechanisms.

These techniques can be considered as creating and diffusing ideology. Advertising favors certain social values among those acceptable to the environment. It uses them to the advantage of the organization, both to justify the consumption of the output and, ultimately, to justify the existence of the organization itself. In this way, advertising can better control the elements of the environment most important to the production exchange.

Public relations and propaganda are essentially the same; the former is less directly concerned with the productive exchange, playing, as it does at the same time, a role in the integrative exchange. The latter is more directly aimed at ideas and values. This is why certain types of psychological action could be quite properly called ideological.

Methods of control in the integrative system

Organizations seek control over the environment not only to ensure production but also to ensure integration. They must control their members; they must have sufficiently effective control to ensure behavior in line with the organization's objectives. Most often, it is in the interests of the organization to establish a stable relationship with those on whom it has conferred a formal role, especially with those individuals or subgroups whose responsibility it is to carry out and ensure the success of the organizational project (i.e., top management).

Essentially, this problem is the same as the one the organization faces concerning production. As mentioned before, the organization seeks to control a part of the environment to its advantage. The results sought are not the same, and the methods might be different; but we shall see that they are not without analogy to those we mentioned for the productive subsystem.[7]

A certain number of constraints can enter into the relationship between the organization and its members. Economic constraints are the most common. Many wage earners, for example, especially after a certain age, are not free to change firms. They are, in fact, forced to stay with the same company. Most of these individuals have no way of escaping the grasp of the big organizations. Our society is progressively eliminating economically independent activities (this is especially the case for farmers who must leave their land). Almost without exception, individuals and groups who cannot fit into the powerful organizations (public administration, unions, big corporations, universities, etc.) are condemned by society to a socially marginal status, or at least economically and culturally inferior positions. There are certainly more constraints in the links between the individual and the organization than one ordinarily perceives. This is obvious in the case of the proletarian worker, but individuals in more important posts make the same discovery when the situation is less favourable for them. In reality, few individuals can refuse or modify the conditions of their relationship to the organization which they have apparently freely joined.

In a liberal society, this contract, which is seen essentially in economic terms, binds the wage earner to the organization in which he works. Everyone recognizes the importance of salary negotiations in employee-employer relations. That money provides the motivation to work has been and continues to be a widely held postulate in employers' circles. The key role of economics in the integration of the firm is supported by the social order. The juridicial apparatus tends to normalize and thus reinforce the effectiveness of such integration mechanisms.

Economically or juridically based relations are not unique to industrial, commercial, or administrative organizations. They are rarely completely absent from integration mechanisms in any organizations. Some organizations that might seem to be the farthest removed from an economically based exchange are often not as far removed as their purpose might suggest. A religious order, for example, ensures the economic security of its members. In looking at this closely, one might be surprised to note the importance of economic exchanges to the integration mechanisms in organizations of this type. It goes without saying that such bonds are vigorously camouflaged and suppressed in the ideology expressed by the leaders.

Organizations use psychological methods in the integration system. Social psychology has shown the integrative role of small groups. In small groups, the interpersonal relations have a relay function between the individual and the organization. This is the same as the leadership effect [*effect d'entrainement*] obtained by face-to-face relations within the hierarchy. Such a topic is related to the problem of authority, which has been the object of a great amount of work.

Furthermore, psychological manipulation, more or less developed and more or less spontaneous, is part of the current arsenal of methods of integration. It is extremely widespread practice in our society (for example, it is a common element in parent-child relationships: 'If you are not good, I will not love you anymore.').

There has been much discussion of the human-relations school that flourished first in the United States and then in Europe after the Second World War. It has been criticized for its simplistic socio-psychological character and for the less-than-honest manipulation it tends to foster. In fact, it has systematized and upholds practices which are present to varying degrees in almost all organizations. For example, the so-called paternalist company has a form of integration that can be summed up as follows: the professionals, employees, and even the workers are given long-term insurance (job and financial security) in exchange for their noncritical acceptance of the rules of the game—mainly, that they must not question the bases of authority nor the way in which they are distributed. A 'long-term contract' of this type cannot seem acceptable, or be accepted, withoug ideological support tending to prove that it is the best situation for the two sides. This example is taken from a type of organization that is widely criticized today. It would be easy to show that almost all organizations use psychological manipulation in one way or another.

The parallel with advertising is evident. Human-relations techniques play the same role in the integrative system that advertising plays in the productive system. Both use techniques formulated by the social sciences in order better to control the uncertainties in the relationship with the environment.

The use of psychological means of integration leads to the manipulation of symbols connected to the values of the society. It is impossible to integrate an organization without employing some of these values. Organizations are led to develop an ideological justification that should be seen as a method of integration.

In this light, three types of organizations can be distinguished:

1 Some organizations make rather limited use of ideological methods of integration, or more precisely, the use of these methods is implicit. There is no creation of ideological tools proper to the organization, but the latter inevitably depends on social values.

2 The second type includes those organizations that use means largely based on external values; for example a research institute that emphasizes scientifically rational values (a universalistically oriented ideology).

3 The third type concerns organizations that tend to develop specific ideological methods of integration. Some organizations are, in fact, based on particularistic values. They develop an ideological logic in order to produce an attachment to the organization through the diffusion of its own 'micro-values' (the mystique of the organization). Clearly, this can only be a limited attempt. The organization cannot avoid supporting its action by the dominant social values.

A few hypotheses can be put forth concerning the factors that encourage the development of ideological and psychological methods of integration. The closer the connection between the output and the culture, and thus social values, the greater the possibility there is of using these methods of integration (of the second type). All the more reason, therefore, that this tendency should be stronger if the object of exchange is to produce or distribute cultural products or services. This becomes even clearer when the explicit goal of the organizational purpose is the promotion of certain values (e.g., a political party or a revolutionary union).

We might also suggest the hypothesis that ideological methods of the third type will develop when the output is not directly and explicitly related to the symbolic systems of the society (e.g., in the case of production of vulgar material goods). The nature of the production tasks makes it difficult, then, to concentrate the attention of the members of an organization on a single technique or product because of overdiversified professional tasks or constantly redefined tasks due to fluctuations in the market. Consequently, the organization finds it difficult to use the attachment of its members to the productive process as an integrating factor. In order to compensate for this, it will tend to develop an integrative ideology based on the specificity of the organization.

If one accepts the distinction between long-term integration[8]—when one's contribution is appreciated over one's entire career, and when remuneration does not immediately follow the individual's contribution—and short-term integration—when the contribution-remuneration exchange does not necessarily imply a lifelong attachment to the organization, then one can hypothesize that the first type of integration favors the development of ideological methods of integration. Indeed, in short-term integration, economic means play the preponderant role. On the other hand, in long-term integration, the individual must give more, for the moment, than he receives. The equality of the exchange must be justified, and the members of the organization must be convinced of the permanency of the system to which they have given their trust. This is why it is so important that the directors develop an ideological logic.

Socialization moves individuals to internalize models and social values. This seems to be especially true in industrial societies where the social bond is formed less by coercion than through symbolic means. This phenomenon is essential to the understanding of the integration mechanisms in organizations. In the case of the short-term integration, the organization has no choice but to take advantage of the dominant values internalized by its members (for example, in a firm, the values of competition, technical rationality, etc.). When there is long-term integration however, the organization can develop more specific methods of integration. It can, for example, find support from some surrounding values that, although not created by it, it has selected and promoted among its members.

These mechanisms clearly show the dependence of any organization on the surrounding cultural environment. Thus, to take the example of American society imbued with the values of aggressiveness and productivity, the industrial firm can easily take advantage of labor's mobility. It finds support in values it has not created, but to which it adapts to its advantage. Certainly the organization helps diffuse these values. In European countries where these values are less dominant, one notes that manpower mobility is essentially a wish expressed by certain entrepreneurs.[9]

We might ask if the effect of domination is greater when the ideological methods are more developed and the central values of the society are explicitly used in the integration mechanisms. We might also examine the consequences of a situation where the output of an organization is linked to values which threaten the social equilibrium. It seems that such organizations would tend to be totalitarian, that is, these organizations tend to monopolize all aspects of industrial life. Prisons are not totalitarian, but this tends to be the case for many organizations whose plan is more 'spiritual' and directly related to the value system; for example, political parties, churches, monasteries, revolutionary groups. It would certainly be easy to show that the more the integrative exchange is composed of symbolic rather than material objects, the more the dominating tendencies of the organization on its members would rely on ideological and psychological manipulation. Such organizations require the greatest integration.

It can be seen that such a perspective is a fundamental reversal of the Weberian models of bureaucratic efficiency. Indeed, for Weber, the rationality of the organization is essentially connected not only to the division of labor, to the interchangeability of roles, to the hierarchization of functions, etc., but also to the abandonment, by individuals, of all reference to the objectives and values that the organization defends. 'Disenchantment with the world' concerns not only the ethics of industrial society, but also the daily life of man at work. On the other hand, in the most efficient large organizations, identification with the professional role loses its importance. It is the internalization of the ends of the organization (that is, the proximity of the members to the organizational purposes and to the social values on which the organization is based) that plays the fundamental role. For Weber, the effectiveness of an organization does not necessarily imply the internalization of the goals by the members of the organization, and thus the necessity to develop psychological and ideological means of integration. It seems that if the opposition between the mechanical and organic models[10] of organization is, in fact, a development in which the first term is more archaic than the second, then these perspectives suggest that there has been a fundamental reversal of perspectives as compared to the first conceptions of bureaucracy.[11]

Finally, the professionalization of members in an organization should favor the development of ideological means of integration, at least in the case where this professionalization is based on universalistic values.[12] (This is the case in scientific laboratories, firms in the front-ranking industries, hospitals, public bodies oriented towards the rationalization of society, etc.) The presence of a social value which is held strongly by individuals makes the professional play an intermediary role in the integration mechanism. The fact that the professionalization of subgroups sometimes leads to certain conflicts between the profession and the organization can be seen as a simple transformation in the functioning of a particular model of integration.

The special position of executives

Organizations have an important reason to establish special links with top management, because the latter are the official agents of the organizational purpose. For the same reason, organizations establish special forms of integration with those who may become top management, that is, with those who will be asked to embody, defend, or develop the organizational purpose. In the light of this fact, we can explain more clearly than we have until now what distinguishes the professionals from other wage-earners, high civil servants from clerks, doctors from the rest of the hospital personnel, professors from the other members of the university, etc.

Take the example of a family enterprise. The content of the organizational purpose is closely identified with the family's interests. The present or future management must show their allegiance to the owning family. The surest way is to choose relatives. The growing technical character of management, however, creates a greater propensity to choose top management from among the employees.

At present, there frequently develops a dissociation of interests between the owner's interests and those of the firm as a social entity. Top management influences the organizational purpose, and it often comes to impose a purpose that is clearly different from the initial purpose of the family or its financial backers. In the modern firm, some of the personnel, for example upper-level staff, are, either presently or potentially, more or less agents of the organizational purpose to the extent that they have the power to contribute to its maintenance or redefinition.

This can explain the specific nature of executive selection. Because some of the personnel play an increasingly important role in the firm's performance, modern psychological methods of selection have been developed. It is logical that the firm use these methods on its professionals, and that it take all precautions to choose and develop men who, as producers or managers, are important to its development. But these methods are not used for executives, since such methods are based on research which tries to adapt individual abilities to specific tasks. They do not take into account the internalization of the organizational purpose. When it comes to choosing managers at the highest level, selection is made by co-opting small subgroups that have a very strong sense of loyalty to the organization. This explains, then, not only the existence of a stable link between the organization and top management, but also its special nature.

Limits on organizational imperialism

We have emphasized the reasons that encourage organizations to develop methods and practices designed to ensure control of certain elements in the environment such as individuals, groups, and other organizations on which the exchange of its output and the integration of its members depend. We must now show why this 'imperialism' is never complete and why this control is rarely 'totalitarian', even though it seems desirable that the individuals and groups it controls should be entirely at its service. In fact, most organizations go only halfway towards this 'ideal.' They meet obstacles that prevent them from completely realizing their goals. For example, organizational logic would suggest that they demand the maximum from their members. In practice, they limit their ambitions to a partial mobilization of individuals and groups towards their production objectives. If organizations do not obtain the maximum from their members, it is because they encounter opposing mechanisms and forces. These restrictions on organizational imperialism fall into two categories: (1) other institutions, other organizations, and, more generally, the functioning of society; and (2) individuals and groups within the organization.

By entering into competition, organizations create a restriction on their own tendencies. For example, by offering the same products or the same jobs, industrial firms limit the effect of domination that a monopoly position gives them over their customers or employees.

In the same way, in areas other than industrial production, the control by organizations over their environment is limited by competition which tends to strengthen the position of the individuals and groups that it wishes to control.

To the extent that organizations serve certain people, groups, and values, they enter into conflict with other organizations which serve different people, groups, and values. Thus, corporations conflict with unions; hospitals with governmental departments, unions, and the 'medical profession'; business associations conflict with unions, government bodies, etc. This fact becomes evident when union-management relations are examined. The corporations defend the values of economic rationality, while the workers' unions defend values of 'private life.'[13] The resulting modes of integration take into account these values to some extent. Equilibria of this kind, based on the antagonistic functioning of organizations, are among the most developed mechanisms of social regulation in our society. The unions can be seen as organizations with a purpose that is oriented directly against imperialist tendencies of the organization toward its personnel. It is only slightly exaggerating to say that the firm tries to obtain the maximum from its members for the minimum remuneration, while the union puts all its energy into obtaining the maximum remuneration for the minimum amount of work. Apart from the ideological justification that each side gives, it should be recognized that many organizational practices correspond to this proposition. Obviously, it is more complex than this since one can find examples of union practices that strengthen the bonds between the personnel and the organization. On the other side, as we have already mentioned, firms are far from pursuing only productivist goals.

In the same way, the activities of individuals and subgroups within the firm tend to limit the grasp of the organizations on the environment. They unite, form cliques, restrict or modify positions taken by hierarchical authorities, join unions—all this with the obvious intention of making certain integration practices more difficult. They end up by 'acquiring rights,' that is, they succeed in altering the content of the organizational purpose by not accepting the legitimacy of the practices to which they object. Their influence could be so great as to lead, in certain cases, to a virtual conquest of the organizational purpose by the members. The change is complete when the organization is diverted from its initial project and comes to function for the benefit of its members or a part of them. Note that this changeover is rarely spectacular, and that it can happen in many ways. One of the most common ways in modern firms is the conquest of strategic positions in the internal power structure by certain men or groups who embody a deviant purpose which, because of this, becomes in its turn the dominant purpose. Another form of action consists of encouraging the penetration of new values into the organization.[14]

Integration: exploitation or participation?
Integration can be seen as an instrument of exploitation. In fact, it is a manifestation of this 'imperialism' of the organization that we have tried to describe and explain above. Through it, the organization tends to control its members more completely and thus to limit their freedom of action to its own advantage. Thus, the doctor who accepts a full-time job in a hospital loses some of the independence of the liberal professions; and the new wage-earner in industry gives up his status as an artisan or independent farmer. In theory, one is all the more rewarded for membership in an organization because one gives up personal goals to serve those of the organization. The more effective the integration, the more it supposes the acceptance of both particular and general norms and values. Integration, then, appears as a boundary-setting mechanism that can be added to the list of forms of social control.

It seems clear that some of the most effective organizations have powerful integration requirements. Some modern corporations, for example, ask not only their management but also their employees and manual laborers to strengthen, or rather transform (for it is not enough to see integration quantitatively; it must also be seen qualitatively), the bond between themselves and the organization. This result is obtained mainly through a greater internalization of the corporation's own norms and objectives. This is most clear, as we have mentioned before, in ideological organizations such as the army, the police, some unions, and political parties that seek to control their members through the development of psychological and ideological methods of integration.

But if these forms of integration are part of the logic of the good functioning of organizations, it is also true that they permit certain members of the organization to influence the organizational purpose. Here we must see what is positive about these forms not only from the point of view of the organization but also for the individual. In this sense, we would say that some forms or levels of integration increase 'participation'. The word is presently very much in fashion although it covers the most varied practices and intentions. We use it here in the only way that is not ambiguous to us: participation is the ability to modify the content of the organizational purpose. It is accession to power—not only in the sense of controlling the firm's future but also the fate of the people connected with the organization. In this sense, and only in this sense, participation is not only a product of the 'imperialism' of organizations of which we have spoken throughout this article. This imperialism is directed against the environment and, consequently, against the members of the organization. It permits their exploitation, that is, the mobilization of the labor force for the benefit of those for whom the organization functions. But participation is also a chance for the individual to gain a little more control over his personal fate in a bureaucratic world.

Thus we can give a precise content to the notion of participation. A comparison is possible with the notion of democracy. The two terms complement each other: one describes a reality at the organizational level; the other essentially describes an analogous reality for political systems. The two refer to both the place of the individual in a power system and the possibility of using his influence to control a part of his own destiny, which is connected to a social order from which, in either case, the individual does not really have the chance to escape.

Notes

[1] Cf. C. Argyris, *Personality and Organization, The Conflict between System and the Individual*, New York, Harper, 1957.

[2] Cf. E. J. Miller and E. K. Rice, *Systems of Organization*, London, Tavistock Publishers, 1967.

[3] This idea is implicit in a number of works and is clearly expressed by some authors. See, for example, A. Etzioni, Vol. I, *Toward a Theory of Organization*, Introduction.

[4] The integrative system conditions the efficiency of the productive system. It largely determines the choice of means that the productive system can use, notably, in that the means are shaped according to the needs of production and exchange.

[5] This is touched upon, although in a substantially different perspective, by F. E. Emery and E. I. Trist, 'La trame causale et l'environnement des organisations,' in *Sociologie du Travail*, No. 4, 1964.

[6] Galbraith speaks of the private planning of the huge American corporations in *The New Industrial State*, Boston, Houghton Mifflin, 1967.

[7] Cf. M. Crozier's article, 'De la bureaucratie comme systéme d'organisation', in *Archives européennes de Sociologie*, 60–1, No. 2, pp. 18–50.

[8] Cf. J. Bonis 'Les cadres, l'entreprise et l'environnement', in *Sociologie du Travail*, August–September, 1969, pp. 241–258 [reprinted in translation in *International Studies of Management & Organization*, Vol. I, No. 1 (Spring 1971), pp. 26–50].

[9] We are not at all suggesting that the low manpower mobility in Europe has only cultural causes. Such obstacles as lack of housing, legal restrictions, distribution of ownership, attachments to certain types of family behavior, etc., all include noncultural characteristics.

[10] T. Burns, 'Des fins et moyens dans la direction des entreprises; Politique intérieure et pathologie de l'organisation', in *Sociologie du Travail*, No. 3, 1962.

[11] Cf. A. Touraine, *La Société Post-Industrielle; Naissance d'une Société*, Paris, Denoël, 1969.

[12] Cf. G. Benguigi, 'La Professionalisation des cadres dans l'industrie,' in *Sociologie du Travail*, No. 2, 1967.

[13] A. Touraine states that 'productivity must be put in opposition not to consumption in general but to "private life" ' in *La Société Post-Industrielle*, p. 117. Also see J. H. Goldthorpe and D. Lockwood, 'Affluence and the British Class Structure', in *Sociological Review*, July 1963; and J. H. Goldthorpe, D. Lockwood, F. Bachoffer, J. Platt, *The Affluent Worker, Industrial Attitudes and Behaviour*, Cambridge University Press, 1968.

[14] The conditions that determine the 'success' of an organization become clear when success is viewed as a response to the environment according to the organizational purpose. This last point is fundamental. For example, measuring the success of industrial firms only in terms of economic efficiency is certainly open to question. Of course, such an analysis can be justified if we look at it from the point of view of the economic system. The firm is thus seen as a component of the system; and one accepts, often without realizing it, that the approach is subject to certain social values—those of economic rationality. From the point of view of the organization, which is our perspective here, efficiency cannot be seen without reference to the purpose of the organization, which implies, among other things, that its evolution must be taken into account.

16 Potential conflict management mechanisms in distribution channels: an interorganizational analysis

L. W. Stern

Introduction

The purpose of this paper is to suggest potential mechanisms that might be employed to manage, reduce, or resolve conflict in distribution channels. Very little work has to date been done in applying to the field of marketing the findings of sociologists, labour relations experts, or political scientists on resolving conflict. Conflict in distribution may be viewed behaviourally, as a form of opposition which is opponent-centred; based on incompatibility of goals, aims, or values of opposing firms; direct; and personal; in which the opponent or opposing firm controls the goal or object desired by both parties. Such conflict—behaviour which thwarts, injures, or destroys an opponent—is present in all socioeconomic systems, including channels of distribution.

For any given socioeconomic system, some degree of conflict may be highly functional for the long-term viability of the system. At some point, excessive conflict becomes dysfunctional and produces adverse effects on the system. Conflict should not be treated as all good or all bad. Boulding nicely characterizes the view taken here:

> 'We are not "against" conflict. It is indeed an essential and for the most part useful element in social life. There is, however, a constant tendency for unmanaged conflict to get out of hand and to become bad for all parties concerned' (Boulding, 1961, p. 1).

In this paper, the potential conflict management mechanisms suggested are organized into categories which are consistent with the various degrees of perceived vertical interdependence among channel members. Viewing vertical interdependence on a continuum from high to low, the categories and the specific mechanisms discussed under each can be outlined as shown in Figure 16.1.

| | Degree of perceived interdependence | | | |
| | High ◄───► Low | | | |
Category	Supra-organizational	Interpenetration	Boundary	Bargaining and negotiation
Specific mechanisms	superordinate goals; conciliation and mediation; arbitration; special-purpose mechanisms: (1) commissions of inquiry (2) observers	membership: exchange-of-persons programmes; ideological: (1) education, (2) propaganda; membership *and* ideological: cooptation	diplomacy	bargaining strategy

Figure 16.1 Interdependence and conflict management mechanisms

As is pointed out below, certain mechanisms facilitate the implementation and reinforce the effectiveness of others (for example, establishing superordinate goals facilitates conciliation and mediation). In addition, productive bargaining and negotiation underlie and make possible the enactment of almost all of the mechanisms proposed.

It is important to note at the outset, however, that if dysfunctional conflict within distribution channels is to be managed, reduced, or resolved, it will be essential for the members involved to come to grips with the underlying causes of the conflict issues which arise among them. And the specific mechanism employed will depend not only on the cause of the conflict but also on the structure of the channel itself. The scope of this paper is, nevertheless, limited to suggesting potential conflict management mechanisms irrespective of issues, causes, or channel structure.

Supraorganizational mechanisms
In channels of distribution characterized by a high degree of interdependence and interaction among members, we might expect to come upon fertile ground for the institutionalization of supraorganizational conflict resolution mechanisms. The supraorganizational mechanisms discussed below are: (1) establishing superordinate goals; (2) employing conciliation and mediation; (3) submitting to arbitration; and (4) establishing special-purpose mechanisms. In order to implement such instruments, channel members would have to view themselves as part of a channel *system* and thereby recognize, overtly, their functional interdependence. Even in these situations, however, members will generally have different sets of active goals (or at least different preference orderings for the same set of goals), and thus the conditions for conflict will continue to exist among them.

Establishing superordinate goals
Superordinate goals are those ends greatly desired by all those caught in dispute or conflict, which cannot be attained by the resources and energies of each of the parties separately, but which require the concerted efforts of all parties involved.

If a superordinate goal or goals could be established within a channel of distribution, this would not only lead directly to a reduction in conflict among members but would provide the motivational basis for adopting other resolution mechanisms. More than any other device, superordinate goals could facilitate functional accommodation. Thus, mediation between groups or organizations in

conflict is likely to be most beneficial when effective appeal can be made to a superior value-consensus which transcends group or organizational differences (for example, the preservation of the system itself, common larger interests, shared norms, and so on). Superordinate goals can also provide the foundation for meaningful contacts, communication, and negotiation—as well as interorganizational problem-solving.

Conflict resolution requires an integration of the needs of both sides to the dispute so that they find a common goal without sacrificing their basic economic and ethical principles. The difficult task is, obviously, to articulate a goal or common interest on which all parties can agree.

The establishment of a superordinate goal requires equitable participation and contribution from all parties in interdependent activities.

If the establishment of superordinate goals is going to lead to effective problem-solving among organizations in a channel, mutual identification must be high among the participants. As Parsons observes: 'The focus of the integrative problem on a trans-organizational level . . . is the problem of the determination of the loyalties of the participants . . .' (1960, p. 47). Clearly, then, the varied loyalties of channel members are limiting factors to the establishment of superordinate goals.

As indicated above, a superordinate goal can be an explicit desire by channel members to resist a threat to the channel's survival or growth from some outside pressure (for example, competitive, legal). In such situations, the channel members set aside their differences for the sake of defence. To some extent, it makes no difference if the threat from the outside is real or is simply perceived; it will tend to increase cohesion within the channel. Not only is it likely to result in the reduction of minor conflicts within the channel, but also it may lead to a heightened sense of identity as an interorganizational system and a greater degree of consensus of opinion and purpose.

It is also likely that the process of meeting a threat external to the system will serve to displace or transfer hostility between and among channel members to the common enemy. Because of the information exchanged and because of the monetary and psychological costs jointly borne by the parties during the time of combating the threat, future relationships between the parties may be significantly different than they were during previous interactions. Channel members may gain empathy by seeing, perhaps for the first time, other channel members' points of view even though these viewpoints are presented in a different context than under normal circumstances. Finally, the original conflict issues—prior to the threat occurrence—may decay over time as energies are directed at the outside threat.

Employing conciliation and mediation

The process of reconciliation presumably leads to the convergence of opposing images held by the conflicting parties. In theory, conciliation is the passive role of attempting to bring harmony and a spirit of cooperation to a negotiation over conflicting issues and primarily involves adjustment of the dispute by the parties themselves. It is likely that, in many distribution channels, independent wholesalers serve as conciliators between their suppliers and their customers and may occasionally serve as mediators. Here, the term intermediary has a double meaning, pertaining to marketing tasks assumed as well as to conciliatory functions performed.

Mediation implies more active intervention by the third party than does conciliation. Mediation is the process whereby the third party attempts to secure settlement of a dispute by persuading the parties either to continue their negotiations or to consider procedural or substantive recommendations that the mediator may make. Thus, conciliation is primarily adjustment of the dispute by the parties themselves, while mediation is guidance by a third party to an acceptable accommodation. In the following discussion, unless otherwise stated, we concentrate on the more intricate process of mediation.

Functional attributes of mediation. Mediation essentially involves operating on the field of the conflicting parties in such a way that opportunities or trading moves are perceived which otherwise might not have been perceived. Solutions might be given an acceptability simply by being suggested by the mediator and hence acquire a degree of saliency which is important in making them mutually acceptable. One party often finds it difficult to accept a proposal suggested by an opposing party, whereas if the same proposal is suggested by a neutral mediator, it can be accepted without difficulty. Effective mediation succeeds in clarifying facts and issues, in keeping parties in contact with each other, in exploring possible bases of agreement, in encouraging parties to agree to specific proposals, and in supervising the implementation of agreements.

The mediator's role. In large part, a mediator of channel conflicts should concern himself with getting the conflicting parties together (perhaps over some noncontroversial procedural problem, such as types of forms used in billing), deflating the conflict situation by providing pertinent facts, raising doubts about positions already assumed, and expanding the area of agreement by suggesting alternative solutions to the problem.

Another function of the mediator is to restructure conflict situations by isolating nonrealistic elements of aggressiveness so that the contenders can deal directly with the divergent claims at issue. Once he has ascertained the real as opposed to the stated positions of contending parties, he can suggest proposals in the area of the real demands or leak information to the various sides about what each side will settle for. Through control of the communications structure, the mediator can reinforce or minimize the intensity of the position of one party as it is transmitted to the other.

To the extent that a mediator exercises independent initiative (as in the case of McKinsey and Company or other consultants), he becomes an entrepreneur of ideas and may, as such, play an extremely important role in structuring the network of interorganizational relationships.

The history of distribution in the United States has shown that, if the disputants allow the conflict to continue long enough, the federal or state government will assume the mediator's role. In the latter case, mediation can rapidly lead to compulsory arbitration or adjudication in the guise of legislation which all parties might find difficult to live with over the long run (for example, the Robinson–Patman Act).

Submitting to arbitration

Arbitration is another supraorganizational conflict management mechanism which can be applied to channel situations. It is felt to be inferior to the mechanism of conciliation and mediation for the resolution of conflict in distribution channels, because imposed resolution often leaves each disputant feeling his position was poorly understood. The 'solution' may be viewed as inequitable, and the dispute may easily surface again in slightly different form.

Arbitration can be compulsory or voluntary. Compulsory arbitration is a process wherein the parties are required by law to submit their dispute to a third party whose decision is final and binding. In a channel context, the government (or the courts) have served to settle disputes, as was the case when the automobile dealers and manufacturers clashed publicly over certain distribution policies and when fair trade pricing was a conflict issue between resellers and manufacturers.

Voluntary arbitration is a process wherein parties voluntarily submit their dispute to a third party whose decision will be considered final and binding.

Conflict resolution through voluntary arbitration requires at least three prior commitments among the disputants:

1 They have to agree that some form of settlement—even one involving the loss of a position—is preferable to continued conflict.

2 They have to agree to resolve the conflict on the basis of legal standards rather than according to political, economic, or social criteria.

3 They have to agree to the jurisdiction of a specific court, commission, or committee.

Thus, in arbitration, a preliminary bargain must be struck, in the sense that the parties have to agree to submit to arbitration. It is hoped that channel members would, in the process of undertaking· such a bargain, understand that the whole question of relying on law and law enforcement to truly resolve conflicts among them is suspect, because it is doubtful whether permanently legislated solutions can be equitably applied to future conflicts in different channel contexts. As Assael (1968) has found, internal (intrachannel) conflict resolution has proven, historically, to be more satisfactory, from both a micro and a macro viewpoint, than external or legally imposed resolution.

Establishing special-purpose mechanisms
Two intriguing supraorganizational mechanisms are suggested in the political science literature. Brief mention is made of them here, because they could prove useful in helping to resolve, manage, or reduce conflict in distribution channels.

Commission of inquiry. Although such commissions are frequently slow in operating, have no effective sanctions, and sometimes serve only as a substitute for action, it is likely that, in situations of considerable friction in the channel, the need for in-depth information, independently gathered, might warrant their establishment. One issue of importance in the drug industry involves the problem of physicians owning pharmacies.

Observers. The dispatch of neutral observers to the scene of hostilities by, say, trade associations comprised of the channel members in dispute might be useful in verifying disputed facts and in acting as a restraining influence. Although such a mechanism is similar to conciliation, the information received about the conflict might be reported to the trade association and published in a factual manner in the trade magazine of the association. With the supposedly fresh insight generated by the information, especially as it relates to the various positions taken on the issue, conciliation may be facilitated.

Interpenetration mechanisms
Organizations with frequent interactions may be more likely to develop patterns of conflict resolution or management in their interrelationships than those whose relationship consists of only occasional events. Interpenetration mechanisms provide means for increasing the number of meaningful interactions among channel members and, concomitantly, for reducing conflict within the channel. In this section, we suggest two primary approaches to interpenetration—membership and ideological.

Membership
According to Lasswell and Kaplan, conflict among groups varies inversely with their mutual permeability. 'The permeability of a group is the ease with which a person can become a participant' (1950, p. 35).

Interaction among the various representatives in trade association-sponsored events is undoubtedly infrequent. What is even more desirable is the creation of a network of primary relations among channel members. The possibility for creating such a network is present within many channels because the relations formed within a channel are functionally important to the members; therefore, as Galtung suggests, their conflict-preventing value may be considerable (1959, p. 74). But even on a relatively infrequent basis, the arranging of interorganizational collaboration on a common task jointly accepted as worthwhile and involving personal association of individuals as functional equals should result in lessened hostility among the organizations. Perhaps one of the most meaningful interpenetration mechanisms, in this respect, might be an exchange of persons programme among channel members, similar to those implemented in international relations.

Exchange of persons. In distribution channels, exchange of persons could take place on several different levels of an organization or at all levels. Thus, as part of his initial executive training programme, the recruit (perhaps fresh from college) could spend a prescribed period of time working in the organization of suppliers, middlemen, and/or customers. A salesman employed by a manufacturer could, on a periodic basis, spend a specified period of time as an employee of a wholesaling or retailing firm selling the latter's assortment of products of which the original manufacturer's product may be only one of several. In like fashion, traffic and inventory personnel could be exchanged as well as other line and staff personnel. For certain types of employees, such as relatively prominent executives, it might even be possible to work out a sabbatical system similar to that of universities, so that these executives could replenish themselves by taking positions either closer to or farther away from the ultimate market in which the product of the particular channel is sold.

The best type of exchange might involve not merely a transfer of persons but common enterprises, jointly initiated and carried out on a relatively large scale.

Ideological

Basically, ideological penetration refers to informational, propaganda, and educational activities aimed at managing, resolving, or reducing conflict. Some of the aims of such activity may be: (1) simply to enhance knowledge and understanding; (2) to cultivate goodwill among channel members, gain prestige, and perhaps to undermine the goodwill and prestige of a competitor competitive channel; and (3) to shape attitudes among the personnel of another channel member so as to influence its management to follow a certain course of action.

Effective ideological penetration, independent of kind, should lead to a reduction of bifurcation of images and to the definition of common symbols among conflicting parties. What the channel propagandist (or educator) may be seeking is some sort of ideological conversion. For example, the effort by many manufacturers and wholesalers to influence retailers to think in terms of return-on-investment criteria rather than in terms of gross profit margins would, if accomplished, represent an ideological conversion, as well as result in changes in retail operating methods. In order to achieve such a conversion, it would be wise for the channel member performing the educational role to:

1   Avoid actions that would have the effect of humiliating the target organization(s);

2   Attempt to achieve a high degree of empathy with respect to the values of members of the target organization(s);

3   Adopt a consistent attitude of trust toward the target organization, including an open statement of one's own plans and intentions;

4   Make visible concessions for one's cause and maintain a consistent set of positive activities which are an attempt at the explicit realization of the goals of the organizations involved and, hopefully, of the channel as a whole.

Specific mechanisms. We have already mentioned the sales training programmes conducted by manufacturers for their middlemen's sales forces. Another specific mechanism that has often been employed to achieve ideological penetration is the wide dissemination of trade publications and reprints.

Also, the development of professional ethics in an industry, either through interactions among trade associations or the Trade Practice Conferences of the Federal Trade Commission, may often serve as a normative structure through which increased coordination is achieved among channel members. Similarly, channel members can coalesce to achieve public relations ends. Such a phenomenon occurs regularly in those industries where the retailers are small and the manufacturers and distributors are large.

All other things being equal, educational programmes will have maximum effects when information is presented as part of the ordinary action of a group or organization carrying out its usual socioeconomic function. Thus, it would appear that ideological conversion, if that is the aim, would be easier in on-the-job training situations where channel members interact directly with one another in the performance of a common task than through trade publications or other general information programmes. A unique approach, which is somewhat in between the on-the-job and the general information approaches, might be the establishment of either libraries or training schools or both by channel members, either individually or collectively. In the case of collective efforts, this would take the form of a supraorganizational mechanism; individual efforts would be an ideological penetration mechanism.

Perhaps ideological penetration can be best accomplished through the process of uncertainty absorption by one channel member for others in the system. This mechanism has been described elsewhere in a channel context and is, therefore, only briefly discussed here. Uncertainty absorption takes place when inferences are drawn from a body of evidence and the inferences, instead of the evidence itself, are then communicated. All channel members face uncertainty in their respective task environments and, as Cyert and March point out, 'firms will devise and negotiate an environment so as to eliminate the uncertainty. Rather than treat the environment as exogenous and to be predicted, they seek ways to make it controllable' (1963, p. 120). There is, however, little likelihood that such a situation will occur. One can expect a high degree of uncertainty to prevail in almost all commercial situations. The problem is to reduce the uncertainty to the point where meaningful predictions are possible, based on probability distributions, and to achieve at least some degree of consensus on a realistic perception of the environment in which firms operate. Once this realistic perceptual consensus is established, one can expect at least some reduction in conflict that was based on incongruent views.

Combinations of membership and ideological penetration

Perhaps the most effective type of interpenetration in terms of changing the goals, attitudes, or behaviour of the target organization occurs when the penetration involves both membership and ideology. An important mechanism in this respect is cooptation.

> 'Cooptation is the process of absorbing new elements into the leadership or policy-determining structure of an organization as a means of averting threats to its stability or existence' (Selznick, 1949, p. 13).

Cooptation may be a response to the pressure of specific centres of power within a channel of distribution.

A channel member, given a position of power and responsibility with regard to the generation of policy decisions throughout the channel, should gain increased awareness and understanding of the problems which the channel as a whole faces. Also, as Thompson and McEwen observe, 'By providing overlapping memberships, cooptation is an important social service for increasing the likelihood that organizations related to one another in complicated ways will in fact find compatible goals.'

> 'By thus reducing the possibilities of antithetical actions by two or more organizations, cooptation aids in the integration of the heterogeneous parts of a complex society. By the same token, cooptation further limits the opportunity for one organization to choose its goals arbitrarily or unilaterally' (Thompson and McEwen, 1969, p. 195).

It might also be said that cooptation of channel members encourages their ideological transformation, so that they subsequently tend to carry the ideology of the coopting unit into their other membership groups. Cooptation makes inroads on the process of deciding goals and means. Not only must the final choice be acceptable to the coopted channel member(s), but to the extent that cooptation is effective, it places an outsider in a position to determine the occasion for a goal decision, to participate in analysing the existing situation, to suggest alternatives, and to take part in the deliberation of consequences. When an established organization is coopted, the coopting organization becomes in some measure dependent upon the coopted organization for administration. Using the administrative machinery of the coopted organization requires one to pursue the interest and goodwill of those who control it, the leaders of the coopted organization. And finally, as Etzioni observes, cooptation may be used to create a semblance of communication from others to those in control without effective communication really existing. Manipulated or fictitious cooptation only conceals the need for real communication and influence (Etzioni, 1958, p. 261). It is perhaps for this latter reason that the term coopted has fallen into such disrepute among students seeking change on college campuses today. The same reaction could easily occur in distribution channels.

It may not, of course, always be feasible or desirable to institute penetration processes similar to those mentioned in this section. If this is the case, channel members may have to rely heavily on activities taking place at the boundaries of their various organizations if conflict is to be reduced or resolved. The following section turns to a discussion of possible boundary mechanisms for resolving conflict or for, at least, coming to grips with conflict situations.

Boundary mechanisms

For the purposes of this section, assume that the relevant boundary of an organization is its legal boundary. Given this assumption, a boundary position can be defined as one for which some role-senders are located in other organizations. The personnel of an organization who are concerned primarily with foreign (external) affairs are called, in this context, boundary persons. Thus, in the role-set of a boundary person are his role-partners in other organizations. Within a channel of distribution, two key classes of boundary personnel are, obviously, salesmen and purchasing agents.

Activities between and among personnel operating at the boundary of organizations within distribution channels may be significant in reducing conflict just as they are significant in creating it. Their boundary roles make these persons continual mediators between organizations, for they should be able to justify the position of either side to the other and thereby should be instrumental in bringing about compromise. In the long run, the roles of these boundary specialists should become routinized through the emergence of opposite numbers, thereby reducing the likelihood of interorganizational conflicts accruing from threats to the status of organizational representatives. What is suggested as a conflict resolution mechanism, then, is the institutionalization of some form of channel diplomacy.

Diplomacy

Using an analogy from international relations, channel diplomacy is the method by which interorganizational relations are conducted, adjusted, and managed by ambassadors, envoys, or other persons operating at the boundaries of member organizations. Channel members must persuade, negotiate with, and exert pressure upon each other if they wish to resolve conflict, because, with the exception of the government, there is generally no superior above them that can impose a settlement. Therefore, they must engage in, cultivate, and rely upon diplomatic procedures. Taken in its widest meaning, the task of diplomacy is fourfold:

1 Diplomacy must determine its objectives in the light of the power actually and potentially available for the pursuit of these objectives.

2 Diplomacy must assess the objectives of other members and the power actually and potentially available for the pursuit of their objectives.

3 Diplomacy must determine to what extent these different objectives are compatible with each other.

4 Diplomacy must employ the means suited to the pursuit of its objectives.

The tasks involved in the implementation of diplomatic procedures and processes are similar to those involved in the implementation of negotiation and bargaining discussed later. The functions of a channel diplomat would, again in the widest interpretation, be to help shape the policies he is to follow, to conduct negotiations with channel members to which he is assigned, to observe and report on everything which may be of interest to the firm employing him, and to provide information concerning his firm to the operatives in counterpart channel organizations.

Strains on boundary personnel

Individuals who operate at the boundaries of organizations are subject to important strains which tend to impede their ability to aid in the resolution of conflict. In a study of such boundary personnel as salesmen, credit expediters, and traffic managers, Kahn, *et al.*, concluded that,

'Lacking formal power over role senders outside his work unit, a person at the boundary has a reduced ability to guarantee that the performance of these outsiders will be as he needs and wishes. In compensation for this lack of formal authority, a boundary person relies heavily of the affective bonds of trust, respect, and liking which he can generate among the outsiders. But these bonds are unusually difficult to create and maintain at the boundary. For the outsiders, the failings of a person's unit are all too easily identified as failures of the person, thus weakening their affective bonds with him.

[A consequence of the role senders' inadequate understanding of boundary positions] is the failure of role senders, especially in other departments, to appreciate the urgency or necessity of a boundary person's requests to them. They are likely to present him with self-interested demands and to be intolerant if these demands are not met.

A person in a boundary position is faced, therefore, with a sizable body of role senders whose demands are hard to predict and hard to control. . . . Most difficult of all, the boundary person faced with such demands has at his disposal only limited power resources with which he may attempt to induce their modification' (Kahn *et al.*, 1964, pp. 123–4).

Assuming that all boundary personnel face strains similar to those enumerated above, the question remains: Who are the most appropriate individuals within an organization to assume the role of diplomat in resolving channel conflicts? It is essential that the status of the diplomat be high enough so that the power which the diplomat holds is at least relatively obvious to the parties with whom he interacts.

To prepare the channel diplomat for this role, it would seem important that he be given thorough indoctrination in and knowledge of organizational procedures and operations if he is to resolve the uncertainty which his role prescribes. In addition, to prevent occupants of these positions from developing too strong an identification with specific channel members, it might be wise to periodically shift such boundary persons among the different members of the channel.

Bargaining and negotiating

It might be reasonably argued that no matter what conflict management mechanism is adopted by policy-makers within a channel, resolution is always the result of bargaining—the making of commitments, offering of rewards, or threatening of punishments or deprivation—between and among the members. Insights into effective bargaining and negotiation should facilitate the employment of the mechanisms suggested previously. And channel members often can be viewed as interest groups in opposition over scarce resources. If channel members do not (or only vaguely) perceive themselves as part of a distribution system and, instead, take the position of interest groups, then a bargaining model is more appropriate to deal with the conflict which arises among them.

In a channel context, the term bargaining refers to the negotiation of an agreement for the exchange of goods or services between two or more organizations. Negotiation is a process through which the parties interact in developing potential agreements to provide guidance and regulation of their future behaviour. Here, the two terms will be used interchangeably, unless otherwise noted.

Within a channel, the bargaining may at first appear to be a fixed-sum game, that is, whatever solution is arrived at will yield the same total benefit, even though the division of returns will vary. However, solutions frequently yield a greater total benefit to the channel in, say, the form of higher sales or lower costs. Bargaining, under these conditions, takes on the characteristics of a variable-sum game. In addition, there is, within a channel:

> '... a curious mixture of cooperation and conflict—cooperation in that both parties with a certain range of possible solutions will be better off with a solution, that is, a bargain, than without one and conflict in that, within the range of possible solutions, the distribution of the total benefit between two parties depends on the particular solution adopted' (Boulding, 1962, p. 314).

The strategy of bargaining

Two questions appear central in developing a bargaining strategy: (1) How much is it necessary to concede? and (2) How can the other side be induced to accept less favourable terms than it wants? Schelling notes that 'to "win", a party must make his commitment appear irrevocable to the other party'. On the other hand, if one party can demonstrate to the other that the latter is not committed, or that he has miscalculated his commitment, the former may undo or revise the latter's commitment (Schelling, 1960, p. 28). If bargaining is going to be effective in leading to integrative problem-solving, it is essential to prevent the other party from holding a committed position in order to claim a disproportionate share of the joint gain. In other words, it is important to attempt to keep the other party flexible or to help him abandon a committed position once it has been taken, because integrative or cooperative bargaining requires free and open exploration without preconceived ideas or dogmatic positions.

A stable bargaining situation depends on the development and maintenance of trust and mutual respect between bargainers. One obvious reason for trusting another channel member is the awareness that this member has incentives for behaving in a trustworthy fashion and that its leaders recognize these incentives. In some cases, trust or distrust is based on what is known about another member's past behaviour. Trust is likely to develop if the other member has engaged in helpful behaviour (as defined by the furtherance of the goals of the affected member), distrust if it has engaged in harmful behaviour.

If a channel member wants to be trusted, it should demonstrate that its helpful actions are freely taken and that it adopts policies harmful to the interest of other channel members only when compelled to do so by forces beyond its control.

Some suggestions which seem useful for establishing trust in channel relations come from the political science literature. One suggestion is the taking of unilateral steps to reduce tension. Adapting Osgood's theory to a channel context, one could say that for such a unilateral act to be effective in inducing another channel member to reciprocate, it should (1) be clearly disadvantageous to the member making it, yet not cripplingly so; (2) be such as to be clearly perceived by the other member as reducing his external threat; (3) be such that reciprocal action by the other member is available and clearly indicated; (4) be announced in advance and widely publicized to all channel members (its nature, its purpose as part of a consistent policy, and the expected reciprocation); and (5) not demand prior commitment to reciprocation by the other member as a condition of its commission (Osgood, 1959).

Compromise, like trust, is a prerequisite in successful bargaining. Negotiations are possible only if each side is prepared to give up something in order to gain some of its objectives. The difficulty with the compromise outcome is that the basic problem may not be solved and may continue to be a source of tension.

The willingness to negotiate a compromise depends, of course, on correct assessment of the conflict situation. Such assessment and the following accommodation is possible only if each party is aware of the relative strength of the others. If implicit assessment is difficult, mediation may help, for one of the key functions of the mediator is to make such indices readily available to the parties. The conflicting parties will be able to negotiate to the extent they share a common system of symbols allowing them to arrive at a common assessment.

With regard to the loss of face problem, the logic of bargaining and compromise is not appropriate for the settlement of ideological differences. The negotiators cannot bargain over an ideological principle, as might be represented by the small business ethic versus the desire for efficiency on the part of large businesses, without compromising their moral position. There is an all-or-none quality to moral principles. Thus, in order to prevent the two types of differences from getting confused, it may be best to send to the channel bargaining table pragmatic, task-oriented men (rather than ideologues, as some top corporate executives must be) with at least some system perspective and intimate understanding of the nature of the channel structure, so that the members can avoid bargaining over ideological issues.

Several major problems face the negotiator, however, even if he is vested with appropriate authority. Thus, negotiators face the dual problems of (1) securing consensus among the operating executive within his own firm; and (2) compromising between the demands for flexibility by conflicting channel members and the demands for rigidity by the executives in his own firm. These same problems serve to place constraints and limitations on negotiation as a conflict resolution mechanism in distribution channel relations.

Constraints and limitations

We have already mentioned one major limitation on the scope of the negotiation in channel relations— the difficulty of settling ideological differences through bargaining. In fact, it is likely that establishing superordinate goals is the only means to settling ideological differences. We have also noted that negotiation is governed by, and operates within, bounds acceptable to the firm from which the negotiator comes. In this respect, leaders on each side in the bargaining situation must avoid courses of action which threaten the leadership positions of their counterparts. Where there is genuine interest in maintaining the bargaining relationships, studies indicate that leaders on both sides clearly take into account the limitations that their opposite numbers must contend with and minimize behaviours that produce embarrassment or problem-creating consequences for them.

Clearly, there is no point in negotiating in the absence of some possibility of success. The problem is more complicated, though, if the purpose of one or more of the parties is not agreement but rather the pursuit of a side effect. Such side effects can be positive or negative, for example, to maintain contact (to keep channels of communication open), to gain more knowledge of the other party's true position, to reveal the intentions of the other side, to deceive (to buy time, for example), to permit a forum for prop-

aganda, or to affect a third party (the government, consumers, suppliers, middlemen outside the negotiation, and so on).

Lastly, although this list is not exhaustive, public debate among the channel members is likely to hurt the chances of achieving an effective accommodation through negotiation. Taking a public position in advance of negotiation lays the groundwork for competition to enter, even when the firms would be expected to interact in a collaborative manner. Taking a public position intensifies the problems mentioned above, for when a negotiator deviates from a fixed public position, it means that he is openly going against the desires of his firm. As we have already taken pains to point out, compromise is a prerequisite to bargaining, and therefore it may be impossible to negotiate successfully in channel situations if one side takes a specific and adamant public position.

Other mechanisms

We have not discussed the conflict resolution mechanisms of (1) avoidance or withdrawal (sometimes referred to as conflict denial or passive settlement); and (2) the use of force, counter-threats, and deterrence (balance-of-power mechanisms). We have also not explored fully the use of law and law enforcement or the creation of authority in a supersystem. These mechanisms have been placed outside the scope of this paper because they are either (1) obvious and may require no purposive effort on the part of channel members to institute; (2) dependent for their initiation on some manifest coercive power on the part of members; or (3) maintain the conflict in a suspended and oftentimes unstable state. Nevertheless, by omitting an examination of them, we do not mean to imply that they are unimportant.

References

Assael, H. (1968), 'The political role of trade associations in distributive conflict resolution', *Journal of Marketing*, vol. 32, April, pp. 21–8.

Boulding, K. E. (1961), 'Opening remarks', in E. Boulding (ed.), *Conflict Management in Organizations*, Ann Arbor, Michigan, Foundation for Research on Human Behavior.

Boulding, K. E. (1962), *Conflict and Defense*, New York, Harper & Brothers.

Cyert, R. M., and March, J. G. (1963), *A Behavioral Theory of the Firm*, Englewood Cliffs, New Jersey, Prentice-Hall, Inc.

Etzioni, A. (1958), 'Administration and the consumer', *Administration Science Quarterly*, vol. 3, September, pp. 251–64.

Galtung, J. (1959), 'Pacifism from a sociological point of view', *Journal of Conflict Resolution*, vol. 3, March, pp. 67–84.

Kahn, R. L., Wolfe, D. M., Quinn, R. P., and Snock, J. D. (1964), *Organizational Stress: Studies in Role Conflict and Ambiguity*, New York, John Wiley & Sons, Inc.

Lasswell, H. D., and Kaplan, A. (1950), *Power and Society,* New Haven, Yale University Press.

Osgood, C. E. (1959), 'Suggestion for winning the real war with communism', *Journal of Conflict Resolution,* vol. 3, December, pp. 295–325.

Parsons, T. (1960), *Structure and Process in Modern Societies,* Glencoe, Ill., The Free Press.

Schelling, T. C. (1960), *The Strategy of Conflict,* Cambridge, Mass., Harvard University Press.

Selznick, P. (1949), *TVA and the Grass Roots,* Berkeley, California, University of California Press.

Thompson, J. D., and McEwen, W. J. (1969), 'Organizational goals and environment', in A. Etzioni (ed.), *Complex Organizations: A Sociological Reader,* 2nd ed., New York, Holt, Rinehart & Winston, Inc.

17 Comparing structures and comparing games
M. Crozier

Summary
In the 1950s the study of organizations was mainly characterized by case studies; in the 1960s by sampling studies focussing on organization structures. The biases inherent in the structure studies suggest the need for a new paradigm which replaces the focus on structures by a focus on the recurring games played by the individuals and groups; what people deal with in these games is not only maximizing pay-offs, but also the tensions created by power relationships.

The insufficiency of the study of structures only, and the greater insight provided by the comparison of games, is illustrated by two examples, one dealing with hemodialysis units in two Belgian and two French hospitals, and one with the politico-administrative system in three French 'departments.' From these examples certain generalizations are drawn as to the 'games' approach: the need to study common types of recurrent games and the need to analyze regulations and boundaries determining the games played. The new research paradigm implies a new way of reasoning about power, in which power is seen not as a commodity, but as a bargaining relationship. It also implies a de-emphasizing of structure as the key element in an organization and an interpretation of the environment in terms of problems to be solved rather in terms of variables determining structure.

Comparing games: a hospital example
It is the validity of this latter paradigm which I would like to question here. I will now use two successive examples to show that a new paradigm, more fruitful heuristically, although less apparently scientific in the simple sense, could be developed. To progress in this direction, one should focus the comparison around *games* and not around *structures* and one should re-examine our theoretical assumptions around the basic problem of power.

Instead of conceiving of organizational behaviour as the answer of a set of individuals with their own personal and collective motivations to the demands of a constraining structure, and their adjustment to its prescribed roles and routines, one could visualize it as the result of the strategy each one of them has adopted in the one or several games in which he participates. An organization can thus be considered as a set of games, more of less explicitly defined, between groups of partners who have to play with each other. These games are played according to some informal rules which cannot be easily predicted from the prescribed roles of the formal structure. One can discover, however, these rules, as well as the pay-offs and the possible rational strategies of the participants, by analyzing the players' recurrent behaviour. This could eventually be formalized according to rough game theory models.[1] But what people deal with in these games can also be expressed in terms of power relationships, which means that it has direct affective connotations and consequences. Games can therefore be understood also as depending on the individual and collective capacities (partly cultural, partly organizational) for dealing with the tensions created by such relationships (Peaucelle, 1969; Crozier, 1973; Ch. 1, 'The Problem of Power').

I would like to take as a first example a recent research done by Kuty (1973) on power relationships between physicians, nurses, and patients in four hemodialysis units in two Belgian and two French hospitals. This research is a mixture of the case study method and of the comparative approach. It focusses, however, on organizational units within hospitals and not on hospitals as organizations. But these units have a high degree of organizational autonomy and by analysing their functioning one can test quite clearly some of the most fundamental aspects of the dominant paradigm.

Here we have four very similar units in four different hospitals settings using the same complex and very constraining technology: hemodialysis kidney machines. This would be a good case for showing the way in which technology commands structure and behaviour; yet not only is it impossible to predict the kind of working arrangements by considering technology only, but Kuty finds two widely different, even opposite, patterns of working arrangements and human and social relations. Two of the units are characterized by clear-cut role distinctions; a hierarchical pattern of power relationships; a strong priority given by the physicians to their technical function; a very poor communications system built on secrecy; and a complete passivity of the patients accompanied by strong secondary psychosomatic reactions. The two other units show a relative blurring of the professional roles; complex interpersonal relationships cutting across these roles and in which patients themselves participate, some of them enjoying very strong bargaining positions; a relatively open and active communication system, and a much lesser degree of psychosomatic reactions on the part of the patients.

According to the dominant paradigm, one should focus on the structure to find out, what kind of variables outside technology could have influenced it. But the formal structure does not vary very much, and inasmuch as it varies, i.e., between the French and the Belgian settings, this is not relevant since one of the hierarchical units is in France and the other in Belgium.[2]

The subject matter of the comparison should not therefore be the structure, but the system, which can be aptly formalized with the model of the game. And the question becomes: Why do the various partners play a formalistic game of isolation and non-communication in two of the units, with the physicians concentrating on their technical expertise and the patients on the expression of psychosomatic symptoms, while in the two other units they play a game of open communication, the patients invading the field of technical expertise and the physicians entering the field of interpersonal relations?

Explaining the difference in games in the hospital example

To answer the above mentioned question, one should try first to understand what kind of problem these people have to solve and what kind of solution corresponds to the game they play. The problem, of course, is to fight a most dramatic fight against death with the help of a new technology which is very effective within certain limits, but only to maintain life, not to cure the disease.[3] The source of uncertainty in this process is less and less its technical dimension, since the use of the machine has been quickly routinized, but more and more the patient's capacity to handle the problem physically and psychologically and the capacity of the physician to help him. Another element which structures the problem is the possibility of restoring the patient's health and independence by a grafting operation. This surgical intervention, however, is still highly

risky, and for it to succeed the psychological as well as the physical state of the patient is very important.

Now two opposite solutions can be given to the problem. One is the technical one: physicians concentrate on their technical and medical expertise; they take all decisions concerning the patient and use their expertise as a charisma to soothe him. This solution is clearly unrealistic, since it does not take into account the large part of uncertainty that the patient controls. But it has the merit of simplifying the problem and making it possible to apply the technology to all cases. With the second solution, the physicians recognize the patient's contribution and by recognizing it, they can strengthen the patient's capacity to handle the situation. This changes completely the bargaining power of the partners: the patient can bargain both directly and by using his influence over other patients. The whole game changes, forcing the physicians and the nurses to be involved. This strains their capacities as well as those of the patients. And the problem becomes that of under what conditions and through what processes this is feasible.

In the four cases studied by Kuty, the key decisions in this respect seem to have been decisions concerning the boundaries of the units. The hierarchical units had chosen early to practice an open admission policy, that is to admit all patients whatever their condition and to concentrate on the use of the machine without taking into account the feasibility of grafting. The open communication units had chosen to be very selective and to admit only those patients who seemed to be good risks for this kind of intervention. They were conversely closely associated with the surgical units that would perform it. In the first case, it is quite clear that an open communications policy would have been extremely difficult to handle, since many of the patients would not have tolerated discussing their cases, in view of the widely different risks they represented. In the second, on the other hand, patients were homogeneous and strong enough to support each other. Furthermore, the involvement of the physicians with grafting meant the predominance of a common goal.

One could still try, of course, to fit this analysis into the dominant paradigm, by combining the influence of technology with the characteristics of the market and showing what kind of organizational structure fits with such a combination. But when entering that kind of argument, one is already changing the mode of reasoning. And one has to go further since the evidence shows, first, the wide margin of choice that may exist for combining the factors; second, that the reason for a choice may be an ideological reason: the charismatic leader of one of the open communication units wanted to promote new kinds of human relations in the hospital; third, that the success of these new arrangements did not depend on this 'structural choice' only, but on the building up of a collective capacity to cooperate and handle the tensions and fears associated with the risk of death. This means that there are other inputs in the system than 'objective' inputs such as the technological variables, but also that what is considered as an output—individual and group behaviour—has to be considered also as an input, and finally, that there is nothing central one can pinpoint as a structure to be detached from the game people play.

The longitudinal analysis made by Kuty of the development of the open communications units is extremely interesting, inasmuch as it shows very concretely the long interplay between the situation and the problem on the one side, and the capacity of the partners and the characteristics of their game on the other side. The units move from a charismatic concentration of the communication, prestige and power relationships network to a more open, multipolar system with the progressive involvement of nurses and patients. But they do it through crises in a sort of trial and error process. One should remark finally that they have not reached a stable 'best way' but have tended to regress frequently according to interpersonal configurations.

One last remark: One may have noticed that the inside game of free communication, tolerance, and lack of intergroup barriers has been made possible only because of the existence of strong barriers at a higher level whose existence and use supposes another very different game played by the physicians and especially by the head of the service, with other units and with the environment.

Such a contrast between two opposite solutions within the same structures, solutions drawn according to some early choices and the development of human capacities to manage the game these choices implied, may appear to be a sort of limit case; but we have several instances of similar oppositions, and in any case they do exemplify the existence of a wider range of solutions for organizational problems and the importance of the key variable for their use: the *collective capacity of the people concerned to handle the tensions these games create*.

An example from French public administration

I would like now to take as a second example a widely different kind of case, the case of the complex politico-administrative system at the 'departmental'

[4] level in France. I have just completed with Jean-Claude Thoenig a research program on this problem which bore on three departmental units (out of 100) where all the influential people were interviewed (about 200 per unit) (Crozier and Thoenig, 1975). The analysis of this case, supported by an extensive background of organizational studies, carried out in a number of French public agencies, may be helpful for reconsidering all the implications of this comparison of games and for showing the method, the mode of reasoning and the emerging new paradigm which is involved in such an approach.

The first issue we were investigating concerned the existence of a joint system incorporating the different participants in the decision making process, that is a relationship of interdependence with some regulating mechanism. We had shown earlier the importance of the interdependence of two roles such as the role of prefect[5] and the role of mayor (Worms, 1966). Here we wanted to prove that these relationships and many similar ones were part of a broader, more complex system.

Empirically, what we could show was first, the existence of complex but very stable games between the different participants and the organizations they represented; second, the interlocking of these games; and third, the existence of some common characteristics which supposed some basic regulations.

To begin with, there emerged from our data and observations the recurrence at the operational level of a very strong model of a prevailing game which can be summarized as follows:

—First, contrary to what one would expect, the very centralized public agencies do not have a close control over their field officers with regard to departmental decision-making. Communications are difficult. Higher ups do not know and do not want to know field officers as long as there are no problems. This is management by exception but without policy.

—Second, there is also no communication between peers. Mayors do not talk openly of their problems and their deals to other mayors. They always try to settle their problems individually. Field officers conversely never put up a common front among themselves, not even within the same corps. They may defend their status and conditions with a jealous fervor, but they keep aloof for their job and decisions.

—Third, the kind of bargaining taking place between these very individualistic decision-makers is basically a divide-and-rule game where one partner has the leading hand because he stands alone in dealing with a collection of individuals. The field officer for Equipment, in charge of Public Works, deals individually with two dozens of mayors in a district and is therefore in a position to orient the relationship the way he feels best. He is supposed to serve them but tells them what they should ask him if they want to get help.

—Fourth, people accept their inferiority in one game in as much as they are always part of other games where they may be in a superior position.

—Fifth, these games are interlocked according to a recurrent cross-control pattern. For example, the field officer for Equipment may impose his views on 'his' mayors, but when one tries to understand what kind of 'policies' he may pursue, one discovers that he is very much influenced indirectly by the local political climate. More precisely, he seems to be very sensitive to the cues he gets from the local influentials, for example the member of the General Council of the area he serves. The departmental director of Equipment, his superior in the bureaucracy, does not want and cannot usually direct him. He can, of course, impose the general standards and the numerous rules; he does not, however, intervene in local policies, except when dealing with the political influentials who in their turn intervene with the field officer.

This criss-crossing is a very cumbersome game where the converging bargaining relationships do not allow for easy and clear understanding. Regulation is not achieved by command, evaluation and control, but indirectly by the results of games where each partner fights for his own interests without regard for his peers and superiors and must cater to the wishes of a stronger partner over whom his superiors and the whole milieu has an influence.

We have moved from the game to some elements of regulation. But if we consider the system as a whole, we discover that the field is not uniform and that, although the model we have described is highly dominant, we also find one recurrent exception to the model. This recurrent exception develops around the elected official who holds a plurality of offices. Such a person has indeed a strategic advantage in a system where communication is slow and difficult and where misunderstanding is general. He who can bargain at two or three different levels where his opposite partners cannot communicate, enjoys a superior bargaining position at each of them and is thus sure to win everywhere if he knows how far he can go. Moreover, since every inside player knows where the advantage lies and why, the 'notable' holding a plurality of offices will be the man to watch—from which fact he will derive a lot of

influence and therefore a capacity to get things done. The system will be structured around such situations of dominance. He will be a sort of gatekeeper whose favorable position comes from the mere fact that he can reward his friends without having to punish his enemies and that everyone thinks he is powerful.

Finally, one can suggest that to the game of divide-and-rule, which is in this case the operational game, there had to be added a game of exception and access, which is the second level game.

There are many other angles in such an extremely complex system where a lot of similar but also opposite games are interlocked with each other. But if one tries to form a simple view by looking at these first elements, one can see very definite common characteristics. First, this is a system where decisions are made in secrecy and which is allergic to public debate. Second, this is a very restrictive system where the problem of access becomes consequently a basic problem. Third, this is a system which hides from any kind of interference; the cross-control game is the best protective device against outside pressure and change. Fourth, this is a system whose small number of influential figures protected from outside publicity can monopolize access and therefore will become indispensable and enjoy very long tenure. This is by consequence a very conservative system. And its conservatism justifies and legitimizes the intervention of the central government and public administration to which it is the necessary counterweight.

Such a reasoning may help understand the extraordinary stability of such a system, however poor its performances, and the extraordinary errors made by people who use the management kind of counseling to impose changes by rationalizing the structure according to some 'one best way' formula of centralizing and decentralizing.

Here again, it is evident that the basic games are more meaningful for explaining action and performances than the formal structure of roles, authority, and decision making powers, and that such basic games are a human invention to answer the problem of cooperation. Its development is conditioned by the nature of the problem, but also by the capacity of the people concerned and their experience and traditions.

The study of games as a general approach to organization research

Can we now generalize? It can be argued that both our examples should be dismissed, since the former does not deal with a formal organization as a unit but with sub-units of an organization, while the latter deals with a loose system encompassing several widely different kinds of organizations. But former experience makes me think, on the contrary, that these examples do exemplify basic problems of all organized systems, of which the classic bureaucratic kind of Weberian organizations are but a special case and to some extent quite a limited one. It is my feeling that we tend to overemphasize the hierarchical model as an explanatory framework, even, and may be all the more, if we are intent on fighting it; we tend, therefore, to miss the triangular cross-control relationships, the recurrent conflicts over goals and boundaries through which the most important regulations and the most decisive orientations are achieved. We also misunderstand the models of government by exception and the real nature of the game at the top of the organization. In such a perspective, the present dominant paradigm has become counterproductive. Because of the kind of framework within which most sociologists are reasoning, they are incapable of asking these new questions seriously.

A reversal of the trend should begin with a reversal of method, which would be, at the same time, the advent of a new kind of research strategy. Instead of focussing on the structure and the allocation of power, formal or informal, one should focus on the games around which meaningful relationships develop and without which the different partners' strategies do not make sense. Focussing on games, however, has the disadvantage of making formalizing much more difficult and of preventing for quite some time any kind of measurement, at least at the organizational level. We have, I think, to accept this and to try to move first from literary description to some kind of qualitative assessment instead of requiring immediately some irrelevant statistical sophistication.

To achieve a real understanding, two main orientations will have to be developed jointly. First of all we ought to know about the most common recurrent games at the operational level and to develop methods to formalize their characteristics. This would lead to an interplay with game theory. From this angle formal structural characteristics can be understood as some of the determinants of the rules of the game in interplay with the socio-psychological capacities of the players.

Second, we ought to focus on the regulations of the games taking place in an organization and on the game of regulation one can discover behind the power play among the decision makers. Drawing boundaries, defining the problem to be solved, will influence the relationship between the players, but it will also have basic consequences for the regulation of the whole and because of the consequences will be deeply structured by the anticipations of the necessary feedbacks. What seems to be clear from our examples already is that the vague assumption of homology between the relationships at the top and the relationships at the bottom of the pyramid is radically false. An organization or a broader system such as the one described is not regulated according to the same principles that are operating at the primary group level. One interesting hypothesis seems to concern the importance of government by exception and the importance of an organization's or system's weaknesses for the building of the regulation game.

A new reading of my observations on French public administration could be done along these lines. The stratification system, which may be one recurrent structural feature, can be analyzed as a choice of boundaries isolating subsystems and structuring the problems to be solved.[6] Centralization is a first kind of regulatory game which develops around the problems that cannot be solved within the sub-systems. But this is a very formalistic game which can handle only part of the exceptions. The real regulation game is the power game around the loopholes of the whole apparatus, and this game is of a completely different nature.

Although differences at first glance seem to be striking, we have found some similarities with this model in the government of large scale private enterprises, where the gap between general management and operational executives seems to be a basic characteristic of the regulation game of the organization.

Cross-cultural comparisons will be decisive in such a perspective. I feel that they will help us understand much better the area of autonomy for human choice for social learning and institutional investment, inasmuch as they will show the differences between the possible solutions to the same problem or the different ways to structure the problem. Up to now these possibilities were stifled by the paralyzing influence of the dominant paradigm, which did not allow for a real search for the autonomy of the human construct as a basic input in the organizational setup.

Outlines for a new paradigm

This kind of research strategy implies two kinds of theoretical orientations, out of which one can see a new paradigm emerging. First of all, there is a new kind of reasoning about power. Power problems were beginning to re-emerge in the early sixties at the end of the functionalist period. But they were quickly discarded because of the elusiveness of the concept and the impossibility of operationalizing and measuring it. March's otherwise very brilliant article on 'the power of power' was most unfortunate in this respect (March, 1963). When power now re-emerges because of the gradual realization of weakness of the central scheme of research, this is still within the framework of the old paradigm, that is, as if it were a commodity whose allocation could be studied from a normative and from a structural point of view (Perrow, 1972; Hinings et al., 1974).

To go one step forward, one should forget about power as a commodity whose amount could be measured but focus instead on power as a bargaining relationship over time within a framework of constraints which the actors cannot easily change. As a bargaining relationship, the power game centers around the predictibility of behaviour. As a bargaining relationship over time, it implies a consideration of strategy which can be viewed as the utilization of the objective and artificial uncertainties which derive from the interplay between the goals chosen by the organization, and the technical means available to it. At a second level, it raises the technical problem of the sources of uncertainty existing objectively, of the way these are dealt with according to the structuring of the problems one is handling, and of the structuring of the information about them.

There is, then, a second kind of theoretical orientation, which is the consideration of an organization as a system of games for solving the problems raised by the contextual constraints, and not only as a social system whose activities are finalized. We have already discussed such an assumption. Let's just add that it raises a whole new set of questions.

The dominant paradigm revolved around the basic question concerning the structure: how contextual variables determine the basic structural features of an organization and how these features command the behaviour of the members and the performances of the organization. The new paradigm emerges first around the idea that the contextual features of the organization should not be considered as variables determining the structure of the organization, but as problems to be solved, and second around the idea that structure is not the necessary nodal point of the organization, but that the games with their rational mathematical features as well as their human parameters will be a much more concrete and rich focal point.

Research questions then become: What are the different systems of games that can solve the same problems—i.e., the meeting of the same contextual constraints? What kind of capacities do they require from the members concerned? How do such capacities develop and how do new games and new systems of games become possible?

Notes

[1] This has been done for the Industrial Monopoly case in 'The Bureaucratic Phenomenon. (Crozier, 1964). Such formalization can be done ex post—i.e., when one knows the outcomes. The strategies and the payoffs can be interesting only for comparative purposes.

[2] This also shows that two different national cultures can be compatible with two very opposite kinds of working arrangements. I did not want to overemphasize this argument, however, inasmuch as the differences, although not negligible, are not as strong as the usual differences between developed societies.

[3] This problem seems in many respects quite similar to the one analyzed by Miller and Gwynne (1972) and described by Miller in this volume (Chapter 2).

[4] A 'department' in France is what elsewhere would be called a 'province.' The entire country is divided into 100 departments.

[5] The prefect is a civil servant who is appointed by the national government to be in charge of one department, that is (1) to direct a staff of civil servants in charge of general administration, (2) to coordinate the work of all field officers of the different specialized ministries, (3) to be the executive officer of the autonomous departmental unit under the theoretically deliberative responsibility of an elected general council, (4) to audit the activities of the mayors.

[6] See a new formulation of this problem in The Stalled Society (Crozier, 1972; Ch. 5: 'The French Bureaucratic Style').

References

P. M. Blau, 1955, The Dynamics of Bureaucracy, Chicago: University of Chicago Press.

P. M. Blau and R. A. Schoenherr, 1971, The Structure of Organizations, New York: Basic Books.

M. Crozier, 1964, The Bureaucratic Phenomenon, Chicago: University of Chicago Press and London: Tavistock Publications.

M. Crozier, 1973, The Stalled Society, New York: The Viking Press.

M. Crozier and J. C. Thoenig, 1975, 'La régulation des systèmes organisés complexes,' Revue Française de Sociologie, 16: July.

A. Gouldner, 1954, Patterns of Industrial Bureaucracy, Glencoe Ill.: Free Press.

C. R. Hinings, D. J. Hickson, J. M. Pennings and R. E. Schenk, 1974, 'Structural Conditions of Intraorganizational Power,' Administrative Science Quarterly, 19: 22–44.

O. Kuty, 1973, 'Le pouvoir du malade: analyse sociologique des unités de rein artificiel,' Doctorate thesis, Paris: Université René Descartes.

J. G. March, 1963, 'The Power of Power,' American Political Science Review, 57

E. J. Miller and G. V. Gwynne, 1972, *A Life Apart: a Pilot Study of Residential Institutions for the Physically Handicapped and the Young Chronic Sick,* London: Tavistock Publications.

J. L. Peaucelle, 1969, 'Théorie des jeux et sociologie des organisations: application aux résultats du phénomène bureaucratique,' *Sociologie du Travail,* II:22–43.

C. Perrow, 1972, *Complex Organizations: a Critical Essay,* Glenview Ill.: Scott, Foresman & Co.

P. Selznick, 1949, *TVA and the Grass Roots,* Berkeley: University of California Press.

J. P. Worms, 1966, 'Le préfet et ses notables', *Sociologie du Travail,* 8:249-275.

18   The self-exciting system
G. Vickers

One thing is clear from a study of systems of all kinds—no trend, literally *no* trend can be expected to continue in the same direction indefinitely, least of all one that increases at an exponential rate, however slow. So anyone who makes proposals based on the assumption that any such trend will continue should be asked to show reasonable grounds for thinking that it will at least last long enough to support whatever proposal or argument he is basing on it.

It is convenient to begin by asking how it is that the system has become, in the West, so powerfully self-exciting.

The system, when stripped of its shield of familiarity, is very odd. Consider first only its two main elements. One of these is a large population of corporations which provide goods and services and recover their costs from the users, with a margin, much of which they are free to accumulate. The other element consists of institutions which also provide goods and services (including the services of government) but which recover their costs from public funds. These funds are drawn partly from the corporations which form the first element and partly from that population of individual men and women whom I have left for the moment standing in the wings of the stage, awaiting their cue to appear.

I will distinguish these two types of institution as user-supported and public-supported. None of our familiar names will precisely fit. 'Public sector' and 'private sector' are the nearest approximations. Yet these are doubly misleading. Some institutions in what is commonly called the public sector, such as the railways and the Post Office, are user-supported, though others, such as the hospitals, are public-supported. In any case, it is misleading to describe as 'private' a sector consisting of autonomous corporations which perform so many public functions, and some of which are publicly controlled and even owned.

The user-supported section of our economy is free to accumulate profits and increasingly finances itself out of these accumulations. These undertakings are still judged primarily by the criteria appropriate to investments; increasing turnover, profits and net wealth are accepted as their primary indices of success. So far from costing anybody anything, they are regarded as the primary producers and accumulators of wealth.

The public-supported sector is still widely regarded as living as a parasite, or perhaps a predator, on the user-supported sector. It abstracts money from the user-supported sector and uses it to provide those goods and services, including government, which the current ethos or the legacy of history regards as impossible or unsuitable to be paid for by the users. It accumulates no money, only enormous debts; and though it does accumulate vast and increasing stores of public wealth, none of these appears in any balance sheet. It is therefore not commonly regarded as either a producer or an accumulator of wealth. On the contrary, everything it does is regarded as a cost to someone.

The distinction between these two worlds was once clearer, more logical and more acceptable. Until little more than a century ago, public power performed its regulative function almost entirely by making and enforcing rules. Its control of operations was largely confined to physical coercion—law and order at home, defence (and attack) abroad. The persistence of this age-old conceptual pattern makes current developments less comprehensible and less acceptable than they would otherwise be.

The relation between these two worlds is turning into a very complex form of symbiosis. Public funds buy directly an increasing share of the user-supported products and pay the wages and salaries of an increasing proportion of all employed persons. Public authority, by redistributing the incomes of all, helps to maintain the purchasing power by which the user-supported section lives. Thus the user-supported section is increasingly dependent on the public-supported sector.

Equally, the public-supported system is increasingly dependent on the user-supported system, from which it has to get an ever-increasing annual income. It provides virtually all the common services by which the user-supported section and the general population live; roads, schools, hospitals and the rest, not to speak of defence and foreign relations. The cost of maintaining all these services would rise even if both their level and the numbers served remained static. Since both numbers and aspirations rise, the public-supported services need annually not merely an increased amount but an increased proportion of the gross national product (GNP). In the West, the public-supported system extracts this at present only by taxation; and it has a far better chance of increasing its revenues from an expansion of taxable revenue than from an increase in the rates of taxation. So it has an intense, though indirect, interest in the expansion of the private sector.

The user-supported sector has a similar interest in expanding revenue and hence in expanding consumption. Competitive businesses learned long ago that they could increase their profits far more easily by expanding their total market than by winning part of a static market from a competitor. (It is rare indeed for any firm to increase its earnings in a market that is contracting or to fail to do so in a market that is expanding.) Further, the user-supported sector is dependent on growth in several other ways. Growth is necessary to capital accretion, which is also the prime attraction for investors. It is necessary to attract and keep good senior staff, who choose growing concerns because they themselves want room to grow. It is in any case the accepted yardstick of success both in the sub-culture of the user-supported sector and generally.

Again those parts of the user-supported sector which use highly capitalized mass-production processes are further dependent on growth, not only because they need long, uninterrupted runs of production but because their processes are so rigid that any output which falls short of what is planned by a quarter or even less is likely to be unprofitable. On the other hand, any demand for more than the planned output is so profitable to achieve and so damaging to refuse that it initiates intensive expansion. Thus a ratchet-like mechanism operates to make every ceiling attained into a future floor, which cannot easily be lowered. Nothing could be more conducive to self-exciting growth.

What of the men and women who individually use and pay for most of the goods and services and who, in their active capacity, fill all the seats in both sectors? Most of these also are at present motivated to increase their personal share of what is provided by the System, both to make their current lives easier and more varied and to secure themselves by accumulating their own reserves. These motivations are increased by the massive efforts of the user-supported sector, which spends £500 million a year of its consumers' money on promoting consumption. For comparison, the public-supported sector in 1968 spent £1,800 million of its tax and ratepayers' money on all forms of education. This weird disparity reflects and contributes to the fact that people in Western cultures value what they buy individually so much more than what they contribute to provide collectively. The motivations of the individual are increased also by disparities of wealth no longer sanctioned by an accepted social order. They are further excited by a cultural norm which plays back to them, from other sources, the motif stated by the advertisements; and in so far as they are also agents in the user-supported sector they are influenced as consumers by the ideology which supports them as producers. To some extent they are still motivated by the search for security in an unsafe world, though for many the reaction to gathering uncertainty is to turn away from it.

There is no doubt that the system is set in a pattern of self-exciting expansion. There is equally no doubt that in the course of producing more goods and services with less effort, it has met many real needs and created or extended the range of many legitimate wants and that it has still much room to do both, even in Western countries. But we still have to ask whether the system can meet the demands which its own expansion is bringing to it, without more radical change than is consistent with the linear expectations of the prophets.

If we examine the pattern of these self-exciting activities, we find that it is very uneven. The user-supported sector is intensely self-exciting for one reason; the public-supported sector is much less self-exciting and when it is excited, responds to quite a different incentive.

The user-supported sector is excited by its own success. Its resources have to be used, its capital must be put to work, its machines must be kept busy, its newspapers must be filled, output must be kept up and up, if mounting overheads are to be carried. It is generally less disastrous to sell at a loss than not to sell at all. The public-supported sector, on the other hand, is not excited but (as it should be) relieved by its successes, and excited by its failures. If a weighty effort brings the school-building programme or the health programme or the defence programme more nearly in line with aspirations, the next budget is likely to shift its priorities, even to abate its total demands. 'Success' does not generate more revenue or leave more accumulated resources waiting to be invested.

Broadly, in cybernetic jargon, feedback is negative in the public-supported sector but positive in the other.

There is, however, one other link between the two systems. The public-supported system is mainly excited by the imbalances created by the user-supported system. The user-supported system disturbs physical and social relationships. The demand for regulation falls on the public-supported system and so does the blame for failing to solve what may be insoluble problems generated by the user-supported system.

Within the user-supported system itself, there is another disparity to be noted. The increase in abundance has taken place in those goods and services which can be multiplied by mechanized and automated processes, not in those which involve personal service or personal skills. This concentration on goods rather than services is masked by the fact that many activities, classed as services, can be mechanized and automated. In America today, for the first time in human history perhaps, more than half the labour force are in 'service' industries. This is noteworthy. The fact remains that in New York it is much easier to get a television set serviced than to call in a doctor.

Briefly then it may be said that the user-supported sector is self-exciting, whilst the public-supported sector is not; that the system is set to produce goods rather than services and impersonal services rather than personal services; that it is much more responsive to individual wants than to collective needs; and that it powerfully resists the creation of any 'good' which can only be achieved by abating rather then redoubling activity.

When we look ahead, it seems clear that the linear progress which so many prophets envisage will challenge the system, in all these respects, in the order of its greatest weaknesses.

The growing GNP contains very different elements, growing at very different rates. At least five need to be distinguished.

The first includes all those extra resources which we need to generate in order merely to stand still—to keep the air no more polluted, the houses no more crowded, and so on. All these cost more yearly, merely to avoid regress. This, however, is inseparable from the second factor, which includes making the environment at least good enough to meet the minimum expectations—already frustrated and mounting—of those who cannot be ignored. This means doing much better than standing still.

The third element is the ever more costly capitalization of the productive machine which is to produce this rising GNP. The fourth is the ever rising expenditure on defence, space exploration and other such exercises.

None of these four activities produces any goods which an individual can choose and buy. Only the second produces any increment of 'good' which an individual can enjoy at all. Only the balance, the fifth element after these four have been satisfied, enlarges that field of choice which the individual exercises, through the market and which in Western countries, he has come to value so much. The question whether this fifth element will rise or fall—and for whom—can be decided only after a careful assessment of the other four, an assessment which is made almost impossible by the doubts which attend the fourth. But whatever the answer given, it will surely show that by far the biggest expansion will go into goods and services which are not chosen by individuals through a market but by public bodies through the political process.

Welfare economics has charted several classes of goods and services of this kind. They include those goods which, if supplied, must be supplied to all, such as lighthouses, sewers, and diplomats. They include goods which, though they benefit the receiver, are even more important to his neighbours, such as the treatment of infectious diseases; and their opposite, the negative good of being protected from harm from another's activities, as by his pollution of water or air. They include goods which only a government wants, like space probes, or which only a government is able and willing to supply, like the largest irrigation schemes; and negative goods of the same kind, such as proceed from traffic control and economic stabilization and the keeping of law and order. They include the preservation of goods which market valuation would destroy, such as open spaces in cities; the prohibition of goods which market valuation would create, like heroin; and the forced consumption of goods, like education, which some people might otherwise not choose, even if it were freely available. Many of the goods just listed can, of course, be supplied through the market; industry can build the roads, the schools and the lighthouses. What the market cannot do in this essential and expanding field is to elicit or restrain their appearance or declare their 'true' value by that process which was once thought to be the prerogative of the market.

Clearly then, one implication of the current trend is a huge increase in the load to be borne by the process of political choice; and the question arises whether the machinery for making these choices, on which Western societies pride themselves, will be able to support without radical change the additional load.

It is convenient to examine some conceptual barriers which at present make these new political tasks even harder than they might be.

Three attitudes seem particularly relevant.

The concept of competition already involves, in the philosophy of both public and private sectors, contradictions which demand resolution. Both still officially regard competition as good.

A further tangle of out-dated assumptions confuses the concept of the market.

Markets are most convenient institutions. Some, notably the money market and the commodity markets, still retain an astonishing pitch of technical perfection. All have an important distributive function. But the market for goods and services retains to some extent, chiefly in America but to some extent even in England, a mystique which it no longer deserves as a mechanism for objective valuation. This helps to retain for it in our thinking a central place which it has long ceased to deserve. The goods and services provided by acts of political choice, though they multiply, are still too often thought of as regrettable exceptions to a general rule. In these fields we must reluctantly leave it to the political process to decide on priorities and within these priorities to decide for each who is to profit and who is to pay. But outside this suspect and subjective area *we know*. The market tells us.

This is no longer tenable. The economist's theory of the market was based on a number of assumptions which were accepted not because they correspond with the real world— some manifestly did not—but because they were simple enough to handle and accurate enough to work in what used to be a substantial area of human activity. The free market in which the choice of consumers was supposed to adjust the products of competing producers was a market in which both consumers and producers were so numerous that no one of them could affect the outcome of the whole: and where consumers' wants were supposed to be fixed and uninfluenced by the market or indeed by anything else. Consumers were supposed to know their wants and to know how best to satisfy them, in any given state of the market. Producers profited and even survived only in so far as they could guess or fill the unfilled need better than their rivals.

This model worked well enough only in fields in which its basic assumptions were not too far from the truth. Notable among these are the assumptions of effective competition and of wants which can be taken as given. The field in which both hold has so narrowed as to be the exception rather than the rule. Competition has lost its mainspring of unused resources. Wants become increasingly a function of supply. In the market, as in politics, advocates of rival values appeal to individuals for their support and do all they can to mould these individuals' valuations to support them. Nowhere outside the totalitarian world are their political choices manipulated so openly or so effectively as are their market choices in the Western world. In politics rival parties criticize each other, whilst the mass media criticize all. But in commerce mutual criticism of products is banned; only in recent years has the rise of consumer protection organizations subjected the commercial suppliers of goods and services to even the mildest informed criticism. The citizen has far more effective means to influence government than the consumer has to influence his economic masters.

But the main factor which displaces market choice by political choice is the increasing cost or benefit – usually cost – which flows from many market transactions to third parties and to society generally, in fields remote from the interest or even the imagination of the parties concerned. It is this which increasingly involves those multi-valued collective choices which are the stuff of politics.

Welfare economics tries with increasing sophistication to 'sum' the individual gains and losses resulting from the public creation of collective goods but does so largely still within the very unsophisticated limits of a false antithesis. *Either*, it is argued, some paternal dictator decides what is good for us *or* some process sums our own individual valuations of these goods and thus disentangles our preferences as the market does in its own area. The antithesis obscures the fact that our preferences between collective goods and individual goods and between one collective good and another, far more than between packets in a supermarket, are not given but are the subject of that mutual persuasion which is the democratic process. Democratic political leaders neither dictate collective goals nor seek to sum what they think individuals want.

Thus the increasing importance of 'collective goods' magnifies the importance of political choice and thus of the political process. It is not the only influence to drive in this direction. For politics is concerned with power and the outstanding characteristic of our ever more crowded and more active world is the increasing power exercised wittingly and unwittingly by each over all. It is time to explore the proliferation of power.

19 Diffusion of innovation
D. Schön

When we speak of 'the formation of social policy', we envisage society as a giant 'decider' and we see social change as a process in which society confronts its changing situation, makes up its mind what is to be done, and carries out its decisions.

There is an entirely different perspective on social change—one shared by anthropologists, economists and students of the history of technology, as well as by some business managers—according to which social change occurs as inventions come into use and fan out over the society. Here, the central metaphor is not 'deciding' but 'spread', 'propagation', or 'contagion'. Diffusion of innovation is a dominant model for the transformation of societies according to which novelty moves out from one or more points to permeate the society as a whole.

Systems for diffusion are critical to the learning capacity of a society. They evolve over time. Their evolution tends to follow changing infrastructure technology—technology for the flows of men, materials, money and information. Theories of diffusion tend to be based on old systems; they lag behind our own expanding competence. They fail, therefore, as guides for policy and action now, but they are remarkably stubborn and resilient.

In what follows, I will examine evolving models for the diffusion of innovations, make explicit some of the assumptions on which they rest, and hold them up against recent experience.

The centre–periphery model

Those who have tried to account for social change via the diffusion of innovations, and those who have sought to develop and promote new systems for diffusion (most notably, in agriculture, medicine, and industrial development) have relied heavily upon the centre-periphery model.

This model rests on three basic elements:

The innovation to be diffused exists, fully realized in its essentials, prior to its diffusion.

Diffusion is the movement of an innovation from a centre out to its ultimate users.

Directed diffusion is a centrally managed process of dissemination, training, and provision of resources and incentives.

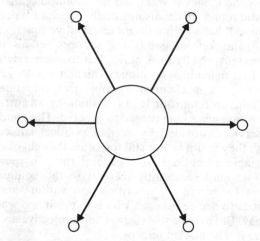

Figure 19.1 The centre-periphery model

Advocates of centre-periphery theory have tended to see diffusion as 'the human interaction in which one person communicates a new idea to another person. Thus, at its most elemental level of conceptualization, the diffusion process consists of (1) a new idea, (2) individual A who knows about the innovation, and (3) individual B who does not know about the innovation. . . .'[1] The prototype of the 'diffuser' is the agricultural extension agent, the medical 'detail man' (who introduces new pharmaceuticals to doctors), salesmen, nurses and doctors, school administrators and teachers. Diffusion studies tend to focus on products or techniques like new plant varieties, weed sprays, insecticides, drugs, and public health practices. But the dominant model remains the US Agricultural Extension program whose perceived success in increasing agricultural productivity in the late 19th and early 20th centuries has made it a paradigm for all later students of directed diffusion.

The effectiveness of a centre-periphery system depends first upon the level of resources and energy at the centre, then upon the number of points at the periphery, the length of the radii or spokes through which diffusion takes place, and the energy required to gain a new adoption. The diffusion capability of an agricultural extension agent, for example, depends upon his own energies and skills, the number and location of the farmers he serves, and the time and effort he must devote to work with each farmer.

Scope depends, as well, on infrastructure technology. The scope of the centre-periphery system varies directly with the level of technology governing the flows of men, materials, money and information. Public health officials, who try to spread new methods of birth control in India, use elephants to reach thousands of small villages over roads difficult to pass at any time and impossible in certain seasons. The use of elephants reflects not only a solution to the transportation problem but an ingenious sense of public relations.

Finally, the scope of a centre-periphery system depends on its capacity for generating and managing feedback. Because the process of diffusion is originally regulated by the center, the effectiveness of the process depends upon the ways in which information moves from the periphery back to the centre.

There are two important variants to the centre-periphery model:

'Johnny Appleseed' Here the primary centre is a kind of bard who roams his territory spreading a new message. Into this category fall the travelling scholars, saints and artisans of the Middle Ages; Voltaire and Thomas Paine; and contemporary bards of radical activism like Saul Alinsky.

The 'magnet' model The 'magnet' attracts agents of diffusion to it, as universities have long since done. With the flowering of science and medicine in the universities of nineteenth-century Germany, for example, students flocked to Germany from all parts of the world and then returned to their own country to teach and practice what they had learned. The United States, Britain and the Soviet Union play magnet, particularly in technology and economics, to developing nations.

The magnet model offers advantages. It permits tighter control of the teaching and greater efficiency in the use of teachers. But it has less control over what happens afterwards, and permits less variation of doctrine to suit the specialized needs of the outposts.

The Johnny Appleseed model allows the teaching

to be adapted to the special conditions of the territories. But there is less opportunity for the development of a critical mass at the centre capable of attracting new adherents.

The travelling centre or the magnet centre may spawn new centres. But in neither case does it monitor or manage the process of dissemination. Once the new centres are established, for better or worse, they pursue their disparate paths.

When the centre-periphery system exceeds the resources or the energy at the centre, overloads the capacity of the radii, or mishandles feedback from the periphery, it fails. Failure takes the form of simple ineffectiveness in diffusion, distortion of the message, or disintegration of the system as a whole.

Detail men working for a drug company communicate with doctors in their territory. When they have insufficient time to reach their quota of doctors, they may reduce their level of effort with each doctor to a point where they are unable to convey the company's message effectively. Or they may lose contact with their own central office, garbling new messages. If, as a result, sales fall off and salesmen lose morale, the system as a whole may fall apart.

The proliferation of centres
This is an elaboration of the centre-periphery model, designed as though to extend the limits and overcome the sources of failure inherent in the simpler model.

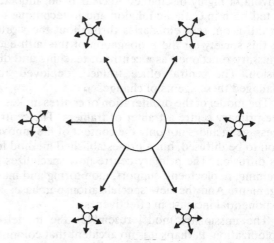

Figure 19.2 Primary and secondary centres

This system retains the basic centre-periphery structure, but differentiates primary from secondary centres. Secondary centres engage in the diffusion of innovations; primary centres support and manage secondary centres. The effect is to multiply many-fold the reach and efficiency of the diffusion system. The system's scope still depends both on the level of energy and resources at the centre, and on infrastructure technology. But there is an exponential increase in the leverage of a given central resource and a given state of infrastructure technology. Each secondary centre now has the scope of what would have been the whole system. The limits to the reach and effectiveness of the new system depend now on the primary centre's ability to generate, support and manage the new centres.

The model of the proliferation of centres has had many prototypes, but among the first and most important was the Roman army. The army's advance guard moved out from Rome to invade new territories, subjugate peoples and establish colonies. The business of the outposts was war and government. As a corollary to subjugation, each outpost established in its territory an approximation to the Roman way of life. There was a centrally established doctrine and a centrally established method for diffusing it. Each outpost functioned as a centre of control and diffusion, linked to the primary centre in Rome.

Among the early Christian missionaries there was a central, pre-established doctrine and a fixed methodology for its dissemination. In the more elaborate and disciplined missionary systems like the sixteenth century Jesuit organization of Ignatius Loyola, a highly disciplined nuclear band, indoctrinated both in Catholic religion and in technique for its diffusion, sent emissaries throughout the world. In this society for the propagation of the faith each emissary functioned as a centre of teaching and diffusion. The central office trained, deployed and managed these agents of change.

The model of the proliferation of centres makes of the primary centre a trainer of trainers. The central message includes not only the content of the innovation to be diffused, but a pre-established method for its diffusion. The primary centre now specializes in training, deployment, support, monitoring and management. And the new specialization purchases an exponential increase in effectiveness.

The missionary model resembles the model of colonization. Perhaps it is no accident that colonization of the New World, from the 16th century on, allied itself with missionary activity. In the colonial model it is an entire way of life that is diffused. Colonists move out from a mother country from which they are monitored, supported and managed. Their diffusion proceeds only secondarily by communicating innovations to others, and primarily by an expansion of the agents of diffusion into their surrounding environments.

The late 19th and early 20th centuries were marked by the flowering of a cluster of highly developed models along the lines of the proliferation of centres:

Industrial expansion

The Communist movement

Imperialism.

All were characterized by highly specialized primary centres and by the exploitation of the new infrastructure technologies of steam and rail for the maintenance of the network of primary and secondary centres. As distinguished from the models of the magnet and Johnny Appleseed, systems for the management and control of secondary centres became predominant.

Industrial expansion came about on a world-wide scale through a form of specialization reminiscent of the Roman army. The central message now took the form of technology both for production and for the management of the business firm. These spread throughout the world as industrial centres established decentralized networks of distribution, marketing, production, manpower and financial control.

The patterns have been varied. Agents of the central firm established new centres throughout the target territories, replicating the central methods of the industry. Or they took over existing decentralized operations and subjugated them to central control. In some cases the firm decentralized whole industrial systems. In other cases it decentralized marketing and distribution and kept production central. The story of the variations is the story of the growth of modern industrial enterprise.

Cutting across all variants, however, there is a dominant pattern in the primary centre's relationship to secondary centres:

The primary centre is a guardian of pre-established doctrine and methodology.

It selects territories for expansion, and deploys and organizes agents of expansion.

It is not only the source and model of operations to be diffused but the developer of methodologies for diffusion.

It trains and incubates new agents of diffusion.

It supports decentralized outposts through capital, information and know-how.

It monitors and manages decentralized operations, setting criteria for performance, monitoring performance, observing and overseeing leadership in the outposts.

It maintains information throughout the network of outposts.

The Coca Cola company is a later model of the type. It functions on a world-wide basis. It has established a name and a product, as well as a method of operation, which permits it to replicate again and again a single system for production, distribution and marketing. The simplicity and uniformity of its central message permits a system of deployment and control capable of encompassing the world as a whole.

The Communist movement

In the early decades of the 20th century, Communism produced a system of diffusion which rivalled industrial expansion in scope and design. It had a fixed doctrine for dissemination, an established methodology for diffusion, and an international system of cells.

The functions of the centre are comparable:

The management of the overall movement

The training of leaders for the cells

Control over the cells through central policy and the maintenance of rewards and punishments

The monitoring and replacement of leadership

Provision of a model for imitation on the part of the cells

Progressive maintenance of the central doctrine and of the methodology for its diffusion

Management of the overall network of cells

The system had special features. Its message was one of economic, social and political revolution, and revolution was its strategy of diffusion. But the centre of diffusion was also a nation. The dissemination of revolutionary doctrine mingled with a struggle for national hegemony.

Imperialism

Nineteenth century imperialism succeeded European colonialism and consisted not only in colonization but in the economic and political domination of colonial peoples. The strategy of empire was one of military domination, followed by military occupation and then by civilian colonial government. Most frequently, imperial government meant extraction of the nation's raw materials in the interests of the

mother country. But it meant, as well, the imposition of the mother country's way of life on the colonial nation. Institutions were exported wholesale and an imperial elite served as a model for subjugated nations, creating both pressures and incentives for adopting the way of life represented by the mother country.

Great Britain's pattern was more widespread and in some ways more impressive than those of other European nations, but the contents of these patterns were basically similar. Great Britain established colonial governments in Africa, Asia, and the Middle East. Commerce and military conquest led to military government and then to the simulacrum of civilian government along the lines of the British model. British civil servants entered the country to create remarkably stable bureaucracies. The British influence premeated the country's institutions in religion, education, business, trade, military organization and even sport. British agents and colonists were both manipulators and models for colonial peoples. And Britain itself became a magnet training ground for them. All of this was in the name of military and economic advantage. Under the ideology of empire, the diffusion of the British way of life was a by-product of the search for advantage.

Not surprisingly, these diffusion systems came to be confused with one another. Critics have seen Communism as a form of imperialism. Historians have described both Communism and imperialism as vehicles for industrial expansion. Perhaps all three were variants of a central process of world-wide westernization, industrialization or modernization.

Why did these variant models develop at about the same time? To answer, we would need to examine the role of the new infrastructure technology of steam and rail and the flowering of industrial production technology. Both had the effect of making the world into 'territory'. We would have to consider the power of the metaphors of the machine and of early biological theories of cell formation and reproduction.

The forms of failure

When the model of the proliferation of centres fails, the secondary centres get out of control. In missionary organizations this takes the form of heresy; in colonialism, revolution: in Communism, deviationism. In industrial organization, failure takes the form of fragmentation, insubordination and the classical problems of centre-branch conflict.

But what looks like heresy or deviationism from the point of view of central, may look to the secondary centre like innovation appropriate to its region.

In this context we can understand the conflicts of colonial outposts with the mother country and the familiar complaints of regional offices that central is unresponsive and out of touch with local problems.

When secondary centres get disconnected from central, the diffusion system fragments and becomes unable to maintain itself and expand. It may still transform dispersed societies. But the transformation no longer consists in diffusion of an established message. It leads, rather, to a variety of regional transformations which bear only a family resemblance to one another.

In failure, the model of the proliferation of centres may become a learning system in spite of itself. But it is a learning system in which the feedback loop is not from secondary to primary centres, but from secondary centres to themselves.

The process as a whole, then, has a pattern something like the following:

1   A primary centre emerges.

2   It develops a diffusion system.
    The primary centre replicates itself in many secondary centres.
    The primary centre specializes in creation and management of secondary centres and in maintenance of the overall network.

3   The diffusion system fragments.
    Central loses control.
    The network disintegrates.
    Secondary centres gain independence (*or* they decline, *or* one of them assumes the role of primary centre.)

Sources of failure
There are variants of the same conditions that lead to failure in the simple centre-periphery model.

The limits of infrastructure
When the network of communications of money, men, information and materials is inadequate to the demands imposed on it, the system must either retrench or fail. The far greater scope of the model of proliferation or centres depends on more advanced infrastructure technology (specifically, on the technologies of transportation and communication developed in the late 19th and early 20th centuries). But the need for rapid central response, or for a more differentiated response to widely varying regional conditions, may overtax the available infrastructure. Or the introduction of new infrastructure technology may disrupt a relatively stable diffusion system.

Constraints on the resources of the centre
The demands on leadership and management may overwhelm the system as the primary centre takes on new responsibilities. The new functions of training, selecting territories and nurturing leadership create problems of balance between the needs for central direction and for attention to special regional problems. Competence in creating networks differs from competence in maintaining them. The transition from one to the other is difficult. There is a tendency to underestimate the *difference* between these kinds of competence and the kinds of competence required by the secondary centres themselves.

The motivation of the agent of diffusion
In the model of the proliferation of centres, the agent of diffusion is of two kinds, the field man who makes first contact and first communicates the central message, and the local or regional entrepreneur who builds up regional centres. The latter are the heads of mission, branch managers, local governors and cell leaders. Their situation, particularly in the early stages, may be something like this:

The environment is always foreign and often hostile. The agents confront local resistances and dangers that central can never know as intensively as they, and that central may ignore altogether. Central always seems to be out of contact and slow in response. The central message may appear strange and inappropriate in the new setting. There are often strong local counter-pressures threatening to engulf the mission. The mission, moreover, feels alienated from the centre of power—where policy is being made and where battles for power are going on. The distance from the centre can be agonizing when there is uncertainty over change of direction at central, or when central seems simply unresponsive to local requirements.

What moves an agent of diffusion to enter a situation like this may be a desire for new territory, attraction to adventure and romance, flight from an intolerable situation at centre, or—perhaps most importantly—a religious attachment to the central message. This 'missionary mentality' may attach itself to empire, to revolution or even to Coca Cola. The more threatening the local system, the more tenuous the contact with central, the more congenial the situation to the missionary—providing the central message remains capable of sustaining its religious burden.

Regional diversity and the rigidity of central doctrine

Territories are different from one another and from central. Does the central message lend itself to modification to take account of regional differences? What are the limits of acceptable deviation? Does the feedback loop between central and the regions permit modification of the central message?

In the Communist Internationale, party-liners came into conflict with partisans who believed in the right of each country to find its own road to revolution. Failure may occur in industrial expansion out of central's insistence on its way of doing business without taking into account the special features of local situations—for example, the special problems created for Coca Cola by the unique demands of the African market or the problems created for the Corn Products Company by the special requirements of agribusiness in Latin America. A colonial administration may fail by refusing to recognize and build on local institutions, such as the institutions of the chief and witchcraft in African tribal societies.

Similar problems of rigidity hold for the *method* to be used in diffusion. There is as much conflict between regional and central over this as over the message to be diffused. Consider, for example, the conflicts between the central business office and regional branches over marketing methods, or the conflict between regional outposts and central offices over methods of diffusing techniques of birth-control.

Resolution of these kinds of conflict may be achieved through central's ability to alter its message in response to local needs. Or the diffusion system may avert the conflicts altogether by adopting a central message which is like a kind of constitution, in the sense that it provides guidance for action and yet lends itself to variations without 'breaking'. In either case, the set of secondary centres comes to look more like a family of overlapping and analogous situations than like a set of replications of a single model.

Normative use of the model

The centre-periphery model, with its extension in the form of the proliferation of centres, is not only historically important. [2] It has also become the dominant normative model for diffusion.

Agricultural development programs in Africa and Latin America, for example, draw on the model of successful agricultural extension programmes in the United States. The model requires centres of technological competence like experimental stations, model farms, central laboratories, land grant universities, and experts in technical assistance, who communicate the new technologies of agriculture to the farmers in their territories.

In the field of medicine and health care, a major current programme rests on the concept of local 'centres of excellence' (medical research and teaching centres) whose purpose is to communicate the new medical technology to peripheral rings of community physicians. The assumption is that the relevant expertise is to be found at the centre and communicated to the periphery through new systems for referring patients from one physician to another, training programs, demonstrations, short courses and the like.

When directed diffusion of innovation is at issue, the centre-periphery model is simply what comes to mind. But a normative theory of diffusion based on the centre-periphery model has inadequacies beyond the historical failings of actual centre-periphery systems. In two crucial respects, the prevailing theories fail to take into account phenomena underlying some of their successes.

Diffusion as communication

Everett Rogers, who simply reflects current thinking on the subject, treats the act of diffusion as an act of communication: 'The essence of the diffusion process is the human interaction in which one person communicates a new idea to a new person.'[3]

The essential process is getting information out, 'communication from A who knows about the innovation to B who does not'. This concept leaves out of account the dynamically conservative plenum into which information moves. The process is more nearly a battle than a communication—a fact recognized, in spite of their failings, by the great 19th century models of the proliferation of centres.

Product or technique as the unit of diffusion

Every social system has prevailing technologies and related theories around which it is organically built. Innovation in any aspect of the system threatens the system as a whole. The more significant innovations are those whose acceptance would require more radical transformation of the system; hence their threat to the system is greater.

Rogers, along with other exponents of centre-periphery theory, considers the diffusion only of new products or techniques which presuppose a relatively stable technological system of which they are components.

A new weed-killer, for example, moves into a system of agricultural technology which includes mechanical ploughing, harvesting and spraying, the use of new genetic varieties, chemical fertilizer, crop rotation, mechanical packing equipment, and motorized transportation of crops. Within such a technological system, middle- to large-sized farms are dominant. The economic constraints on farming, as well as the impact of previous technological innovations, have already sharply reduced available farm labour. The acceptance of a new weed-killer depends on equipment which would permit its use over relatively large areas with relatively little labour.

If the weed-killer could be shown to be relatively effective and innocuous in its side-effects, and if it promised an increase in land productivity or a further reduction in farm labour, then managers of middle- to large-sized farms might accept it fairly readily. Its diffusion might then very well consist of disseminating information, conducting trials, influencing opinion leaders, and the like. But this would be because the weed-killer meshes with a pre-existing technological system whose objectives it seems likely to enhance with relatively little disruption. For that system, it is not, in the sense we have been using the term, a very significant innovation.

The situation is quite different where the introduction of the innovation requires significant disruption of the entire technological-social system and the system of ideas related to it. In such a case, diffusion of an innovation looks less like the dissemination of information than like a sequence of related disruptions of complex systems, resulting in each case in a new configuration. Here the unit of diffusion is not a product or technique but a whole technological system.

Systems as units of diffusion

Where the unit of diffusion is more nearly a complete technological system than a single product or technique, the process involved in the diffusion of significant innovation resembles the generation and diffusion of industries. For purposes of comparison, let us examine the development and diffusion of a new industry—the granite industry in New England in the late eighteenth and early nineteenth centuries.

The story of the rise and fall of the Cape Ann granite industry is only one chapter in the industry's diffusion throughout New England. But that chapter is a microcosm, displaying processes which are common in the diffusion of new industrial systems.

The crucial role of war   The industry rose and fell in the interval between two major wars—the Revolutionary War and World War I. The first

created the extraordinary conditions of mobility which brought the carriers of stone-cutting technology to the New World. The second set in motion a second revolution in building which displaced the first.

The role of the inventor   Tarbox was a prototype of the independent inventor whose contribution triggered the new industry, although he himself was only dimly aware of his own importance and failed to gain any long-term profit from it.

The role of pulses of special demand   The new prison of Charlestown sparked Governor Robbins' search, which led to the take-off of the Quincy operation. That operation, in turn, providing a new supply of relatively cheap granite cut to dimension, meshed with and reinforced a growing demand for new fireproof buildings which came with the development of Boston. Thenceforth, the demand and the industry mutually reinforced each other's growth.

The interaction of deliberate intervention and unforeseen occurrence   Governor Robbins took on himself the management of a segment of a process of diffusion, when he brought Tarbox to Quincy to teach the local cutters his new method. Entrepreneurs like Torrey, moving out from Quincy, sought deliberately to create new, profitable centres of industry and, in so doing, triggered the industry's spread. The industry's take-off and full development depended on waves of new demand which no one had anticipated or sought deliberately to create.

The clustering of innovations and the requirements for infrastructure   The growth of the industry in Cape Ann after 1823 depended not only on the new stone-cutting technology but on blasting methods, wire rope and hoisting equipment—and later on steam-powered drills and hoists—which permitted the exploitation of granite in quarries as deep as 500 feet. Requirements for transport drew first on oxen and then on rail technology, and led to the creation of the wharf and the sloop traffic to Boston. The growth of water and rail transport permitted Cape Ann products to travel as far as Washington, DC, and permitted the development of a widespread market whose growth fed into the industry's.

The system of the granite industry grew in interaction with other related systems: the systems of steel, rail transport, steam power, the growing urban systems of the cities of the Atlantic coast, and the migration system, together with its technology, which permitted the entry of successive waves of cheap labour.

No one system caused the others to come into being. Each fed on and reinforced the others. There were precipitating events—the prison, the discovery of Tarbox—but no one of them can be said to have 'caused' the development of the industry. Similarly, individuals and associations intervened at various times and tried, more or less consciously, to forward the industry's diffusion. But no man or group can be said to have directed or managed that diffusion. Each chapter in the diffusion of the granite industry represented a complex reconfiguration of related systems. The development of the industry in Vermont, for example, was analogous but by no means identical to its development at Cape Ann.

Every complex that is in the broadest terms an industry represents just such a socio-technical system as the granite industry on Cape Ann. The agricultural industry, the food industry, the primary metals industry, the nuclear industry, all are systems of technology, production, distribution, marketing, employment and finance. They have developed over time through processes not unlike the one described above. Major non-industrial institutions in our society—institutions for health care, education, and social welfare, for example—represent developing socio-technical systems of a similar kind.

Taken function by function, and (fulfilling these functions) institution by institution, our society represents a dynamically conservative plenum into which innovations must find their way if they are to be diffused. Within such a plenum, potential innovations can be ranked, as we have already suggested, in a kind of target diagram depending on the magnitude of the disruption their acceptance would cause. Innovations lying near the periphery are likely to undergo a diffusion process very much like the ones described by Rogers—a process whose principal features have to do with the dissemination of information, the communication of information from A who knows about the invention to B who does not. But for innovations located near the centre of the diagram, which precipitate system-wide changes, the process of diffusion is a battle for broad and complex transformation. And within such a process, the assumptions underlying the classical diffusion model do not hold:

The innovation does not by any means entirely antedate the diffusion process; it evolves significantly within that process.

The process does not look like the fanning out of innovation from a single source. Many sources of related and reinforcing innovations are likely to be involved.

And the process does not consist primarily in centrally managed dissemination of information. This element is usually present, but subordinate to the reorientation of existing socio-technical systems. Deliberate entrepreneurial intervention usually intermeshes with the emergence of new demands comparable in their force to the dynamic conservatism of the established system itself.[4]

Under *these* circumstances, the problem of directed diffusion is to set in motion and guide a chain of related processes of social learning in which sequences of deliberate entrepreneurial intervention interact with unanticipated and inadvertent processes, all more adequately treated under the metaphor of battle than communication.

Recent steps in the evolution of diffusion systems

Theories of diffusion have characteristically lagged behind the reality of emerging systems. The image of the county agent, the detail man and the public health officer still dominate accounts of historical processes of diffusion as they do normative theories of diffusion. Prevailing models of directed diffusion still rest on the great social inventions of the late nineteenth and early twentieth centuries.

As we have seen, these models of directed diffusion do not adequately describe the diffusion systems from which they are derived, when the unit of diffusion is a central rather than a peripheral innovation, or a system as broad as the granite industry.

Even in their reality, moreover, the great nineteenth century proliferation-of-centres systems were inherently limited. They suffered from dependence on limited resources and competence at the primary centre, from the rigidity of central doctrine, and from a feedback loop within which information moved primarily between secondary and primary centres. As a consequence, the great institutions for diffusion, such as industry, the church, and world Communism, tend to read their own adaptations as failures of central control.

The development of more nearly adequate theories for the diffusion of innovation must begin by taking account of the existing systems which are already in advance of theories in good currency.

The business firm, as we have seen, evolves toward an advanced learning system. And business firms are very much vehicles for diffusion; marketing is diffusion by another name. Over about the last fifty years, the unit of diffusion around which business firms have organized has evolved from a highly specific product, to a more aggregated product, to constellations of products which bear only a family resemblance to one another, and finally to functional business systems. Concepts of organization, management and planning have evolved along with the unit of diffusion. The business firm, which attained its first great growth through the proliferation of centres, moves toward new models of diffusion as functional systems become central.

During the last decade in which the constellation firm has reached full development and the business systems firm has begun, a very different though in some ways comparable evolution has occurred in domains of society usually considered unrelated or downright antithetical to business. This evolution has followed the pressures for social revolution stemming from a cluster of interrelated movements for civil rights, black power, peace, disarmament and student revolt. These are all national or international causes, but at regional and local levels they have been allied with movements against urban renewal, dislocation of neighbourhoods by superhighways and abuses of community interests and rights too numerous to mention. The organizations involved range from SNCC (Student Non-violent Co-ordinating Committee), CORE (Council on Racial Equality), the Black Panthers, the SCLC (Southern Christian Leadership Council), the Urban League, the NAACP (National Association for the Advancement of Coloured People), to the SDS (Students for a Democratic Society), PAX, Peace and Freedom Party, and include portions (or at times all) of organizations like ADA (Awareness for Democratic Action), UAW (United Auto Workers), and the Welfare Rights movement.

Typically, we cannot say precisely whether this is a movement or a set of related movements. It is a process of social evolution that takes place in the interstices of established organizations; or rather, established organizations become from time to time the instruments through which the movement works itself out.

There is a pattern to the evolution of the movement. Its precursors lie in the radicalism of the 1930s, in the traditional civil rights organizations and in the labour movement. But the new ingredients which began to make themselves felt in the last decade came to their first point of high visibility in the Mississippi summer of 1964, and in the first visible and successful demonstrations and protest marches of Martin Luther King. Here the themes were militant but non-violent activism in the name of civil rights. The events took place in the heart of southern racist country.

The evolution of the movement has proceeded through new pulses of activity centering around new issues. Each new pulse has tended to draw with it new leadership and new groups of participants. The Mississippi summer and the marches and demonstrations in the south gave way to more militant actions in northern ghettos. The Free Speech Movement in Berkeley announced a wave of disruption on university campuses. A small group of college students carried along a more massive following. Civil rights and black power came to be allied with the movement against the war in Vietnam. Clergymen and academics joined blacks and students. Senator McCarthy's candidacy presented a rallying point for the young—but the campaign emphasized the split between the young and the blacks. The withdrawal of President Johnson established the effectiveness of the movement. McCarthy's defeat raised doubts over the validity of 'action within the system'. There was a chain reaction of campus disruptions triggered by SDS, but involving broadening segments of the entire student and faculty populations.

Seen as a system for diffusing innovations, the Movement has had a number of remarkable features:

It has no clearly established centre. Centres rise and fall on a shifting *ad hoc* basis, around new issues and leaders. At various times, the centres have been Martin Luther King and the SCLC, SNCC, the Free Speech Movement and SDS. In a period of months, centres and leaders emerge, come into prominence, and fade away. Often there appear to be multiple or overlapping centres interacting loosely with one another. A group of college students from Columbia and Cornell undertake an explicit pilgrimage to university campuses to carry a message—the substance and methodology of revolution as they conceive it. But this putative centre may be upstaged by the next impetus from an entirely different source.

Neither is there a stable, centrally established message. There is no settled content—of theory, technology or methodology—whose diffusion is the movement's work. Instead, there is a shifting and evolving doctrine—a family of related doctrines. Orthodox Marxism, the theory of power elites, the radical sociology of an Alinsky, the radical critique of a man like Naom Chomsky, the doctrines of participation and advocacy, the Black Manifesto, the elaborations of guerrilla ideology and tactics, the rationale for mysticism and for the use of drugs, the philosophical radicalism of Marcuse, the essays in radical politics of the New Left, all flow and work together and change rapidly over time. In any given action or event, like the Harvard strike of 1969, it is impossible to separate out clear strands of theory or social innovation whose diffusion is the work of that event. Taking one conceptual threat, for example, the doctrine of racial justice, the history of the message has been manifold and changing, from the militant non-violence of King to the theories of Cleaver and the fragmentation of central doctrine in black nationalism, separatism, black revolution and integrationism. But this shifting and evolving message has proved to be compatible with continuity of action and organization around issues of race.

The system of the movement cannot be described as the diffusion of an established message from a centre to a periphery. The movement must be seen as a loosely connected, shifting and evolving whole in which centres come and go and messages emerge, rise and fall. Yet the movement transforms both itself and the institutions with which it comes into contact. The movement is a learning system in which both secondary and primary messages evolve rapidly, along with the organization of diffusion itself.

Its remarkable behaviour and its international scope depend upon the *infrastructure technology* on the basis of which it operates. It is possible to know at Berkeley tomorrow what happened at Cornell yesterday. Third World factions in Algeria maintain connections with American blacks in Cleveland and in Cuba. Television permits simultaneous international witnessing of events, and makes events 'major' because they are so witnessed. Jet transport permits an international traffic in leaders, spokesmen and participants. An underground press, with readership in the millions, services blacks, students and radicals of all shades and persuasions. Telephones permit connection and co-ordination of events across the nation. Records, tapes, and transistor radios spread words and music through which all shades of opinion and feeling find expression. Informal networks of students, blacks and radicals employ these technologies to establish a remarkable level of connectedness among individuals, organizations and communities throughout the world. The connectedness permitted by highly developed infrastructure technology allows the movement to retain cohesiveness in the face of shifts in the centres of leadership and the central doctrine. Because of the ease with which innovation can diffuse itself throughout the system as a whole, the movement can adopt an ethos in which transformation around the new is a value in itself.

The learning system of the movement is survival-prone because of its fluidity and its apparent lack of structure. Its ability to transform itself allows it to continue to function with vitality as issues and situations change around it. Its lack of a single fixed centre makes it difficult to attack. Its scope is no longer limited by the energy or the resources at the fixed centre, nor by the capacity of the 'spokes' connecting the primary centre to secondary ones.

Like the constellation firm, the movement represents a set of overlapping and evolving innovations, rather than a set of like instances or applications of a single innovation. Its innovations bear a family resemblance to one another.

Like the business firm organized around a functional system, the movement represents a complex network of components capable of transforming itself by related interacting innovations in its elements. It internalizes what would otherwise be a series of conflicts and interactions among separate systems. In so doing, it raises the potential for systems innovation and raises the level of requirement for critical management and co-ordination. Both the movement and the business system firm represent network organizations, but what the business system firm accomplishes through formal organization, the movement carries out informally. The business system firm attempts to achieve through formal organization what has grown up in the movement as an informal structure. The movement is to old-style political parties what the business firm has been to the classical product-based firm of the thirties and forties.

Taking the business systems firm and the movement as family-resembling, though apparently antithetical, models of learning systems, we discover an interesting contrast with classical models for the diffusion of innovation.

Classical models for the diffusion of innovations	*Business systems firms and the movement*
The unit of innovation is a product or technique.	The unit of innovation is a functional system.
The pattern of diffusion is centre-periphery.	The pattern of diffusion is systems transformation.
Relatively fixed centre and leadership.	Shifting centre, *ad hoc* leadership.

Classical models for the diffusion of innovations	Business systems firms and the movement
Relatively stable message; pattern of replication of a central message.	Evolving message; family resemblance of messages.
Scope limited by resource and energy at the centre and by capacity of 'spokes'.	Scope limited only by infrastructure technology.
'Feedback' loop moves from secondary to primary centre and back to all secondary centres.	'Feedback' loops operate locally and universally throughout the systems network.

The principal problem of design shifts from the design of a product or technique to the design of a network. The person's principal allegiance shifts from membership in an organization to membership in a network. And the pattern of social learning shifts from successive 'sweeps' of limited innovations from a centre throughout a periphery, to the formation of self-transforming networks.

Notes

[1] Everett Rogers *Diffusion of Innovations*, The Macmillan Co., 1962, pp. 13–14.

[2] In fact, later evolutionary developments in diffusion systems do not necessarily eliminate earlier forms; the simple centre-periphery model still functions in education and business. And the proliferation of centres, which flowered in the nineteenth century, had its precursors in early history.

[3] Rogers *op. cit.*, p. 14.

[4] The whole matter is complicated somewhat by the fact that the reaction of a system to an innovation depends on the ways in which the innovation is perceived by those within the system. The threat inherent in a significant innovation may or may not be apparent at the outset. Where it is apparent, the system is likely to respond by ignoring or by actively resisting the innovation. But where the threat is not apparent, the system may accept the innovation fairly readily as a kind of Trojan horse, only to experience far-reaching and unanticipated disruption as a consequence. Such appears to have been the case in the well-known story of the adoption of the steel axe by Yir Yoront: acceptance of the attractive and apparently innocuous implement led to a chain reaction of cultural disruption. Consumer acceptance of television in our own society may turn out to have been a similar phenomenon.

Or again, the system may be structured in such a way that only a certain element of it, and a relatively powerless one, experiences disruption as a consequence of acceptance. The acceptance of mechanical equipment, chemical fertilizer and weed-killer by cotton planters in the Mississippi Delta turned out to transform the Delta cotton system and in the process to dislocate thousands of black plantation workers. But these were unable to make their resistance felt.

So that our earlier conclusion must be somewhat modified. The diffusion of a significant innovation behaves like our model rather than the Rogers model where the innovation creates a perceptible threat of disruption to elements of the system powerful enough to oppose it.

20 Meta-power and relational control in social life
T. Baumgartner, W. Buckley and T. R. Burns

Introduction

Power and social control are typically conceptualized and investigated in terms of interpersonal or intergroup relationships in which one actor tries to get another to do something, usually against the latter's will (e.g., Blau, 1964). The object of power is more or less direct behavioral control. However, such an approach to the study of power captures only a part of the power activities of groups, organizations, and states.

A large, and historically more important part involves attempts to structure or re-structure the social and cultural matrix within which power activities are to be played out. A given institutional or socio-cultural structure may be viewed as the macroscopic resultant of the application of power to determine permissible or acceptable activities and relationships of individuals and groups to one another and to forms of property or resources. This system also defines the distribution of benefits and costs for categories of persons and groups.

Our approach in this paper views the exercise of power as oriented substantially toward the attempted shaping of this structure of social relationships (in the broadest sense including economic and political relationships) (see also Baumgartner et al., 1975a, 1975b, 1975c). We refer to the exercise of such 'meta-power' as relational control, that is control over social relationships and social structure. Relational control is used by particular groups to promote or stabilize their advantages or dominance over others or to ensure the effective functioning of a social system. Relational control constitutes, in part, the 'historical forces' underlying the given institutional structure of societies and the dynamics of new institutional forms continually struggling to emerge.

Although relational control has specific behavioral consequences and may be used as a means of behavioral control, the purpose of the exercise of relation control is generally the long-term structuring of social process and its outcomes: the individual and collective actions of those whose social relationships are structured (Buckley, et al., 1974). Among other things, it may be used to encourage cooperative social organization on the one hand, or to produce competition or conflict between actors on the other, and generally, to increase power in relation to others[1].

The Hobbesian problem has to do with such structuring of social relations. However, as commonly expressed it poses misleading questions, for it assumes an already existing social situation and directs attention away from the multiple processes that produce such situations and change them. Social theorists typically assume certain initial conditions and single out a particular social control mechanism, attempting to construct a theory of social order on that basis. For example (and we recognize that in this summary form, we fail to do justice to the subtleties of their arguments):

1   Hobbes starts out with atomistic actors in each-gainst-all (conflictive) relationships and ends up with social order based on coercive compliance. Note that for liberal economics, this is the alternative model to that of the market. If the market model does not apply or operate effectively, as in the production of public goods, then the state intervenes to tax citizens and purchase what cannot be obtained through the market mechanism.

2   Coleman (1966) also starts out with atomistic actors in competition. However, peaceful exchange and social integration obtain if value systems or preferences differ in complementary ways. This is basically the liberal viewpoint with market type economic and political systems providing the social exchange mechanisms for societal integration. (But, as Samuelson and others have shown, such systems will not produce sufficient amounts of public goods (Buckley et al., 1974). Hence, it is argued that the state steps in (with sociological and political conditions unspecified) and produces sufficient amounts of public goods. An 'optimal mixed economy' is the final result).

3   Parsons (1951) assumes shared value systems, promoting normative compliance and cohesive

204   T. BAUMGARTNER, W. BUCKLEY AND T. R. BURNS

social order. The manner in which such value systems are obtained or produced in the first place, and the concrete processes whereby they are maintained or eroded are questions not systematically addressed by Parsons.

In considering concrete conflict situations—e.g., those involving management and labor or those occurring in the international sphere—one finds that typologies such as that of Ellis (1971) with coercive, exchange, and normative 'solutions' to the Hobbesian problem, although suggestive, are too static and narrowly conceived for a rich and systematic analysis of social order. The management/labor relationship, for example, entails 'exchange', and by necessity a considerable degree of cooperation. The state, in regulating this relationship, uses coercion, normative pressure, and positive sanctions as well as a variety of other devices such as mediation, arbitration, and adjudication both to prevent costly social disorder and to maintain the hierarchical character of the relationship.

The approach presented in this paper makes up a broader attempt—developed more systematically elsewhere (Buckley *et al.*, 1973; Baumgartner *et al.*, 1975*d*)—to conceptualize and model, from a modern systems perspective, the larger processes of control and self-regulation on the national and international level. Our work, and this paper in particular emphasizes (1) the degree to which social fragmentation as well as social integration are themselves *human products*—and in general, the degree to which social structures are the resultant of more or less intentional, purposeful management of social relationships by power groups; and (2) the *variety of social control mechanisms* used in building up and maintaining social order and human cooperation. Many important questions have to do with these processes, how they operate, interact with one another, change, and so forth. Therefore, we take as a research task, preliminary to the eventual analysis of social order, the conceptualization and analysis of control activities in human groups pertaining to the regulation and maintenance of certain social relationships. For this purpose, we conceptualize an interaction system and then distinguish the three bases of relational control with respect to such systems: control of action opportunities, control of differential payoffs or outcomes of interaction, and control of cultural orientations and ideology.

Any ongoing social system entails a *system of interaction* within a *social structure* (encompassing economic, political, and other bases of power difference). The interaction system, involving actors A, B, C, . . . can be conceptualized as consisting of at least three system components: their action and interaction possibilities, the likely outcomes or payoffs of their interaction in specific exchange situations, and a culture of normatively defined as well as emergent values and orientations among the actors which, among other things, define qualities of their established or anticipated social relationships. In our general model, the *behavioral outcomes* of the interaction system are a function of the states of its three system components:

1   the interaction *situation*—the action possibilities available to B and C, (focusing for the moment on only two actors and their interaction system): for instance, the possibilities for B and C to communicate, combine, and cooperate or to segregate and compete or conflict; or the symmetry of their action opportunities within a certain institutional framework, that is, whether or not B and C have more or less equal rights, perquisites, and in general, power resources.

2   the interaction *payoffs* or outcome structure—the promotion of certain actions and the discouragement of others through the structuring of gains and losses associated with them, for instance the promotion of competitive private interests or shared group interests.

3   the actors' attitudes and *orientations* toward one another—the promotion of distrust or an individualistic self-interest ideology or of trust and a social cooperation ideology; or the promotion of vertical orientation and loyalty to 'superior' persons or groups as opposed to horizontal cooperation with other actors in co-equal situations.

These three system properties are mutually interrelated and can probably be separated only analytically.

In investigating and conceptualizing the power to carry out direct behavioral control, one focuses typically on differences in resources, skills, strategies, etc., among actors *within* a matrix of rules and structural constraints (which typically remain in the background or are taken for granted). In the study of relational control, one is also interested in differences among actors in resources, skills, strategies, and so forth, but focuses on interactions and the mobilization of power resources to *manipulate* the matrix of rules, the conditions of interaction, and the distribution of resources which, among other things, define the power and control possibilities for the exercise of behaviorial control. The ability to exercise relational control is a *meta-power* setting the limits of lower order power (Baumgartner *et al.,* 1957*d*). Clearly, although an actor B may have social power *within* an interaction situation or 'game' (e.g., greater ability than others to select a preferred outcome or to realize his will over the opposition of others within that social structural context), he may or may not have power to *structure* social relationships, to alter the 'type of game' the actors play, the rules and institutions and conditions governing interactions or exchanges among the actors involved.

In this paper, we focus primarily on situations where an elite A, a power group in a social structure, manipulates one or more of the components of an interaction system involving B, C, D, . . . so as to structure social relationships and their action outputs. In a word, A exercises meta-power.

Much of what we discuss here has been pointed out previously in one way or another by other social scientists. What our work tries to offer is a more systematic perspective and the theoretical linkage of apparently unrelated phenomena.

Relational control: the structuring of social relationships

An actor A may be in a position to influence and structure one or more of the states of the B/C interaction system using such powers to structure a particular type of relationship between B and C, e.g., to produce competition or conflict between them. The choice A makes in this regard depends on his interests and value structure in the setting, which, of course, may be determined or influenced by a yet higher power or authority. Although in our illustrations some consideration is given to the basis of A's interests in exercising relational control, this matter is of secondary importance in this particular paper. The primary focus is on relational control, its nature and its realization in concrete social processes.

While the emphasis here is primarily on an external power A exercising relational control, groups or persons having or anticipating social relationships to one another may exercise relational control with respect to their own relationships. In other words, A need not be a power agent distinct from B and C. A may (1) be drawn from B and C as a 'leader', or (2) consist of B and C themselves, their 'collective power', acting in relation to their relationship, negotiating and deciding on its nature. Clearly, in the first case, A has meta-power which the other actors to a greater or lesser degree lack, which puts him in a position to structure interaction situations to his own advantage.

Below we consider a number of instances of relational control in order to suggest the general applicability of our conceptualization as well as to point up the various properties of relationships which are the object of control and which are structured through the manipulation or management of one or more components of interaction systems.

The properties of social relationships which we investigate here are:

1 *the solidarity or predisposition for cooperation in social relationships*. In Section 1 we examine the structuring of distrustful, noncooperative relationships through 'fragmenting' or 'divide and rule' strategies. Section 2 takes up the structuring of relationships in which actors are predisposed, to some degree, to trust in one another, take one another's interests into account, and cooperate. In Section 3 we consider the use of both integrative and alienative strategies, structuring intra- and inter-group relationships in order to accomplish group formation or greater group cohesiveness and coordination.

2 *asymmetry in social relationships*. In Section 4 we examine the structuring of unequal exchange relationships, using the example of employer/employee exchange in capitalist societies as well as an international example.

1 *Structuring uncooperative social relationships* (Baumgartner *et al.,* 1975*a*)

Strategies of social fragmentation, including divide and rule strategies, entail A's use of his relational powers to alienate B and C socially from one another, that is, to create or maintain a Hobbesian situation of 'war of each against all'[2]. A structures the relationship between B and C so as to foster conflict of interest, social disorganization, and distrust, which A, as a power of authority, exploits to his advantage, e.g., in order to achieve or maintain domination over them[3]. A's control activities may go so far as to foster resource-squandering competition or conflict between B and C, thereby weakening them. In any case, they are prevented from collectively increasing their potential power (through cooperation) with respect to their own relationship and to A.

Such social fragmentation is accomplished in any of the three ways that A can exercise relational control with respect to the B/C interaction system.

Structuring segregative interaction situations: constraint on association and organization. A structures the interaction *situation* so as to make it difficult, if not impossible, for the actors to join together, organize, and cooperate in order to resolve conflicts of interest, problems of scarcity, or oppression. For instance, the actors are not allowed to associate or to communicate, must use individual rather than collective decision procedures[4], or cannot make binding agreements or contracts.

As Simmel has emphasized (1950, p. 163), the association itself is feared—even if there is no clear and present danger that it is a challenge to the ruling power—simply because there is the possibility, the potentiality, that it might be put to such a purpose:

'Pliny, in his correspondence with Trajan, states explicitly that the Christians are dangerous because they form an association, otherwise they are harmless.'

Eighteenth and nineteenth century slave systems in the Americas offer extreme illustrations of divide and rule strategies of control (Genovese, 1965; Elkins, 1968; Patterson, 1967; Davis, 1966; Aptheker, 1969). In general, the formation of corporate groups among slaves was not encouraged and was in most instances actively suppressed. Every conceivable device was used to prevent slaves from consorting with each other or exchanging intelligence. Negroes could not assemble without permission or supervision. Dirks points out (1974, p. 34) in the case of the West Indies[5]:

'Outside of work situations, the household, and the mission congregations formed late in the 18th century, organized groups are not in evidence among slaves. Indeed, planters actively discouraged slaves from congregating in large numbers or forming organized bodies in other than task performance. Unsupervised assemblies, particularly night gatherings, were banned. These legal prohibitions were not always rigorously enforced but groups detected under suspicious circumstances were dealt with promptly.'

Strategies to reduce the density and opportunities of interacting among subordinates have been used often by rulers whenever feasible (although, as we discuss later, particularly in regard to the factory context, such strategies may be unavailable or less attractive under certain socio-economic conditions). It is common practice under authoritarian regimes to impose 'martial law' restriction against *unauthorized association* or *assembly* of more than a few people so as to prevent the exchange and discussion of information and opinion, coordination or organization of activities or in general any political activity not controlled by the government. Parties or labour unions, while often espousing democratic principles, establish an organizational system of vertical links with very few horizontal links, in a word, a system of extreme compartmentalization so that groups at the same level find it difficult to communicate or to coordinate with one another except through higher authorities. Divide and rule patterns are institutionalized in bureaucratic forms of social organization.

Structuring competitive or conflictive payoff structures. A structures the interaction payoffs of B and C in such a way as to establish competitive or conflictive preferences, thus increasing the likelihood of distrust and of non-cooperation between the actors (especially under the conditions discussed above) and prompting thereby his own interests in relation to them.

This strategy of social fragmentation is repeatedly emphasized by students of slave systems. Dirks writes (1974, p. 39):

'Widespread deprivation and mutual distrust made the recruitment of reliable co-conspirators (for revolt) difficult. Numerous attempts to overthrow the control of planters were frustrated by slaves who took opportunities (offered by planters) for manumission and cash rewards by turning in plotters.'

In addition, there were daily rewards and incentives as well as punishments differentiating slaves who cooperated with their masters from those who did not: on the positive side, monetary rewards or gratuities, allocations of small plots of ground to cultivate their own crops during spare hours, promotion in the slave hierarchy, travel passes, etc.; on the negative side, beatings, branding, torture and death.

The maintenance of a slave hierarchy of positions (personal servants, general domestic workers, drivers, and field workers) with differential rewards and privileges—holding out hope of mobility and even a small chance of freedom—encouraged many blacks to identify their interest with those of their owners rather than with their fellow slaves. Aptheker points out (1969, p. 61):

'Carefully selected slaves were the personal servants, male and female, who often were assigned to and did serve, a particular member of the master's family throughout his or her life. Here, as was natural, there frequently developed a strong attachment, and it was very largely from this group that spies and traitors were obtained by the ruling class. Betrayal always brought substantial economic reward and invariably freedom—the greatest gift in the possession of the slaveholders.'

Simmel describes several interesting examples of rulers manipulating rewards and honors for purposes of maintaining their power as well as exploiting their subordinates. Inca rulers used the procedure of dividing newly conquered tribes approximately in half and placing a chief over each of them with a disparity in rank so as to provoke rivalry between the heads. This served to prevent any united action against the ruler on the part of the subjected tribes (Simmel, 1950, p. 165).

In general, division of the population into multi-level status hierarchies has been a common device to generate schisms and to inhibit political co-operation of those who are beneath the top dogs even at the same time that the structure may contribute to the coordination of reciprocal relationships and productive activities. Such a system constrains the amount, form and content of interaction between individuals and groups in different positions of the structure. Thus, stratification in status and pay both within an enterprise or industry as well as across enterprises and industries has served to fragment the labour movement; not to speak of sexual, ethnic, religious, racial and other sources of cleavage—the 'cultural superstructure'—that rulers cleverly manipulate to maintain their dominance (Blauner, 1972, p. 32). Typically, the social fragmentation is not viewed as 'dysfunctional' by its creators and those (the rulers) who are in the best position to change it (Wachtel, 1974).

Propagating non-cooperative ideologies. Through the use of ideologies, control or communication media, ritual and myth, a power of authority group may foster orientations or attitudes of individualism, independence, and self-reliance, rather than of collectivism and social interdependence. When, in addition, a competitive payoff structure and segregative interaction conditions are encouraged, the *emergent ideology* of private decision-making and action, and of minimal trust and cooperation, promotes non-cooperative type outcomes which are far from optimal from a collective point of view.

A transparent case of power groups propagating ideologies to support their domination is that of slavery. Slave masters in the US South succeeded in instilling their paternalistic ethos and values in the minds and behavior of their subjects (Genovese, 1974). Using propaganda, laws and customs, and ritual patterns of dominance and 'courtesy', they drummed into their subjects the concepts of their dependent but 'mutually considerate' ties with their masters year after year, generation after generation (Aptheker, 1969). These patterns ultimately served both master and slave, the master's objective to stabilize domination and the slave's desire for protection against abuse of power and brutalization.

As Genovese suggests, paternalism undermined the solidarity of the slaves by linking individuals to oppressors. The slaves looked to their rulers rather than to one another (not that there was a lack of mutual dependence among slaves) for protection, economic amenities, and solutions to various problems requiring resources. By accepting the ethos and values of paternalism, they helped to legitimize and stabilize class domination (Genovese, 1974; Woodward, 1974). Of course, the hierarchy of slave positions and the impediments to corporate group formation among slaves reinforced such orientations.

In many instances, the ideological/cultural barriers to subordinate group formation and collective action are not produced by rulers but, nonetheless, are used by them to constrain association and organization of subordinate groups and to obstruct processes that would overcome existing divisions.

Examples of rulers *actively* exploiting racial, ethnic, or ideological cleavages so as to inhibit organization or political cooperation of subordinate groups fill the pages of history. (1) Dominant groups *recruit* mutually hostile persons or groups for subordinate status. For example, slaves were often recruited with a view to tribal and language divisions, which would weaken or prevent effective slave opposition. A result was (Patterson, 1967, p. 281):

'... that the different tribal stock hated "one another so mortally that some of them would rather die in the hands of the English than join with other Africans in an attempt to shake off their yoke".'

(2) Rulers *build social organization* upon 'natural' conflicts: vertical ordering of interaction with rulers who allocate resources and 'resolve' conflicts; establishment of separate institutions which duplicate 'natural' cleavages—school systems, trade unions, racially segregated promotion systems within plants, etc.; promulgation of laws limiting or outlawing collective decision-making and anit-competitive and solidarity meetings of segmented groups and their respective organizations. Through social organizational means, the cleavages are *institutionalized*, inhibiting collective action among subordinate groups with essentially common interests in their opposition to their rulers. (The discussion above and that immediately following point up that the bases of social divisions are rarely independent.)

Elsewhere, we have investigated in some detail divide and rule strategies of different degrees of sophistication (Baumgartner *et al.*, 1975a). We have also explored how accidental or historically derived fragmentation, much like a manipulated one, may contribute to the maintenance of a system of domination or, as pointed out above, serve as a basis for divisive institutions.

2 Structuring cooperative social relationships

In contrast to the divide and rule strategy, A's goals or interests may lead him to try to structure conditions regarding B and C that lead to cooperative processes and outcomes. Thus, in order to exploit their subordinates more effectively for productive or defence purposes, rulers must often organize them, even though this organization, potentially, can be used by them to oppose their rulers. Thus, there is often a contradiction or a dilemma facing rulers between, on the one hand, maximizing systematic power or the social product by bringing about or maintaining social organization among subordinates and, on the other, maximizing domination by segmenting B and C through divide and rule strategies (Baumgartner et al., 1975a). Rulers concerned only with domination are not faced with this dilemma. However, if the system they control comes into competition or threatening conflict with other systems or groups, they are likely to be motivated to try to increase their system's output, thus causing the dilemma. There may also be internal reasons for improving the social organization of production. For instance, the goals or needs of the ruling elite may be unrealizable under a more fragmented system of productive relations; in order to increase production, they reduce or transform the alienative relationships among producers or producer groups.

In response to the dilemma and to the power implications of greater integration, rulers or leaders frequently develop or evolve new control strategies, techniques, and institutions enabling them to increase the level of cooperation in society while remaining firmly in control:

1   A structures the associations between B and C by controlling the nature and extent of the cooperative process itself, for instance through limiting it to the productive domain, discouraging cooperation outside that context, or by supervising strictly the association of B and C[6].

2   Economic and other rewards are allocated so as to create status and wage hierarchies which inhibit political coordination at the same time that productive cooperation is encouraged.

3   Talented and ambitious individuals who might become opposition leaders and draw on the potential power of a more integrated system for opposition, particularly if their own careers or ambitions are blocked, are brought ('coopted') into the administrative apparatus or rewarded through patronage. Non-conformists can be singled out, iso-lated, or forced into exile (Oberschall, 1973).

4   Religious or other ideological specialists influence socialization processes, legitimizing beliefs stressing subordination and obedience to those in 'authority', rather than orientation to other subordinate persons or groups.

5   Laws are invoked or drafted that limit the action possibilities of subordinate organizations, e.g. limiting collective bargaining and action of trade unions to 'legitimate' issues.

As a new regime develops, its control over subordinate associations typically becomes institutionalized in law, custom, and ideology. Consider, for example, the history of labour unionization in the USA and its limitations controlled by the Taft-Hartley Act and other legal restrictions. In these and other ways, often entailing sophisticated strategies of divide and rule, authorities may permit, indeed, encourage, a certain degree of *social integration and coordination*—even in political affairs—and therefore provide the cooperative basis essential to more developed (interdependent) forms of human production. At the same time, such strategies are designed to prevent maximal cooperation of subordinate groups to challenge the power of their rulers. In a word, *the level of social integration for production is raised at the same time that the society remains stratified politically* (Baumgartner et al., 1975a).

In a related paper (Buckley et al., 1974), we have investigated the ways that human groups to varying degrees try to structure cooperative social relationships among group members, particularly in situations where non-cooperative behavior, e.g. competitive panics as in the case of a crowd in a burning theatre, is self-defeating or, in general, in situations where self-interest contradicts group or collective interest and where cooperation may be problematic. Certain social control processes found operating in many groups increase the likelihood of cooperative interactions[7]. These processes operate on the various components of human action: perceptions and knowledge, preference or value structure, decision procedures, and action possibilities. For example, social groups create new action opportunities for their members as well as constrain their action and interaction possibilities; evaluation and preference structures are restructured through persuasion, activation of social sentiments and the application of selective sanctions in groups; and the decision-making actions of individuals are coordinated or collectivized through various forms of group decision-making including voting and authoritative rule

(Buckley *et al.*, 1974; Burns and Meeker, 1976). Below we discuss briefly the three ways in which A can structure more cooperative relationships.

Structuring cooperative interaction situations. In as much as social trust and effective social controls are crucial to overcoming pressures toward non-cooperative behavior, particularly in situations of scarcity, group leaders may try to *structure interaction situations* so that individual members interact generally in small groups within which interpersonal trust and cooperative predispositions can be developed and monitored. Thus, members of large organized groups interact in 'small groups', 'cells', 'units', etc., with internal social controls and co-ordination. These units in turn are coordinated with one another through relatively small higher level units and so on, making up a multi-level control system capable of large-scale productive cooperation (Baumgartner *et al.*, 1975*b*). An army is a good example of a permanently structured, large-scale social organization whose actions must be based on 'irrational' behavior from its many constituents. In battle, each soldier is faced with the choice of fleeing to save himself, or staying to fight with others and risking his life. The organization of the army into squads, platoons, companies, etc., each having representatives (squad leaders, platoon leaders, company commanders, etc.) who meet, in small groups, at a higher level of organization is designed in part to create and maintain social solidarity and mutual trust within reasonable size units (of course, there are additional social control mechanisms including in some armies the threat of execution). If the squad members act 'irrationally' and fight in battle, if the squad leaders trust their counterparts to remain in the battle and therefore are disposed to remain themselves and so on at each level of the organization, the army will, as a whole, be capable of acting 'rationally' upon this pyramid of 'irrationality' (see Shils and Janowitz, 1948).

A control agent A may intervene directly in the B/C relationship to facilitate communication, collective decision-making and binding agreements among the actors. In industrial societies, the state regulates a number of crucial relationships which have potential for serious conflict and social disruption[8], particularly labor/management relationships[9]. Its motive to regulate may derive from interests it shares with one or both parties in maintaining good relations and/or it may derive from broader interests in the 'general welfare' that depends on B/C cooperation (for example, an industrialized society's dependence on at least minimal management/labour cooperation).

Thus, in advanced capitalist societies, the state attempts to structure the conditions of business transactions so as to facilitate and stabilize economic transactions. For example, the state intervenes in market systems, regulating business activity, to insure, among other things the honouring of debts and contracts (e.g., regarding the quality of goods, delivery, service, payments, and other aspects of exchange), maintenance of minimum standards of quality (in the case of food products, drugs, housing, etc.), and prevention of the use of false measures, misrepresentation, and false payments (false checks, counterfeit bills, etc.). Such conditions engender trust and more or less predictable patterns of interaction[10], make business agreements easier to arrive at (especially long term agreements) and in general promote the development of trade and production. A contract entails promises by two or more persons that are enforceable by law (*Encyclopaedia Britannica*, 1973, 6, pp. 424–425):

'Business and social pressures, such as the fear of losing goodwill or credit standing probably provide the strongest inducements for persons to perform the promises they make. Nevertheless, the enforcement of contracts is generally considered one of the most important functions of the judicial institution, *and there can be no doubt that in performing this role, the courts contribute to the stability of commercial transaction.*'

One cannot emphasize enough the obvious importance of social and legal conditions favorable to commerce and productive cooperation, namely a system of customs, rules, and laws to produce at least some minimal trust and cooperativeness of actors, a system of standardized weights and measures as well as a system of dependable money and money institutions. These control systems are essential to maintaining and developing the complex and ever-changing nexus of actual as well as *potential* exchange relationships in capitalist market systems, and cannot be taken for granted in any complete analysis[11].

Structuring cooperative payoffs. Using resources which the group itself allocates to him or which are delegated from outside the group, A may apply selective sanctions in order to produce a payoff structure *conducive to B/C cooperation* (Burns and Buckley, 1974; Buckley *et al.*, 1974).

Sanctions applied by group leaders change the outcomes of acts and, therefore, preference structure. For example, members of a group receive social approval or avoid disapproval by conforming to anti-competitive and cooperative norms. Norms and sanctions against 'rate-busting' in factories, 'apple polishers' and 'teacher's pets' in schools, and 'stool pigeons' and 'traitors' in groups of any kind, represent social disapproval of and attempts to control conduct that advances the individual's interest at the expense of other group members or of the group as a whole (Blau, 1964, p. 255). Organized groups such as the Mafia, exercising considerable power in relations to members, can effectively enforce such norms. Loosely coupled groups (e.g., the 'criminal sub-culture') generally have fewer sanctioning resources, and unrelated criminals brought together in a momentary criminal act obviously have the fewest.

Examples of governments using financial inducements, especially in the absence of sufficient political or constitutional power (as in the case of federally constituted states), to prod subordinate political units to search for and adopt collective solutions to pressing problems are numerous and widespread:

(1) regional land use planning and regional solutions to problems of refuse disposal, transportation, etc., are encouraged in many countries by granting special subsidies to regional units; (2) badly needed school district consolidations, for example in Quebec and Germany, were brought about through the use of subsidies financing new consolidated facilities, or by the threat of retracting current subsidies to individual schools if the case consolidation failed to be accomplished in the immediate future; (3) government subsidies for expensive research facilities may be granted, as in Switzerland recently, only after the various universities agreed upon institutional specialization and programme allocation, thus reducing competitive duplication.

Propagating cooperative ideologies. The power or authority A may persuade or socialize B and C to show collective interest over individual interests (as suggested in the examples above of normative influence; see Burns, 1973). In some groups particularly, a premium is placed on trustworthiness and cooperative behavior. Members are socialized to orient strongly toward the group and to control personal ambitions, selfishness and competitiveness in the interest of the collective (as well as to consider, in some instances, the 'external' power or authority as an opponent).

In general, social control over the perception of action possibilities and their outcomes or over the valuation bases of preference can bring about the same result: a structuring of preference relations (Buckley et al., 1974). Thus, group ideology and myths may serve to structure and *to coordinate individuals' perceptions and evaluations* (or the value criteria and cognitive models underlying them) and, therefore, constitute social control mechanisms. Actors may 'know' one another's orientations and behavioral dispositions on the basis of information provided them by an 'authority'. The belief that everyone else is cooperating typically enhances the likelihood of cooperation. The larger and more socially fragmented the group, the more the maintenance of learned expectations about others and perceptions of social reality depend on socially defined 'authorities' and the use of mass media.

Social interactions often entail processes of changing sentiments or activating sentiments and social norms (e.g., through personal appeals and moral persuasion) to the effect that preference structures are transformed in the manner described above. Thus, the leaders of a social or religious movement who persuade persons touched by it to rank 'cooperation' over 'competition' and 'sharing' over 'exploitation' in effect alter value structures such as those of the 'zero-sum' or competitive types. Religious and political leaders often play such 'integrative roles' in social groups.

While the emphasis above has been placed on the persuasion and socialization of group members, a device often used to insure a high level of trust and cohesiveness among members is to recruit persons deemed trustworthy. For example, persons may be included in or excluded from a group on the basis of certain characteristics they possess (race, ethnicity, religion, kinship, political attitudes) *which are believed to relate to trustworthiness*. Continued membership in a group may also depend on a person's behavior in the group: a human group tends to exclude members who, for example, refuse to carry their weight or in general to comply with important social norms (the usual social control mechanisms having proved ineffective). Obviously, if groups requiring mutual trust and cooperation for their activities were not to control group membership by excluding persons believed to be untrustworthy, mutual distrust and the erosion of social controls would develop among the members (distrust can spread especially in cases where 'untrustworthy' members cannot be readily identified).

3 Structuring between-group relations: The problem of group 'boundary maintenance'

In this section, we consider situations where both

integrative and alienative strategies are utilized in a patterned manner. Of particular interest are situations where there are attempts at the coordinated structuring of in-group and between-group relationships so as to accomplish group formation or greater group cohesiveness and coordination in the context of other competing or hostile groups. The resultant social structures define the action opportunities and powers of individuals and sub-groups in specific social matrices entailing exchange, competition, and conflict.

When a group A has a conflictive or hostile relationship with another, group B, members of each are expected to interact with the adversary or its agents accordingly. That is, there are definite social controls to insure a certain type of relationship between members of group A and members of group B. Individual members from the two groups typically are not permitted to interact except in a group context: hence, there is *group* interaction rather than interactions between individuals. Of course, highly trustworthy members (leaders and their agents) may be permitted to engage in more interpersonal relationships.

Even in non-conflictive situations, the leadership of a group may try to control or regulate relationships to outsiders in order to prevent erosion of group solidarity and coordination by external powers supporting one or another subgroup against the central leadership or against one another. For example, prior to the federal constitution of 1848, the Swiss cantons had the power to make their own foreign policy. This set-up threatened federal unity, since each member could and did look for outside support, and the collectivity developed tendencies toward disintegration. The constitutions of 1848 and 1872 went a long way toward giving the central government *control over relationships with foreign entities, including rights of supervision over such relationships that did develop between subunits and foreign entities.*

'By the constitutional restriction of cantonal freedom in foreign policy, it became more difficult for other countries to interfere in the internal affairs of Switzerland with the help of individual cantons and parties. This meant that the period of foreign tutelage was at an end. As the creators of the new federal state had wished, the Swiss people now stood united in the face of the outer world, as a people with a fully developed national feeling' (Bonjour *et al.,* 1952 pp. 273–274).

To limit further the interaction possibilities of subordinate political units or individual citizens with foreign states, the new constitution forbade the conclusion of future agreements to provide mercenaries and determined that members of the federal authorities, military service, and federal civil service were not allowed to accept pensions, salaries, gifts, titles, or other orders of merit from foreign governments. This served to restrict the development of special obligations or emotional ties with foreign governments that could influence the options and choices of the Swiss government (Bonjour *et al.,* 1952, p. 274).

Some groups may attempt to eliminate all relations with 'outsiders' which might contaminate or in any way adversely affect group interactions and sense of group solidarity and identity. Such exclusiveness may be achieved either by completely withdrawing or refusing to have anything to do with the 'outsiders' (see earlier discussion on recruitment and exclusiveness). For example, the group rejects and even destroys all things representing or associated with outsiders, particularly dominant outsiders. Anderson (1974, p. 13) writes:

'Sometimes the desire to maintain a boundary is symbolized with physical withdrawal: the Maya Indians in Quintana Roo studied by Villa Rojas [. . .] have withdrawn into a remote part of the Yucatan peninsula and discourage members of the dominant Mexican Yucatec society from venturing into their area.'

Some of the Mayas manifest an extreme form of exclusion. For instance, after the Mexican army evacuated their sacred city of Chan Santa Cruz following the Revolution, the Indians destroyed anything that represented the larger society (quoted from Villa Rojas in Anderson, 1974, p. 13):

'Again masters of their old capital the natives set about destroying the public benefits instituted there by the Federal Government: the magnificent public reservoir was blown up with dynamite; the Vigia Chico railway was put out of service, and the locomotives torn apart, and the coaches burned, and finally in order to isolate themselves completely from the outside world, the telegraph and telephone lines were cut, and the wire put to other uses.'

Anderson goes on to point out (1974, p. 13):

'Many exclusive systems, like the Mayas in highland Chiapas, Quintana Roo or Guatemala manifest their exclusiveness by wearing distinct costumes, worshipping different saints and pursuing specific fiestas. If one knows the costumes, one can immediately tell which community a person comes from. In addition, boundary maintenance has also been signified by expulsions of the ladino (Spanish-speaking) populations from several Indian communities . . .'

Quite often a group has economic ties with one or more other groups viewed as adversary or contaminating 'foreign elements'. In this case it may maintain a specific 'business-like' relationship with 'outsiders', for example, conducting trade in an impersonal, often calculating manner (Burns, 1973). In a word, a specific as opposed to a diffuse solidary relationship is maintained, limiting interaction to what is necessary to accomplish the limited task, that made the transaction desirable or necessary ('silent barter' is an extreme form of such limited interaction). Anderson (1974, p. 14) reports that in a Norwegian factory studied by Lysgaard, the 'workers' collective' formed a subsystem. The members of this group recognized and *maintained a clearcut boundary between themselves and management and* other personnel groups, such as the foremen, whom they viewed as the representatives of management. Their social world was one of 'us and them', and *diffuse social relationships across the group boundary were discouraged*. The workers obviously needed to interact with foremen and management, but the exchanges were 'impersonal' and limited in content. In general, social constraints may prevent or inhibit the development of close or cooperative relationships between persons who come into contact with one another, for example, in their everyday work (Burns, 1973). Possession of certain social attributes such as those of age, sex, religion, tribe, or ethnic group serve to dissociate some actors from (or on the other hand, to associate them with) other categories of persons or groups in the situation.

Groups may attempt to expand their boundaries—to form a larger unit of association in which trusting and basically cooperative relationships obtain (at least to the extent they are normatively regulated under the broader umbrella). In the development of human groups, clans *extend* lineage and family structures. Persons belonging to the same clan were expected to aid one another whenever possible, and if deemed necessary, the entire clan might be called on to avenge a wrong done to one member. The clan's main functions were to regulate marriage, extend obligatory relationships beyond extended family, facilitate concerted action in projects requiring more manpower than was available in extended family or local groups. The formation of larger, more inclusive groups within which relational control, cooperative exchange, and the coordination of action can be facilitated and resources mobilized is characteristic of the development of human societies (Burns *et al.*, 1973). EEC, OPEC, and the UN are contemporary examples of such group formation.

4 The structuring of unequal exchange relationships (Baumgartner and Burns, 1974, 1975; Baumgartner *et al.*, 1975c)

In the previous sections, we have focused on the structuring of cooperative and non-cooperative relationships, including within-group and between-group relationships. In this section, we examine briefly two instances of the *structuring of asymmetric relationships*. In the first, an example of employer/employee exchange in capitalist society, we describe the unequal allocation of the social products of productive activity and point out how the exchange process both reflects asymmetric structuring of exchange and contributes to the maintenance of the unequal relationship. In addition, we consider briefly a few of the ideological and socio-political mechanisms which contribute to the maintenance of the asymmetric relationship, that is contribute to relational control.

The second example relates to the establishment of the trade relationship between England and Portugal in the 17th century through which, in part, England attained dominant status, while it helped push Portugal into a position of obscurity and backwardness.

Some actors in a system of social relationships enjoy an initial power advantage. For example, the exercise of asymmetrical control by nation states over resources and valuables in different spheres (economic, military, and cultural) is partly the result of natural resource endowment (mineral deposits), climatological conditions (e.g., affecting agricultural production), and geographic location which can give a state proximity to and control over important lines of communication. Partly it is the result of historical developments that lead to the accumulation of productive capacity in some countries but not others: that bring forth a well-educated, cohesive, disciplined and well-motivated labour force in a few countries while preventing its development in others; that permit the development of cultural traits and socio-political structures and behavior flexible enough to let some societies adapt to changing conditions while other societies fail to react effectively to such challenges; that bring certain nations into possession of positions of recognized ideological, spiritual and cultural leadership (Baumgartner and Burns, 1975; Baumgartner *et al.*, 1975d).

Actors can use their power advantage to structure the rules, institutions, and other conditions of interaction or exchange to their benefit (typically on a long term basis), as when A provides B necessities or needed support for which B concedes to A meta-powers or action opportunities to develop meta-power. That is, A provides B with goods and services which offer only short-term benefits (e.g., in consumption) whereas A gains in return goods, resources, or conditions which have long term advantageous structural effects (e.g., the establishment or maintenance of an unequal or dependent relationship between A and B). For example, nations in advantageous positions can use their control over political influence, economic resources, and markets as well as cultural values and their position in the structure of international relations to establish and manipulate economic, political and military alliances and international organizations. They can see to it that their exports gain favorable access to important markets, their imports come from secure and cheap sources, and their financial and direct investments are profitable and protected from losses. Thus, most favored nation status, preferential tariffs, quotas, product boycotts, and rules for differential pricing, etc., establish a *structural framework within which* international economic exchange takes place.

We say A *dominates* B if A is in a position to establish, maintain, or change the relationship between A and B as well as relationships between B and other actors, against B's will[12]. Other actors may be interested in establishing and maintaining the unequal A/B relationship and therefore assist or support A in structuring it in such a way.

1 Employer/employee relationships in capitalist societies: Structured inequality (Baumgartner and Burns, 1974). In employer/employee exchange, the employee (B) submits his or her labour power (Y) to the control of the employer (A) and the latter provides the employee with part of the revenue (r) derived from operating the means of production and providing goods and services to 'consumers'. The exchange is not an equal one in a structural sense, for it provides the employer with action opportunities and powers both within the productive system and in the larger social system which are not made available to the employee. In particular, *the employer gains the meta-power to structure relationships in the productive system as well as in the larger social system* (e.g., in the latter case, by trading economic concessions and favours for political advantage). On the other hand, a worker or workers as a class gain(s) little or no *power leverage* from the income he or they receive(s)—certainly not for bargaining with the employers or with other power agents in the larger system, especially *when most of the income is gained and utilized individually and must be allocated to personal consumption.*

Legally, both employer and employee meet in the 'market place' with 'equal' buying and selling rights. However, the exchange is *asymmetrical* not only because the employer retains exclusive control over the physical means of production, but because he

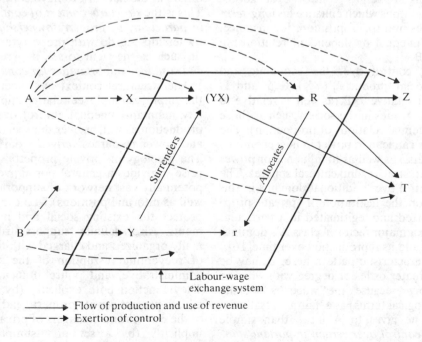

Figure 20.1 Structure of exchange between employer and employee

gains control over the actions of employees and *the economic and non-economic products, spin-offs and spill-overs, of such action applied to the means of production.* In particular (see Figure 20.1), such a process leaves A controlling the means of production (X), B's labor power (Y) which A has purchased, the products (YX) derived from the conjunction of labor power and the means of production, revenue (R) from the sale of products as well as other valuables or sources of valuables (Z) and (T) in different spheres that obtain from operation of the system in its socio-economic environment (including externalities)[13, 14].

The social relationship between A and B is based on unequal control over or access to the means of production and to social products (YX), R, Z, and T[15]. Workers create or contribute to the creation of valuables of which they do not receive a share or for which they are not 'paid', constituting the origin and essence of surplus *values*.

A allocates to B in exchange for his or her labor power a certain income or certain goods, r (derived from operation of the means of production but detached from them). B has the right to use as he sees fit his income and other goods which he or she receives from the employer in exchange for his or her labor power. But, in general, A provides B with resources (to obtain goods and services) offering only *short-term,* individualistic consumptive benefits whereas A gains in return control over goods, resources, or conditions which enhance his *long-term* action capabilities and social position, for instance, to maintain an unequal or dependent relationship between A and B.

By extending control over the economic and non-economic social 'products', (YX), R, Z and T, A gains in power relative to B (as well as relative to other more static groups in the society such as those associated with feudal relations of production). The *extension process* can lead to power in new economic domains ('markets') as well as to influence or power in political, administrative, and cultural spheres. The extension of control over additional domains in this manner, based on the institution of 'private property' conceptualized and legitimated in a particular social context, is a major factor in class A's domination over class B and its reproduction over time[16].

We note a characteristic pattern here. B may be 'satisfied' to a greater or lesser degree with what he receives, possibly because the wage is socially defined (in ideological terms) as a 'fair' or a 'satisfactory' one. But he gives to A more than simple labour: *A gains control over certain important spin-offs and spill-overs resulting from B's productive activity*[17]. (Of course, these need not all be positive. They may be negative or entail risks of negative outcomes.) On the other hand, the income and other benefits B receives (or acquires control over) do not provide generally for an enhancement of B's position relative to A. Of course, a few employees may acquire resources and skills in the productive process which make them essential to the employer or even better, acquire skills that are valuable and transferable, thereby improving their bargaining position. Even though A imparts these skills to B or provides the conditions for B to acquire them, A cannot 'own' B or claim a percentage of B's gains in the future.

An important exception to the system of unequal distribution of *cooperative exchange benefits* may be found in the case where B retains, through the *institution of patenting,* control over many of the positive gains (income, prestige, etc.) from his or her labor. Increasingly, however, employers have patents written in the name of the firm rather than in the name of the inventor. This is another instance of the extension of employer's control over employees' energy, skills, and creative output and its *ramifications in society.*

The structural context of control relationships. Control over a domain X (material or non-material) is based on a network of social relations. An actor or class of actors is implicitly or explicitly recognized by others in the network to have control rights over X. This is the *structural context of control relations and, in particular, of property ownership.* The rights of ownership—to do with property as the owner sees fit, such as the right to sell it—are *socially defined and sustained opportunities for control over it*[18].

The structural context of property rights and of the employer/employee relationship in capitalist society maintains unequal control over the means of production as well as over the spectrum of valuables and power resources *derived* from operating them. The ideology of 'private property' and 'free enterprise' provides a general normative pressure and a potentially vast network of supporters (in formal as well as informal positions) who can be mobilized to protect the existing social and material arrangements. Also, definite 'support structures' are formally organized and charged with the responsibility of preventing disruption of the system: judicial, administrative, and police branches of the state. They function both explicitly (by legal directives, e.g., to protect private property and the prerogatives of the owners and managers of private property) and implicitly (by a set of assumptions underlying policies and operations with respect to business enterprises) to maintain the position of employers in autonomous private properties and their rights to operate their firms without 'undue interference' from workers, consumers, or the general public[19]. In particular, the police and courts of the capitalist state operate to guarantee that, should ideology and persuasion fail, the structure of socio-economic relations and the configuration of constraints outlined above would be maintained 'by other means': namely, 'legitimized force'. As Adams (1972, p. 21) points out:

> 'When in the contemporary capitalist state we say that A "owns something", we actually know that his ownership rests on property laws that are sanctioned by a government [. . .] In fact, of course, they (A) do better than control it; they have the judicial and police powers of state on their side to sanction individuals who would illegally take the property away.'

The structural context of the A/B relationship maintains unequal control over the means of production not only by denying access to them but also by preventing B from using organized power in relation to A so as to gain greater access to or control over the means of production. For instance, the legislature and courts limit the areas in which employees or labour unions may exercise their collective powers (e.g., to strike). Employees, although having gained the right to organize and negotiate about their wages and certain features of their working conditions, have been constrained by ideological and institutional means from exercising their full powers in regard to such matters as (1) the dismissal of workers in response to economic recession or overproduction; (2) the replacement of men by machines; (3) the organization and reorganization (division of labour, group and organizational structure, etc.) of enterprises; and (4) the introduction of new technologies[20]. Similarly, employees have been limited in regard to the type of collective acts they may use against employees, thereby restricting their control over areas (such as consumption) which undoubtedly would have enhanced their power relative to employers. For example, the prohibition (Taft-Hartley Act of 1947 and Landrum-Griffin Act of 1959) against organizing a secondary boycott of an employer's products denied employees one of their most effective means for gaining power in relation to the employer.

Because of structural inequality, the relationship between the classes [A] and [B] is one of domination. Members of [A] enjoy freedoms to exercise control over the means of production, to extend control or influence over additional domains, and in general, to structure relationships both within enterprises as well as in the larger social system. Members and subsets of [B] are subject to constraints in the exercise of collective power in relation to A's (or [A]), and *in general, have few opportunities in the present ideological and institutional context effectively to restructure or transform social relationships*[21]. In a word, they lack meta-power and the capacity to exercise substantial relational control both within productive enterprises in which they are employed as well as in the larger social system.

2 Portugal and England: the structuring of an unequal exchange relationship (Baumgartner and Burns, 1975; Sideri, 1970). Over a span of 60 years in the 17th century, from the time Portugal regained its independence from Spain (1640) until the Methuen Treaty of 1703, England was able to take advantage of the political and military weakness of Portugal to conclude a series of treaties that locked Portugal into a dependent relationship to England. In exchange for politcal support and military protection from England, Portugal—that is, its royal house and domestic allies—made economic concessions with long-term negative developmental implications. Portugal opened its ports, as well as those in its African and Indian possessions, to English ships, granted English merchants special privileges in Portugal, making Portuguese merchants vulnerable to foreign competition, agreed to purchase in England all the ships needed for the Portuguese fleets, and gave up the right to protect its own infant textile industry. By elevating England to supplier of ships, Portugal limited itself to an exclusive supply contract for a strategic resource with a country that competed worldwide with Portugal for superiority in trade and colonization on the basis of possession and development of that resource. In sacrificing its infant cloth industry, it gave up a manufacturing sector which in many countries developed subsequently into a leading sector of industrialization. And, of course, this stopped short a technological learning process, perpetuating and developing a technological gap still existing today.

Portuguese economic concessions did not in general damage the *immediate* economic interests of the ruling dynasty and its supporting class. In particular, the expansion of wine production improved the income and economic power of the landed aristocracy and the Church. These would have a strong interest in the future in maintaining guaranteed access for their products to the English market (and their continued economic and political dominance would assure appropriate policies)[22]. The costs of the concessions fell heavily upon the non-landowning merchant and capitalist classes. It also indirectly kept low the income levels of wage-earning workers in agriculture, manufacturing, and services. Consequently, the growth of these sectors and classes was made more difficult, if not altogether prevented. This, in turn, inhibited the future development of new political, social, and cultural interests *that would have vigorously pressured for a structural change of the socio-political fabric of Portugal*[23].The economic base of Portugal stagnated or even atrophied while that of competing countries, e.g., England, was rapidly developing. Portugal lost its opportunities for establishing an independent economic base which would have provided the underpinning for its political and military power and for the control and development of its empire. *The circle was thus closed: future threats from hostile internal or external forces would drive Portugal to seek renewal and reinforcement of its special relationship to England.* The basically weak position of Portugal (and its rulers)—the reason for the initial quest for outside support—would lead again and again to the exchange of economic concessions for political and military support.

The pattern of specialization in production and trade with Portugal specializing in wine production and England in the production of 'hardware and other goods' had also differing economic consequences. Portugal was forced to import large quantities of foodstuffs. However, payment deficits and the resultant outflow of Brazilian gold to England prevented Portuguese capital accumulation[24]. This in turn was partly the reason for the inability of Portugal to finance the development of its colonies for its own benefit. The expansion of English textile production was reinforced by the opportunity to deliver to the Portuguese market. This contributed to further cost reductions and stimulated additional technological advances, increasing the ability of English producers to penetrate and control old markets and create new ones. *This set the stage for further expansions in a spiral of development, leaving a stagnant Portugal further and further behind.* Portugal's situation corresponded to a trade structure that maximizes the power of the trading partner. The outcome resulted from a long process in which England used its initial power advantages to structure its exchange relations with Portugal in such a way as to increase its power advantage and ultimate economic and political gains.

Conclusion

We have focused here on three main bases of relational control, the structuring and managing of social relationships whereby dominant groups attempt to control or regulate social systems: control of possibilities for contact and social organization of various subgroups in the system, control of differential payoffs or the distribution of valuables accruing to subgroups, and control of cultural orientations and predispositions of actors toward one another.

A main concern of ours in this paper has been to focus research interest on the development of social system structures as the resultant of the more or less intentional, purposeful management of social relationships and structures by power groups—a meta-level of power which, when successful, promotes the attainment of more substantive dominant group goals and interests, whether for good or ill vis-à-vis the larger social system. The characteristic politico-economic structures and processes of a social system at any time can be seen as the resultants of the evolution of such meta-power.

As we have shown, the exercise of meta-power may manifest itself through a divide and rule strategy, or through the structuring of cooperative and unifying social relationships. These represent the two horns of an inherent control dilemma: a divide and rule strategy promotes greater domination but decreases system integration and productive effectiveness; whereas the structuring of cooperation and unification has the opposite effects. A number of national and international examples were given.

In the case of Portugal and England in the 17th century, relational control is revealed in the negotiations, exchanges, and power and control processes which led to the structuring of an asymmetric social relationship between them. This contributed to the development of England while it retarded Portugal in the development of its productive potential and social structure, perpetuating Portuguese dependence to this day. Elsewhere (Baumgartner *et al.,* 1975*d*), we examine more fully from a dynamic perspective the exercise of relational control and structuring processes, investigating historical processes and conditions under which certain social structures emerge and develop, are maintained or decay, and are replaced or transformed.

Notes

[1] Although the concepts of power and control are typically used to refer to conditions and activities related to self-interested influence, we use them in a more general sense, determining in specific analyses purposes to which power and control are put.
[2] A more comprehensive treatment of divide and rule appears in Baumgartner *et al.,* 1975*a*.
[3] In social class terms, A by virtue of his social position, has

resources available (e.g., control over institutional conditions and the allocation of valuables) to impede B/C cooperation, whereas B and C, in their social positions lack sufficient resources to provide for maximum cooperation in relation to A and to counteract A's divide and rule strategies. Such an abstract characterization can be applied to many systems of domination, specifically to employer/employee and seller/consumer relationships.

[4] Committees, juries, conferences, legislative bodies and other voting systems as well as formal organizations are a few of the mechanisms for collective decision-making and for coordination of social behavior.

[5] Many of the opportunities made available to slaves—to build microsocial structures such as nuclear family units, to own property and to engage in trade, to pursue careers in a slave hierarchy, manumission, etc.—served as social control mechanisms assuring domination of the slave owners over their slaves on the one hand and maintenance of a high level of worker morale and productivity on the other.

[6] We cannot take up here the more specific problem of how rulers decide on and implement what they believe to be an 'optimal mixture' of productive cooperation and political fragmentation. Also, we would want to investigate the feed-back and control processes A utilizes in order to regulate the degree and type of cooperation or association between B and C. Regulated or supervised association, to be effective, requires such processes.

[7] The social controls structuring the response potentialities or predispositions of actors may be based on the direct relationships and control processes among the actors. Those with enduring and multiplex (many-stranded) social relationships are likely to take one another into account, to communicate and to cooperate in achieving jointly satisfying outcomes, to the extent possible in any given situation. That is, the form and context of the interaction are established and maintained by the actors themselves—and hence are distinguishable from more exogenous control forms by *self-regulating processes*. Each actor involved has a personal interest in maintaining the relationships and, therefore, of avoiding actions such as cheating or exploitation which could permanently disrupt them.

Social controls may depend on institutional and ideological conditions exogenous to group relations. The weaker the commonality of interests and endogenous controls among the actors, the more social control must be accomplished through *external* mechanisms, making, for instance, norms and collective decision-making (e.g., voting) obligatory.

[8] Other important social relationships that are regulated by the state are landlord/tenant, creditor/debtor, etc., and in non-economic spheres, citizen/citizen and family (husband/wife; parent/child) relationships, especially as regulation through norms and sanctions exercised by extended kinship systems, church, and community have declined in importance.

The need for orderly and non-violent disposition of human conflict in industrialized and urbanized societies has led to the development of political, judicial, and administrative institutions serving as *social control and integrative devices* (Stone, 1966, p. 294): '. . . more specifically, [. . .] it

lies behind the *prohibition* (subject to few exceptions) of *self-help* by individuals in the assertion of their legal rights, and the duty of courts to pass upon all disputes and *not* turn disputants away on the ground that no legal solution is available. It enters, too, as one general element in all criminal penalties, and as the main specific element in such crimes as disorderly behavior, riot and unlawful assembly as well as related applications of the tort of nuisance.'

[9] We have examined elsewhere (Baumgartner *et al.*, 1975) state regulation of labor management relationships, in particular the structuring of interaction situations between management and labor. Such relational control varies from the establishment of a framework facilitating collective negotiation and decision-making between the parties to almost complete reliance on administrative action (arbitration and adjudication), determining and imposing settlements concerning both the terms of exchange and the nature of the relationship between management and labor. These are devices to inhibit conflict escalation and violence and, in general, to maintain cooperation in the face of inherent conflict. The state is especially interested in preventing losses from strikes, lock-outs, etc., in a world of limited resources and high economic interdependence.

Of course, such stabilizing mechanisms typically work to the disadvantage of those in subordinate positions who experience deprivation and wish to change the situation but are compelled to engage in 'disruptive' conflict to do so. And, in any case, the state is not neutral generally in its regulation of economic relationships. Not only do its laws and administrative actions favor some sectors and industries over others, but both formally and informally it tends to support business interests over those of workers and other groups in the society (consumers, etc.). Thus, the state seeks to maintain a cooperative relationship at the same time that it lends support to capitalist freedoms—freedom to accumulate, contract labor, freedom of exchange, freedom to dispose of wealth and property as the owner or managerial authority sees fit, freedom to exercise relational control and to carry out structuring activities within productive enterprises as well as in the larger social system—to capital's long-term advantage (see Section 4).

[10] Of course, in small cohesive communities, shared cultural norms and values or common goals may foster such exchange relations without state intervention (see Note 7).

[11] Contrary to the 'market ethic' and the image of economic processes suggested by orthodox economic theory, pure unconstrained selfishness and pursuit of self-interest disrupts commerce and exchange by promoting dishonesty. This may take the form of using false measures, false payments, misrepresentation, and refusal to honor debts and promises. Such behavior (or merely its likelihood) engenders distrust, makes agreements more difficult to arrive at and in general interferes with and retards the development of trade and production.

[12] In building up and maintaining unequal relationships, rulers often try to recruit persons for subordinate positions, who are oriented vertically to 'superior' persons or groups, or predisposed to be compliant.

[13] This analysis is structurally as well as temporally simplistic in

that it fails to distinguish within the classes [A] and [B]; for example, between managers of the conglomerates and small businessmen or between technicians and other professional employees and blue-collar workers. It also fails to consider emergent groups and divisions.

In considering more elaborate social structures and structural change, one makes use of the same theoretical perspective and arguments as sketched above (see Baumgartner and Burns, 1973; Burns et al., 1973). For example, 'technocrats' are an emergent group of increasing importance. They include technicians (engineers, lawyers, accountants, psychologists, etc.) and administrators. Although their relationship to the means of production is not one of ownership, they occupy, by virtue of their knowledge, skills, and education, strategic positions in the control over, and development of, economic and technical processes in a modern industrial society. In some instances, they have substituted for or taken the place of 'owners' or titular chiefs. Therefore, they belong to or are closer to group A in the diagram above them to the class of B's who, as blue collar and office employees, are merely 'dependent participants' (see Note 15).

Technocrats operate at present within the ideological and institutional constraints of capitalism. However, their knowledge and skills and bargaining power based on their importance to the operation of the system puts them in a better position than most 'employees' to get the system to serve their interests.

[14] Dashed lines indicate control over a given sphere; solid lines trace the flow of production, selling, use of revenue, and ramifications of production processes. The short dashed lines suggest the exercise of partial control by B over the spheres X and r (see also Note 16).

[15] As Zeitlin (1967 p. 37) points out: 'The origin of the system, then, rests on the social process which separated the worker from his means of subsistence and production, while these means come under the exclusive control of the capitalist.' Although our argument in this paper refers ostensibly to contemporary capitalist society with private ownership and management of the means of production, it may be extended to industrial societies without significant private ownership (e.g., communist countries in Eastern Europe). The argument applies wherever there is substantial differential control over the means of production (as represented in Figure 20.1), with a few actors making most of the key economic and technological decisions, and the remainder excluded, reduced to a condition of 'dependent participation' (Touraine, 1972, p. 9). This inequality of control is justified in most eastern European countries by ideology (e.g., concepts such as 'dictatorship of the proletariat' and 'rational socialist management') and sustained institutionally in ways similar to those described above.

[16] With the development of effective trade unionism and the 'democratic welfare state' in many contemporary capitalist societies, there has been a definite shift in the relations diagrammed in Figure 20.1, in that employees have gained greater influence over certain aspects of the operation of the means of production, e.g. their wages and certain of their working conditions (the shift is indicated by the short arrow from B to X). Yet, in many important respects, A dominates and in some, such as the introduction of new technologies and the organization of work, A continues to enjoy more or less absolute dominion. The structure of contemporary capitalism remains basically unchanged in spite of a number of important reforms under 'welfare capitalism'.

[17] It may be that B (and possibly A also) feel that the exchange is an equal or a 'fair' one (e.g., on the basis of social norms or ideology regarding equal or fair exchange). However, our concern here is with the power and meta-power ramifications of such exchange and not the subjective feelings of those involved (see Baumgartner and Burns, 1974).

[18] Property and ownership, of course, have a range of meanings and forms in different social systems, depending on what complex of control rights are socially established and maintained (Burns et al., 1973).

The concept of 'private property' and property rights can be applied generally to systems at different levels (Anfossi, 1974): the case of the owner or manager of the means of production exchanging with workers as well as the case of two or more countries 'trading' with one another where in the latter case, the resources, the gains and losses, etc., of a nation are its 'private property' (see pp. 35–37).

[19] The basis of support are many: ideological, institutional, exchange links, and common interests.

The business firm's economic importance to a community and to government revenues (as well as to party financing) give it political leverage to counteract community and employee pressures as well as government attempts at control. It can effectively threaten the government, community, or an employee group with movement of its 'private plant' elsewhere or a 'necessary' contraction of operations or employment—with all of the serious implications such acts have for jobs and income, tax revenues, and political climate—unless the government or community ceases to 'interfere' or to apply pressure.

The business firm's importance to community and government extends to state and national levels, guaranteeing that administrative and judicial officials, regardless of their ideological inclinations, will feel considerable responsibility and social pressure to keep the system operating: that is, to support existing property relations and the socio-economic structure and to pursue fiscal, monetary, and other policies which promote business prosperity and produce a state of confidence that encourages new investment. Were the government or courts to initiate policies and decisions which jeopardize business confidence and well-being, serious social problems and economic disruption would result, with adverse consequences for jobs, tax revenues, and political climate. The well-being of corporations and financial institutions under such circumstances becomes identified with the national interest (Stone 1971, p. 32) (as well as with the political interest of those in government who are eager to keep or advance their positions).

Hence, although there may be considerable divergence in interest about specific issues and problems (economic or social), there is a well-understood shared interest of the government executive and of the corporate executive to keep the system functioning. The same holds in the case of labor union leaders. This convergence of 'general interest' and commitment to the effective functioning of the system serves to maintain through relational control capitalist structure and institutions (with minor corrections and reforms deemed essential to 'more effective performance' and to perpetuation of the system). This shared commitment among the highest circles of the society is an essential underpinning of the system.

[20] Workers generally lack the rights to determine how they are organized (e.g., on the assembly line), how they relate to one another, to productive activities, and to the products of their labour and the multiple ramifications referred to earlier (see Figure 20.1). Such relational control is the prerogative of management, which it defends vigorously in terms of 'property rights', 'technical needs', etc. This is not to overlook important recent developments entailing the *delegation* to workers by top management of relational control rights to work out such arrangements *within certain constraints*.

[21] Indeed, the work place is the most authoritarian milieu in democratic societies (with the obvious exception of the military and total institutions such as prisons and mental hospitals). Employees are forced to lead a double existence: outside their work they may enjoy considerable freedom, independence and self-confidence, *although their capacity to structure and restructure social life on any significant level is quite limited*; in their places of work, they are subject to strict authority and control, particularly those at the lower end of the hierarchy, and to forces of technological and social change over which they have no control—in Touraine's phrase, 'dependent participation'.

[22] The desire of conservative interests to expand wine trade (and to keep the volume of manufactured imports up to provide customs revenue) coincided with the English determination to firmly establish its dominant economic, political, and military position, particularly after the Portuguese efforts at industrialization in the last decades of the 17th century. The discovery of gold in Brazil could finance any future trade deficit of Portugal and at the same time alleviate the English shortage of bullion. The convergence of internal and external interests contributed to the structuring of a particular English/Portuguese relationship, as exemplified by the Methuen Treaty of 1703. On the one hand, the relationship helped to preserve the established social and economic structures of Portugal, assuring non-development in the future and, on the other, it reinforced Portugal's dependence on England. *The internal and external structural arrangements reinforced one another in such a way as to stabilize and maintain themselves in an overall system of dependence.*

[23] Following 1670, the Portuguese government made a brief effort to modernize and industrialize Portugal by introducing protectionist legislation. This was not only because of negative Portuguese balance-of-payments but because of recognition of the harmful effects of the treaties with England which created a privileged and prominent expatriate English merchant class. Portuguese cloth soon managed to be competitive with English cloth even at reduced prices. Portuguese production increased dramatically (helped in part by new laws of incorporation). Imports of English cloth fell, particularly because the Portuguese substitutes were successful in those categories in which England specialized.

In spite of these initial gains, the required transformation of the Portuguese economy and class structure was prevented by several factors: (1) the political opposition of the landed gentry and the Church, both groups having extensive agricultural interests and substantial internal power. The Church also feared the increased influence of immigrant artisans and Jewish entrepreneurs. (2) The absence of a strong indigenous merchant class. (This condition was itself the consequence of earlier Anglo-Portuguese treaties with their privileges for English competitors). Thus, there was no substantial base of political pressure or support for new governmental policies favouring commerce and manufacturing. (3) The lack of administrative skills to follow through on initial successes of new policies.

[24] Portugal overcame balance-of-trade deficits by using Brazilian gold. However, this served to stimulate English production and to have, in general, widespread positive ramifications. This arrangement can be contrasted to one where Portugal would have been stimulated to produce another export commodity or to reduce its imports from England. Thus, while the trade of gold for manufactured goods may be 'equal' in the sense of bringing equal satisfaction to both or in the sense of 'fair market price', the goods exchanged had significantly different long-term consequences for the relative social and economic development of the two societies (see Baumgartner and Burns, 1974, 1975).

References

Adams, R. M., 1972, *Power: Its conditions, strategy, and evolution* (Manuscript.)

Anderson, B., 1974, *Parts and wholes* (Unpublished mimeo).

Anfossi, A., 1974, *Reflections on the social foundations of economic concepts* (Paper presented at the 8th World Congress of Sociology, Toronto.)

Aptheker, H., 1969, *American Negro slave revolts*. New York, International Publishers.

Baumgartner, T.; Buckley, W.; Burns, T., 1975a, 'Divide et impera', *Theory and society*. (In press.) 1975b, 'Relational control: The human structuring of cooperation and conflict' *Journal of Conflict Resolution*. (In press.) 1975c, 'Toward a systems theory of unequal exchange, uneven development and dependency relationships', in: J. Rose (ed.). *Proceedings: Third International Congress on Cybernetics and Systems,* Bucharest.

Baumgartner, T.; *et al.,* 1975d, 'Meta-power and the development of hierarchical control in social systems' in: T. Burns and W. Buckley (eds.), *Power and hierarchical control*, London, Sage.

Baumgartner, T.; Burns, T., 1973, *Socio-economic power, market prices, and the distribution of income* (Mimeo). 1974, *Structural determinants of unequal exchange* (Paper presented at the annual Convention of the Eastern Economic Association, Albany, NY.). 1975, 'The structuring of international relations', *International Studies Quarterly*. (In press.)

Blau, P., 1964, *Exchange and power,* New York, Wiley.

Blauner, R., 1972, *Marxian theory and race relations* (Paper read at the Annual Meeting of the American Sociological Association, New Orleans, La.).

Bonjour, E.; Offler, H. S.; Potter, G. R., 1952, *A short history of Switzerland,* Oxford, Oxford University Press.

Buckley, W.; Burns, T.; Meeker, L. D., 1973, *A mathematical theory of social behavior: Application to problems of power, cooperation and conflict, and social order* (Mimeo). 1974, 'Structural resolutions of collective action problems', *Behavioral Science* 19 (September): 277–297.

Burns, T., 1973, 'A structural theory of social exchange', *Acta Sociologica* 16: 188–208.

Burns, T.; Buckley, W., 1974, 'The prisoners' dilemma game as a system of social domination', *Journal of Peace Research* 11 (September): 221–228.

Burns, T.; Downs, R.; Laughlin, C., Jr., 1973, *Political structure and political process: An evolutionary perspective* (Mimeo).

Burns, T.; Meeker, L. D., 1976, 'A theory of multi-level, multiple objective evaluation and decision-making', *International Journal of General Systems* 3.

Coleman, J. S., 1966, 'Foundations for a theory of collective choice', *American journal of sociology* 71: 615–627.

Davis, D. B., 1966, *The problem of slavery in Western culture*, Ithaca, NY, Cornell University Press.

Dirks, R. T., 1974, *Resource fluctuation and planter-slaver competition in the British West Indies* (Mimeo).

Elkins, S., 1968, *Slavery*, Chicago, Ill., University of Chicago Press.

Ellis, D. P., 1971, 'The Hobbesian problem of order: A critical appraisal of the normative solution', *American Sociological Review* 36: 692–703.

Encyclopaedia Britannica (EB), 1973, Chicago, Ill., Benton.

Genovese, E. D., 1965, *Political economy of slavery,* New York, Pantheon.

Michels, R., 1949, *Political parties,* Glencoe, Ill., Free Press.

Oberschall, A., 1973, *Social conflicts and social movements,* Englewood Cliffs, NJ, Prentice-Hall.

Parsons, T., 1951, *The social system,* Glencoe, Ill., Free Press.

Patterson, O., 1967, *The sociology of slavery,* London, MacGibbon and Kee.

Shils, E. A.; Janowitz, M., 1948, 'Cohesion and disintegration in the Wehrmacht in World War II', *Public Opinion Quarterly:* 280–315.

Sideri, S., 1970, *Trade and power,* Rotterdam, University Press.

Simmel, G., 1950, in K. H. Wolff (ed.), *The sociology of Georg Simmel,* New York, Free Press.

Stone, A., 1971, 'How capitalism rules', *Monthly Review* 23: 31–36.

Stone, J., 1966, *Social dimensions of law and justice,* Stanford, Calif., Stanford University Press.

Touraine, A., 1972, Cited in T. Bottomore, 'Three authors in search of a proletariat', *New York Review of Books*, April 6: 31.

Wachtel, H. M., 1974, 'Class consciousness and stratification in the labor process', *Review of Radical Political Economics* 6: 1–31.

Zeitlin, I., 1967, *Marxism: A re-examination,* New York, Van Nostrand Reinhold.

Keyword index